BUSINESS ETHICS 95/96

Seventh Edition

Editor

John E. Richardson
Pepperdine University

Dr. John E. Richardson is Associate Professor of Management in the School of Business and Management at Pepperdine University. He is president of his own consulting firm and has consulted with organizations such as Bell and Howell, Dayton-Hudson, Epson, and the U.S. Navy, as well as with various service, nonprofit, and franchise organizations. Dr. Richardson is a member of the American Management Association, the American Marketing Association, the Society for Business Ethics, and Beta Gamma Sigma honorary business fraternity.

Annual Editions
A Library of Information from the Public Press

Cover illustration by Mike Eagle

Dushkin Publishing Group/
Brown & Benchmark Publishers
Sluice Dock, Guilford, Connecticut 06437

The Annual Editions Series

Annual Editions is a series of over 65 volumes designed to provide the reader with convenient, low-cost access to a wide range of current, carefully selected articles from some of the most important magazines, newspapers, and journals published today. Annual Editions are updated on an annual basis through a continuous monitoring of over 300 periodical sources. All Annual Editions have a number of features designed to make them particularly useful, including topic guides, annotated tables of contents, unit overviews, and indexes. For the teacher using Annual Editions in the classroom, an Instructor's Resource Guide with test questions is available for each volume.

VOLUMES AVAILABLE

Africa
Aging
American Foreign Policy
American Government
American History, Pre-Civil War
American History, Post-Civil War
Anthropology
Archaeology
Biology
Biopsychology
Business Ethics
Canadian Politics
Child Growth and Development
China
Comparative Politics
Computers in Education
Computers in Business
Computers in Society
Criminal Justice
Developing World
Drugs, Society, and Behavior
Dying, Death, and Bereavement
Early Childhood Education
Economics
Educating Exceptional Children
Education
Educational Psychology
Environment
Geography
Global Issues
Health
Human Development
Human Resources
Human Sexuality
India and South Asia

International Business
Japan and the Pacific Rim
Latin America
Life Management
Macroeconomics
Management
Marketing
Marriage and Family
Mass Media
Microeconomics
Middle East and the Islamic World
Money and Banking
Multicultural Education
Nutrition
Personal Growth and Behavior
Physical Anthropology
Psychology
Public Administration
Race and Ethnic Relations
Russia, the Eurasian Republics, and Central/Eastern Europe
Social Problems
Sociology
State and Local Government
Urban Society
Violence and Terrorism
Western Civilization, Pre-Reformation
Western Civilization, Post-Reformation
Western Europe
World History, Pre-Modern
World History, Modern
World Politics

Cataloging in Publication Data
Main entry under title: Annual Editions: Business ethics. 1995/96.
    1. Business ethics—Periodicals. I. Richardson, John E., *comp.* II. Title: Business ethics.
ISBN 1–56134–347–1   658.408   91–649227

Seventh Edition

Printed in the United States of America

Printed on Recycled Paper

To the Reader

In publishing ANNUAL EDITIONS we recognize the enormous role played by the magazines, newspapers, and journals of the *public press* in providing current, first-rate educational information in a broad spectrum of interest areas. Within the articles, the best scientists, practitioners, researchers, and commentators draw issues into new perspective as accepted theories and viewpoints are called into account by new events, recent discoveries change old facts, and fresh debate breaks out over important controversies.

Many of the articles resulting from this enormous editorial effort are appropriate for students, researchers, and professionals seeking accurate, current material to help bridge the gap between principles and theories and the real world. These articles, however, become more useful for study when those of lasting value are carefully *collected, organized, indexed,* and *reproduced* in a *low-cost format*, which provides easy and permanent access when the material is needed. That is the role played by *Annual Editions*. Under the direction of each volume's *Editor*, who is an expert in the subject area, and with the guidance of an *Advisory Board*, we seek each year to provide in each ANNUAL EDITION a current, well-balanced, carefully selected collection of the best of the public press for your study and enjoyment. We think you'll find this volume useful, and we hope you'll take a moment to let us know what you think.

Recent events have brought ethics to the forefront as a topic of discussion throughout the United States. And, undoubtedly, the area of society that is getting the closest scrutiny regarding its ethical practices is the business sector. Both the print and broadcast media have offered a constant stream of facts and opinions concerning recent unethical goings-on in the business world. Insider trading scandals on Wall Street, the marketing of unsafe products, money laundering, and questionable contracting practices are just a few examples of events that have recently tarnished the image of business.

As corporate America struggles to find its ethical identity in a business environment that grows increasingly complex, managers are confronted with some poignant questions that have definite ethical ramifications. Does a company have any obligation to help solve social problems such as poverty, pollution, and urban decay? What ethical responsibilities should a multinational corporation assume in foreign countries? What obligation does a manufacturer have to the consumer with respect to product defects and safety?

These are just a few of the issues that make the study of business ethics important and challenging. A significant goal of *Annual Editions: Business Ethics 95/96* is to present some different perspectives on understanding basic concepts and concerns of business ethics and to provide ideas on how to incorporate these concepts into the policies and decision-making processes of businesses. The articles reprinted in this publication have been carefully chosen from a variety of public press sources to furnish current information on business ethics.

This volume contains a number of features designed to make it useful for students, researchers, and professionals. These include a *topic guide* for locating articles on specific subjects related to business ethics, the *table of contents abstracts* with summaries of each article and key concepts in bold italics, and a comprehensive *index*.

The articles are organized into five units. Selections that focus on similar issues are concentrated into subsections within the broader units. Each unit is preceded by an overview which provides background for informed reading of the articles, emphasizes critical issues, and presents *challenge questions* focusing on major themes running through the selections.

Your comments, opinions, and recommendations about *Annual Editions: Business Ethics 95/96* will be greatly appreciated and will help shape future editions. Please take a moment to complete and return the postpaid article rating form on the last page of this book. Any book can be improved, and with your help this one will continue to be.

John E. Richardson
Editor

Contents

Unit 1

Ethics, Values, and Social Responsibility in Business

Seven selections provide an introduction to business ethics and social responsibility

To the Reader   iv

Topic Guide   2

Overview   4

1. **Business Ethics: A Manager's Primer,** Gene Laczniak, *Business,* January–March 1983.   6

   Gene Laczniak offers some solid and pragmatic advice for managers facing **ethical dilemmas.** He also discusses how the process of ethical behavior in an organization stems from the diverse and sometimes **conflicting determinants of personal values, organizational pressure, and societal values.**

2. **Principles of Business Ethics: Their Role in Decision Making and an Initial Consensus,** Archie B. Carroll, *Management Decisions,* Volume 28, Number 8, 1990.   13

   Archie Carroll lucidly delineates how such approaches as the **Golden Rule,** intuition, and **utilitarianism,** as well as other ethical principles, are used in business decision making.

3. **Principles for Infusing Ethics in Your Company,** Judy C. Nixon and Judy F. West, *Business Forum,* Fall 1993.   18

   The authors believe an organization manages its reputation by creating an **ethical corporate culture** and communicating its ethical expectations clearly to its **employees** and the public.

4. **What Is Virtue?** Kenneth L. Woodward, *Newsweek,* June 13, 1994.   21

   Kenneth Woodward feels that virtue too often is confused with **values.** Whereas "values" can be a morally neutral term, "virtue" is a quality of character by which individuals habitually recognize and do the right thing.

5. **Integrity: An Essential Executive Quality,** Donald G. Zauderer, *Business Forum,* Fall 1992.   23

   The author believes that **managers** who lack integrity place themselves and their organizations at risk. He identifies several traits of managers that compromise integrity and suggests some specific actions that can help build a **culture** where integrity can be regularly practiced.

6. **The Trouble with Business Ethics,** Tom Peters, *The Orange County Register,* September 22, 1989.   28

   Tom Peters discusses the complexity of business ethics. He believes that a central ethical issue in the **workplace** is protecting and supporting the unempowered—especially the **frontline worker** and the **consumer.**

7. **Ethics in Practice,** Kenneth R. Andrews, *Harvard Business Review,* September/October 1989.   30

   The author believes that **management's values** are evident in every strategic decision made. He also feels that when management focuses its total loyalty on **the maximization of profit,** it becomes the principal obstacle to achieving higher standards of ethical practice.

The concepts in bold italics are developed in the article. For further expansion please refer to the Topic Guide and the Index.

Unit 2

Ethical Issues and Dilemmas Involving Employees in the Workplace

Twenty selections organized within seven subsections examine crucial employee-related issues and their ethical implications for management's decision-making practices and policies.

Overview   36

A. EMPLOYEE RIGHTS AND DUTIES

8. **The New Deal: What Companies and Employees Owe One Another,** Brian O'Reilly, *Fortune,* June 13, 1994.   38

   The author believes that although **worker loyalty** and **job security** are dwindling phenomena in the workplace, employers who deliver honesty and satisfying work can expect a new form of commitment from workers.

9. **Are You Guilty of Electronic Trespassing?** Deborah L. Jacobs, *Management Review,* April 1994.   43

   The author discusses how companies have used high-tech tools to cut costs and **deter theft.** Too often, however, some managers have unwittingly used these tools to invade an **employee's privacy.**

10. **A Reluctant Invasion,** Doug Wallace, *Business Ethics,* January/February 1993.   49

    The article presents a situation where a manager—after laying off an employee—learns that the employee is **HIV positive.** How can a manager help an employee without invading his or her **privacy**?

B. EMPLOYEE CRIME

11. **Ethics and Employee Theft,** William J. Kehoe, from *Reducing Employee Theft: A Guide to Financial and Organizational Controls,* Quorum Books, 1991.   52

    William Kehoe delineates how **employee theft** is a problem for both **managers** and their **employees.** He believes that when ethics are instilled within the organization—and the **culture** becomes one of pride and honesty—employee theft will be deterred.

12. **Crime and Punishment: A Hard Look at White-Collar Crime,** Barbara Ettorre, *Management Review,* May 1994.   56

    Barbara Ettorre reveals that even though **federal sentencing guidelines** have become more severe for **white-collar criminals,** many American companies are perplexed about developing ways to effectively deter this type of misconduct.

C. SEXUAL TREATMENT OF EMPLOYEES

13. **Six Myths of Sexual Harassment,** Jan Bohren, *Management Review,* May 1993.   63

    The author explores some of the myths surrounding **sexual harassment.** He also suggests preventive steps for **management** to take to deal with sexual harassment in the workplace.

14. **Ten Steps to Follow When Investigating a Sexual Harassment Complaint,** Stuart H. Brody and William Lee Kinnally Jr., *Ethikos,* January/February 1994.   66

    The authors lay down some specific steps to follow when investigating a **sexual harassment** complaint.

15. **Women Make Strides, but Men Stay Firmly in Top Company Jobs,** Rochelle Sharpe, *Wall Street Journal,* March 29, 1994.   69

    Rochelle Sharpe observes that thirty years after the **Civil Rights Act** barred **sex discrimination** in the workplace, it can be noted that women have moved into nonclerical white-collar jobs in droves—however, female management gains have been impeded by a **male-dominated culture.**

The concepts in bold italics are developed in the article. For further expansion please refer to the Topic Guide and the Index.

D. DISCRIMINATORY AND PREJUDICIAL EMPLOYMENT PRACTICES

16. **Many Minorities Feel Torn by Experience of Affirmative Action,** Sonia L. Nazario, *Wall Street Journal,* June 27, 1989.   72

    There is much ambivalence among **minorities** about **affirmative action,** relates Sonia Nazario. Some minority members feel that it has opened doors that would otherwise have remained shut. However, others believe that affirmative action has brought with it the unwelcome baggage of making it appear that they were hired or promoted only because of race, resulting in unwarranted skepticism about their abilities.

17. **White, Male, and Worried,** *Business Week,* January 31, 1994.   74

    The article delineates a present casualty of diversity in the workplace—**white males.** White men are slowly **becoming a workforce minority** and are thus worrying about their future opportunities, as well as feeling resentful that the rules are changing too fast.

18. **Ageism: The New Diversity Issue,** Genevieve Capowski, *Management Review,* October 1994.   79

    The author reveals that diversity issues do not end with **sexism and racism.** As the American population ages, new concerns about staffing shortages, mandatory retirement, and **age discrimination** are being brought into the limelight.

E. DOWNSIZING OF THE WORKFORCE

19. **Burned-Out Bosses,** Lee Smith, *Fortune,* July 25, 1994.   85

    Lee Smith reflects that while companies have devoted vast resources to deal with the trauma of **downsizing,** most of that effort goes to the benefit of the most obvious victims—those let go. Over time, survivors may suffer more psychological damage than the departed.

20. **The Pain of Downsizing,** John A. Byrne, *Business Week,* May 9, 1994.   88

    The author conveys that, despite signs of economic recovery, **corporate bloodletting** is being carried out on an unprecedented scale. The article gives an inside assessment of the trauma of large-scale **layoffs** at a major telecommunications corporation.

21. **"You're Fired,"** Doug Wallace, *Business Ethics,* January/February 1992.   94

    This article describes an actual case where an employee is **fired unfairly** for what he suspects is a result of an ethical stance he had once taken. The reader is given the opportunity to interact with the case and to decide what action the employee should take.

F. WHISTLE-BLOWING IN THE ORGANIZATION

22. **Changing Unethical Organizational Behavior,** Richard P. Nielsen, *The Executive (The Academy of Management),* May 1989.   96

    Richard Nielsen depicts some intervention strategies that can be used to change unethical behavior (secret and public **whistle-blowing,** for example), provides some cases of how each strategy can be implemented, and describes some important limitations of the strategies.

The concepts in bold italics are developed in the article. For further expansion please refer to the Topic Guide and the Index.

23. **Whistleblowers: Who's the Real Bad Guy?** Barbara Ettorre, *Management Review,* May 1994.   104

Most **whistle-blowers,** according to the author, are well-educated, well-liked, and committed employees, yet they are still treated as tattletales, sneaks, and troublemakers. The article scrutinizes ways for companies to encourage **ethical behavior** without encouraging "snitching."

G. *HANDLING ETHICAL DILEMMAS AT WORK*

24. **Implementing Business Ethics,** Patrick E. Murphy, *Journal of Business Ethics,* 7, 1988.   110

A pragmatic approach to implementing business ethics is presented. For a successful implementation of ethics, there must be **top management support** and a **corporate culture** that is supportive of **codes of ethics, conferences and training programs,** and an ethical audit.

25. **Right vs. Wrong,** Lori A. Tansey, *Managing Your Career,* Spring/Summer 1994.   119

The author offers two **ethical dilemmas** for the reader to wrestle with and then discusses some important considerations that can be helpful in handling ethical issues.

26. **Signs and Signals of Unethical Behavior,** John Paul Fraedrich, *Business Forum,* Spring 1992.   122

The author analyzes some of the causes behind individuals' and companies' making **unethical decisions** and suggests steps necessary to better confront **ethical dilemmas.**

27. **What Would You Do? A Twisted Arm,** Doug Wallace, *Business Ethics,* January/February 1994.   126

An **ethical dilemma** is presented where a manager is **threatened into contributing** a specified amount of money for a particular cause. "Here's the contribution we expect," the memo read. "What you give will have a bearing on your future compensation."

Overview   128

A. *CHANGING PERSPECTIVES IN BUSINESS AND SOCIETY*

28. **The New Crisis in Business Ethics,** Kenneth Labich, *Fortune,* April 20, 1992.   130

During these tough **economic** times, according to the author, more **managers** are cutting ethical corners and putting more heat on subordinates. The result has been an eruption of questionable and sometimes **criminal behavior** throughout corporate America.

29. **The New World of Work,** *Business Week,* October 17, 1994.   133

Vast changes in the **economy,** technology, and the **workforce** have altered work itself—not just in the United States, but around the **world.**

30. **Family Friendliness,** *U.S. News & World Report,* February 22, 1993.   137

The article reflects the important role that companies play in **family life.** Flextime, job sharing, telecommuting, and elder care have moved off the pages of human-resources journals onto boardroom agendas.

Unit 3

Business and Society: Contemporary Ethical, Social, and Environmental Issues

Twelve articles organized within three subsections provide an analysis of important ethical, social, and environmental issues affecting both domestic and multinational business operations.

The concepts in bold italics are developed in the article. For further expansion please refer to the Topic Guide and the Index.

31. **Business Rethinks, Refines, Recycles, and Recoups,** **141**
Ted J. Rakstis, *Kiwanis Magazine,* August 1993.
Ted Rakstis explores how *"the green movement"* is branching "further into offices, shops, and factories as the working world learns that recycling makes both dollars and sense."

32. **Environmentalists Are on the Run,** Ann Reilly Dowd, **145**
Fortune, September 19, 1994.
The author delineates that, for the first time in years, *environmentalists* are on the defensive. Business leaders, local officials, and angry citizens are demanding an end to *legislation* based on silly science and bad economics.

B. *MAJOR CONTEMPORARY DILEMMAS*

33. **Combating Drugs in the Workplace,** Minda Zetlin, **149**
Management Review, August 1991.
Some *drug-abuse incidents* are not clear-cut, presenting problems not only of good *management,* but also of good ethics. The author presents five dilemmas relating to drug-related issues drawn from real-life *workplace* situations.

34. **Embracing Diversity,** Charles Garfield, *Executive Excellence,* October 1994. **156**
Charles Garfield believes that demographic changes in the *workplace* and in the *marketplace* compel us to learn more about one another. Moreover, diversity—whether in the form of gender, culture, ethnicity, or some other attribute—has broad implications for how work is viewed, organized, and approached.

35. **The Aging of America Is Making 'Elder Care' a Big Workplace Issue,** Sue Shellenbarger, *Wall Street Journal,* February 16, 1994. **158**
The article reflects the views of some authorities that, in the coming years, elder care may be the biggest personnel issue that companies will face in maintaining productivity from day to day. It may have a greater impact upon the workplace than child care or any other *work-family issue* so far.

C. *GLOBAL ETHICS*

36. **Is U.S. Business Obsessed with Ethics?** David Vogel, **161**
Across the Board, November/December 1993.
David Vogel elucidates how the norms of ethical behavior tend to vary widely in different capitalistic nations and why some *foreign managers* resent the distinctive American *ethical practices* being forced on them.

37. **Ethics: Are Standards Lower Overseas?** Andrew W. Singer, *Across the Board,* September 1991. **165**
The author scrutinizes the common perception that U.S. standards and *values* are higher than those *overseas.* Is this accurate?

The concepts in bold italics are developed in the article. For further expansion please refer to the Topic Guide and the Index.

38. Ethics in the Trenches, Robert D. Haas, *Across the Board,*   169
May 1994.
Robert D. Haas, chairman and CEO of Levi Strauss, discusses
how Levi's developed and adopted a set of ***global-sourcing
guidelines*** that established standards that their contractors must
meet to ensure that their practices are compatible with Levi's
values.

39. Levi Tries to Make Sure Contract Plants in Asia Treat   171
Workers Well, G. Pascal Zachary, *Wall Street Journal,* July
28, 1994.
The author describes Levi Strauss's concern about ***foreign contract workers' rights.*** For example, the article gives an account
about an inspector for Levi's in Malaysia who searches for ***health
and safety hazards*** and abuses of worker rights—rather than just
examining Levi's jeans and shirts for flaws.

Unit 4

Ethics and Social Responsibility in the Marketplace

Seven selections organized within two subsections
describe the practice of incorporating ethics into
the marketplace.

Overview   174

A.   MARKETING STRATEGY AND ETHICS

40. Marketing by Professionals: Some Ethical Issues and   176
Prescriptions, Patrick E. Murphy and Gene R. Laczniak,
Business Insights, Spring/Summer 1990.
Some of the critical ***ethical issues*** faced by professionals in their
marketing and advertising practices are addressed. Specific
suggestions that can help advertising and marketing by professionals to remain on a high ethical plane are provided.

41. Three Ethical Challenges for Sales Managers, Gene R.   182
Laczniak and Patrick E. Murphy, *Ethikos,* March/April 1994.
The authors describe three areas of ethical challenge for ***sales
managers:*** administration of sales territories, setting of sales
quotas, and ***competitive*** considerations.

42. The Green Movement Sows Demand for Ecofurniture,   185
Cheryl Powell, *Wall Street Journal,* September 2, 1994.
The author discusses how ***environmentally friendly furniture*** is
gaining a following in the ***marketplace.***

B.   ETHICAL PRACTICES IN THE MARKETPLACE

43. Managing for Organizational Integrity, Lynn Sharp   186
Paine, *Harvard Business Review,* March/April 1994.
Lynn Paine advocates that, by supporting ethically sound behavior, ***managers*** can strengthen the relationships and ***reputations***
their companies depend on.

44. Managing by Values, *Business Week,* August 1, 1994.   196
The article examines why Levi Strauss has long enjoyed a
reputation for being a ***socially responsible employer.*** Levi's
CEO, Robert Haas, believes that the corporation should be an
ethical creature—an organism capable of both reaping profits and
making a better place to live.

The concepts in bold italics are developed in the article. For further expansion please refer to the Topic Guide and the Index.

45. **The Ethics of Bootstrapping,** Scott Cook, *Inc,* September 1992.   **201**

Scott Cook founded Intuit, maker of the check-writing software product Quicken, with $151,000 in 1984. Cook freely shares his experience as the man behind a little, struggling, start-up venture that faced *ethical questions* almost every day.

46. **The 5th Annual Business Ethics Awards for Excellence in Ethics,** Margaret Kaeter, *Business Ethics,* November/December 1993.   **204**

Business Ethics magazine recently honored three *consumer product companies* for their exemplary leadership: Merck, for putting human lives above profit; Aveda, for building *environmentalism* into every aspect of its operation; and Levi Strauss, for its commitment to human rights at home and *abroad.*

Unit 5

Developing the Future Ethos and Social Responsibility of Business

Five selections consider guidelines and principles for developing the future ethos and social responsibility of business.

Overview   **208**

47. **The Challenge of Ethical Behavior in Organizations,** Ronald R. Sims, *Journal of Business Ethics,* July 1992.   **210**

The author lays out some of the challenges that *ethical organizations* will face in the future: *international competition,* new technologies, increased *quality, employee motivation and commitment,* and managing a diverse work force. Also, the author presents some suggestions for creating and maintaining an ethically oriented culture.

48. **Creating Ethical Corporate Structures,** Patrick E. Murphy, *Sloan Management Review,* Winter 1989.   **219**

The author believes that "*ethical business practices* stem from ethical *corporate cultures.*" He discusses several companies' experiences with three types of ethics-enhancing structures: corporate credos, *ethics training programs and workshops,* and tailored corporate *codes of ethics.*

49. **Can a Company Be Too Ethical?** Andrew W. Singer, *Across the Board,* April 1993.   **226**

Andrew Singer discusses the frequent criticism made against some companies—for instance, Control Data Corporation—for ignoring core business concerns at the expense of so-called humanitarian projects. He scrutinizes how ethics is tied to *social responsibility* as it relates to "*stakeholders,*" including employees, customers, suppliers, and the community in which one operates.

50. **High Explosives,** Craig Cox, *Business Ethics,* January/February 1994.   **232**

Craig Cox believes that the path to *business success* has been littered with *ethical land mines.* He offers ten explosive issues that need to be avoided and provides a route through which a business can be safely guided through the minefield.

51. **How to Make Diversity Pay,** Faye Rice, *Fortune,* August 8, 1994.   **236**

The author delineates that, while many companies dawdle, smart ones are betting that a *diversified workforce* will prove vital in the twenty-first century.

Index   **241**
Article Review Form   **244**
Article Rating Form   **245**

The concepts in bold italics are developed in the article. For further expansion please refer to the Topic Guide and the Index.

Topic Guide

This topic guide suggests how the selections in this book relate to topics of traditional concern to students and professionals in the field of business ethics. It is useful for locating articles that relate to each other for reading and research. The guide is arranged alphabetically according to topic. Articles may, of course, treat topics that do not appear in the topic guide. In turn, entries in the topic guide do not necessarily constitute a comprehensive listing of all the contents of each selection.

TOPIC AREA	TREATED IN:	TOPIC AREA	TREATED IN:
Codes of Ethics (Codes of Conduct)	1. Business Ethics: A Manager's Primer 5. Integrity 7. Ethics in Practice 11. Ethics and Employee Theft 24. Implementing Business Ethics 25. Right vs. Wrong 36. Is U.S. Business Obsessed with Ethics? 40. Marketing by Professionals 41. Three Ethical Challenges for Sales Managers 43. Managing for Organizational Integrity 47. Challenge of Ethical Behavior in Organizations 48. Creating Ethical Corporate Structures 50. High Explosives	**Employee Health and Safety** **Employee Rights**	13. Six Myths of Sexual Harassment 14. Investigating a Sexual Harassment Complaint 29. New World of Work 39. Levi Tries 2. Principles of Business Ethics 3. Principles for Infusing Ethics 5. Integrity 6. Trouble with Business Ethics 8. New Deal 9. Are You Guilty of Electronic Trespassing? 10. Reluctant Invasion 11. Ethics and Employee Theft 14. Investigating a Sexual Harassment Complaint
Conflicts of Interest	2. Principles of Business Ethics 6. Trouble with Business Ethics 9. Are You Guilty of Electronic Trespassing? 21. "You're Fired" 23. Whistleblowers 26. Signs and Signals of Unethical Behavior 27. What Would You Do? A Twisted Arm 32. Environmentalists Are on the Run 35. Aging of America 45. Ethics of Bootstrapping 48. Creating Ethical Corporate Structures		17. White, Male, and Worried 18. Ageism 27. What Would You Do? A Twisted Arm 29. New World of Work 30. Family Friendliness 33. Combating Drugs In the Workplace 34. Embracing Diversity 39. Levi Tries 44. Managing by Values 48. Creating Ethical Corporate Structures 49. Can a Company Be Too Ethical? 50. High Explosives 51. How to Make Diversity Pay
Consumer Protection	6. Trouble with Business Ethics 23. Whistleblowers 40. Marketing by Professionals 42. Green Movement 45. Ethics of Bootstrapping	**Environmental Disregard and Pollution**	2. Principles of Business Ethics 31. Business Rethinks, Refines 32. Environmentalists Are on the Run 38. Ethics in the Trenches 39. Levi Tries 42. Green Movement 43. Managing for Organizational Integrity 46. Fifth Annual Business Ethics Awards 47. Challenge of Ethical Behavior in Organizations 50. High Explosives
Discrimination	5. Integrity 10. Reluctant Invasion 15. Women Make Strides 16. Many Minorities Feel Torn 17. White, Male, and Worried 18. Ageism 21. "You're Fired" 41. Three Ethical Challenges for Sales Managers 44. Managing by Values 47. Challenge of Ethical Behavior in Organizations 51. How to Make Diversity Pay	**Equal Employment Opportunities**	15. Women Make Strides 16. Many Minorities Feel Torn 17. White, Male, and Worried 18. Ageism 33. Combating Drugs In the Workplace 34. Embracing Diversity 46. Business Ethics Awards 50. High Explosives 51. How to Make Diversity Pay
Downsizing	12. Crime and Punishment 19. Burned-Out Bosses 20. Pain of Downsizing 21. "You're Fired" 25. Right vs. Wrong 28. New Crisis in Business Ethics 29. New World of Work 30. Family Friendliness 50. High Explosives 51. How to Make Diversity Pay	**Ethical Dilemmas**	2. Principles of Business Ethics 6. Trouble with Business Ethics 8. New Deal 12. Crime and Punishment 16. Many Minorities Feel Torn 23. Whistleblowers 25. Right vs. Wrong 26. Signs and Signals of Unethical Behavior 27. What Would You Do? A Twisted Arm

TOPIC AREA	TREATED IN:	TOPIC AREA	TREATED IN:
Ethical Dilemmas (cont.)	35. Aging of America 38. Ethics in the Trenches 43. Managing for Organizational Integrity 50. High Explosives	**Multinational Corporations and Global Business Ethics**	16. Many Minorities Feel Torn 24. Implementing Business Ethics 29. New World of Work 36. Is U.S. Business Obsessed with Ethics? 37. Ethics: Are Standards Lower Overseas? 38. Ethics in the Trenches 39. Levi Tries 46. Business Ethics Awards 49. Challenge of Ethical Behavior in Organizations 50. High Explosives
Ethical Training	4. What Is Virtue? 11. Ethics and Employee Theft 12. Crime and Punishment 13. Six Myths of Sexual Harassment 23. Whistleblowers 24. Implementing Business Ethics 25. Right vs. Wrong 26. Signs and Signals of Unethical Behavior 28. New Crisis in Business Ethics 43. Managing for Organizational Integrity 47. Challenge of Ethical Behavior in Organizations		
		Product Safety and Quality	28. New Crisis in Business Ethics 32. Environmentalists Are on the Run 39. Levi Tries 42. Green Movement 43. Managing for Organizational Integrity 45. Ethics of Bootstrapping 46. Business Ethics Awards 47. Challenge of Ethical Behavior in Organizations 50. High Explosives
Illegal Business Practices	15. Women Make Strides 16. Many Minorities Feel Torn 25. Right vs. Wrong 43. Managing for Organizational Integrity		
Insider Information	7. Ethics in Practice 47. Challenge of Ethical Behavior in Organizations 48. Creating Ethical Corporate Structures 50. High Explosives	**Sexual Harassment and Discrimination**	2. Principles of Business Ethics 5. Integrity 13. Six Myths of Sexual Harassment 14. Investigating a Sexual Harassment Complaint 15. Women Make Strides 44. Managing by Values 49. Can a Company Be Too Ethical? 50. High Explosives
Insider Trading	11. Ethics and Employee Theft 47. Challenge of Ethical Behavior in Organizations		
Legal and Legislative Environment	1. Business Ethics: A Manager's Primer 7. Ethics in Practice 12. Crime and Punishment 15. Women Make Strides 16. Many Minorities Feel Torn 17. White, Male, and Worried 18. Ageism 23. Whistleblowers 24. Implementing Business Ethics 28. New Crisis in Business Ethics 32. Environmentalists Are on the Run 33. Combating Drugs In the Workplace 37. Ethics: Are Standards Lower Overseas? 41. Three Ethical Challenges for Sales Managers 43. Managing for Organizational Integrity 49. Can a Company Be Too Ethical? 50. High Explosives	**Value System(s)**	3. Principles for Infusing Ethics 4. What Is Virtue? 38. Ethics in the Trenches 43. Managing for Organizational Integrity 44. Managing by Values
		Whistle-Blowing	1. Business Ethics: A Manager's Primer 22. Changing Unethical Organizational Behavior 23. Whistleblowers 25. Right vs. Wrong 28. New Crisis in Business Ethics 36. Is U.S. Business Obsessed with Ethics? 41. Three Ethical Challenges for Sales Managers 47. Challenge of Ethical Behavior in Organizations
Marketing Practices	1. Business Ethics: A Manager's Primer 7. Ethics in Practice 21. "You're Fired" 23. Whistleblowers 24. Implementing Business Ethics 25. Right vs. Wrong 31. Business Rethinks, Refines 34. Embracing Diversity 38. Ethics in the Trenches 41. Three Ethical Challenges for Sales Managers 42. Green Movement 43. Managing for Organizational Integrity 44. Managing by Values 45. Ethics of Bootstrapping 46. Business Ethics Awards 49. Can a Company Be Too Ethical? 50. High Explosives	**White-Collar Crimes**	7. Ethics in Practice 9. Are You Guilty of Electronic Trespassing? 11. Ethics and Employee Theft 12. Crime and Punishment 28. New Crisis in Business Ethics
		Women and the Workplace	14. Investigating a Sexual Harassment Complaint 15. Women Make Strides 17. White, Male, and Worried 29. New World of Work 30. Family Friendliness 34. Embracing Diversity 35. Aging of America 51. How to Make Diversity Pay

Ethics, Values, and Social Responsibility in Business

Ethical decision making in an organization does not occur in a vacuum. As individuals and as managers, we formulate our ethics (that is, the standards of "right" and "wrong" behavior that we set for ourselves) based upon family, peer, and religious influences; our past experiences; and our own unique value systems. When we make ethical decisions within the organizational context, many times there are situational factors and potential conflicts of interest that further complicate the process.

Decisions do not only have personal ramifications—they also have social consequences. Social responsibility is really ethics at the organizational level, since it refers to the obligation that an organization has to make choices and to take actions that will contribute to the good of society, as well as to the good of the organization. Authentic social responsibility is not initiated because of forced compliance to specific laws and regulations. In contrast to legal responsibility, social responsibility involves a voluntary response from an organization that is above and beyond what is specified by the law.

The seven selections in this unit provide an overview of the interrelationships of ethics, values, and social responsibility in business. The lead article in this section, "Business Ethics: A Manager's Primer," offers practical and insightful suggestions to managers, enabling them to approach the subject of business ethics with more confidence. The next four articles discuss the significance of ethical principles and values in personal and organizational decision making. In "The Trouble with Business Ethics," Tom Peters discusses very candidly the complexity of business ethics. The last unit article underlines the importance of management's values being an integral part of the organizational decision-making process.

Looking Ahead: Challenge Questions

Do you believe that corporations are more socially responsible today than they were 10 years ago? Why or why not?

In what specific ways do you see companies practicing social responsibility? Do you think most companies are overt or covert in their social responsibility activities?

After reading "Integrity: An Essential Executive Quality," do you believe that there is a necessary correlation with being ethical and making a profit? Why or why not?

In "The Trouble with Business Ethics," Tom Peters advocates that a central ethical issue in the workplace is protecting and supporting the *unempowered*—especially the frontline worker and the consumer. In what respects do you agree or disagree with this contention?

What are the economic and social implications of "management accountability" as part of the decision-making process? Does a company have any obligation to help remedy social problems, such as poverty, urban decay, and pollution? Explain your response.

From an organizational perspective, what do you think are the major arguments for and against social responsibility?

Business Ethics: A Manager's Primer

The application of different ethical maxims to a given situation may produce divergent ethical judgments. The 14 propositions given here should enable management to deal with the subject of business ethics with confidence.

Gene Laczniak

Dr. Laczniak *is Associate Professor of Business and Chairman of the Department of Marketing at Marquette University, Milwaukee, Wisconsin. The author would like to acknowledge the helpful comments of Professors T.R. Martin and Patrick E. Murphy of Marquette University in the development of this article.*

Too many business managers have been shortchanged in their business education. They have been cheated because during their college years their business professors failed to integrate ethical issues into management education. While some practicing managers have taken courses in "business ethics" or "social responsibility," they typically have not learned to appreciate fully the crucial role that ethics plays in business decision making. To a large degree this has happened because many business educators shy away from integrating ethics into mainstream business classes such as marketing, finance, and production.

Why do educators find it so difficult to teach business ethics or, for that matter, to address ethical issues when dealing with other topics of business strategy? Largely for the following three reasons. First, many business educators pride themselves on their analytical approach; in contrast, addressing ethics is associated with a softer type of analysis, and occasionally with a preachy mentality. This might be deemed the *soapbox* factor. A second closely related cause is that the foundation for meaningful remedies in the area of business ethics is perceived as subjective and unscientific. In other words, many business professors feel that ethics is too elusive a subject for extended lecture treatment. This constitutes the *soft* factor. Third, some business educators believe that dealing with business ethics in the classroom will have little or no lasting effect upon the morality of their students; this might be labeled the *superfluous* factor. Consequently, a great many business educators have not given business ethics its proper due in the classroom because of their perceptions that the subject is soapboxish, soft, and superfluous.

This article compiles and analyzes some propositions that are useful for understanding business ethics. These propositions are grouped into three categories: (1) propositions that serve as useful foundations; (2) descriptive propositions; and (3) proscriptive propositions.

Propositions That Serve as Useful Foundations

Proposition 1: Ethical conflicts and choices are inherent in business decison making. This proposition is a logical springboard for appreciating the importance of business ethics because it legitimates the inseparability of business decisions and moral consequences. Substantial support for this postulation is available. One classic study of business ethics reported that at some point in their careers 75% of the responding managers felt a conflict between profit considerations and being ethical.[1] Later studies noted that the majority of managers questioned also felt this pressure to be unethical.[2] Similarly, another widely publicized study indicated that 65% of the managers surveyed sometimes felt pressure to compromise their personal ethical standards.[3]

More importantly, this proposition can provide the business manager with the motivation to discover and analyze the numerous ethical implications of current business practices. For example:

• Is it ethical for pharmaceutical companies to market infant formula in developing countries as an alternative to breast feeding when it is common knowledge that sanitary containers and unpolluted water are frequently not available and that babies will be deprived of the immunological benefits inherent in breast milk?

• Is it proper for a public relations firm to attempt to bolster the worldwide image of a country accused of numerous human rights violations?

• Is it moral for a firm to ship a product designated unsafe in one market, such as the United States, to another market where the regulations do not apply?

Every business manager can add examples to the ones just noted. The point is that this proposition emphasizes that the ethical implications of business practices are legion.

"...a high organizational ethic could induce a manager with low integrity to behave more properly."

Proposition 2: Proper ethical behavior exists on a plane above the law. The law merely specifies the lowest common denominator of acceptable behavior. This proposition undercuts the argument that legality is the only criterion for judging acceptable behavior. If this proposition does *not* hold, the study of ethics is extraneous. While some members of the legal profession may challege this postulate, the entire field of moral philosophy rests on its inherent truth. This proposition provides a rationale for examining the compelling argument that ethical propriety and legality do not necessarily coincide. For example, it is not *illegal* to exhort children to ask their parents to buy a product promoted *via* a commercial on a children's television show. Whether such a practice is *unethical*, because it exploits the gullibility of children, can be vigorously debated.

In addition, this proposition provides an opportunity to explore some fundamental differences between legal and ethical perspectives. For instance, the law is a *reactive* institution that applies to situations only after they have occurred. Ethics is usually more *proactive*, attempting to provide guidance prior to a situation's occurrence. Similarly, within the law, a transgression must be proven beyond a reasonable doubt, whereas from an ethical perspective, an action is morally wrong independent of conclusive proof that it in fact took place. For example, suppose the quality control manager of an electrical supply house knowingly sends out Christmas tree lights that could potentially short out because of a design defect and thereby cause a fire. The lights, however, do not malfunction. Legally, the manager is not culpable because no harm occurred; ethically, a violation of trust has clearly occurred. Thus this proposition embodies the concept that the realm of ethics provides guidance for managerial actions and supplements the requirements provided by law.

Proposition 3: There is no single satisfactory standard of ethical action agreeable to everyone that a manager can use to make specific operational decisions. Few business executives would question this generalization. This proposition establishes that advocating a particular moral doctrine is not the point of examining the issue of ethics. Rather, while there are many ethical perspectives of great worth, the issue of morality *in general* is at question. In other words, the power and impact implicit in managerial decisions demands an examination of the responsibility for those actions. Thus, ethical considerations are properly examined in reference to the managerial process.

Proposition 4: Managers should be familiar with a wide variety of ethical standards. Several ethical maxims are used as the theoretical foundation for a variety of industry statements on ethics. Typical of the more simplistic maxims are:

The utilitarian principle—Act in a way that results in the greatest good for the greatest number.

The professional ethic—Take only actions that would be viewed as proper by a disinterested panel of professional colleagues.

The golden rule—Act in the way you would expect others to act toward you.

Kant's categorical imperative—Act in such a way that the action taken under the circumstances could be a universal law or rule of behavior.

The TV test—A manager should always ask, "Would I feel comfortable explaining to a national TV audience why I took this action?"

Obviously, these maxims are difficult to apply to specific situations and can sometimes lead to conflicting resolutions, particularly if analyzed in the context of a *case situation*. For example, consider the case of a sales representative who, against stated company policy, routinely pads his expense account vouchers 10% to 15%. However, he does this with the knowledge that his fellow sales representatives and his supervisor do the same thing and tacitly approve of this action. In this circumstance, does the golden rule justify the behavior? Wouldn't the professional ethic imply that the practice should cease? This is a rudimentary illustration, but it underscores the fact that various modes of moral reasoning exist and that the application of different ethical maxims to a given situation may produce divergent ethical judgments.

Proposition 5: The discussion of business cases or of situations having ethical implications can make managers more ethically sensitive. Perhaps this is the most debatable of the five propositions ventured thus far because a certain substantial segment of business educators and managers would question its truth. The position of this group is that academic course work cannot instill integrity in a future manager. They believe that students come into the classroom with a relatively intransigent morality. Therefore, classroom efforts directed at personal values are an exercise in futility.[4]

Notice, however, that the proposition as stated promises only the *potential* for increased sensitivity to ethical concerns, not wholesale changes in morality. One expert provides some limited support for this proposition when he reports that a sample of MBA graduates who took a course in business ethics seemed to develop ethical sensitivity over a period of time.[5] Furthermore, other researchers have contended that the academic community has the reponsibility to provide courses in business ethics regardless of their effect.[6] In the view of these experts, such offerings will not transform personalities overnight but will stimulate thinking about ethical issues. In short, sufficient justification exists for encouraging discussion among managers about business ethics, and for the expectation that the effort will have some moral payoff in the business world.

In summary, the five foundation propositions provide a rationale for business ethics as (1) an area of significant managerial concern, (2) distinct from the realm of law, (3) an area, like many areas of management, that has few pat answers but (4) worth exploring because of its relevance to effective and responsible management decision making.

Descriptive Propositions

With these five foundation propositions, the business manager is now ready to address the specific process of ethical behavior as it occurs in the organization. Unfortunately, little can be definitively stated about how ethical or unethical behavior evolves in a business firm. In part, this is why business ethics are considered subjective or soft—a dimension that was referred to earlier. Nevertheless, a few useful, general propositions can be established for ethics in the organization.

Proposition 6: There are diverse and sometimes conflicting determinants of ethical action. These stem primarily from the individual, from the organization, from professional norms, and from the values of society. This proposition underscores the multiple influences that characterize the business environment and shape ethical actions; it also highlights the complexity of pressures that can be part of resolving an ethical question. Consider, for example, the following sample situation:

Smith University holds as part of its endowment portfolio a large block of stock in the multinational Jones Company. The stock was donated to Smith University by the founder of the Jones Company. The Jones Company is heavily involved in apartheid-ruled South Africa. Members of the university community, especially students and faculty, are pressuring the university to immediately sell all its Jones Company stock. Some members of the community where Smith University is located have even threatened to picket Smith classes. Mr. Courtney, vice president of Finance at Smith and a former diplomat, knows Jones Company to be a model corporate citizen in South Africa, treating black and white employees alike. However, the management of Jones Company supports the existing South African government. Furthermore, Courtney believes the Jones Company stock is extremely depressed at this time and that its sale would not be in the best interest of the endowment fund, the major source of student scholarships. Should Courtney and Smith University sell the stock immediately?

Notice the multiple pressures that may be present in a situation such as this: *Societal* pressures dictate selling the securities. Moreover, Courtney's *personal* beliefs, stemming from his religion and philosophy, make him shudder at the inflexibility of the South African government. On the other hand, *organizational* pressures dictate restraint, since Courtney and other officers of the university feel the Jones securities will soon appreciate in value. Similarly, from a *professional* viewpoint, Courtney knows that the sale of the Jones stock would be a symbolic act at best and at worst a slap in the face to a company that has been a Good Samaritan in South Africa and a close friend to the university. How does Courtney resolve these conflicting pressures? No precise answer exists. Somehow he takes the various viewpoints into consideration and recommends an action with which he is comfortable. It is even possible that his recommendation, whatever it is, will be overruled at a higher level of the organization.

The foregoing examination of Proposition 6 suggests another proposition. In the last analysis, Courtney must make a decision that will have ethical consequences. Ultimately, the factors and subfactors to which ethics are attributable—influences such as religion, professional norms, societal expectations, and organizational pressures—somehow combine to shape an *individual* decision that is associated with Courtney and according to which Courtney could be morally judged. This leads to the next proposition.

Proposition 7: Individual values are the final standard, although not necessarily the determining reason for ethical behavior. The upshot of Proposition 7 is that multifaceted influences affecting the likelihood of ethical action by the decision maker will ultimately be reflected in an individual decision. The action taken will be perceived by others as embodying the ethical values of the decision maker. Introduction of this proposition helps businesspeople realize the individual responsibility inherent in managerial decision making. In other words, no matter what factors lead a manager to make a particular decision, there is a measure of individual responsibility that cannot be denied because in the last analysis the decision was made by a given manager. For example, the product manager who knowingly sends a shipment of unsafe products to retail stores cannot avoid individual culpability by claiming that economic pressures in the organization necessitated the action.

One major organizational implication of Proposition 7 is that management should strive to maintain a laudatory *organizational* ethic because this dimension is somewhat controllable by the organization. This lessens the likelihood that organizational considerations will pressure the individual manager to compromise his or her personal beliefs and behave unethically. Conversely, a high organizational ethic could induce a manager with low integrity to behave more properly. For example, the American Telephone and Telegraph Corporation (AT & T) provides all employees with a copy of a booklet that states that if employees report to outside sources the improper behavior of AT & T management or employees, no disciplinary or retaliatory action will ever be taken.

Proposition 8: Consensus regarding what constitutes proper ethical behavior in a decision-making situation diminishes as the level of analysis proceeds from abstract to specific. Put another way, it is easy to get a group of managers to agree *in general* that a practice is improper; however, casting that practice in a specific set of circumstances usually reduces consensus. For example, almost all

"...younger, middle managers feel greater pressures to compromise their personal ethics."

businesspeople will agree that stealing by employees is wrong. But consider the following specific question: Is it alright for a manager to unwittingly take a few pens and pads of paper home for personal use? What about a stapler? A calculator? A typewriter? What if the pens will be used by orphans to play games at a charity picnic? Where does one draw the line?

Even a simplistic example like this can cause debate. The difficulty is compounded as the circumstances become more involved. In any event, Proposition 8 emphasizes the uncertain environment in which managers necessarily function as they attempt to make the ethically proper decision. Consider the following ethical precepts—with which all businesspeople would agree—along with the complication introduced by some hypothetical situation-specific examples.

• *Business has the obligation to honestly report financial progress and potential to holders of company debt and equity. Situation:* The annual report of the Columbia Railroad Co. reports that the firm has financially outperformed all its competitors. This was largely due to the sale of some highly appreciated Manhattan real estate. The income from this transaction is noted with only a footnote in the financial statement. Columbia avoided having the income classified as a special treatment "extraordinary item" because of some complex legal maneuvers and

because it has other real estate assets that might provide similar profits in the future. Should the income from the real estate be highlighted more clearly in the annual report?

• *Business has the obligation to treat potential, current, and past employees fairly. Situation:* Employee Harry Harris is apprehended stealing tools and equipment valued at $500 from the company. Company policy calls for dismissal in such instances. However, Harris is 63 years old—two years from pension—and has had a clean slate until this incident. Is it ethical for the company to fire him at this point in his career?

• *Business has the obligation to provide consumers with facts relevant to the informed purchase of a product or service. Situation:* The Doe Co. manufactures Clean & Gleem, an all-purpose cleaning concentrate that consumers mix with four parts water. Clean & Gleem has been sold this way for 25 years. A recent issue of *Consumer Reports* indicates that Clean & Gleem will clean just as effectively if mixed with eight parts water. Thus, consumers need only use half as much concentrate. Should the Doe Co. inform customers of this fact? Would it be unethical not to do so?

In summary, Proposition 8 and these examples of some specific "tough choice" cases provide some insight into the difficulty of steering an ethically proper course.

Proposition 9: The moral tone of an organization is set by top management. Stated another way, the organization is but a lengthened shadow of the morality of persons in charge. For instance, one study found that managers ranked the behavior of superiors as the strongest single factor in deterring unethical behavior.[7] Similar results are reported in more recent studies.[8]

The organizational implications of this proposition are clear. If employees take their cues concerning ethical behavior from top management, then the first line of responsibility for setting high ethical standards falls to these corporate executives. The following example partially embodies the proposition:

An employee embezzled $20,000 over several years. When confronted with the incriminating evidence, the employee was not contrite and expressed the belief that he was just as entitled to the company's money as any member of top management. He pointed out that upper management dipped into petty cash for lunch money, used company stamps to mail Christmas cards, and had company personnel help with yard work at their personal residences.

Numerous other real-world examples of this proposition abound. The J.C. Penney Co. is a classic illustration of a company with a reputation for high ethical standards along with a record unblemished by any major scandal. Much of the credit must go to the founder, who was so convinced that ethics and profit were compatible that the company's outlets were originally called the "Golden

Rule" stores. In contrast, many of the so-called "dirty tricks" and the political whip cracking of the Nixon administration can be explained by the win-at-all-costs philosophy of the men at the top.

Proposition 10: The lower the organizational level of a manager, the greater the perceived pressure to act unethically. At first glance, this proposition might seem contradictory to Proposition 9. After all, if the moral tone of an organization resides in top management, why the concern with the subsidiary levels of management? The answer lies in the fact that while a *general ethical climate* is established by an organization's superiors, many of the operational decisions that have ethical implications will actually be made at levels other than top management. Thus because the frequency of decision making is greater, the lower-level manager may simply have more opportunities to behave ethically or unethically. Furthermore, it may be that the areas of responsibility of middle management are treated as profit centers for purposes of evaluation. Consequently, anything that takes away from profit—including ethical behavior—is perceived by lower-level management as an impediment to organizational advancement and recognition.

Surveys of managers seem to confirm that ethical conflict is felt most strongly by lower-level managers.[9] Thus, top management's exhortations and policy regarding ethics will be a factor in ethical behavior at these levels of management, but only *one* factor. If organizational advancement and salary adjustments are made primarily by the rule of bottom-line unit performance, pressure will exist on middle managers to compromise ethical standards if profit can be served. In this sense, the "ethical buck" stops at the bottom rather than the top of the organization.

Top management should recognize that ethical pressure points will exist at all levels of the organization. Therefore, a sanctimonious statement of a manager's standards does not discharge a firm's duty to foster high ethical standards. Efforts should be made to communicate to all levels of management that ethical behavior will be monitored and will be rewarded accordingly. This proposition reminds business managers that they will be involved in potential ethical conflicts when they enter the organization. The proposition also implies that mechanisms, such as codes or policy statements, that could be used by top management to communicate an ethical commitment "down the line" should be examined for their usefulness to middle management.

Within the context of Proposition 10, it is interesting to note that some analysts have speculated that managers behave more ethically as they grow older—a kind of "mellowing" factor. Since managers in top management are usually older than those at the lower level, this might partially explain why the younger, middle managers feel greater pressures to compromise their personal ethics. Similarly, one can reason that top-level managers have attained career success already; thus they have the luxury

of subscribing to high ethical norms, while lower-level managers must still prove themselves, which perhaps requires a more aggressive (and likely less ethical) posture. This "mellowing" hypothesis is controversial and does not yet merit the status of a proposition.

"...ethical propriety and legality do not necessarily coincide."

Proposition 11: Individual managers perceive themselves as more ethical than their colleagues. This postulate is the product of many studies of ethics in management. Typically, it evolves because of the following situation: An individual manager is interviewed by a researcher or reporter about a specific questionable practice, such as the use of invisible ink to track questionnaires after respondents have been promised confidentiality. The manager responds that X% of his colleagues would participate in such a practice but, of course, he or she would not. Thus, more than anything else, this proposition emphasizes the human tendency of managers to discuss ethics in a manner that will protect themselves from incrimination or to rationalize their own uprightness.

One implication of this proposition is that the actual ethical norms of businesspeople are probably more accurately reported in what they say their typical colleague would do in a situation than in what they report they themselves would do. The introduction of this proposition serves to remind the business manager of the difficulty of maintaining one's objectivity when one is involved in analyzing ethical questions that hold personal ramifications. Propositions 6 through 11 are limited in number but in fact establish some fundamental insights into the realm of business ethics. Namely:

• Multiple factors influence ethical decision making. Some are controllable, some are not. Ultimately, the final decision regarding an ethical question is strongly motivated by the manager's individual values.
• Consensus regarding ethical propriety is difficult to achieve when evaluating many specific situations; moreover, managers have a tendency to overstate their own ethical sensitivity.
• Ethical pressures are felt most acutely by lower- and middle-level managers who look to top management for behavioral cues but are themselves confronted with many difficult decisions.

Proscriptive Propositions Concerning Ethics

Propositions regarding business ethics, while easy to postulate, are difficult to propose with the confidence that they will have a significant impact on the organization. One is reminded of the quip by Mark Twain, "To be good is noble. To tell people to be good is even nobler and much less trouble." Nevertheless, organizations with a reputation for impeccable ethical conduct have cultivated and enhanced their outstanding moral demeanor with organizational adjustments that have had an impact on ethical performance. The following propositions focus on such organizational strategies.

Proposition 12: Effective codes of ethics should contain meaningful and clearly stated provisions along with enforced sanctions for noncompliance. A code of ethics or some other formal statement of ethical concern is the minimum commitment to organizational social responsibility all firms should be expected to make. Unfortunately, the vast majority of executives have little confidence in the effectiveness of codes in improving morality because of their vagueness and the difficulty of enforcing them.[10] All too often such codes have become meaningless public relations gimmicks. Still, codes are not without value. They represent a public commitment regarding the prohibition of practices and can diffuse potential ethical problems. For example, consider the purchasing agent who wonders whether it is proper to accept a bottle of 12-year-old Scotch whiskey at Christmastime from a sales representative. He may reason that there is no explicit quid pro quo expected and that since the gift is given at holiday time, the practice is acceptable. Nevertheless, the manager makes this assessment half-heartedly, because he knows the sales representative's firm has several contracts pending and the practice looks suspicious. A specific code statement that prohibits the giving or receiving of gifts with a value of more than $5 would have eliminated the ethical question concerning the gift.

Successful codes tend to be those that are specific *and* enforced. To anticipate every ethical contingency that can arise in a business situation and to hope to include it in a code is both naive and unrealistic. However, certain specific ethical problems tend to arise in particular industries, and these problems require the special scrutiny of management. For instance:
- Producers of heavily sugared products must face the question of how ethical it is to advertise to children, given both the persuasibility of this group and their susceptibility to tooth decay.
- Companies selling whole life insurance must question the ethics of promoting a financial institution that can lock an individual into a low return on investment in perpetuity.

Almost every business environment suggests some relatively unique ethical questions.

The question of code enforcement is a matter of behavioral psychology. Unless members of the organization see a code of ethics monitored and subsequently enforced with visible sanctions, they will ascribe little organizational importance to the code. The implication of

Proposition 12 is that a code of ethics that is not enforced is a code of ethics without teeth, and it will be treated as such by personnel at all levels in an organization.

Proposition 13: Employees must have a nonpunitive, fail-safe mechanism for reporting ethical abuses in the organization. This postulate raises the issue of "whistle blowing" and its role in the firm. On one hand, no corporation likes to have its dirty linen aired in public without an opportunity to examine internally its own transgressions. On the other hand, a real commitment to ethical propriety demands that clear abuses of organiza-

---

"Successful codes tend to be those that are specific *and* enforced."

---

tional morality will be condemned and dealt with accordingly, no matter how they come to light. In recent years, too many corporate Serpicos have gone public with substantial abuses, only to be hounded by their own organizations. Organizations dedicated to high ethical standards should provide mechanisms that will assure channels of communication and subsequent protection for whistle blowers. Operationally, this sort of program requires the explicit support of high-level administrators. If top management might be involved in the transgressions, employees should be made aware of an audit committee of the board (chaired by a member independent of management, such as an outside director) to whom information can be given.

Admittedly, such a program can be difficult for management to accept. The possibility of undue negative publicity caused by an overzealous or alarmist employee is a risk. Some issues are difficult to resolve. For example, a financial auditor discovers a foreign payoff that was made several years ago by the now retired chief executive officer. Should this skeleton be allowed to leave the corporate closet? Yet, such dilemmas are the price of developing a climate of ethical responsibility in the organization.

Proposition 14: Every organization should appoint a top-level manager or director to be responsible for acting as an ethical advocate in the organization. In an organization committed to high moral standards, ethical responsibility falls into everyone's domain. But as with many things, unless someone is appointed to direct the effort the responsibility dissolves among the many. One researcher has insightfully proposed the concept of the ethics advocate—a top manager or director whose responsibility would be to elucidate the ethical implications of management's decisions.[11] For example, if a corporation is planning to shut down a plant in a particular community, the ethical advocate would seek to clarify what, if any, moral responsibility the company had to the community where the plant was located. Similarly, the representative would outline what ethical responsibilities the company has to the employees who might be discharged because of the plant shutdown. In short, the ethical advocate would serve as the verbal conscience of the corporation. Both Cummins Engine Co. and the Monsanto Corp. have introduced such positions into their organizations.

Notice that these three propositions—Propositions 12, 13, and 14—provide the business manager with a battery of questions that can be used to initially evaluate the ethical posture of an organization:

• Does the organization have a code of ethics? Is it specific? Is it enforced?
• Has the organization attempted to identify ethical concerns unique to its industry and operations?
• What is the organization's policy toward whistle blowers? What mechanisms are available to report ethical abuses? Internal channels? External channels?
• Has top management communicated its concern for a commitment to high ethical standards? How has this been practically demonstrated?
• Is there someone in the organization who serves as an ethical advocate or ombudsman? What are this person's specific responsibilities?

Conclusion

Certainly, it can be said that there is not a great deal of definitive knowledge regarding the process that leads managers to behave ethically. It is also conceded that the precise philosophical perspective managers ought to use to make ethical decisions is open to debate. Whether it be moral intuition, a particular theory of distributive justice, utilitarianism, or some other framework, reasonable people can disagree on whether a particular decision is ethically proper or not. A few will also continue to maintain that such discussions and frameworks will never have a pragmatic influence on managerial behavior. In this sense the study of business ethics remains somewhat soft, relatively subjective, arguably superfluous, and prone to a soapbox mentality.

Nevertheless, the strength of such arguments is overstated. While business ethics may be an area that is relatively soft, certain solid propositions that are supported in multiple research studies and in the practices of progressive companies can be transmitted to current and future business managers. Rather than embodying a soapbox mentality, the purpose of these propositions is to sensitize the manager to some of the realities of ethics in the organization. The fact that ethical questions are unavoidable, that subordinates look to top management for behavioral cues, and so on, are bits of managerial acumen that should be well-ingrained in the future business executive. These propositions also describe some pragmatic mechanisms that have been utilized by organizations to develop a progressive ethical climate. Numerous executives testify to the worth of these propositions as an aide to moral responsibility. Thus one may realistically view business ethics as an area consisting of a limited number of solid, successfully adapted propositions that can sensitize managers to their ethical responsibility as organizational decision makers. On these propositions business practitioners can begin to build, supplement, and amplify the necessary discussion of ethics that must take place in the boardroom and beyond.

1. Raymond C. Baumhart, "How Ethical Are Businessmen?" *Harvard Business Review* (July-August 1961): 6.

2. Steven N. Brenner and Earl A. Molander, "Is the Ethics of Business Changing?" *Harvard Business Review* (January-February 1977): 52-71.

3. Archie B. Carroll, "A Survey of Managerial Ethics: Is Business Morality Watergate Morality?" *Business and Society Review* (Spring 1975).

4. Mary Susan Miller and Edward A. Miller, "It's Too Late for Ethics Courses in Business Schools," *Business and Society Review* (Spring 1976): 39-43.

5. Theodore V. Purcell, "Do Courses in Ethics Pay Off?" *California Management Review* (Summer 1977).

6. Richard A. Konrad, "Are Business Ethics Worth Studying?" *Business and Society Review* (Fall 1978): 54-57.

7. Baumhart, "How Ethical are Businessmen?" 6.

8. John W. Newstrom and William A. Ruch, "The Ethics of Management and the Management of Ethics," *MSU Business Topics* (Winter 1975): 29-37.

9. Carroll, "A Survey of Managerial Ethics"; Brenner and Molander, "Is the Ethics of Business Changing?" 52-71.

10. Brenner and Molander, "Is the Ethics of Business Changing?" 52-71.

11. Theodore V. Purcell, "A Practical Guide to Ethics in Business," *Business and Society Review* (Spring 1975): 43-50; "Electing an 'Angels Advocate' to the Board," *Management Review* (May 1976): 4-11.

Principles of Business Ethics:

Their Role in Decision Making and an Initial Consensus

Do as you would be done by? Don't get found out? Follow your intuition? What ethical principles do managers really use in business decisions?

Archie B. Carroll

Dr Archie B. Carroll is Professor of Management and holder of the Robert W. Scherer Chair of Management and Corporate Public Affairs at the University of Georgia, USA.

Our principles are the springs of our actions; our actions, the springs of our happiness or misery. Too much care, therefore, cannot be taken in forming our principles.

Skelton

One clear conclusion that has emerged from society's and businesses' preoccupation with business ethics over the last decade is that managers at all levels need help in making ethical decisions in the workplace. It has long been established that decision making is at the heart of management. Managers need to make many decisions in their everyday working lives in which reside questions of right or wrong, fairness, justice, or, as some business ethicists say, the allocation of harms and benefits.

There are dozens of workplace issues in which ethical questions are now coming to the forefront. A recent survey conducted by Ronald Berenbeim, for The Conference Board, identified seven key issues on which at least 80 per cent of his 300 respondents agreed represented ethical issues in business today. These seven issues comprised employee conflicts of interest, inappropriate gifts to corporate personnel, sexual harassment, unauthorised payments, affirmative action, employee privacy, and environmental issues[1].

The purpose of the current discussion is to describe briefly how principles of business ethics are used in a decision-making process, and to report on a survey that was conducted among a group of managers and prospective managers. The survey was designed to present the respondents with a number of alternative business ethical principles, and then to ascertain the usefulness or power of these principles to the respondents. The respondents then ranked the principles in terms of usefulness to them in their work. Finally, we describe the consensus that seems to emerge from the findings of the study.

The Principles Approach

There are several different ways in which managers may go about improving the ethics of their decision making. One popular approach, which we shall call The Principles Approach, is based upon the idea that managers need to compare their proposed actions, decisions or behaviours with certain principles of ethics. This raises the question

From *Management Decisions*, Vol. 28, No. 8, 1990, pp. 20-24. © 1990 by MCB University Press Limited. Reprinted by permission.

of *what is* a principle of business ethics and *how* might it be applied?

A principle of business ethics is a guideline or rule which, if applied when you are faced with an ethical dilemma, will assist you in making an ethical decision. Examples of principles which have been articulated and discussed by business philosophers and ethicists include the utilitarian principle, the justice principle and the rights principle. These principles, along with others, have been described in detail elsewhere; and our purpose here is not to add to that body of thought[2].

In addition to a comparison of personal or corporate behaviour with an ethical principle is the notion of standards or norms of acceptability. These norms might be personal, organisational or societal in terms of their origin. The process of ethical decision making entails, therefore, a consideration of (1) the action, behaviour or decision being considered, (2) standards or norms against which a comparison might be made, and (3) a principle of business ethics which provides guidance as to what is most important in the decision being made: e.g. utilitarianism, justice, rights. Often, decision making is made based upon comparisons of (1) and (2) or (1) and (3).

Such a principles approach might yield a process of ethical decision making similar to that shown in Figure 1. Note here that the term "ethics screen" is used to imply a filtering process wherein actions, behaviours or decisions are compared with standards or norms, and ethical principles or guides with decision making. The proposed decision, action or behaviour then "passes" or "fails" the ethics screen, and results in the course of action being deemed acceptable or unacceptable.

The Survey

The purpose of the survey described here was to see if prospective managers (senior level business students) and actual practising managers would reach any kind of consensus on what principles of business ethics they found useful. On separate occasions, the two groups were presented with the same set of descriptions of ethical principles which were adapted from earlier work by T.K. Das and Steiner and Steiner[3]. Thirty-four business students and 88 middle managers ranked the principles presented in Figure 2. The eleven principles listed were extracted from 14 principles studied earlier by Das.

Figure 3 presents the ethical principles that were considered most important by the 88 managers. Included in the ranking is a brief statement as to what each means. These are reported here first because they come from

Figure 1. *A Process of Ethical Decision Making*

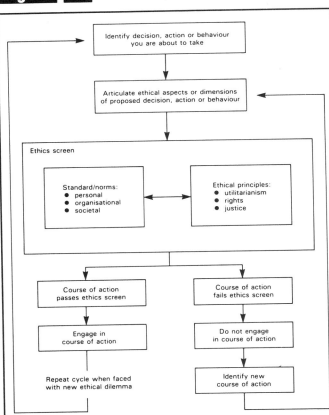

Source: Adapted from Archie B. Carroll *Business & Society: Ethics & Stakeholder Management* (South-Western Publishing Co., 1989), p. 128. Used with permission

actual practising managers and must therefore be deemed most credible.

Figure 4 summarises the ranking done by the managers, along with the ranking done by a sample of business students from a large Southeastern university. Also included is the ranking which was done in the T.K. Das study among a large group of Southwestern business students. The researcher regrets that the surveys of managers and Southeastern students did not include all of the principles listed by Das, but most of them (11 out of 14) were on the survey and this provides some useful comparisons.

Some Consensus Emerges

Several interesting findings emerge from these three surveys. Most notable is the fact that there is consensus among the three groups on the Golden Rule and the Disclosure Rule as the top two ranking ethical principles among those considered. Further, the Intuition Ethic and Categorical Imperative were ranked third and fourth by the managerial group and drew strong support from both

Figure 2. *Ranking Ethical Principles*

Below are listed 11 different ethical principles that may be used in business decision making. Rank them in terms of how powerful or useful they would be for you.

Principle

*Name of Principle**

1. You should not adopt principles of action unless they can, without inconsistency, be adopted by everyone else.

Categorical Imperative

2. Individuals should act to further their self-interests so long as they do not violate the law.

Conventionalist Ethic

3. Do unto others as you would have them do unto you;

Golden Rule

4. If it feels good, do it.

Hedonistic Ethic

5. If you are comfortable with an action or decision after asking yourself whether you would mind if all your associates, friends, and family were aware of it, then you should act or decide.

Disclosure Rule

6. You do what your "gut feeling" tells you to do.

Intuition Ethic

7. If the end justifies the means, then you should act.

Means-Ends Ethic

8. You should take whatever advantage you are strong enough and powerful enough to take without respect for ordinary social conventions and laws.

Might-Equals-Right Ethic

9. This is an age of large-scale organisations — be loyal to the organisation.

Organisation Ethic

10. You should do only that which can be explained before a committee of your professional peers.

Professional Ethic

11. You should follow the principle of "the greatest good for the greatest number".

Utilitarian Principle

* The names of these principles were not included on the survey sheet. They are supplied here just for purposes of explanation.

Figure 3. *Ethical Principles Ranked According to Value by Practising Managers. N=88*

1. **The Golden Rule**

   Do unto others as you would have them do unto you.

2. **Disclosure Rule**

   If you are comfortable with an action or decision after asking yourself whether you would mind if all your associations, friends, and family were aware of it, then you should act or decide.

3. **The Intuition Ethic**

   You do what your "gut feeling" tells you to do.

4. **The Categorical Imperative**

   You should not adopt principles of action unless they can, without inconsistency, be adopted by everyone else.

(tie) 5. **The Professional Ethic**

   You should do only that which can be explained before a committee of your professional peers.

(tie) 6. **The Utilitarian Principle**

   You should follow the principle of "the greatest good for the greatest number."

Figure 4. *Ranking of Ethical Principles by Three Groups*

Principle	Managers $n=88$	SE Students $n=34$	SW Students $n=265$
Golden Rule	1	1	1
Disclosure Rule	2	2	2
Intuition Ethic	3	5	6
Categorical Imperative	4	6	8
Professional Ethic	5(tie)	4	7
Utilitarian Ethic	5(tie)	3	3
Proportionality Ethic	*	*	4
Organisation Ethic	*	*	5

* Not on Managers or SE survey

student groups. Likewise the Professional Ethic and Utilitarian Ethic, which tied for fifth by the Managers, were strongly supported by the SE student group and partially supported by the SW group. The SW group placed two principles in the fourth and fifth position which were not on the survey of the other two groups.

It is worth noting that the *Golden Rule* — "Do unto others [as] you would have them do unto you"—is a fairly straightforward, easy to understand principle. Further, it guides the individual decision maker to behaviour, actions or decisions which he or she should be able to assess as acceptable or not based upon some direct comparisons with what he or she would consider ethical or fair. There is nothing esoteric about this. All it requires — and this is sometimes seen by some as difficult — is that the decision maker affords others the same kind and degree of consideration that he or she would think is right in similar personal circumstances.

The Golden Rule is among the oldest of the principles of living

The Golden Rule simply argues that, if you want to be treated fairly, treat others fairly; if you want to be told the truth, tell others the truth; if you want your privacy protected, respect the privacy of others. The key is impartiality. According to this principle we are not to make an exception of ourselves. In essence, then, the Golden Rule personalises business relations and brings the ideal of fairness into business deliberations[4].

Perhaps the reason the Golden Rule is so popular is that it is rooted in history and is among the oldest of the principles of living. Further, it is universal in the sense that it requires no specific religious beliefs or faith. Almost since time began, religious leaders and philosophers have advocated the Golden Rule in one form or another. The following is illustrative[5]:

— The Hindu *Mahabharata* professes: ''Men gifted with intelligence and purified souls should always treat others as they themselves wish to be treated''.

— Confucius summed up the rules of life as follows: ''What you do not want done to yourself, do not do to others''.

— In the *Bible* Jesus taught in the book of Matthew: ''So in every thing, do to others what you would have them do to you''.

— Rabbi Hillel, when asked by a supplicant to be taught the Law, answered: ''What thou thyself hatest, do not to thy neighbour. That is the whole Law. The rest is commentary. Go and learn it.''

It is easy to see, therefore, why Martin Luther could say that the Golden Rule is part of the ''natural law'', because

it is a moral rule which anyone can recognise without any particular religious teaching. That this thousands-of-years-old wisdom should surface as the number one ethical principle is indeed suggestive of the enduring understanding of how humanity should treat humanity. Some things just never change, it is said.

Intuition is the immediate thought we have before rational thought or inference

The *Disclosure Rule*, which could be seen as complementary to the Golden Rule, moves the focus of attention to how others whose opinions you respect would regard your decision, action or behaviour. According to the Disclosure Rule, you are probably on a sound ethical footing if you are still comfortable with a proposed action or decision after asking yourself whether you would mind if all your associates, friends, and family were aware of it. The concept of public exposure is a powerful tool; and, though it does not provide ironclad assurance that you are acting ethically, it does provide some strong indication of how the action is likely to be viewed.

The third-ranked principle by the managers studied was the *Intuition Ethic*. Whereas the previous two principles required some degree of rational thought about how the decision maker would like to be treated and how others might regard the proposed action, the intuition ethic is driven by one's quick and ready insight. Intuition, sometimes thought of as ''gut feeling'', is the immediate thought we have before engaging in rational thought or inference.

A person should not adopt principles unless they can be adopted by everyone else

Intuition is probably the result of an endowment of moral consciousness we each have, combined with experience and wisdom gained over time. It is a kind of awareness that might be the sum total of all that the decision maker is or has experienced. It is very possible that the intuition ethic might yield an evaluation of a proposed action that embodies considerations of the Golden Rule and the Disclosure Rule as well as other principles. Managers are often driven to make quick decisions, and it is tempting to believe that they go on their own "gut feeling" when time does not permit a more careful assessment based upon other principles or guidelines.

Technically, Immanuel Kant stated the *Categorical Imperative* as follows: "Act only according to that maxim by which you can at the same time will that it should become a universal law." Stated in another way, this principle argues that a person should not adopt principles of action or behaviour unless they can, without inconsistency, be adopted by everyone else. This principle is useful in terms of the manager searching for universal guidelines of consistency, but it really does not provide pointed guidance in a decision making situation. In a sense the categorical imperative is an abstract guideline that could be imposed upon other, more useful, principles.

The *Professional Ethic* holds that you should do only that which can be explained before a committee of your professional peers. In a sense this is a more restricted version of the disclosure rule and, though useful, is not as rigorous because of the possibility that those in similar areas of work might be more understanding of ethical lapses than the general public. In other words, you could more easily find someone in your own profession or line of work to agree with your proposed action than perhaps among your friends or family who are not immediately familiar with the constraints you are up against.

Finally the *Utilitarian Principle*, which argues for the greatest good for the greatest number, is idealistic, somewhat abstract, but quite difficult to apply. How is one ever able to determine what decision or course of action reflects the greatest good for the greatest number? This principle is extremely attractive on first thought, but is very difficult to apply and use.

Summing Up

There are a number of useful ethical principles around should managers wish to use them. First, managers must *wish* to use them. All the principles in existence will not suffice if the individual leader or decision maker is not interested in being ethical. An underlying assumption to the use of the ethical principles is, then, that the manager wishes to do the right thing.

A process of ethical decision making was presented, and this entailed the manager subjecting his or her proposed action to an ethics screen composed of an assortment of ethical principles and standards of acceptability. The process should help the manager to think through or "model" what the decision making process should look like when ethical considerations are included. There is no guarantee that the ethics screen will filter out all proposed actions that may be poorly formulated. It does,

however, add a measure of ethical process to decision making. It requires the manager to "think ethically" when making decisions.

Finally, a small set of ethical principles rose to the surface as most valuable when considered by a group of practising managers and soon-to-be-managers. The three principles which were ranked highest were quite straightforward and easily understood — treat others as you want to be treated, do only what you would feel comfortable with if those whom you care most about knew it, and follow your intuition. We should add in closing, however, that the modern concern for principles of ethical decision making that are neatly wrapped in a ready-to-use package cannot really be met. Though we desire to have such precision and closure, with no loose ends or puzzling leftovers, we simply cannot identify or agree upon rules, slogans, proverbs or principles that will eliminate all thought and deep introspection.

There are ethical principles that managers can agree upon as useful for management decision making. The real challenge seems to be in their use. As Herman Nelson once said ". . . it is in the application of principles which anyone can understand that management proves itself good or bad". This quite certainly applies here. As so often is the case with successful managers or organisations, the acid test is with implementation.

References

1. Berenbeim, R.E., *Corporate Ethics*, The Conference Board, New York, 1987, p. 3.
2. De George, R.T., *Business Ethics*, 2nd Ed., Macmillan, New York, 1986.
3. Steiner, G.A. and Steiner, J.F., *Business, Government and Society: A Managerial Perspective*, Random House, New York, 1980, pp. 383-9; Das, T.K., "Ethical Preferences among Business Students: A Comparative Study of Fourteen Ethical Principles", *Southern Management Association Proceedings*, 13-16 November, 1985, pp. 11-12.
4. Barry, V., *Moral Issues in Business*, Wadsworth, Belmont, California, 1979, pp. 50-51.
5. Shinn, R.L., *The Sermon on the Mount*, United Church Press, Philadelphia, 1962, pp. 76-7.
6. *The Forbes Scrapbook of Thoughts on the Business of Life*, Forbes, New York, 1976, p. 356.

Application Questions

(1) Complete the ranking of ethical principles exercise (Figure 2 in the article). Do these principles vary according to the situation?
(2) Outline your personal ethical standpoint on privacy, environmental issues and unauthorised payments. Do they always coincide with practice in your organisation?
(3) Should principles ever be compromised?

Principles for Infusing Ethics in Your Company

Ground Rules for Company Z

Play fairly.
Don't hit others.
Return things to their proper place.
Clean up after yourself.
Don't steal.
Be accountable for your actions.

Judy C. Nixon
Judy F. West

JUDY C. NIXON, Ph.D., is a professor of management at the University of Tennessee at Chattanooga.

JUDY F. WEST, Ph.D., is a professor of management at the same institution.

In today's organizations, ethical issues permeate every department and are every person's responsibility. Therefore, the reputation of the firm is actually determined by the employees—even though the CEO is charged with being the "ethics leader." The firm's reputation is among its most valuable assets, and it is now understood that high ethical principles contribute to increased corporate performance. Read on, and you'll find a blueprint for instilling or enhancing ethical principles in your firm.

An organization manages its reputation by creating an atmosphere of high ethical principles and communicating its ethics expectations to its employees and the public. The effectiveness of its communications program is essential to produce maximum employee performance. However, while performance has been emphasized for decades in business circles, ethics has not always been viewed as an enhancement to employee performance. This has been a serious mistake.

Management by objective has served as a guideline for performance. However, it focuses on outcomes—meeting or exceeding set profit and production goals—regardless of "corner cutting" devices used. Ethical performance, perhaps, was not a consideration, nor was the purpose of the performance communicated clearly to participating employees. The message that middle managers—the ones often tangled in unethical acts—frequently received was all that really mattered was that they achieve set objectives through their daily operations. However, the trend appears to have changed. According to a 1991 survey conducted under the sponsorship of the Conference Board, training sessions for middle managers were the most popular initiative being undertaken to help them develop a sensitivity to, and an awareness of, acceptable ethical behavior.[1]

Incorporating Ethical Values

The Conference Board survey of 1,900 international firms (264 corporations responded) revealed that 84 percent of the United States respondents had codes of ethics. Among the 84 percent, 45 percent had implemented their code since 1987. However, having a written code is only a base; communication, encouragement, oversight, review, and revision are imperative and must be ongoing to change attitudes, build trust, and establish and maintain high ethics—all of which can lead to high profits in the long run.[2]

Are businesses changing philosophies? Mark Pastin, director of the Lincoln Center for Ethics at Arizona State University, states that a reward philosophy can be most productive in the long run. This reward philosophy is based on realism, not a Pollyannaish optimism, and can foster a realistic raising of sights. However, the old ground rules that the organization really operates on must be penetrated. This penetration requires a decision to retain existing ground rules or replace them.[3]

To verify whether changes occurred in 25 firms, Pastin and other leading researchers conducted a three-year international study. The purpose was to determine "connectors" between high ethical performance and high economic performance. Once identified, the connectors were used to help develop principles that work synergistically to improve both ethics and economic outcomes. Ethical firms that were studied included Cadbury Schweppes, 3M, Arco, Motorola, Hilby Wilson Inc., Northern Chemical Company, Interwestern Management, Apple Computer, as well as public (governor's office, mayor's office) and semipublic (chamber of commerce, industry association) organizations.

Highlighting Four Principles

Four principles are presented that have worked, and are working, for organizations that adapt, implement, communicate, review, and revise them as situations require. Albeit, not all principles need undergo all of the processes simultaneously; rather, they are considered perhaps singly or in a selected group. An environment is created that allows all employees to become thinking persons who can choose from among the "best" to make the "best" even "better" over time.

Pastin emphasizes that these principles establish an agenda that thinking managers can use to test the principles against hard problems, revise or reject them, and try again. Thinking managers carry the principles as questions, not as question killers, and persistently seek criticism, new principles, and new questions. Most firms operate as a closed "reality," meaning that their managers are comfortable with their peers (but not entirely comfortable). In contrast, thinking managers in high-ethics firms are comfortable with extremely diverse groups that are—or should be—interested in their firms' activities.

Assuming that firms choose to be identified as high-ethics firms, they should be at ease and willing to divulge any and all information about operations to diverse internal and external stakeholder groups. That assumption carries over to the ethics of the internal and external stakeholders. High-ethics firms make the assumption that their stakeholders also are ethical. Therefore, the following principles should guide managers' decision-making processes.

"High-ethics firms are obsessed with fairness."

Principle 1: High-ethics firms are at ease interacting with diverse internal and external stakeholder groups.

These firms' ground rules make the strengths of these stakeholder groups part of their own strengths.

As Richard Capen states, the ease in interacting is established by setting standards of integrity and trust in a straightforward, everyday proposition.[4] Trust cannot be legislated, nor can it be mandated by the courts. Four specific tasks must be completed: build trust, be optimistic, be an encourager, and lead by personal example.

Build Trust

Trust is the essential foundation; it is the ultimate value that protects an orderly, civilized society from chaos and anarchy. It must be embedded in every action taken; it has ramifications in every decision. It is never guaranteed but must be constructed carefully, nurtured vigorously, and reinforced daily. It begins at birth and is a lifetime process to be inherited by future leaders to perpetuate survival.

Be Optimistic

Ease in interacting is perpetuated in attitudes of optimism. Managers must look optimistically both within and outside the firm for interests that can be folded into the firm's purposes and activities to help them achieve the highest ethical and economic goals for the public, stakeholders, and employees. An attitude of dedication to serving others must be instilled in each employee. Attitude can make the difference between success and failure. Attitudes are constantly communi-

cated verbally, in writing, and nonverbally—in every action and every decision.

Be An Encourager

An encourager is a thoughtful listener (the larger half of successful communication), a caring adviser, and a special friend. An encourager must interact. Pastin cites four examples of the encourager's interaction with diverse groups.

Control Data started intensive computer training programs for unemployed minority youth in neighborhoods where it operated. Motorola shared proprietary cost-reduction and quality-assurance programs with its employees' health care providers. Diesel Engines adopted a strategy designed to clean the air and enhance its competitive position simultaneously. Recognizing that every employee desires to be treated as an individual, Interwestern Management emphasizes autonomy, recognizes uniqueness in all aspects of the business, and makes a virtue of individualism. An encourager can do amazing things to lift another's spirits, to temper a blow to one's ego, to help one overcome a terrible setback, or to achieve seemingly impossible goals.

Lead By Personal Example

The fourth ethical task is the need to lead by personal example. From the CEO downward, all employees must articulate clearly their understanding of the firm's values. The firm should be viewed both as a business and a public trust that is built on the highest standards of ethics and integrity. All employees should strive to excel in all that they do to ensure that the name of the firm is synonymous with the "best." To be the best, all employees must be truthful and candid; all must be decisive and courageous; all must keep promises, be loyal, respect human dignity, pursue excellence, be compassionate, and be fair. Pastin states that in high-ethics firms, fairness is the bread and butter of management.

Principle 2: High-ethics firms are obsessed with fairness.

Their ground rules emphasize that the other person's interests count as much as their own. They waste little energy managing conflicts because the amount of control and management needed is proportional to the number of people who believe they have been treated unfairly. Cadbury Schweppes and Hilby Wilson, Inc. are good examples.

Cadbury Schweppes has achieved labor peace in a hostile labor environment by assiduously maintaining fairness with employees at all levels. "Despite bargaining with over twenty unions, it has better labor-management relations than any non-unionized U.S. firm we know of, and it does this with a lean management cadre."[5]

Hilby Wilson, Inc. is a land syndication company that puts its own interests on the line by its willingness to invest in any land that it offers for sale.

Because they are empathetic with other firms about their ethical decisions, these firms' interactions with others are fairer, and fewer adjustments are necessary. They reduce the causes of conflicts by having basic confidence that they treat people equitably when imbalances inevitably occur. Each person has a right to fair treatment and should seek it forthrightly. Fairness is effected by those responsible. Although the source of responsibility is impossible to pinpoint in many firms, it is most visible in high-ethics firms.

Principle 3: In high-ethics firms, responsibility is individual rather than collective; individuals assume personal responsibility for actions of the firm.

These firms' ground rules mandate that individuals be responsible to themselves. Robert Akers, former chairman of IBM, indicates that responsibility involves putting first things first. He cites Vince Lombardi's quote that he expected his players to have three kinds of loyalty: to God, to their families, and to the Green Bay Packers, *in that order*. He expected them to act responsibly.[6]

Responsibility is the glue that holds the organization together; responsibility involves taking actions and being happy to take credit for those actions. Individuals act on behalf of the organization as its representatives—its agents. In their actions, *vis-a-vis* others, they *are* the organization. Thinking managers "make the activity happen" by adopting four key qualities: persistence, consistency, coherence, and commitment. Also, they use the five-"s" model: shared values, strategy, structure, systems, and staff. All must work *together* consistently, coherently, and in the same direction. Shared ethical values—a foundation—provide vision that makes consumers want to buy; employees happy to go to work in the morning; the community feel

---

"Ethical organizations operate on ground rules that encourage them to communicate and treat diverse constituencies fairly, promote individual responsibility, and enact a purpose."

---

proud and supportive; regulators wish to enable rather than limit; and investors want to buy shares.[7]

Individuals must maintain—and continually renew or re-express—their responsibility or value systems. These values must be substantiated by strategies, structures, and systems designed to bring them into actual practice. Responsibility must be persistent to ensure consistent application of the values in the development of strategy, structure, and systems and a solid coherence among them. Management's responsibility is to gain and maintain the commitment of staff. A positive ethical perspective must be maintained and renewed. Each individual must act responsibly to fulfill the organization's purpose.

Principle 4: The high-ethics firm sees its activities in terms of a purpose.

This purpose requires a way of operating that members of the firm value. The purpose of the activities ties the firm to its environment.

Purpose encourages each person to take an honest look at how many employees view themselves as engaged in work that truly matters. From those to whom the work matters, find out why. From those to whom the work does not

matter, find out what does matter and whether alignment with the firm is possible. Purpose is difficult to determine because many times it is unknown. When it is known, it may be buried under layers of belief, rationalization, and fear of disclosure. To find purpose, one must persist in asking why, try to see the pattern and underlying assumptions, and become an excellent reverse engineer. One must seek the alignment and self-motivation that produce the most ethical and effective action.

Ethical organizations operate on ground rules that encourage them to communicate and treat diverse constituencies fairly, promote individual responsibility, and enact a purpose. They thrive on individuality. They subscribe to the simple kindergarten principles stated by Robert Fulghum: Share everything. Play fair. Don't hit people. Put things back where you found them. Clean up your own mess. Don't take things that aren't yours. Say you're sorry when you hurt somebody. Live a balanced life—learn and think and draw and paint and sing and dance and play and work some every day. When you go out into the world, watch out for traffic, hold hands, and stick together. Everything you need to know is in there somewhere.[8]

One can take these items, extrapolate them into sophisticated adult terms, and apply them to one's life, to family, to work, to government, and to the world, They hold clear and true for businesses as well as individuals.

1 Berenbeim, Ronald, "The Corporate Ethics Test," *Business and Society Review*, 1992, 81,77-80.
2 Hoffman, W. Michael, "Developing the Ethical Corporations," *Bell Atlantic Quarterly*, 1986, 3 (1).
3 Pastin, Mark, "Lessons from High-Profit, High Ethics Companies: An Agenda for Management Action," *Business Ethics: Reading and Cases*, 1990, New York, McGraw-Hill Publishing Company.
4 Capen, Richard G. Jr., "Ethical Values," *Vital Speeches of the Day*, 1990, 56 (22), 685-687.
5 Pastin, *op. cit.*
6 Akers, Robert, "Confronting Ethical Dilemmas," *Vital Speeches of the Day*, 1990, 56 (23), 102.
7 Ibid.
8 Fulghum, Robert, *All I Ever Really Need to Know I Learned in Kindergarten*, 1989, Boston, G.K. Hall & Co.

What Is Virtue?

You can't lose it, like virginity, and don't confuse it with 'values,' which vary. Throughout a long, rich history, it's meant doing the right thing.

KENNETH L. WOODWARD

VIRTUE: FOR TOO MANY AMERIcans, the word suggests only a bygone bluenose era, prim lectures on sexual purity—at best, something you "lose" when you finally give in or give up. But for the ancient Greeks, the great medieval theologians and a growing number of contemporary philosophers as well, virtue has little to do with sexuality. For these thinkers, the cultivation of virtue makes individuals happy, wise, courageous, competent. The result is a good person, a responsible citizen and parent, a trusted leader, possibly even a saint. Without a virtuous people, according to this tradition, society cannot function well. And without a virtuous society, individuals cannot realize either their own or the common good. That, in theory, is what the "politics of virtue" is all about."

But before politicians embrace virtue as their latest election-year slogan, they would do well to tune in to contemporary philosophy. Despite the call for virtue, we live in an age of moral relativism. According to the dominant school of moral philosophy, the skepticism engendered by the Enlightenment has reduced all ideas of right and wrong to matters of personal taste, emotional preference or cultural choice. Since the truth cannot be known, neither can the good. In this view, the most any government can do is carve out rules that—like a traffic cop—ensure that a rough justice prevails among its citizens. Within agreed-upon social limits, therefore, people are free to make what they will of their private lives. In the United States, this outlook has produced a strong emphasis on rights over responsibilities, and it influences much of contemporary political theory.

Against this moral relativism, advocates of the "ethics of virtue" argue that some personal choices are morally superior to others. The issue, as they see it, is not the right to choose but the right way to make choices. The disorder of contemporary American society, they insist, is proof that the "Enlightenment Project," as philosopher Alasdair MacIntyre of the University of Notre Dame puts it, has failed. What he and a variety of other influential thinkers like James Q. Wilson of UCLA, Martha Nussbaum of Brown University, Charles Taylor of McGill University in Canada and Bernard Williams of Oxford in England propose is the renewal of the idea of virtue—or character—as the basis for both personal and social ethics.

For the ordinary citizen, virtue is easily confused with "values." Since personal values differ, Americans argue over whose values ought to be taught. But "values" is a morally neutral term that merely indicates preference and can be quite banal. To choose vanilla over chocolate is not the same as deciding how to raise children, though both express values. A virtue, by contrast, is a quality of character by which individuals habitually recognize and *do* the right thing. "Instead of talking about 'family values'," says Wilson, "everybody would be better off talking about the virtues that a decent family tries to inculcate." To Wilson and thinkers like him, these are the four classical virtues, old as Aristotle and just as compelling today: prudence, justice, fortitude and temperance.

But they do need modern translation. Prudence, for example, is not cautious calculation but practical wisdom—recogniz-

ing and making the right choice in specific situations. It is the master virtue that makes all others possible. Justice, as the Greeks thought of it, includes fairness, honesty and keeping promises. Fortitude is courage—guts—not only in combat but, as Lincoln exemplified during the Civil War, in pursuit of the right path despite great risks. And temperance involves much more than moderation in drink. It is self-discipline, the control of all the human passions and sensual pleasures—anger and frustration as well as food, drink and sex. A person of good character, then, is someone who through repeated good acts achieves an appropriate balance of these virtues in his life. Like a successful tennis professional, the virtuous person plays a consistently good game.

Traditional though they may be, the four virtues are not written on stone tablets. In "After Virtue," the most widely read American book on moral philosophy of the previous decade, MacIntyre points out that different societies emphasize different virtues—and often add new ones. Loyalty, for example, was a highly desired virtue in the clannish world of Homeric Greece as well as feudal Europe. Obedience to God's commands was central to ancient Israel. Christianity added three theological virtues—faith, hope and charity—to Aristotle's four. To this day, Catholic candidates for sainthood are judged by those seven virtues—plus one that the Greeks never admired: humility. And in his own influential book, "The Moral Sense," Wilson adds compassion as the virtue by which we habitually extend to strangers that concern we readily show for family and friends.

1. ETHICS, VALUES, AND SOCIAL RESPONSIBILITY IN BUSINESS

Can virtue be taught like academic subjects? This is what a number of public-school districts are asking themselves in response to parental demands that the classroom foster the formation of good character—as it did in the 19th century. Plato, whose philosophy focused on ideas, was inclined to think it could. But Aristotle was the wiser man. Unlike science and other intellectual pursuits, he reasoned, moral virtue is acquired only through practice. "We become just by doing just acts, temperate by doing temperate acts, brave by doing brave acts," he wrote. Children, Aristotle observed, learn virtue by following rules of good behavior, hearing stories of virtuous people—like those in Bill Bennett's book—and imitating virtuous models: parents, friends and worthy public figures. A child born to bad parents or a citizen of a corrupt society, he concluded, had little chance of becoming a virtuous adult.

In short, an ethics of virtue cannot be learned alone. Nor can it be taught from textbooks. Good character comes from living in communities—family, neighborhood, religious and civic institutions—where virtue is encouraged and rewarded. For much of American history, that responsibility fell disproportionately on women: in the home, of course, but also in Sunday schools and one-room schoolhouses. But contemporary America is as far from its small-town past as ancient Athens is from midtown Manhattan. Sociologically, all of the core institutions that once transmitted moral education are in disrepair. The family has fractured; neighborhoods have disappeared or turned surly; many schools can barely educate, and even many churches wonder what to teach. "You can't have strong virtues without strong institutions," says Jean Bethke Elshtain, professor of political science at Vanderbilt University. "And you can't have strong institutions without moral authority."

But many Americans are unprepared to recognize any moral authority outside themselves. Even so, they are not without their value systems. Believers have their God, movement feminists their liberation, intellectuals their ideas, professionals their careers. In ethics, says MacIntyre, what we have are merely shards of competing moral traditions, none of them coherent. Among them the most prevalent is "the ethics of authenticity," a phrase that Canadian philosopher Charles Taylor uses to describe those whose controlling moral purpose is personal self-fulfillment. But even this narcissistic goal, popular since the '60s, cannot do without the virtues it refuses to recognize. As Wilson puts it, "Self-fulfillment presupposes that you have a self worth fulfilling."

The ethics of virtue has its problems too. Sometimes virtues clash, as justice and compassion often do. Choices must be made, one good placed above another. Judgments must be made, too, on the behavior of others in society, even if it rubs the tarnish off their self-esteem. No ethical system is perfect, which is why religion persists, with its ethic of forgiveness. But the rising national debate over character may bring at least this much: a public rethinking of the kind of people we really want to be.

With Susan Miller in New York

INTEGRITY

AN ESSENTIAL EXECUTIVE QUALITY

Donald G. Zauderer

DONALD G. ZAUDERER, Ph.D., is director of the Key Executive Program at The American University in Washington, D.C. He thanks Lisa Levy, Tim Evanson, Jeff Fishel, Carol Blum, Pete Phillips, Morley Segal, and Rabbi Bruce Lustig for their contributions and comments during the preparation of this article.

What has happened to the notion of "integrity" in our nation? This author identifies 13 traits of business managers which compromise integrity and he presents specific actions that can help build a culture where integrity is practiced on a constant basis.

Stories about the absence of managerial integrity are dominating the mass media. We are reading about corruption in the Savings and Loan industry, insider trading on Wall Street, manipulative and harmful leveraged buy outs in American industry. In the political world, we are reading about negative campaigning, unlawful surveillance among political rivals, congressmen bouncing checks and failing to pay House restaurant charges. Many CEOs are being criticized for taking excessive bonuses while at the same time laying off large numbers of mid-level managers and production workers due to recessionary pressures. Even universities are under attack for raising tuition costs, charging the government for entertainment and decorating projects, approving sweetheart severance and retirement packages for administrators, and failing to emphasize quality education.

Philip Cushman, commenting in the *American Psychologist* on the breakdown in integrity claims that Americans have become emotionally and spiritually disoriented—preoccupied with how an issue affects the individual rather than how it affects the community or society.[1] Donald M. Wolfe, in yet a stronger statement contends in his article on integrity that, "The exploitative mentality has become so pervasive, and the impact of organizational practices so potent, that organizations cannot be trusted to ensure the commonweal—to protect the environment, to provide fair and human treatment for employees, to protect the safety and security of clients and customers, to refrain from misappropriation of public funds, and the like."[2] Both Cushman and Wolfe are arguing that there has been a serious erosion, accentuated in the last ten years, in the moral fabric of managers and leaders in the private and public sectors.

An Ancient Theme

Concerns such as these are not new—or unique to contemporary America. It is a pervasive theme going back to ancient times. In the book of Genesis, we learn that God formed humans with two inclinations—one good and one evil. Some Old Testament scholars see these inclinations as biological drives woven into the psychological fabric of every human being.[3]

In making decisions, managers are often faced with opposite and compelling inclinations, an internal struggle between modern versions of good and evil. Greed drove some Savings and Loan chieftains to misappropriate the savings of depositors. From all indications, they were not concerned about protecting their depositors, preserving the credibility of the banking system, or protecting the public trust that is essential to effective financial management. The concern for private gain prevailed over any concern for the public good.

Integrity is often overlooked or assumed in corporate life. There are few training programs focusing on ethical responsibility. Performance appraisal systems, corporate codes, and orientation programs often say little about principles of conduct in dealing with others. Often, a person's integrity is given little attention when compared to other characteristics in selecting candidates for positions. Corporations provide little guidance and, thus, many managers are operating without a solid infrastructure of principles guiding their behavior. If good and evil are pervasive themes in our personal and organizational lives, then corporations should consider doing more to help their managers make choices that reflect the "good"—thus preserving the good name of both the individual and the corporation.

This is a tall order. How does one get started? The logical first step is to get some understanding of what integrity means in broad terms, and then move toward clarifying those principles of conduct which might guide behavior in corporate life. In essence, corporations need to declare that certain principles define the nature of a manager's responsibility with respect to how he or she deals with others. Clarifying relational obligations is the first step in building an environment where a culture of integrity prevails over a culture of excessive and amoral self-interest.

The ideas put forth here are not intended as complete or definitive. Rather, they can provide a basis for initiating a dialogue about what set of principles might guide behavior in your organization.

From *Business Forum*, Fall 1992, pp. 12-16. © 1992 by the School of Business and Economics, California State University, Los Angeles. Reprinted by permission.

What is Integrity?

The word integrity is derived from the latin word *integri*, meaning wholeness. It is defined as a "state of being whole or undiminished." It is also defined as a state of "soundness of and adherence to moral principle."[4] Since integrity is an aspect of one's character and behavior, the definitions are highly related. It has been argued that one's character cannot become whole and integrated unless it is grounded in a solid infrastructure of moral values.[5]

What are these values? While there is no universal agreement on what moral principles should guide our behavior, we can gain perspective by integrating ancient classical ideas with modern thought. The Old Testament, recounting a thousand years of events, focuses on the struggle between good and evil. Confucius, writing in the years 551-479 BC proclaimed, "What you do not want done to yourself, do not do to others." Saint Matthew is quoted in the New Testament with an admonition that today is translated into what we call The Golden Rule: Do unto others as you would have them do unto you. Aristotle, writing over 2000 years ago, placed considerable emphasis on his conception of "happiness." In Aristotelian terms, happiness is described as a "kind of virtuous activity of the soul."[6] The term "activity" is particularly important because of its emphasis on moral action in a social environment. The major function of virtue, according to Aristotle, is to influence others to perform noble actions, and to create a society where people can develop to their full potential.[7] To achieve this end, he recommended that citizens become fully engaged in both study and the political life of the community. Wealth and the possession of goods were not considered an appropriate end, but simply served as instruments to achieve "happiness."[8]

While Aristotle focused on learning, political and social involvement, and good deeds, Immanuel Kant, writing in the 18th century, emphasized moral duties and obligations in our relationship with others. In his view, the first duty of individuals is to treat others as ends and not as means. Implicit in his statement is the belief that "no person's rights should be subordinated to anyone else."[9] If executives see workers simply as means to their own accumulation of wealth, it is quite natural to minimize their share of increased profits; to mini-mize developmental opportunities unless it is of immediate benefit to them; or to invest as little as possible in the safety and security of the worker. Alternatively, seeing the employee as an end induces one to think of him or her as a partner, whose interests you attempt to fully integrate with the interests of the organization.

One of IBMs core values, "Respect for the individual," has its roots in Kantian logic. Kant introduces a set of moral duties and obligations that should guide our relationships with each other. Principles such as honesty, generosity, and keeping one's word, are some ways in which we treat people as an end rather than a means.

Contemporary philosopher Mark Halfin further emphasizes the importance of intention in defining integrity. He defines integrity as reflected in one who "maintains a consistent commitment to do what is best—especially under conditions of adversity."[10] In attempting to do what is best, people of integrity intend to embrace noble ideals and just principles; and acknowledge and confront all relevant moral considerations when faced with a dilemma. Halfin adds two important dimensions to the conversation: It is the *intention* to do what is best based on personal analysis and reflection that matters; and it involves *doing* what is perceived to be best—even under conditions of adversity. Naturally, integrity is most severely tested under adverse conditions. One, then, does not have to be morally pure or perfect in judgment to have integrity. Rather, one's integrity is determined by the intention to do what is right.

Halfin's notion of holding onto principle under adversity, is further emphasized by authors Nancy Adler and Frederick Bird who indicated that "Individuals demonstrate integrity when they withstand pressure from others while taking risks in defense of behavior they conscientiously consider to be best."[11] Integrity is risky business. Should an employee tell government inspectors about transgressions of environmental law even though it might threaten his or her job? Should a boss spend time on employee development despite the criticisms of peers who believe it is a waste of time? Should a male confront other males about sexual harassment, and risk the criticism of peers? Integrity implies the disposition to take risks in defense of relational duties and obligations; having the courage to stand up, to maintain a course of principled action, even under attack or severe criticism.

Each of the sources adds a distinct and unique element to the emerging definition of integrity. The following summarizes their contributions:

The Old Testament: Consciously struggle to subdue the evil inclination.
The New Testament: Live according to the principal of The Golden Rule.
Aristotle: Maintain concern for the community; engage in political and social life to improve the community; inspire others to do good deeds.
Kant: Establish, affirm, and exemplify moral duties and obligations toward others; treat others as ends and not as a means.
Halfin: Maintain a consistent commitment to do what is right, especially under conditions of adversity; confront all moral considerations before taking action.
Adler and Bird: Take risks to defend just principles and ideals.

Specific Behaviors

The preceding discussion has focused on general guidelines. But how does one move from guidelines to specific behaviors? What specific behaviors reflect high integrity? How does one's integrity affect the trust of others and the strength of the commonweal?

In attempting to identify specific behaviors, a far reaching search of literature that included religion, philosophy, biographies of great leaders, psychology, and business and government ethics was conducted. Cross-cutting moral themes and principles were identified and are described in the following list: (The behaviors are expressed in a negative form—the opposite behavior follows in italics.) A manager's integrity is compromised when he or she:

Displays Arrogance by becoming puffed up with their own importance, exaggerating their worth to the organization, and speaking only with people at same or higher level. (*Posess humility*)

Promotes Self-Interest by exploiting the organization for own purpose and focusing on "what's in it for me" when considering actions. (*Maintain concern for the greater good*)

Practices Deception by making untrue statements, taking credit for the work of others, and using misleading facts to defend positions. (*Be truthful*)

Breaches Agreements by delivering

services late, or failing to follow an agreed upon decision process. (*Fulfill commitments*)

Deals Unfairly by making judgments without researching facts, discriminating in hiring and promotion, and assigning the most interesting projects to a favored few. (*Strive for fairness*)

Shifts Blame by declining to acknowledge personal responsibility, falsely accusing others, and denigrating the reputation of colleagues. (*Take responsibility*)

Diminishes Dignity by withholding recognition, declining to invite or accept input, exhibiting discourteous and impolite behavior. (*Have respect for the individual*)

Retains Envy by begrudging other's success, and competing at every opportunity. (*Celebrate the good fortune of others*)

Neglects Employee Development by providing superficial performance appraisals and failing to coach or train staff. (*Develop others*)

Avoids Risks by refusing to confront unjust actions, or declining to stand up for principle. (*Reproach unjust acts*)

Holds Grudges by failing to let go of hard feelings, and finding ways to get even. (*Be forgiving*)

Declines to Extend Self by withholding help and assistance in times that matter, and being ungenerous in rewards. (*Extend self for others*)

Displays Arrogance
Arrogant managers nourish their ego at every opportunity. They focus on the size of their offices, the quality of their furniture, the location of their parking place, and other symbols of status. They take advice from superiors, but spurn the counsel of peers and subordinates. Arrogant managers may try to intimidate subordinates with hard questions, taking delight in catching flaws in facts or logic. Their agenda is simple: to puff up their own importance. The effect is predictable. It diminishes the dignity and self-esteem of subordinates, and limits the real potential contribution of the manager.

Subordinates resent arrogant bosses, and may even retaliate. A relationship that starts with trust, loyalty, and commitment will degenerate into one characterized by suspicion, betrayal, and lack of dedication.

Promotes Self-Interest
Some people pursue their self-interest to the detriment of the organization. As an example, financier Charles Keating bolstered his financial position by recklessly using his savings and loan money to finance risky ventures. The cost to the public was immense—notably in dollars and confidence in the entire savings and loan system.

There are many ways to exploit the system for personal gain. Doctors might order unnecessary tests to increase their income. Lawyers might complicate divorce proceedings to increase billable hours. Managers may grossly under-reward subordinates to enhance their reputations for efficiency. Professors may devote little time preparing for their classes in order to pursue the larger rewards of publication. And corporate CEOs may curtail research and development to improve short-term profits and be rewarded with a generous year-end bonus. In the long term, these actions erode public trust and confidence in our institutions.

"Managers who lack integrity place themselves and their organizations at risk."

Practices Deception
Some managers regularly deceive colleagues, vendors, and clients. This deception takes many forms. They assign projects without revealing obstacles and potential risks; provide staff with false information on why management promoted someone else; or promise services to clients without any intention to deliver. Similarly, they provide subcontractors with false information on the real scope of work; provide employees with misleading information on their career potential; or promise and rescind offers to participate in important decisions. A manager who builds a career on deception will eventually stand alone.

Breaches Agreements
Managers who are unable to meet commitments lose a precious asset, their reputations. Some renege on promises to grant subordinates specialized training, career guidance or developmental assignments. Managers who regularly fail to follow through on agreements such as these will lose credibility, trust, and effectiveness in the organization. These managers will find that peers and subordinates will no longer be inclined to respond to their needs in a timely manner.

Deals Unfairly
Some managers deal unfairly with associates. They may provide access to a favored few, base salaries and bonuses on general perception instead of concrete results, promote staff with the "right" cultural, educational, and religious background, and reward those who tell them what they want to hear. In such situations, some subordinates flourish while others feel rejected and alienated. When managers treat some staff unfairly, they inadvertently demotivate part of their staff and reduce total team effectiveness.

Shifts Blame
Some managers blame others for every problem. They furnish plausible explanations about how someone else's actions contributed to declining profits, high overhead or client dissatisfaction. They rarely acknowledge their role in the problem and expect others to accept the blame. Subordinates will resent the finger pointing, and the loyalty they once brought to the job will be replaced by alienation and distrust.

Diminishes Dignity
Some managers specialize in diminishing others. They take credit for the work of employees, make decisions without meaningful participation, decline to return phone calls of their subordinates, and insist on reviewing all decisions. These actions diminish the self-esteem of subordinates.

In some cases managers practice discrimination. They stereotype African Americans, Hispanics, Asians, American Indians, women, or anyone else with a different color, gender, or cultural background. They may stereotype minority staff as lazy, indecisive, ungenerous, fragile, or ineffective. Armed with these discriminatory assumptions, managers disregard the special talents of subordinates. This practice diminishes the self worth of employees, and by becoming a self-fulfilling prophesy, limits opportunities for advancement. To make matters worse, the organization will fail to get the maximum value of each employee.

Retains Envy
Managers inevitably try to compare the

salaries, perquisites and resources with those of their colleagues who have similar rank. They may find that someone else has a larger staff, bigger office or more generous expense account. Some will become consumed with envy and look for ways to redress the inequity. They may press the boss for better conditions, refrain from cooperating with peers, or withhold their best effort on important projects. As a consequence, their relationships will deteriorate up and down the organization.

The wise Solomon said that "envy is the rottenest of bones," implying that unrestrained feelings of envy always damage relationships. Managers who cannot transform these feelings will be unable to build a loyal following.

Neglects Employee Development

Some managers neglect to develop subordinates. For example, they rarely clarify job expectations, provide subordinates with well grounded feedback on performance, or discuss career aspirations within the context of organizational needs and opportunities.

Employees soon understand that they are at a dead-end. They may conclude that if the manager is not concerned about them, they will care less about him or her. Managers who invest little time in people will get little back from them.

Avoids Risks

It takes courage to speak the truth, especially when it may bring reprisals. For example, a manager of environmental affairs at a major oil company was fired for failing to remove documents from a plastics facility in order to conceal facts in an investigation. His superiors had forced him to choose between losing his job and taking the ethically correct action.

While confronting every action of injustice would be foolhardy, some managers damage the organization by staying silent in the face of an unjust or unethical act. Their silence, in effect, creates a precedent for similar acts of questionable integrity. Peers and subordinates with lax standards can then operate freely, increasing the risk that decisions will embarrass or weaken the organization. In the case of the oil company, for example, the fired employee went to court and was awarded $1.375 million in damages.

Holds Grudges

Life in organizations is sometimes like a hockey game. Players bash one another in attempting to gain a competitive edge. Managers are wounded when senior executives pass them over for promotion, criticize them in public, withhold information, or second guess decisions. Managers can also be angered when subordinates embarrass them by bungling a presentation with senior management. In addition, peers can wound colleagues by raising embarrassing questions in high-level meetings.

Some managers respond to these events by "getting even." They may strike back by withholding information from the boss, being inaccessible to a

---

"Organizations can do a great deal to build a climate where considerations of integrity are taken into account in decision-making."

---

subordinate; or providing a peer with half-hearted cooperation. Managers who want to get even can always find a way—usually at a cost to their reputations.

Such acts will lead superiors to doubt the manager's ability to remain cool under pressure. Subordinates will play it safe to guard against retribution. These outcomes can damage a manager's reputation as a mature professional who can be trusted to exercise good judgment.

Declines to Extend Self

Some managers rarely extend themselves for others. They focus attention on their personal objectives, and feel no sense of responsibility for assisting subordinates. For example, the regional vice president of a restaurant chain heard about a newly appointed high potential manager who was facing a serious turnover problem. With some coaching, the manager could have identified the problem. The regional V.P. never provided the needed assistance, and the manager left the business out of frustration.

People in organizations need all types of help. They may need special mentoring on how to transition into a new job, get along with a difficult boss, or balance the responsibilities of work and home. A manager who declines to extend assistance relinquishes an opportunity to empower employees and gain their loyalty.

Summing Up

Managers who lack integrity place themselves and their organizations at risk. When they transgress norms of integrity, they risk losing the trust, loyalty, and commitment of employees, suppliers and customers. The best preventative is for organizations to define the moral standards expected of everyone and to develop programs that reinforce these standards.

Many companies understand that integrity is a key element in building strategic advantage. John F. Akers, Chairman of IBM, contends that IBM has built its business on a basis of trust and confidence."[12] IBM has always understood that integrity has helped the organization build strategic advantage, avoid adverse publicity, and maintain an identity as competent, successful, and ethical.

Organizations can do a great deal to build a climate where considerations of integrity are taken into account in decision-making. The following are some actions that help build a culture where integrity is practiced on a consistent basis:

Communicate the Message from Senior Management. The words and actions of senior leaders have an enormous impact in building a culture of integrity. If senior managers are models of integrity, they will earn the right to emphasize it in speeches, memos, and policy statements. Their actions and words will be the single most important factor in determining the ethical climate of the organization.

Develop Codes of Ethical Conduct. Many corporations have established core value statements or codes of ethical conduct to communicate their expectations. Digital Corporation, for example, in its statement of philosophy emphasizes "fair personnel practices, meeting commitments to customers and employees, developing people, honest and straight forward communication with customers, being honest, fair and open with suppliers, never criticizing the competition publicly, and striving to do what is right in every situation."[13]

Develop Procedures for Discussing/ Reporting Incidents. Statements of corporate policies and procedures are another means of reinforcing ethical codes of business conduct. Boeing Corporation has an elaborate statement of business conduct, and has established a channel that enables employees to report infractions or concerns. IBM Corporation has a wide ranging set of guidelines for business conduct, and each employee must certify in writing every year that he or she has read it. The IBM Speak Up and Open Door Programs also allow employees to pursue a complaint with any higher level of management. All complaints are investigated and threats of retribution are not tolerated. Employees who transgress corporate standards face disciplinary action—even the potential for dismissal.

Establish Integrity as an Assessment Criteria.

When employees understand that integrity is an evaluative criteria, they will pay more attention to this aspect of their performance.

Build Ethical Considerations into Long-Range Planning.

Corporations can benefit from considering ethical issues when discussing alternatives for future action. Researcher Susan Harrison writes that corporations should "identify ethical issues in which the company is or may be involved, how each issue may impact the company, the probability of occurrence, and an appropriate response to the ethical issue."[14] This analysis can legiti-

mate ethics as a consideration in corporate decision-making; and can prepare the corporation for defending its actions on moral grounds.

Include Ethics and Business Conduct in Corporate Training.

Training is often the only action that corporations take to reinforce their business conduct guidelines. By itself, it will not be effective in raising the standards of ethical conduct. Together with other actions discussed above, it can contribute to improving the ethical climate in the corporation. Such training programs can introduce corporate values and beliefs. Through the use of videos, case studies, simulations, and other methods, training can provide employees with a heightened awareness of the ethical implications of their actions, and provide them with guidance on how to exercise ethical judgment.

All of these actions will reinforce the message that employees at every level are expected to bring integrity to their jobs, and to their relationships with fellow workers, suppliers, customers, and the community. In the long run, the corporate strategic advantage will be enhanced by its reputation for integrity.

It's time to reconsider the words of John Gardner in *On Leadership:*

We must hope too that our leaders will help us keep alive traditional values that are not so easy to embrace in laws—our feeling about individual moral responsibility, about caring for others, about honor and integrity, and tolerance and mutual respect, and about individual fulfillment within a framework of shared values.

Notes

1 Cushman, Philip, "Why the Self is Empty: Toward a Historically Situated Psychology," *American Psychologist,* May 1990, 604.
2 Wolfe, Donald M., "Is There Integrity in the Bottom Line: Managing Obstacles to Executive Integrity," Suresh Srivastva and Associates, *Executive Integrity: The Search for High Human Values in Organizational Life,* San Francisco, Jossey-Bass, Inc, 1988, 152.
3 Goldman, Norman Saul, *An Investigation Into a Rabbinic Understanding of Yetzer Hara and the Unconscious,* Eastern Baptist Theological Seminar, 1980, 35.
4 Stein, Jess, (ed.), *The Random House Dictionary of the English Language,* New York, New York, Random House, 1967.
5 Taylor, Gabriele, "Integrity," *Proceedings of the Aristotelian Society,* 55 (1981), 143-159.
6 Aristotle, *The Nichomachean Ethics,* London, Penguin Books, 1975, 81.
7 Ibid, 339.
8 Ibid, 69.
9 Kant, Immanual, *The Groundwork of the Metaphysic of Morals,* trans. H.J. Paton, New York, Harper & Row, 1964, 63-67.
10 Halfin, Mark S., Integrity: *A Philosophical Inquiry,* Philadelphia, PA, Temple University Press, 36.
11 Adler, Nancy J., Bird, Frederick B., "International Dimensions of Executive Integrity: Who Is Responsible for the World?," Srivastva, Suresh and Associates, *Executive Integrity: The Search for High Human Values in Organizational Life,* San Francisco, Jossey-Bass, 1988, 252.
12 IBM Corporation, *Business Conduct Guidelines,* September 1990, 5.
13 Digital Corporation, *Personnel Policies and Procedures Manual,* 1990.
14 Harrison, Susan J., "What Corporate America is Teaching About Ethics," *Academy of Management Executive,* 1981, Vol. 5, No. 1, 29.

The trouble with business ethics

Debate frequently is more hot air than substance

Tom Peters

Tom Peters' most recent book is "Thriving on Chaos."

Ethics is a hot business topic, and that is a potential boon to us all. Unfortunately, the heightened awareness has spawned an industry of mindless, "do good, be good" writings. But dealing with ethics isn't so easy. The point was driven home after I accepted an invitation to speak about ethics to business students. I spent many a restless night grappling with the easy simplifications that ignore messy reality. This set of somewhat disjointed observations is one byproduct.

• Ethics is not principally about headline issues—responding to the Tylenol poisoning or handling insider information. Ethical concerns surround us all the time, on parade whenever we deal with people in the course of the average day. How we work out the "little stuff" will determine our response, if called upon, to a Tylenol-sized crisis. When disaster strikes, it's far too late to seek out ethical touchstones.

• High ethical standards—business or otherwise—are, above all, about treating people decently. To me (as a person, businessperson and business owner) that means respect for a person's privacy, dignity, opinions and natural desire to grow; and people's respect for (and by) co-workers.

• Diversity must be honored. To be sure, it is important to be clear about your own compass heading; but don't ever forget that other people have profoundly different—and equally decent—ethical guidance mechanisms.

• People, even the saints, are egocentric and selfish; we were designed "wrong" in part from the start. Any ethical framework in action had best take into account the troublesome but immutable fact of man's inherently flawed character.

• Corporations are created and exist to serve people—insiders and outsiders—period.

• By their very nature, organizations run roughshod over people. Organizations produce powerlessness and humiliation for most participants with more skill than they use by producing widgets.

• Though all men and women are created equal, some surely have more power than others. Thus, a central ethical issue in the workplace (and beyond) is the protection of and support for the unempowered—especially the front-line worker and the customer.

• For employees and managers alike, fighting the impersonal "they"/"them" (in every bureaucratic institution) is almost always justified on ethical grounds.

• While one can point to ethically superior (and profitable) firms, such as Herman Miller, most of us will spend most of our working life in compromised—i.e., politicized—organizations. Dealing with "office politics," "brown-nosing," etc., is a perpetual ethical morass. A "pure" ethical stance in the face of most firms' political behavior will lead you out the door in short order, with only the convent, monastery or ashram as alternatives. The line between ethical purity and arrogant egocentrism (i.e., a holier-than-thou stance toward the tumult of everyday life) is a fine one.

• Though I sing the praises of an "action bias," ethical behavior demands that we tread somewhat softly in all of our affairs. Unintended consequences and the secondary and tertiary effects of most actions and policies far outnumber intended and first-order effects. I sometimes think—as a manager, as a "change agent"—that dropping out is the only decent/ethical path; our best-intended plans so often cause more harm than good. (Think about it: Leaving the world no worse off than when you arrived is no mean feat.)

• The pursuit of high ethical standards in business might well be served by the elimination of many business schools. The implicit thrust of most MBA programs is that great systems and great techniques win out over great people.

• Can we live up to the spirit of the Bill of Rights in our work places? Can "good business ethics" and "good real-life ethics"—and profit—coincide on a routine basis? One would hope that the answer is yes, although respect for the individual has hardly been the cornerstone of American industry's traditional approach to its work force.

• Capitalism and democracy in society

are messy. But I believe they have far fewer downsides and far more upsides than any alternative so far concocted. The same can be said for capitalism and democracy inside the firm—e.g., whole-sale participation, widespread owner-ship.

• Great novels, not management books, might help. There are no easy answers, but there are fertile fields for gathering ideas. If you wish to be appropriately humbled about life and relation-ships and the possibility of ethical behavior, read Dostoyevsky, Forster or Garcia Marquez instead of Drucker, Blanchard or Peters. Then reconsider your latest magisterial proclamation.

• Each of us is ultimately lonely. In the end, it's up to each of us and each of us alone to figure out who we are, who we are not and to act more or less consis-tently on those conclusions.

In my view, anyone who is not very confused all the time about ethical issues is out of touch with the frightful (and joyous) richness of the world. But at least being actively confused means that we are actively considering our ethical stance and that of the institutions we associate with. That's a good start.

Ethics in Practice

*The values of a company's leaders are evident
in every strategic decision they make.*

Kenneth R. Andrews

*Kenneth R. Andrews is the Donald K. David Professor of
Business Administration, Emeritus, at the Harvard Busi-
ness School. He was editor of HBR from 1979 to 1985. This
article is adapted from his introduction to* Ethics in
Practice: Managing the Moral Corporation *(Harvard
Business School Press, 1989).*

As the 1990s overtake us, public interest in ethics is at
a historic high. While the press calls attention to
blatant derelictions on Wall Street, in the defense
industry, and in the Pentagon, and to questionable
activities in the White House, in the attorney general's office, and in Congress, observers wonder
whether our society is sicker than usual. Probably
not. The standards applied to corporate behavior
have risen over time, and that has raised the average
rectitude of businesspersons and politicians both. It
has been a long time since we could say with Mark
Twain that we have the best Senate money can buy or
agree with muckrakers like Upton Sinclair that our
large companies are the fiefdoms of robber barons.
But illegal and unethical behavior persists, even as
efforts to expose it often succeed in making its rewards short-lived.

Why is business ethics a problem that snares not
just a few mature criminals or crooks in the making
but a host of apparently good people who lead exemplary private lives while concealing information
about dangerous products or systematically falsifying costs? My observation suggests that the problem
of corporate ethics has three aspects: the development of the executive as a moral person; the influence
of the corporation as a moral environment; and the
actions needed to map a high road to economic and
ethical performance—and to mount guardrails to
keep corporate wayfarers on track.

Sometimes it is said that wrongdoing in business is an individual failure: a person of the
proper moral fiber, properly brought up, simply
would not cheat. Because of poor selection, a
few bad apples are bound to appear in any big barrel. But these corporate misfits can subsequently

be scooped out. Chief executive officers, we used to
think, have a right to rely on the character of individual employees without being distracted from business objectives. Moral character is shaped by family,
church, and education long before an individual joins
a company to make a living.

In an ideal world, we might end here. In the real
world, moral development is an unsolved problem at
home, at school, at church—and at work. Two-career
families, television, and the virtual disappearance of
the dinner table as a forum for discussing moral issues have clearly outmoded instruction in basic principles at Mother's knee—if that fabled tutorial was
ever as effective as folklore would have it. We cannot
expect our battered school systems to take over the
moral role of the family. Even religion is less help
than it once might have been when membership in a
distinct community promoted—or coerced—conventional moral behavior. Society's increasing seculari-
zation, the profusion of sects, the conservative
church's divergence from new lifestyles, pervasive
distrust of the religious right—all these mean that we
cannot depend on uniform religious instruction to
armor business recruits against temptation.

Nor does higher education take up the slack, even
in disciplines in which moral indoctrination once
flourished. Great literature can be a self-evident

 ## Why do so many good people get caught falsifying costs?

source of ethical instruction, for it informs the mind
and heart together about the complexities of moral
choice. Emotionally engaged with fictional or historic characters who must choose between death and
dishonor, integrity and personal advancement, power
and responsibility, self and others, we expand our
own moral imaginations as well. Yet professors of literature rarely offer guidance in ethical interpretation, preferring instead to stress technical, aesthetic,
or historical analysis.

Moral philosophy, which is the proper academic home for ethical instruction, is even more remote, with few professors choosing to teach applied ethics. When you add to that the discipline's studied disengagement from the world of practical affairs, it is not surprising that most students (or managers) find little in the subject to attract them.

What does attract students—in large numbers—is economics, with its theory of human behavior that relates all motivation to personal pleasure, satisfaction, and self-interest. And since self-interest is more easily served than not by muscling aside the self-interest of others, the Darwinian implications of conventional economic theory are essentially immoral. Competition produces and requires the will to win. Careerism focuses attention on advantage. Immature individuals of all ages are prey to the moral flabbiness that William James said attends exclusive service to the bitch goddess Success.

Spurred in part by recent notorious examples of such flabbiness, many business schools are making determined efforts to reintroduce ethics in elective and required courses. But even if these efforts were further along than they are, boards of directors and senior managers would be unwise to assume that recruits could enter the corporate environment without need for additional education. The role of any school is to prepare its graduates for a lifetime of learning from experience that will go better and faster than it would have done without formal education. No matter how much colleges and business schools expand their investment in moral instruction, most education in business ethics (as in all other aspects of business acumen) will occur in the organizations in which people spend their lives.

Making ethical decisions is easy when the facts are clear and the choices black and white. But it is a different story when the situation is clouded by ambiguity, incomplete information, multiple points of view, and conflicting responsibilities. In such situations—which managers experience all the time—ethical decisions depend on both the decision-making process itself and on the experience, intelligence, and integrity of the decision maker.

Responsible moral judgment cannot be transferred to decision makers ready-made. Developing it in business turns out to be partly an administrative process involving: recognition of a decision's ethical implications; discussion to expose different points of view; and testing the tentative decision's adequacy in balancing self-interest and consideration of others, its import for future policy, and its consonance with the company's traditional values. But after all this, if a clear consensus has not emerged, then the executive in charge must decide, drawing on his or her intuition and conviction. This being so, the caliber of the decision maker is decisive—especially when an immediate decision must arise from instinct rather than from discussion.

This existential resolution requires the would-be moral individual to be the final authority in a situation where conflicting ethical principles are joined. It does not rule out prior consultation with others or recognition that, in a hierarchical organization, you might be overruled.

Ethical decisions therefore require of individuals three qualities that can be identified and developed. The first is competence to recognize ethical issues and to think through the consequences of alternative resolutions. The second is self-confidence to seek out different points of view and then to decide what is right at a given time and place, in a particular set of relationships and circumstances. The third is what William James called tough-mindedness, which in management is the willingness to make decisions when all that needs to be known cannot be known and when the questions that press for answers have no established and incontrovertible solutions.

Unfortunately, moral individuals in the modern corporation are too often on their own. But these individuals cannot be expected to remain autonomous, no matter how well endowed they are, without positive organized support. The stubborn persistence of ethical problems obscures the simplicity of the solution—once the leaders of a company decide to do something about their ethical standards. Ethical dereliction, sleaziness, or inertia is not merely an individual failure but a management problem as well.

When they first come to work, individuals whose moral judgment may ultimately determine their company's ethical character enter a community whose values will influence their own. The economic function of the corporation is necessarily one of those values. But if it is the only value, ethical inquiry cannot flourish. If management believes that the invisible hand of the market adequately moderates the injury done by the pursuit of self-interest, ethical policy can be dismissed as irrelevant. And if what people see (while they are hearing about maximizing shareholder wealth) are managers dedicated to their own survival and compensation, they will naturally be more concerned about rewards than about fairness.

For the individual, the impact of the need to succeed is doubtless more direct than the influence of neoclassical economic theory. But just as the corporation itself is saddled with the need to establish competitive advantage over time (after reinvestment of what could otherwise be the immediate profit by which the financial community and many shareholders judge its performance), aspiring managers will also be influenced by the way they are judged. A highly moral and humane chief executive can preside over an amoral organization because the incentive system focuses attention on short-term quantifiable results.

Under pressures to get ahead, the individual (of whose native integrity we are hopeful) is tempted to pursue advancement at the expense of others, to cut corners, to seek to win at all cost, to make things seem better than they are – to take advantage, in sum, of a myopic evaluation of performance. People will do what they are rewarded for doing. The quantifiable results of managerial activity are always much more visible than the quality and future consequences of the means by which they are attained.

By contrast, when the corporation is defined as a socioeconomic institution with responsibilities to other constituencies (employees, customers, and communities, for example), policy can be established to regulate the single-minded pursuit of maximum immediate profit. The leaders of such a company speak of social responsibility, promulgate ethical policy, and make their personal values available for emulation by their juniors. They are respectful of neoclassical economic theory, but find it only partially useful as a management guide.

As the corporation grows beyond its leader's daily direct influence, the ethical consequences of size and geographical deployment come into play. Control and enforcement of all policy becomes more difficult, but this is especially true with regard to policy established for corporate ethics. Layers of responsibility bring communication problems. The possibility of penalty engenders a lack of candor. Distance from headquarters complicates the evaluation of performance, driving it to numbers. When operations are dispersed among different cultures and countries in which corruption assumes exotic guises, a consensus about moral values is hard to achieve and maintain.

Moreover, decentralization in and of itself has ethical consequences, not least because it absolutely requires trust and latitude for error. The inability to monitor the performance of executives assigned to tasks their superiors cannot know in detail results inexorably in delegation. Corporate leaders are accustomed to relying on the business acumen of profit-center managers, whose results the leaders watch with a practiced eye. Those concerned with maintaining their companies' ethical standards are just as dependent on the judgment and moral character of the managers to whom authority is delegated. Beyond keeping your fingers crossed, what can you do?

Fortunately for the future of the corporation, this microcosm of society can be, within limits, what its leadership and membership make it. The corporation is an organization in which people influence one another to establish accepted values and ways of doing things. It is not a democracy, but to be fully effective, the authority of its leaders must be supported by their followers. Its leadership has more power than elected officials do to choose who will join or remain in the association. Its members expect direction to be proposed even as they threaten resistance to change. Careless or lazy managements let their organizations drift, continuing their economic performance along lines previously established and leaving their ethics to chance. Resolute managements find they can surmount the problems I have dwelt on – once they have separated these problems from their camouflage.

It is possible to carve out of our pluralistic, multicultured society a coherent community with a strategy that defines both its economic purposes and the standards of competence, quality, and humanity that govern its activities. The character of a corporation may well be more malleable than an individual's. Certainly its culture can be shaped. Intractable persons can be replaced or retired. Those committed to the company's goals can generate formal and informal sanctions to constrain and alienate those who are not.

Shaping such a community begins with the personal influence of the chief executive and that of the managers who are heads of business units, staff departments, or any other suborganizations to which authority is delegated. The determination of explicit ethical policy comes next, followed by the same management procedures that are used to execute any body of policy in effective organizations.

▌ How can you tell whether managers merit your trust?

The way the chief executive exercises moral judgment is universally acknowledged to be more influential than written policy. The CEO who orders the immediate recall of a product, at the cost of millions of dollars in sales because of a quality defect affecting a limited number of untraceable shipments, sends one kind of message. The executive who suppresses information about a producer's actual or potential ill effects or, knowingly or not, condones overcharging, sends another.

Policy is implicit in behavior. The ethical aspects of product quality, personnel, advertising, and marketing decisions are immediately plain. CEOs say much more than they know in the most casual contacts with those who watch their every move. Pretense is futile. "Do not *say* things," Emerson once wrote. "What you *are* stands over you the while, and thunders so that I can not hear what you say to the contrary." It follows that "if you would not be known to do anything, never do it."

The modest person might respond to this attribution of transparency with a "who, me?" Self-confident sophisticates will refuse to consider themselves so easily read. Almost all executives underestimate their power and do not recognize deference in others. The import of this, of course, is that a CEO should be conscious of how the position amplifies his or her most casual judgments, jokes, and silences. But an even more important implication—given that people cannot hide their characters—is that the selection of a chief executive (indeed of any aspirant to management responsibility) should include an explicit estimate of his or her character. If you ask how to do that, Emerson would reply, "Just look."

Once a company's leaders have decided that its ethical intentions and performance will be managed, rather than left untended in the corrosive environment of unprincipled competition, they must determine their corporate policy and make it explicit much as they do in other areas. The need for written policy is especially urgent in companies without a strong tradition to draw on or where a new era must be launched—after a public scandal, say, or an internal investigation of questionable behavior. Codes of ethics are now commonplace. But in and of themselves they are not effective, and this is especially true when they are so broadly stated that they can be dismissed as merely cosmetic.

Internal policies specifically addressed to points of industry, company, and functional vulnerability make compliance easier to audit and training easier to conduct. Where particular practices are of major concern—price fixing, for example, or bribery of government officials or procurement—compliance can be made a condition of employment and certified annually by employees' signatures. Still, the most pervasive problems cannot be foreseen, nor can the proper procedures be so spelled out in advance as to tell the person on the line what to do. Unreasonably repressive rules undermine trust, which remains indispensable.

What executives can do is advance awareness of the kinds of problems that are foreseeable. Since policy cannot be effective unless it is understood, some companies use corporate training sessions to discuss the problems of applying their ethical standards. In difficult situations, judgment in making the leap from general policy statements to situationally specific action can be informed by discussion. Such discussion, if carefully conducted, can reveal the inadequacy or ambiguity of present policy, new areas in which the company must take a unified stand, and new ways to support individuals in making the right decisions.

As in all policy formulation and implementation, the deportment of the CEO, the development of relevant policy—and training in its meaning and application—are not enough. In companies determined to sustain or raise ethical standards, management expands the information system to illuminate pressure points—the rate of manufacturing defects, product returns and warranty claims, special instances of quality shortfalls, results of competitive benchmarking inquiries—whatever makes good sense in the special circumstances of the company.

Because trust is indispensable, ethical aspirations must be supported by information that serves not only to inform but also to control. Control need not be so much coercive as customary, representing not suspicion but a normal interest in the quality of operations. Experienced executives do not substitute trust for the awareness that policy is often distorted in practice. Ample information, like full visibility, is a powerful deterrent.

This is why purposely ethical organizations expand the traditional sphere of external and internal audits (which is wherever fraud may occur) to include compliance with corporate ethical standards. Even more important, such organizations pay attention to every kind of obstacle that limits performance and to problems needing ventilation so that help can be provided.

To obtain information that is deeply guarded to avoid penalty, internal auditors—long since taught not to prowl about as police or detectives—must be people with enough management experience to be sensitive to the manager's need for economically viable decisions. For example, they should have imagination enough to envision ethical outcomes from bread-and-butter profit and pricing decisions, equal opportunity and payoff dilemmas, or downsizing crunches. Establishing an audit and control climate that takes as a given an open exchange of information between the company's operating levels and policy-setting levels is not difficult—once, that is, the need to do so is recognized and persons of adequate experience and respect are assigned to the work.

But no matter how much empathy audit teams exhibit, discipline ultimately requires action. The secretary who steals petty cash, the successful salesman who falsifies his expense account, the accountant and her boss who alter cost records, and, more problematically, the chronically sleazy operator who never does anything actually illegal—all must be dealt with cleanly, with minimum attention to allegedly extenuating circumstances. It is true that hasty punishment may be unjust and absolve superiors improperly of their secondary responsibility for wrongdoing. But long delay or waffling in the effort to be humane obscures the message the organization requires whenever violations occur. Trying to conceal a major lapse or safeguarding the names of people who have been fired is kind to the offender but blunts the salutary impact of disclosure.

For the executive, the administration of discipline incurs one ethical dilemma after another: How do you weigh consideration for the offending individual, for example, and how do you weigh the future of the organization? A company dramatizes its uncompromising adherence to lawful and ethical behavior when it severs employees who commit offenses that were classified in advance as unforgivable. When such a decision is fair, the grapevine makes its equity clear even when more formal publicity is inappropriate. Tough decisions should not be postponed simply because they are painful. The steady support of corporate integrity is never without emotional cost.

In a large, decentralized organization, consistently ethical performance requires difficult decisions from not only the current CEO but also a succession of chief executives. Here the board of directors enters the scene. The board has the opportunity to provide a succession of CEOs whose personal values and characters are consistently adequate for sustaining and developing established traditions for ethical conduct. Once in place, chief executives must rely on two resources for getting done what they cannot do personally: the character of their associates and the influence of policy and the measures that are taken to make policy effective.

An adequate corporate strategy must include non-economic goals. An economic strategy is the optimal match of a company's product and market opportunities with its resources and distinctive competence. (That both are continually changing is of course true.) But economic strategy is humanized and made attainable by deciding what kind of organization the company will be—its character, the values it espouses, its relationships to customers, employees, communities, and shareholders. The personal values and ethical aspirations of the company's leaders, though probably not specifically stated, are implicit in all strategic decisions. They show through the choices management makes and reveal themselves as the company goes about its business. That is why this communication should be deliberate and purposeful rather than random.

Although codes of ethics, ethical policy for specific vulnerabilities, and disciplined enforcement are important, they do not contain in themselves the final emotional power of commitment. Commitment to quality objectives—among them compliance with law and high ethical standards—is an organizational achievement. It is inspired by pride more than by the profit that rightful pride produces. Once the scope of strategic decisions is thus enlarged, their ethical

component is no longer at odds with a decision right for many reasons.

s former editor of HBR, I am acutely aware of how difficult it is to persuade business-people to write or speak about corporate ethics. I am not comfortable doing so myself. To generalize the ethical aspects of a business decision, leaving behind the concrete particulars that make it real, is too often to sermonize, to simplify, or to rationalize away the plain fact that many instances of competing ethical claims have no satisfactory solution. But we also hear little public comment from business leaders of integrity when incontestable breaches of conduct are made known—and silence suggests to cynics an absence of concern.

The impediments to explicit discussion of ethics in business are many, beginning with the chief executive's keen awareness that someday he or she may be betrayed by someone in his or her own organization. Moral exhortation and oral piety are offensive, especially when attended by hypocrisy or real vulnerability to criticism. Any successful or energetic individual will sometime encounter questions about his or her methods and motives, for even well-intentioned behavior may be judged unethical from some point of view. The need for cooperation among people with different beliefs diminishes discussion of religion and related ethical issues. That persons with management responsibility must find the principles to resolve conflicting ethical claims in their own minds and hearts is an unwelcome discovery. Most of us keep quiet about it.

In summary, my ideas are quite simple. Perhaps the most important is that management's total loyalty to the maximization of profit is the principal obstacle to achieving higher standards of ethical practice. Defining the purpose of the corporation as exclusively economic is a deadly oversimplification, which allows overemphasis on self-interest at the expense of consideration of others.

> Ultimately, executives resolve conflicting claims in their own minds and hearts.

The practice of management requires a prolonged play of judgment. Executives must find in their own will, experience, and intelligence the principles they apply in balancing conflicting claims. Wise men and women will submit their views to others, for open discussion of problems reveals unsuspected ethical dimensions and develops alternative viewpoints that should be taken into account. Ultimately, however, executives must make a decision, relying on their own judgment to settle infinitely debatable issues. Inquiry into character should therefore be part of all executive selection – as well as all executive development within the corporation.

And so it goes. That much and that little. The encouraging outcome is that promulgating and institutionalizing ethical policy are not so difficult as, for example, escaping the compulsion of greed. Once undertaken, the process can be as straightforward as the articulation and implementation of policy in any sphere. Any company has the opportunity to develop a unique corporate strategy summarizing its chief purposes and policies. That strategy can encompass not only the economic role it will play in national and international markets but also the kind of company it will be as a human organization. It will embrace as well, though perhaps not publicly, the nature and scope of the leadership to which the company is to be entrusted.

To be implemented successfully over time, any strategy must command the creativity, energy, and desire of the company's members. Strategic decisions that are economically or ethically unsound will not long sustain such commitment.

Ethical Issues and Dilemmas Involving Employees in the Workplace

- **Employee Rights and Duties (Articles 8–10)**
- **Employee Crime (Articles 11 and 12)**
- **Sexual Treatment of Employees (Articles 13–15)**
- **Discriminatory and Prejudicial Employment Practices (Articles 16–18)**
- **Downsizing of the Workforce (Articles 19–21)**
- **Whistle-Blowing in the Organization (Articles 22 and 23)**
- **Handling Ethical Dilemmas at Work (Articles 24–27)**

LaRue Tone Hosmer, in *The Ethics of Management,* lucidly states that ethical problems in business are truly managerial dilemmas because they represent a conflict, or at least the possibility of a conflict, between the *economic performance* of an organization and its *social performance.* Whereas the economic performance is measured by revenues, costs, and profits, the social performance is judged by the fulfillment of obligations to persons both within and outside the organization.

Units 2 through 4 discuss some of the critical ethical dilemmas that management faces in making decisions in the workplace, in the marketplace, and within the global society. This unit focuses on the relationships and obligations of employers and employees to each other.

Organizational decision makers are ethical when they act with equity, fairness, and impartiality, treating the rights of their employees with respect. An organization's hiring and firing practices, treatment of women and minorities, allowance of employees' privacy, and wages and working conditions are areas in which it has ethical responsibilities.

The employee also has ethical obligations in his or her relationship to the employer. A conflict of interest can occur when an employee allows a gratuity or favor to sway him or her in selecting a contract or purchasing a piece of equipment, making a choice that may not be in the best interests of the organization. Other possible ethical dilemmas for employees include espionage and the betrayal of secrets (especially to competitors), the theft of equipment, and the abuse of expense accounts.

The articles in this unit are broken down into seven subsections on different types of ethical dilemmas in the workplace. "The New Deal: What Companies and Employees Owe One Another" begins the first subsection by discussing the importance of employers' reexamining the balance between employee and employer rights. The next

article reflects how some employers' high-tech tools that are used to deter theft are sometimes on a collision course with employees' right to privacy. The last article in this subsection presents an ethical dilemma in which a manager wrestles with finding a way to help an employee without invading his privacy.

In the subsection *Employee Crime,* two articles explore computer sabotage, employee theft, and destruction of company property and resources. Suggestions are provided on some ways to deal with these crimes.

The first two selections in the subsection *Sexual Treatment of Employees* take a close look at the sexual treatment of employees in the workplace. The articles reveal various myths about sexual harassment and some forms that sexual harassment and sexual abuse take in office and business environments; they also provide ideas on how to deal with and stop sexual harassment. The last subsection article evaluates the extent and type of gains that women are making in various jobs in the workplace.

The first article in the subsection *Discriminatory and Prejudicial Employment Practices* evaluates affirmative action over the past 25 years and relates the ambivalence that many minorities have about affirmative action. "White, Male, and Worried" reveals how white men are slowly becoming a minority in the workplace and their worry about their future opportunities. The last subsection article discloses that as the American population ages, new concerns about age discrimination issues are being brought into the limelight.

In the subsection *Downsizing of the Workforce,* "Burned-Out Bosses" reflects that the survivors of downsizings may suffer more psychological damage than the departed victims. The next article suggests key issues to consider and provides possible strategies to be used in revamping and resizing organizational structure and design. "You're Fired" describes an actual situation where an employee is

fired unfairly and is in the process of deciding what course of action to take.

The two selections included in the *Whistle-Blowing in the Organization* subsection analyze the ethical dilemma and possible ramifications of whistle-blowing.

The first article, "Implementing Business Ethics," in the last subsection of this unit, examines the benefits of establishing a corporate culture that includes business ethics as an integral part of its ongoing organizational strategy. The last three articles present some real-world ethical dilemmas for the reader to ponder as well as provide some suggestions about how to be better prepared to confront and handle ethical dilemmas.

Looking Ahead: Challenge Questions

Ethical dilemmas occur when a manager or an employee is faced with two or more conflicting ethical choices. In your opinion, what ethical dilemmas do managers face most frequently? What ethical dilemmas do employees face most often?

How prevalent do you feel that the myths given in "Six Myths of Sexual Harassment" are in today's companies? Explain.

What forms of sexual and minority discrimination are most prevalent in today's workplace? Do you think there are particular job situations or occupations where discrimination is more widespread and conspicuous? Why or why not?

Whistle-blowing occurs when an employee discloses illegal, immoral, or illegitimate organizational practices or activities. Under what circumstances do you believe whistle-blowing is appropriate? Why?

THE
NEW DEAL

WHAT COMPANIES AND EMPLOYEES OWE ONE ANOTHER

Brian O'Reilly

DOES THIS sound familiar? You're expendable. We don't want to fire you, but we will if we have to. Competition is brutal, so we must redesign the way we work to do more with less. Sorry, that's just the way it is. And one more thing—you're invaluable. Your devotion to our customers is the salvation of this company. We're depending on you to be innovative, risk-taking, and committed to our goals. Okay?

It is understandably not okay with legions of workers encountering this widespread replacement of the job compact of the previous era, the one that traded loyalty for job security. That deal is virtually dead, but top managers rarely realize how debilitating their one-sided version of the new deal is. Daniel Yankelovich, the marketing and opinion researcher, is one of many who have observed a vast drop over the past few years in workers' commitment to employers. Says he: "Companies are unaware of the dreadful impact they are having. They don't realize they are violating an unwritten but important social contract they have with workers."

The bill will come due soon. Until recently the brass could regret but tolerate

REPORTER ASSOCIATE *John Wyatt*

> Loyalty? Job security? They're nearly dead. But employers that deliver honesty and satisfying work can expect a new form of commitment from workers.

sullen workers. In a recession the folks had no place to go. And Pat Milligan, a partner at Towers Perrin, a human resources consulting firm, observes that there is always a period after a contract is broken when people will try to adhere to the old rules and work hard.

But now, says Milligan, employees are getting restless. "The economy is picking up. Workers are saying to management: 'I have choices now. Tell me what the new re-

lationship is so I can decide if I want to stay.' And companies that don't articulate the new deal beyond the paycheck and the pension won't get the best people."

The encouraging news is that certain companies are crafting a new deal that works—sometimes. It makes no one feel warm and fuzzy, but it seems to minimize debilitating fury and anxiety. In its most naked form it goes like this: "There will never be job security. You will be employed by us as long as you add value to the organization, and *you* are continuously responsible for finding ways to add value. In return, you have the right to demand interesting and important work, the freedom and resources to perform it well, pay that reflects your contribution, and the experience and training needed to be employable here or elsewhere."

For some companies and some workers, that is exhilarating and liberating. It requires companies to relinquish much of the control they have held over employees and give genuine authority to work teams. Companies must work harder than ever to make themselves attractive places to work. Employees become far more responsible for their work and careers: No more parent-child relationships, say the consultants, but adult to adult. If the old arrangement sounded like binding nuptial vows, the new one suggests a series of casual, thrilling—if often temporary—encounters.

For others the arrangement is troubling. Attractive, mobile, young technical experts and professionals may fare well, at least for a while. But down the road, will those folks be cast aside for someone younger, more attractive, more current? Or will wisdom, not technical expertise, be what keeps people employed 20 years hence? No one knows. Says Kevin Sullivan, senior vice president at Apple Computer: "Experience or knowledge? It's a dilemma."

Companies that make explicit the new rules discover they can elicit a new form of commitment and hard work from employees—but relations may be far less warm, loyal, or familial. Says a young project manager at Prudential in central New Jersey: "We're cold and calculating and looking out for ourselves. If the economy picked up, I'd consider a job elsewhere much sooner than before. I wouldn't bat an eye."

Most companies are only edging toward the new deal but already find that winning commitment without the old carrot of lifetime job security can be extraordinarily difficult. Chevron vice chairman James Sullivan knows why he joined the company 33 years ago: "I chose Chevron because the work was interesting and because I'd have lifetime employment." Sullivan was lucky. Chevron reduced its work force by nearly half, to about 50,000 people, after the merger with Gulf in 1984. It cut staff by another 6,500 in the past two years. But the impact on employee loyalty has been severe. "On employee commitment, I'd give us a B-minus," Sullivan says.

THOUGH profitability is up sharply, Chevron decided that isn't enough. The company has bravely posted the results of employee morale surveys in company bulletins and in the lobby of headquarters in San Francisco, and has vowed to improve them by developing a new relationship with workers. "It's not easy," Sullivan says candidly. "Until you try to write about it or talk about it, you don't realize how inept you are." Nonetheless, candor and communication are essential, he has found. Chief Executive Kenneth Derr and other bigwigs hold periodic meetings with employees at facilities far and wide, and toil to explain how business is changing and how this affects career advancement and security.

Some others are more bashful. At a big industrial company in the Midwest, top managers can't bring themselves to declare that the old loyalty-security pact is dead. They have drafted dozens and dozens of unpublished versions of a new compact with employees. They are working on yet another.

Should we mourn the death of the old ties? Anyone disemployed or haunted by memories of the Great Depression will miss lifetime job security, but the security-loyalty-paternalism pact of yore wasn't all that terrific either. The old deal often became stultifying. Corporate tolerance for unproductive workers produced ludicrous, and ultimately demeaning, arrangements. Du Pont would stick surplus executives in window offices and tell them to "count boxcars," a none-too-delicate message that their careers were sidelined. The head of human resources at a publishing company recalls, aghast, how the company used to park unproductive 35-year-old executives in useless jobs and leave them there. "We made no attempt to steer them to something useful."

Although constant anxiety about job loss is unfair to workers and counterproductive, ironclad job security definitely doesn't produce the agile and competitive work force today's economy demands. For decades, until January 1988, a big New York bank promised workers that anyone with 20 years' experience would never be laid off. Imagine what sort of worker such a policy attracted and what behavior it encouraged. Says a human resources executive at the bank: "That was okay when we were clerically intensive and needed the mindset of a grunt. But as the organization changed in the Eighties and technology became important, we found that the people who came for security wouldn't adopt new ways of doing things."

UNDOING those bank workers' sense of entitlement "is like moving the Rock of Gibraltar," he says. Once older clerical workers heard they wouldn't get tenure, they agreed to accept training and new methods of working—reluctantly. But their resentment and sense of betrayal lingers. "These are adults, living independent lives with families and mortgages," says the executive. "But they are emotionally and intellectually blocked. Some are still furious and won't go the extra mile for themselves or for customers." Some still don't get it at all, he has found; a bank worker in his 40s who recently lost his job told his superiors that he assumed they would find him another spot. "He acted like we owe it to him to deliver a new job," says the executive. "We don't."

At AT&T, after ten years of upheaval since divestiture and the elimination of more than 100,000 jobs, the new message—that employees are responsible for their own survival—is slowly sinking in. For an electrical engineer who has worked at Bell Labs in Holmdel, New Jersey, for more than 20 years, it requires a stressful and demoralizing adjustment.

He can be notified at any time that his job is "at risk." That means that Bell Labs is cutting back people in his area or discipline, that his skills are obsolete, and that he had one of the poorer job evaluations in recent years. Even if there are no layoffs and his evaluations are good, he cannot relax. His engineering projects typically last a year or two, and when they end he must find another project to work on. If he can't find another job at the company within a few months, he must leave.

Now he hustles all the time, concerned that he won't have the necessary skills to win a berth on a new project when the current one ends. It is a persistent worry but not a paralyzing fear so far. He says, "They don't expect me to see 15 years into the future. But they expect me to recognize that the box I'm working on now will be a microchip in a year, with ten times as much software, and to be ready." His concerns, in order of urgency: "What project will I be on in six months, what will my role in the project be—electrical engineer, software writer, tester—and will I have a job?"

To stay current he tries to take engineering and other courses that AT&T offers, but sometimes work leaves little time. "If I

HOW LONG THEY STAY

Average length of time with current employer for managers and professionals

FORTUNE CHART / SOURCES: WYATT CO.; BUREAU OF LABOR STATISTICS

think I need to learn more about power circuits, and my boss says no, he really needs me now, it's still my responsibility. I'll take the course at night or on weekends." And if he chooses to master a technology that AT&T turns out not to need? "It's my problem."

A few miles away, at a big Prudential office, paternalism has died an even harder death. "Five years ago we played softball and basketball on company fields, and it was enough to make us loyal because we had job security," says a young manager there. But the company has eliminated 5,000 jobs nationally since then, and a quarter of the manager's co-workers have been fired.

"The message we're getting now is that the company doesn't owe you anything," she says. "Consultants have told us the company is not there for your emotional support, that they don't owe you raises or job security, just honesty. And that a day's pay for a day's work is honest." The result? "Everyone is shocked. The drones are panicking and looking for somebody to tell them what to do. The better ones are looking for opportunity."

She adds, "The people who will survive have realized we have to look out for ourselves. If you see a good assignment, you have to get it yourself. You have to fight for it. Make contacts . . . If there's a good assignment opening up and I'm not done with my current project, I'll work on the new one at night or on weekends. If I don't do that, I can't complain about not getting new skills."

She and her peers resent the upheaval Prudential is causing, but surprisingly, it's not a disaster. She is still committed to doing a good job. She is driven partly by her own professionalism and competitiveness. "It's like I'm running a marathon and trying to beat my own time."

Gradually, too, she has realized that she is freer to do her work than before. "The old days could be obnoxious. You had to kiss ass and dress right to get ahead. Now none of that matters anymore. If you work hard, you'll find a place." Maybe not at Prudential, though. Rumors say the company will relocate her operation to another office 20 miles north. She worries about the effect of a longer commute on her family. If asked to move, she will quit and find work closer to home. Any qualms? "I don't owe them anything."

Can companies establish this new-age, no-tenure employment compact without poisoning relations with employees? Intel discovered that it helps if the company never had the old implied contract in place to begin with. Like innumerable Silicon Valley firms, the semiconductor maker was founded and staffed by professionals who swarmed out of other companies. Intel never hinted at lifetime job security and didn't demand lifetime loyalty.

Nevertheless, a big round of layoffs in the early 1980s was traumatic, and even Intel realized it could not be cavalier about employee relations. Particularly useful, the company found, is sharing as much information as possible with employees so they can make intelligent career decisions. Intel has quarterly BUMs, or business update meetings, with all its workers, to outline Intel's recent financial health, and twice-yearly SLRPs, describing strategic long-range plans, for executives. A key part of every manager's job is to help co-workers understand if demand for their skills is shifting, and to encourage necessary training. But the message to employees is clear, says human resources VP Kirby Dyess: "You own your own employability. You are responsible."

NOTE the wording. Many companies tell workers they are responsible for their own careers. That's what Intel used to say. But "career" implied constant, upward movement through one broad discipline. Intel's organization chart has become so flat, there aren't many upper berths to aspire to. Anybody who wants to keep a job must be prepared to go anywhere. Lest anyone ignore that gospel, it is coming home to its in-house evangelists. After a SLRP last year, Dyess realized her HR operation had been growing faster than the company and would have to be cut back. In April 1993, a year before the cutbacks would start, she met with her staff to explain the cuts and to tell them they should keep an eye out for new work. Says Dyess: "Some people are concerned. Some are excited—it's a chance to get into a whole new line of work."

At Reuters, which had a more conventional contract with workers for many years, managers found that switching to a new employment arrangement requires explanation, sensitivity, and time. "Because we were doing well financially, employees' first reaction was, 'Why are you doing this to us?' " says Celia Berk, who heads employee programs and training for the company's operations in North and South America.

"But we decided that if you measure yourself just by financial results, you can't tell if you're creating an opportunity for rivals." Now the company measures itself on client satisfaction, employee effectiveness and satisfaction, operating efficiency, and contribution to shareholder value, in that order. Employee satisfaction is deliberately not at the top of the list, Berk explains. "You could argue that IBM had satisfied employees. It's obviously not enough."

That new measurement system is changing much of how business gets done at Reuters, and the company is exploring ways to link it to employment security and pay. "But we recognized you can't just announce the end of job security without explaining what you'll do in its place," says Berk. "The company isn't entitled to blind loyalty." The company held workshops to explain the new approach and to teach employees how to think about their careers. Reuters developed a set of explicit brochures that show what is expected of managers (for example: "Encourages continuous improvement . . . Looks beyond the short term"), and another set for senior managers ("Promotes innovation . . . Defines and implements strategy beyond a 12-month time frame"). It revamped its training programs. "We had to rethink adult learning. Not everybody learns well in a classroom."

Wire service employees, measured and rewarded in part on customer satisfaction—customers are newspapers and financial houses—were sent out to clients' offices to observe how they use the Reuters service. Elaborate evaluation procedures solicited comments from supervisors, peers, and subordinates. Criteria were tightly focused: One manager got nicked in a recent evaluation for "failing to use information technology in strategic ways." Supervisors were required to provide candid guidance to their charges. "If a reporter comes to us and says she wants to study Russian, we owe it to her to explain if she will never be Moscow bureau chief," says Berk.

And yes, she says, they fired people. "A few. You have to. Everybody in the organization knows who the drones are. If you don't deal with them, people gauge how much in control the company is. But you can't line everybody up, tell them to salute, and fire anybody who doesn't respond right away. Some people take time to adapt."

In the absence of job security, it turns out, targeted firings are far more palatable to workers than wide-swath layoffs. Companies should probably do more firing—most employees feel it's necessary. Sirota & Alper Associates, a New York City firm that measures employee sentiment, among other things, found that failure to get rid of nonperformers damages morale. Says David Sirota: "When we talk to employees, one of the biggest complaints we get is that companies do a poor job of facing up to poor performers. It's always the most negative finding. Even in the most militant unions, they complain about it. Workers don't want absolute security."

But firing people fairly means evaluating them fairly, and evaluation and measurement remain large failures of the new employment model. Even the best-intentioned companies flub it. At an AT&T division near Bedminster, New Jersey, employees were told that those with the poorest evaluations over the past two years would have to go. Dozens of workers who had migrated to the division from other AT&T operations in recent years discovered that the grading curves shaping their earlier evaluations were all different. In some operations, B's were rare and C's were common. In others, B was average and C was for comatose. But the rule held firm. Some of the worst workers were kept, some of the best lost their jobs. Says a survivor: "This year, at evaluation time, everybody is going to be hysterical."

Can this new, more entrepreneurial employment arrangement really work in the long term? Hardly any companies have enough experience with it to say. The new

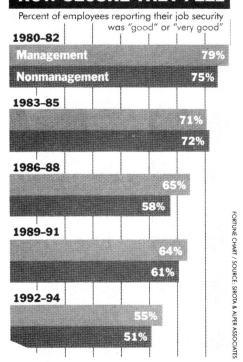

HOW SECURE THEY FEEL

Percent of employees reporting their job security was "good" or "very good"

1980–82	
Management	79%
Nonmanagement	75%
1983–85	
	71%
	72%
1986–88	
	65%
	58%
1989–91	
	64%
	61%
1992–94	
	55%
	51%

FORTUNE CHART / SOURCE: SIROTA & ALPER ASSOCIATES

code rests on important assumptions that may be flawed: that workers are professionals, so their current psychological dependence on employers can be redirected to commitment to their craft; that their work will increase their skills; that their skills are highly transferable between companies or industries.

Apple can woo Stanford grads with the prospect of working on the hottest new device because new hires are confident they can move effortlessly to another company down the street. Their confidence seems reasonable, since 75% of Apple employees are engineers, MBAs, or other professionals.

But it may not be justified. In rapidly evolving professions like electrical engineering and biotech, work on the hottest company projects by itself may not keep you up to speed. Many techies have discovered that their skills have peaked five years after graduation and that they will be replaced by more recent graduates. "It's a real problem," says a top manager who asked not to be identified.

And if you're not a hot, young Silicon Valley engineer, the problem may be worse. Philip Breslin, retired manager of labor relations at Bethlehem Steel, says, "Work at most companies is more prosaic and less glamorous than that. For the assistant purchasing manager at a widget factory, it's hard to make the work fascinating enough to substitute for job security." Besides, says Breslin, jobs for many workers aren't transferable even in the same industry, because each company winds up developing unique ways of handling chores.

An antidote for some of those shortcomings appears to be a team-based approach to managing projects. Even if the widget maker can't make purchasing glamorous, says Breslin, "in many situations, team building is a substitute for pay raises and security. Not because it makes me employable elsewhere, but because it provides me with an identification with a group of people all trying to accomplish a set of goals." At Southwest Airlines, pilots sometimes help clean the plane, notes Charles O'Reilly, a Stanford management professor. "It signals a unity of purpose to the cleaning crew—that their work is as important as flying the plane."

The rapidly readjusting manager at Prudential says teamwork is important in other ways too. "My motivation comes from my co-workers," she says. Pay and job security are tied in part to how the team performs, and while she feels no loyalty to management, she is willing to work hard to help her teammates.

INCLUDING TEAMMATES in arriving at an individual's evaluation gives workers a better sense of job security too, says David Noer, a vice president at the Center for Creative Leadership, in Greensboro, North Carolina. Peers are often a better judge of who is contributing and who is not. "Qualitative, boss-down evaluations are wrong," he says. "AT&T would have been better off with team-based appraisals."

One of the great unanswered questions of the new work arrangement is how 40ish and 50ish workers will fare if continually forced back into in-house or external labor

markets to compete with younger, cheaper workers. James Medoff, a labor economist at Harvard, says older workers' generous paychecks are at some risk. For years a tacit agreement was in place in most companies, he says: "You get paid less than you're worth in the first half of your career and more than you're worth in the second half." Workers let go at 45 may find their new jobs don't pay more with age and feel cheated.

Growing old may not be a catastrophe for job-hoppers, though. Don McDermott, head of a human resources consulting company in Red Bank, New Jersey, says many companies that fired older workers are finding that the youngsters put in their place can't handle the job. Kirby Dyess at Intel says she has studied data looking for evidence that older workers have a harder time shifting between jobs there than younger ones, and hasn't found any.

Says Dyess: "The people who have a problem are the ones who never moved out of a job category, who never took a course, never got a degree, never took risks." That doesn't mean that Intel employees automatically get rewarded for getting old. "Salaries are variable. If I switch jobs in the company, I may find my new position doesn't pay as well as the last one. Nothing guarantees that my paycheck keeps getting bigger."

Will anyone ever spend 30 years with the same company again? Yes. Even the most aggressive exponents of the new employment contract say there will be plenty of lifers. Argues Hal Burlingame, executive vice president for human resources at AT&T: "People will have very long careers here. It just won't be static."

Not everyone gets a gold watch. What may evolve are two or three classes of employees, all with varying degrees of connectedness to the organization, and each getting a very different package of compensation and reward. Peter Moore, managing partner of Inferential Focus, a social trends think tank in New York City, says every company must identify "the critical intellectual strengths it needs to be successful over the long term. You lock those people in—make them captive to the organization, fully employed, compensated, and benefited." Even they may not be retained forever, says Moore. "I have one client where 80% of its revenues comes from businesses it wasn't in three years ago. So who is core in that company?"

Other tasks, advertising or data processing perhaps, get farmed out to a regular stable of individuals or organizations who are paid on a contract basis for results. And a third set of workers—telemarketers, widget assemblers, clerks, and so on—come in part time or as needed.

2. ETHICAL ISSUES AND DILEMMAS: Employee Rights and Duties

WHAT MANY companies find is that if they won't offer security, they'd better offer freedom, and lots of it. American Express surveyed workers and found what they wanted more than anything else was free time. Some customer service agents and credit analysts there are now free to set their own hours and work dusk to dawn if they choose. Amex travel agents often work at home on computer terminals, answering calls from customers who don't have a clue. Michael Connors, a senior vice president (and full-timer), says their productivity has not diminished at all. Workers who want to improve job skills can drop in to career resource centers at several Amex facilities.

Intel discovered the best way to keep valued workers is to set them free occasionally.

Every seven years Intel employees get an 11-week paid sabbatical. Yes, there is a seven-year itch, says Dyess, and workers run the risk of burnout if they can't get away.

Is there a place in all this for loyalty—workers devoted to the company instead of their own résumé, or companies carrying workers whose contribution has peaked? Probably. Companies in anything but the rankest commodity business will always have to ask workers to invest in skills that are virtually useless elsewhere. Says Robert Paulson, head of McKinsey's aerospace practice in Los Angeles: "Companies are forced to make what they cannot buy. And what they make or do that others cannot is what makes them unique and gives them competitive advantage." A genuine commitment by companies to retrain workers with unusual skills is helpful, but not everyone can be recycled. Companies that fail to demonstrate some sort of fidelity to those workers won't find many new recruits for similar assignments.

There aren't any easy answers to problems caused for employees by competition and the rapidly changing skills that companies need to survive. But all workers deserve at least an honest explanation of how that change will affect them and what their employer will or won't do to help. "Employees don't expect the impossible," says Robert Levering, co-author of *The 100 Best Companies to Work for in America*, "but they do demand the possible. And good, two-way communication is probably the most important thing companies can do."

It's not just fair, it's practical too. Chevron has discovered that when it candidly explains its problems to employees, their commitment to the company and their work increases, even if the news is bad. And managers who demonstrate they care about their workers might just find they get loyalty in return.

Are You Guilty Of Electronic Trespassing?

Companies are using high-tech tools to cut costs and deter theft. But in the process, they may be invading their employees' privacy. Here's how to walk the fine line.

DEBORAH L. JACOBS

Deborah Jacobs is a Brooklyn, N.Y.-based business writer who specializes in legal issues.

I n this era of increasing employee disloyalty, espionage and theft, you may feel justified in keeping tighter reigns on your staff through a variety of monitoring techniques. If so, you wouldn't be alone. More than one company in five eavesdrops electronically on its employees—by searching employee computer files, voice mail, electronic mail and other networking communications—according to a survey of 301 businesses by *Macworld* magazine.

Granted, most survey respondents use electronic searches only occasionally. Just 3.1 percent said they had monitored their employees 50 or more times during the past two years. But many others—more than 70 percent—used some electronic eavesdropping method at least once during the same period. And companies often have good reason to use various electronic monitoring—say, an extension phone to evaluate customer service

ILLUSTRATIONS: MARK TUCHMAN

representatives' telephone calls or a hidden video to observe a suspected thief's activities.

But there's a trade-off: Companies are at risk of invading their employees' privacy and finding themselves at risk of lawsuits.

Since most lawsuits are settled out of court, it's difficult to document the actual number of privacy disputes that exist. More courts, however, are ruling in favor of the employee, lawyers say.

A CASE IN POINT: a lawsuit four years ago against a family-owned liquor store near Camden, Ark. Newell and Juanita Spears, the husband and wife owners, suspected that a recent theft was an inside job and used an extension phone in their home next door to monitor and record employees' calls from work. During a three-month period, they recorded more than 22 hours of conversations. These included an illicit deal by one female employee to sell a keg of liquor at a discounted price. But the recorder also picked up several steamy phone calls between that employee and the customer with whom she made the deal. The tapes revealed that the two were having an extramarital affair. The Spears fired the employee. She and her lover sued them for violation of a federal law known as the Wiretap Act.

Ruling against the employers, the court found that the store owners had gone too far— by listening in longer than necessary for their investigation and by informing the employee's spouse. Since the Spears had only hinted that they might monitor phone calls from the store—and they never specifically announced their plans to do so—the court rejected their defense that the employee had consented to the monitoring. Both the employee and her lover had "a reasonable expectation that their telephone conversations were private," the court stated. Taping and disclosing the sexually provocative calls served no business purpose, it concluded.

The court ordered the business to pay $40,000, as well as the legal expenses of the two individuals who brought the case. It could have been a lot worse. Other losing companies are

> **BRIEFCASE**
>
> E-mail, fax machines and other technologies make it easy for a company to collect information about its employees. Yet companies often end up on the wrong side of a lawsuit when they are sued for violating an employee's privacy.

shelling out multi-million-dollar payments, including back pay, out-of-pocket costs and punitive damages. Even when a company wins, it may have to spend tens—or even hundreds— of thousands of dollars to defend its activities.

There's no federal law that covers all aspects of an employee's right to privacy in the workplace. But the proliferation of leading-edge technologies has intensified the search for boundaries between permissible monitoring and illegal snooping. To date, a patchwork of laws in some states prohibits eavesdropping, drug testing and other forms of privacy invasion.

And, if it's not enough for employees who believe their privacy has been invaded, there are still other weapons in their legal arsenal. If employees say you've used the investigation or information gathered against them, they may tack on other claims to their privacy lawsuits. These include charges of defamation, discrimination based on age, sex, or race, and the 1990 Americans with Disabilities Act (ADA).

Let's say, for example, that in the course of listening in on a phone call to investigate theft, you discover that a worker has AIDS or takes anti-depressants. Penalizing him or her because of this might violate the ADA, which prohibits discrimination against people with a range of mental and physical impairments.

Making inquiries and taking disciplinary actions linked to an employee's sexual orientation, marital status or social life are also legal

The proliferation of leading-edge technologies has intensified the search for boundaries between permissible monitoring and illegal snooping.

mine fields. And a growing number of state and local laws are addressing the issue. In New York, for instance, a 1992 law prohibits discriminating against employees for legal activities in their private lives, which could mean anything from having a homosexual relationship to campaigning for abortion rights. Enforcing that law, the state attorney general sued Wal-Mart last July on behalf of two of the company's employees who were fired for dating. The attorney general argued that Wal-Mart's policy of prohibiting employees from dating violates the new state law.

State Your Purpose

Of course, e-mail, fax machines and other technologies make it easy to collect a lot of information that you may find useful, but which may not serve a legitimate business purpose or which could be considered an invasion of privacy. Consider call-accounting systems, which allow companies to collect detailed and employee-specific telephone records. Should an employer be allowed to count the number of calls employees make to their spouse, or trace a call to a substance-abuse hotline, while collecting telephone records to audit the phone bill?

That's what makes the line between monitoring and snooping so fuzzy. But you stand a greater chance of defending your use of potentially intrusive searches if you have a valid business purpose for conducting them in the first place. For example, you might be able to search a locker to maintain a drug-free workplace, listen in on telephone calls to conduct performance reviews and read faxes to prevent the unauthorized use of your company's equipment. On occasion, you might be able to justify videotaping employees in order to investigate illegal gambling, theft or misuse of proprietary information.

But just how much privacy are employees entitled to? Again, there are no definite answers, but a lot depends on what they've come to expect based on your company policy or practices, says Ira Shepard, a lawyer with the Washington, D.C., firm of Schmeltzer, Aptaker & Shepard.

A current Cook County Circuit Court case will soon be trying to answer this very question. Last September more than 40 Kmart employees sued for invasion of privacy, breach of contract and intentional infliction of emotional distress. They are accusing Kmart of hiring private investigators to pose as workers. The employees charge that the investigators at the

Manteno, Ill., store gathered information about everything from employees' living arrangements to their recreation plans.

In general, however, employers have the right to search desks, file cabinets and offices since it's assumed they were provided for business use. In contrast, most courts have found that employees have the right to expect that they won't be snooped on in the lavatories, lockers and, to a lesser extent, lunch rooms and lounges, which are considered private and provided for their own use.

However, your company's policies and practices can change employees' expectations. If your company handbook makes a specific reference to the privacy of employees' desks, for instance, you could create a right of privacy where a court might otherwise disagree. By the same reasoning, an employee who gives his supervisor the combination to his locker might negate any expectations about privacy that would ordinarily apply.

The Honesty Policy

You can outline your expectations—and reduce the risk of privacy lawsuits—by letting employees know in advance that you intend to monitor their activities, says Robert Ellis Smith, an attorney and editor of *The Privacy Journal*, a Rhode Island newsletter. That way, you both know what to expect and a court will deem that employees have consented to your actions. Smith favors articulating specific reasons and time limits for the surveillance, and then sticking to them.

John Shyer, an attorney with Latham & Watkins in New York, favors a more sweeping approach. He says it's a good idea to remind employees via memo, policy statement or handbook that company property—whether desks, file cabinets, fax machines, e-mail or phone mail—are provided by the company for business use. This way, you reserve the right to inspect property and monitor computer messages for whatever business purpose you may later identify, whether it involves tracking down misuse of trade secrets or drug dealing. To make sure employees know the ground rules, have them sign a statement that they've read and understand them, Shyer advises.

Knowing the most common activities that can subject a company to a lawsuit is an important first step in preventing them. Below are some of the most prevalent pitfalls:

▶ *LISTENING IN.* Listening to employees' business-related telephone calls made to and from the company is one of the most common forms of workplace monitoring. Companies dependent on extensive telephone work—such as telemarketers and insurance companies—often listen in on sales representatives or customer service people to evaluate the success of their training and the quality of their interaction with the public. Other companies, trying to cut costs, listen in on staffers to make sure they're not using the phone lines for excessive personal calls.

The wiretap law, at issue in the case involving the Arkansas liquor store, permits employers to listen to calls "in the ordinary course of business," although the meaning of that phrase is subject to interpretation. Some state laws specifically require that employees be notified of the practice in advance. As the Arkansas case suggests, that's a good preventive measure even if your state doesn't require advance notice.

But what you do with the information you collect can require tricky judgments. Suppose that in the course of collecting information about illegal gambling, you overhear an employee talking with his psychiatrist. If, in this case, the material serves no business purpose, you should destroy it. If you uncover criminal behavior, turn it over to law enforcement authorities, Smith advises.

The line between snooping and violating an employee's privacy becomes even blurrier when you discover misconduct other than what you were looking for. Let's say, for example, that you were listening in to monitor excessive use of the company phone and found that a staffer was goofing off or passing on trade secrets to a competitor. In that event, Smith recommends informing the employee of your findings and taking disciplinary action. He advises avoiding Draconian measures, like termination, in order to keep a potentially dicey situation from escalating into a pricey lawsuit.

► *READING COMPUTER-TO-COMPUTER MESSAGES.* Most privacy lawsuits arise because employees assume their messages sent via e-mail, voice mail or faxes to be private, but find out that they aren't. Epson America ran into trouble three years ago when an administrator in its Torrance, Calif., headquarters discovered her supervisor reading her e-mail messages. The employee, Alana Shoars, accused her boss of invading her privacy and threatened to report him to higher management. He responded by firing Shoars, prompting her to file a wrongful termination claim.

In a separate lawsuit, under California's privacy law, Shoars is seeking $3,000 for each of the hundreds of messages that were read. So far, the company has prevailed in both cases. The court found that Epson had a right to read its employees' e-mail. Shoars is appealing the case.

If you don't want employees using the computer systems for personal use—a policy that would, of course, minimize disruption and increase productivity—be sure to distribute rules that these systems are for business use only, urges Shyer. You can remind employees of your policy every time they sign on by programming the system to display a message reiterating these rules.

A more lenient—and employee-friendly—alternative: create bulletin boards that employees can use to send personal messages, or passwords that allow them to protect their personal messages. Passwords also can be used to protect some voice mail messages. But even if you permit employees to send personal messages, be sure to retain the right to intercept them when you have to repair the telephone or computer equipment. That warning also puts employees on notice that their privacy is not guaranteed.

► *ELECTRONIC SNOOPING.* Theoretically, a firm can use video monitors and phone bugs to serve a legitimate business purpose, such as checking up on an employee suspected of theft. But even then, the act of videotaping may prompt a lawsuit, especially when it takes place in an area like a locker room, which many employees presume is private.

For example, two employees of Sheraton-Boston Hotel filed a lawsuit last year, accusing the company of invading their privacy by covertly videotaping them in the hotel locker room. Sheraton was looking for drug dealers, says the hotel's lawyer, Allen C.B. Horsley of LeBeouf, Lamb, Lieby & MacRae in Boston. Horsley says the hotel placed the camera in the "least intrusive" place, taping activity in a small area of the locker room. Yet this happened to be a spot where two employees retreated to do their homework. The videotape, which identified the drug dealers, also picked up these two innocents. The case is pending before the Superior Court of Massachusetts.

Unfortunately, very few laws on the books cover workplace surveillance. Connecticut, one of the few states to specifically address the subject, prohibits electronic surveillance, including video monitoring, in any area "designed for the health and comfort of employees or for safeguarding of their possessions, including rest rooms, locker rooms and lounges."

Proposed amendments to the federal wire-tap law, pending in both houses of Congress, would prohibit most instances of secret electronic monitoring, as well as most monitoring in bathrooms, locker rooms and dressing rooms. Companies would have to let employees know that the monitoring system exists, and would sometimes be required to give them a signal (for example, with a beep tone) when the monitoring occurs. Introduced by Senator Paul Simon (D-Ill.) and Representative Pat Williams (D-Mont.), it is backed by civil libertarians and employee rights groups.

➤ *TESTING FOR DRUGS.* Drug testing is a controversial and evolving field, with associated moral and legal problems. Given the risks, most lawyers discourage the practice of random testing for drugs or alcohol. Generally speaking, it's prudent to randomly test existing employees only when their positions involve public safety, such as a guard at a nuclear plant or a forklift operator, says Robert A. Naeve, a lawyer with Morrison & Foerster in Irvine, Calif.

However, you can generally order an existing employee to submit to a drug test if you have "reasonable suspicion" that he or she is abusing unlawful drugs or controlled substances, says Naeve. Should the test be positive, the test and any resulting discipline are likely to be upheld in court if the employee sues for invasion of privacy, he says.

Trouble is, lawyers disagree as to what constitutes reasonable suspicion. Naeve, for his part, would strictly limit testing to cases in which employees look as if they are abusing—that is, they have a staggered gait, dilated pupils or smell of marijuana. Outside of California, a state with strict privacy protections, some lawyers say drug testing might be prompted by behavior such as falling asleep on the job, shortness of attention or an increase in workplace accidents.

If drug testing seems the way to go, adopt a written policy and get employees to acknowledge it in writing. This sets the rules and puts your staff on notice about what to expect. That alone will not protect you in the event of a lawsuit, but it could help with your defense. Rules for drug testing vary enormously from state to state, however, so it's best to have your lawyer help prepare and implement a drug policy.

When conducting any drug test be sure to use the least intrusive means possible: It's good employee relations, it lessens the likelihood of a lawsuit, and it can help your case if you are sued. So if you're worried that an employee will alter the samples submitted for a urine test, ask employees to remove their jackets and empty their pockets instead of having an observer or video camera record their every move. And don't risk a defamation lawsuit by publicizing the test results—they could be false-positive—to people who don't need to know, warns John B. Lewis, a lawyer with Arter & Hadden in Cleveland. (Asking what prescription medicine the employee has been taking is usually permissible—and sometimes necessary to evaluate test results—but asking why the employee has been taking those drugs can lead to problems in some states, adds Lewis.)

WORKBOOK

The following resources provide additional information:

➤ *Privacy & American Business* is a new bi-monthly newsletter. Cost: $295. Write: The Center for Social and Legal Research, Two University Plaza, Suite 414, Hackensack, NJ 07601. Call: 201-996-1154.

➤ *Privacy Journal* reports monthly on recent developments, pending legislation and privacy abuses. Cost: $109. Write: P.O. Box 28577, Providence, RI 02908. Call: 401-274-7861.

➤ *Employee Privacy Rights,* excerpted from a law firm's 1992 seminar book on employment law. Free. Write: John D. Shyer, Latham & Watkins, 885 Third Ave., New York, NY 10022. Call: 212-906-1200.

➤ *Privacy in the Workplace,* a 150-page loose-leaf, reviews the pertinent state and federal statutes related to privacy. These are 1992 materials. Cost: $119. Write: The Employers Group, P.O. Box 15013, 1150 South Olive St., Los Angeles, CA 90015. Call: 213-748-0421.

➤ *Employee Privacy Law,* is a 1,191-page treatise that discusses cases and catalogs state laws that cover privacy issues. Cost: $125. Write: Clark Boardman Callaghan, 155 Pfingsten Rd., Deerfield, IL 60015. Call: 800-221-9428.

➤ *Access to and Use and Disclosure of Electronic Mail on Company Computer Systems: A Tool Kit for Formulating Your Company's Policy,* supplies sample e-mail policies. Cost: $20 for members, $45 for non-members. Write: The Electronic Messaging Association. 1655 North Fort Myer Dr., Suite 850, Arlington, VA 22209. Call: 703-524-5550.

➤ *Workplace Testing.* Author Diane Arthur gives clearly written details (no legalese) on using major types of tests: drug and alcohol, psychological, personality, integrity, physical. Cost: $49.95. Call AMA: 800-262-9699.

What you do with any information collected can add complications—and additional claims—to a privacy lawsuit. Robert R. Belair, an attorney with the law firm of Mullenholz, Brimsek in Washington, D.C., recalls a case in which a company's investigation strongly suggested that an employee was stealing. The company fired the employee and sent a message to every manager in its chain of stores, telling them that their colleague had been fired for theft.

The former employee sued for privacy invasion. In retrospect, the company made two mistakes, says Belair. First, it characterized the employee's action as theft, when he hadn't been convicted of a crime; he was simply discharged due to suspicion of theft. A safer course would have been to say the employee was discharged for suspicion of theft, and then describe what led the company to that belief. Second, the business disseminated the information to people who really didn't need to know about it, Belair says.

To avoid defamation lawsuits stemming from such information leaks, restrict access to those who need to see it. And try not to keep information after it is no longer relevant.

Finally, before taking any action that might be construed as an invasion of privacy, follow what Shyer calls "the Golden Rule" of the workplace: Put yourself in the shoes of the employee and consider how you would react.

WHAT WOULD YOU DO?

A Reluctant Invasion

Sam had every right to hide the fact he was HIV positive.
But when Jackie learned of his condition after laying him off, her hands were tied.
How could she help him without invading his privacy?

ILLUSTRATION BY CARL WESLEY.

DOUG WALLACE

Doug Wallace does frequent consulting work on corporate ethics, and was formerly the vice president for social policy at Norwest Bank in Minneapolis.

All cases used in What Would You Do? *depict actual events, although individual and company names are changed to protect privacy. Please contact Craig Cox at the Business* Ethics *office if you have a case to suggest or if you would like to become a guest commentator.*

THE CASE

He first heard about it during a phone call from Jackie Davies, director of human resources. He remembered because the halting cadence of Jackie's speech seemed strangely out of character. Finally, he stopped her in the middle of one of those painfully hesi-tant sentences and suggested that they talk face to face over lunch. She seemed relieved.

As they sat down at the restaurant later, Jackie began. "Sorry to bother you with this one, Riley, but I didn't know where else to turn. In a moment, you'll see why."

"Well, that's why I'm here," he replied.

As general counsel of Excel, Inc., Riley Trevor was often sought out by managers of the firm to help them think through tough problems. Over the last few years he had helped this major high-tech contracting firm deal with many sticky and unusual legal arrangements with its clients and, as a result, his judgments were highly respected. He also had increasingly been consulted on personnel issues as the organization navigated through the rocky swells of a whitewater economy.

Jackie described the situation. Because of a continued slow decline in con-tracts, the company had decided to trim a few people from its 620-employee payroll. One of the positions slated to go was occupied by Sam Spevac, who had been with the firm for a little over a year. Sam had a good record, but efforts to locate him in another position just didn't succeed. He was given the customary two-week termination notice and a severance package that included the extension of health care benefits for six months.

It all seemed fairly routine, Jackie said. But within a couple of hours of notifying Sam, a colleague of his named George contacted Jackie to talk about Sam's situation. He told her, "We really need Sam. His work is important and we can't understand why you are selecting this position to eliminate. Some of us think there may be some politics mixed up in this."

At the time, Jackie wondered why this issue had come up at the last minute. To reassure herself, she checked into it thor-

Laying off Sam was a routine matter, until Jackie learned he was HIV positive.

oughly and learned that the decision was squeaky clean. She got back to George, at which time he raised the real issue.

"Sam is HIV infected," he said. "We don't think it's right that he's going without a safety net. There are two of us that know and Sam didn't want it disclosed. He doesn't know I am talking with you. In fact, he doesn't even know that I know."

Jackie looked up from her lunch plate. "That's what I wanted to talk with you about, Riley. Sam is already off the payroll. I am concerned about what happens when his health benefits terminate, but at the same time I'm not supposed to know this information about him—he never told anyone except a close friend at work. You have a professional obligation to keep client information private, and, besides, you have been helpful in the past to me in problem-solving. That's why I came to you." '

After some discussion, Riley came up with a suggestion. "Why don't you ask Sam to come in to review his benefits package and give him an opportunity to reveal the situation himself," he said. "If he does, you have a new ballgame."

A couple of days later, Jackie did just that. But she was disappointed with the results. "He never said boo," she told Riley. "We're back to square one. And now he's already out the door."

They both recognized the conflicting ethical values that were at stake, respecting Sam's autonomy and their own concern for the potential precariousness of his situation, particularly after his health benefits ran out.

"Let's put our heads together and see what we should do," Riley said. "There must be another way."

PAUL JOHNSON
Retired General Counsel for Green Giant and H.B. Fuller Companies, Minneapolis, Minnesota.

The first and obvious thing is Sam's right to keep confidential his condition. It's already been breached and should not be breached further. He has made it clear that he does not want his condition disclosed. And one can't assume greater wisdom than other people and say, "Hey, I'm going to do something for you in spite of yourself."

Second, relative to whether he has been discriminated against because of his HIV condition, Jackie was satisfied that it was fair. Still, I would document all this very clearly for fear that it might turn around on me and I might be involved in a lawsuit.

Next, the obligation to Sam as an employee is not all that great. He's been there for one year. If they took him back, they are exposing the company, the stockholders, and probably other employees to big costs, and the question is whether that is fair to those people.

However, I frankly think they have a greater obligation to him as a person than as an employee. Therefore, what I would do (as Jackie) would be to go back to George and explain to him the fairness of the decision, and tell him that we need to respect Sam's wishes. He has made it clear what he wants to do. Then I would suggest that George go back to the mutual friend of Sam's and say that if he can convince Sam to come forward, that I (Jackie) would like to see what I could do in terms of putting together some help for Sam.

If Sam then does come forward to reveal his condition and ask for help, Jackie should try to tap all the resources that are available to her in terms of helping him as a person.

ED MICKENS
Editor of Working It Out, *a newsletter that focuses on gays and lesbians in the workplace, New York, New York.*

I would have to come down squarely on the side of Sam's privacy. He has the American Bar Association on his side, from a legal perspective. But the fact that Sam didn't tell his employer about his status—even though he has the ABA on his side—demonstrates his mistrust regarding the law. People with positive HIV status know that discrimination is rampant, despite the law.

My heart breaks for Sam. He's afraid and not without good reason. He may not be able to get insurance again. I don't know when he learned his status, but it's common that when people do learn of an HIV-positive status that they go into a state of shock and depression and denial that can last for years. Sam has to learn how to stand up for himself. He must make the choices. What we need to do is protect his right to those choices, starting with his right to privacy.

Now, what's the company to do? Since the information came extra legally—George violated Sam's privacy—the same channels need to be used if the company really wants to do something. George has to go to the originator of the information. There is another party involved here. What we have just seen is that information goes from one to two to four in a very short time. You can be sure that more people know about this. The company is going to have to deal with this secret perception, because other employees are saying, "Oh, how unfair for the company to do this to Sam." This is a classic case where the company was not prepared to deal with an HIV situation.

For the future, what I would do is to set a clear policy that the company does not discriminate on the basis of sexual orientation and to back up this policy with a program of education about AIDS and HIV, to get everything out into the open. It's good practice for all employees in terms of their own health interests and reducing discrimination, and also would reduce fear among those who are HIV positive. This is not the last time the company will come across this issue.

DOUG WALLACE'S COMMENTS
This is as close as you can come to a classic dilemma that ethicists love to debate. On the one hand, a persuasive case can be made on behalf of Sam's right to privacy, which rises from ethical theory that there are some principles (such as individual autonomy) that are essential to the human enterprise, that must be honored, and for that reason they are principles that we have an obligation to keep. A classic deontological orientation. On the other hand, one can also make the argument (as Paul Johnson does) that we have a responsibility to be beneficent. This reflects another ethical theory (teleological) which asserts that bringing about a good end is the right thing to do, even though in doing so it might violate some principle (such as individual autonomy).

In this real context, both of our commentators went for action that reflected a combination of these two points of view. The question about honoring Sam's autonomy, his right to privacy, is answered firmly by both. In the end, both advance very similar approaches—That they would go back through the original chain of communication to provide an opportunity for greater reflection and possible reconsideration on the part of Sam.

Beyond that, Ed makes a strong case for the company to position itself to be better prepared to prevent this sort of dilemma in the future with the development of clear policy and training, what I call anticipatory ethics. Anticipatory ethics requires creative planning skills rather than those needed to manage a crisis, which this has become. He would put a program into place to help establish the integrity of the company in its handling of persons who are

> **We may have an obligation for caring that transcends institutional and legal boundaries.**

HIV positive, and in its fair and even-handed treatment of persons regardless of sexual orientation.

On the other hand, Paul accentuates the need for action based upon one human being's obligation to aid another. He poses an interesting distinction which has been discussed more than once in this column. He reminds us that, beyond our responsibility to the organization, we may have an obligation for caring that transcends institutional and legal boundaries.

Ed also reminds us that, in the midst of trauma, we may not always be acting in our own best interests. In those situations, actions that look like they are autonomous may actually be self-deceptive. Sharing our painful human situation with others may be risky, but sometimes it can also transform the character of the human condition by bringing out the very best in one another.

WHAT ACTUALLY HAPPENED?

RILEY TREVOR, the general counsel, made a decision to extend the health care benefits another year. He did this as a matter of fact, without any fanfare or attention. He and the director of human resources maintained confidentiality about Sam's condition. They also did get back to George and reassured him that the process of selecting Sam as one of the persons whose position was to be eliminated was clean. When Riley told me of how the case ended, he seemed quite pleased with the result and felt that he and the organization had done the best it could under the circumstances.

Ethics and Employee Theft

William J. Kehoe

It is obvious by now that employee theft is a pervasive problem. *Time* speaks of a "light-fingered work ethic."[1] James Walls, in *Vital Speeches of the Day,* calls the workplace "America's hot bed of crime."[2] Robert Cameron, in *Venture* magazine, says, "You come to the point where you just cross your fingers and hope they won't rob you blind."[3] The "they" to whom he refers are employees, and the "hot bed of crime" is your business.

THE CONCEPT OF EMPLOYEE THEFT

Employee theft may be tangible, as in the case of an employee taking inventory, supplies, or cash moneys from a firm; less tangible, as in the case of an employee falsifying records or expense reports for personal benefit when such benefit has not been earned; or intangible, as in the case of time theft or demotivating colleagues, thereby reducing their effectiveness to the firm.

Whether tangible or intangible, employee theft occurs when an employee takes from the firm something to which he or she is not entitled and that, if known to the firm, would not be granted to the employee. At one extreme is an employee taking a 50-cent box of paper clips for personal use to another extreme of an employee who takes machinery valued at $50,000. Although the profit consequences of the former are not as severe as the latter, both acts of theft have moral consequences to the firm and to the employee, and each will change both the firm and the employee.

ETHICS AND THEFT

To understand the moral consequences of employee theft, an examination of the concept of ethics is a starting point. Ethics have been defined as "a systematic attempt, through the use of reason, to make sense of our individual and social moral experience, in such a way as to determine the rules that ought to govern human conduct and the values worth pursuing in life."[4]

Ethics are concerned with evaluating actions and decisions from the perspective of moral principles and values. In its simplest meaning, being ethical is doing the right thing rather than the wrong thing. It is being moral, honest, correct, and fair in everything a person undertakes. It is living with a set of values and principles that guide the decisions and actions of a person. Such values and principles include the following:

• Obey the law
• Do not harm others
• Respect the rights and property of others
• Never lie, cheat, or steal
• Keep promises and contracts
• Be fair to all people
• Help those in need
• Encourage and reinforce these values and principles in others

These values and principles, at the simplest level of ethics, have been called "moral common sense."[5] When applied to the situation of employee theft, the concept of ethics at the level of moral common sense would suggest that employees should not steal. Such is a principle that is valued. A person, both in personal life and in employment life, should not steal, and when faced with the potential of theft, an ethical person, using moral common sense, does the right thing rather than the wrong thing and does not steal.

But employees do steal, and employee theft is a real problem, noted earlier in this book to be valued at more than $40 billion a year and to be increasing at a 15 percent annual rate. The notion of moral common sense does not stand in the face of the magnitude of employee theft. Moral common sense is a simple, straightforward notion. Its simplicity, however, which would have sufficed at an earlier age, does not hold today. Employee theft is a major problem, a problem not prevented or resolved by applying moral common sense, a problem exacerbated by rationalization, and perhaps better understood by lifting the analysis from the fundamental level of moral common sense to the more complex levels of ethical relativism, rules (deontology), and consequences (teleology).

THE CONCEPT OF ETHICAL RELATIVISM

Rationalization

A justification used by some employees to rationalize their act of theft is that others are doing it too. This is the "when in Rome, do as the Romans do" rationalization. Because the employee perceives that other employees are partaking in theft, he or she rationalizes that the act is appropriate. That is, he or she develops the belief that it is morally acceptable to steal from the employer because everyone else is perceived to be stealing as well.

Added to the "everyone is doing it" rationalization are other reasons to justify the act. Examples of some of the reasons employees give for stealing are as follows:

- They are not fairly compensated
- Items taken are of small value (e.g., small parts, office supplies, food stuffs, and the like) and will not be missed by the employer
- The employer expects (i.e., approves) that employees will steal or participate in shrinking the inventory and has arranged insurance coverage to offset the loss
- They will not be caught in the theft and, if detected, will be lightly punished, if at all, by the firm
- The company has engaged in unfair labor practices or is planning a reduction in force; hence they should take (i.e., steal) whatever is available as a form of compensation
- The company is bad or in some other way evil and needs to be justifiably punished by the employee through theft
- The company is big and impersonal, and the employee is hardly known; therefore, stealing is justified to strike back at the big, impersonal entity

These reasons become part of a person's system of belief—a system of belief that is assumed by the person to be widely held, logical, and axiomatic—a system of belief used to justify the act of theft.

Ethical Relativism

In justifying the act of theft on the basis that "everyone is doing it," the employee is applying ethical relativism as the logic in use. The concept of ethical relativism is anchored in the notion that "people in different cultures, as well as people within a given culture, hold divergent moral views on particular issues."[6] For example, in the United States it is morally unacceptable to engage in bribery, but in another country it may be morally acceptable and a common business practice. An example within the United States is the divergent views on the issue of capital punishment. People on each side of the issue have reasons to justify or condemn the practice and are able to articulate reasons in ways they perceive to be logical.

The concept of ethical relativism gives explanation as to why, within a single firm, there may be employed people who hold divergent views on theft. For instance, some employees' system of belief or logic leads them to

morally accept stealing from the firm. On the other hand, some employees have moral standards such that, no matter how they view the firm or how it has treated them, to steal from the firm is wrong and is never considered.

Although the concept of ethical relativism gives explanation as to why, within a single firm, some employees may steal while others do not, the concept does not justify employee theft. Rather, as in most cultures, it may be argued that stealing in our culture is morally unacceptable. Said another way, people in a variety of cultures, including ours, hold the view that theft is morally unacceptable or wrong. Given that theft as a concept is wrong, employee theft also is morally unacceptable and wrong.

RULES AND CONSEQUENCES

The basic argument that employee theft is morally unacceptable and wrong has been framed at the level of moral common sense. The ethical analysis, however, must rise to a higher level to fully explore the concept of employee theft from the viewpoint of ethics and to present ethical theories useful in both understanding and preventing employee theft. Specifically, the higher level of analysis considers rules (deontological theory) and consequences (teleological theory).

Rules

Deontological theory is concerned with the rules used in making a decision or taking an action—in other words, the rules that might be used by a person when deciding whether or not to participate in employee theft. Here, two rules are considered: the categorical imperative and the golden rule.

- The categorical imperative requires that people never take actions that they would not recommend to others.[7] That is, people should not take an action (e.g., participate in employee theft) unless they believe that it could be recommended to others. In short, would the person be able to stand at the next company meeting, admit employee theft, and recommend it to others? If the answer is no, the action fails the categorical imperative and probably is not ethical. Not being able to tell others is "a clarion call that what is planned or has been done may not be ethical. The categorical imperative, is one of the best and simplest tests of ethics and should, perhaps, be the first test of ethics to be employed when in doubt about a particular action or decision."[8]
- The golden rule—do unto others as you would have them do unto you—advises people to act in the way they would want others to act toward them. Employees considering theft should ask, under the test of the golden rule, whether they would want the firm to

steal from them. If the answer is no, then, under the golden rule, employee theft is not justified.

In each of the deontological theories, the categorical imperative and the golden rule, the person is faced with a *yes* or *no* alternative. If the answer to the ethical question posed by these theories is no, then the action is not ethical and is one in which the employee should not participate. The practice of employee theft fails both the categorical imperative and the golden rule. But what of the consequences of employee theft? Might there be consequences that justify the practice?

Consequences

Teleological theory is concerned with the consequences of an action or decision. Here two concepts are considered—the utilitarian principle and egoism.

- The utilitarian principle asks that an individual act in a way to produce the greatest good for the greatest number.[9] Employee theft produces ill-gotten gain for the individual, but does not produce good for the greatest number. An employee seeking to do an act for the greatest number would do something to benefit the company, its customers, and its community. Employee theft does not benefit the company (i.e., the greater entity) and only benefits the individual in the form of profit from the ill-gotten gain. Here again, an employee, when contemplating a theft, is faced with a yes or no situation under the utilitarian principle. Will the act produce the greatest good for the greatest number? If the answer is no, the act fails the utilitarian principle and, most likely, is not ethical.

- The concept of egoism is about self-interest. It is divided into psychological egoism—that individuals do act to benefit themselves—and ethical egoism—that individuals ought to act to benefit themselves.[10] Some would argue that we are a very egoist society, a society in which individuals put themselves first in all that they do. In the situation of employee theft, individuals are egoists, in that they perceive the act of theft to be in their best interest, no matter how ill-gotten the gain or the hurt to another person. An egoist "does not care about the welfare of others except insofar as it affects her or his own welfare."[11] This explanation fits a thief, a person who, by the very act of theft, demonstrates a lack of care and respect for others.

THE ETHICAL PERSPECTIVE

The consequences of doing good to others (utilitarianism) and self-interest (egoism) give insight to employee theft. A person who has concern for and wants to do good for others (utilitarianism) may be less likely to steal from an employer than a person who is egotistical in orientation. Likewise, people who care about what others would think of them if the theft be known (categorical imperative) and who act in a way they would want to be treated by others (golden rule) are, again, less likely to steal than a person who does not have these concerns. These thoughts, taken together with the earlier discussion of moral common sense, give understanding of employee theft from an ethical perspective.

An application of the ethical perspective in employee theft is found in the written honesty tests reported to be in use in more than 5,000 companies nationwide.[12] These tests, which were administered to 3.5 million job applicants in 1988, cost $5 to $15 each and may be used on a preemployment or after employment basis.[13] Designed from the ethical theories presented above, the tests attempt to measure a person's ethics and morality. Although no single answer in the tests indicates a thief, those who administer and score the tests look for patterns in the answers. Series of questions measure whether the person has concern for others, his or her disposition to honesty in both small- and large-value situations, and his or her logic-in-use, or how he or she reasons through an ethical situation. Scores are determined for each person and placed within a range to indicate whether he or she is more likely to be honest or to be dishonest.

Honesty tests are an application of ethics in dealing with the problem of employee theft. The tests are based on ethical theory and, by posing a series of ethical situations, attempt to measure a person's tendency toward honesty. Ryan A. Kuhn, president of Reid Psychological Systems in Chicago, has done a great deal of research on the psychology of theft, and his company is probably the industry leader in the honesty-test field. His research findings are useful in helping us understand more about the typical thief. For example, he has learned that people who steal believe that others do it frequently, fantasize about committing the act frequently, and do not believe that thieves should be disciplined for their acts. He also says that dishonest people typically bring other problems with them into the workplace. They are far more likely to demonstrate pathological psychological profiles, to abuse drugs, to quit or be fired, to experience hostile encounters, and to file bogus insurance and worker's compensation claims. The *Reid Report,* the original pencil-and-paper honesty test that typically reduces theft incidences and turnover by about 50 percent, costs between $7 and $15 to use—a small price to pay for extremely valuable information.

THE EMPLOYER IN EMPLOYEE THEFT

Thus far, the focus has been on the employee. Of equal importance in an ethical analysis of employee theft is the employer and the ethical obligations of the employer. These include honesty, prevention, fairness, and instilling ethics in the organization.

Management Honesty

We have previously established that management honesty is of paramount importance. In a study that examined management honesty as a factor in preventing employee theft, the conclusion was that "if employees think top management is behaving honestly, they will probably think they are expected to behave honestly. But if employees perceive that top management is dishonest, they will be more inclined to justify and excuse their own dishonesty."[14]

Thus dishonesty in management will, in time, induce employee dishonesty. Through the actions of management, employees will be moved or conditioned toward honesty or dishonesty. It is imperative that management set an example. If managers participate in such things as insider trading, price fixing, check kiting, expense padding, time and material theft, and other acts of white-collar crime, there is a danger that these dishonest actions of management eventually will induce employees toward dishonesty. Management dishonesty, ultimately, will be manifest as employee theft. Therefore, to prevent employees from stealing based on the perception of a dishonest management, leaders in the organization must maintain the highest levels of honesty.

Management Prevention

Management is morally obliged to recognize their responsibility to their employees in preventing the opportunities for employee theft. Managers should "spot the temptations that might induce employees to steal and isolate these temptations so they can be eliminated."[15] As stated before, eliminating temptation can be done by establishing internal controls and security systems within the organization. These controls include inventory systems, security systems, financial controls, employment-screening systems, and the like. Management must be concerned with prevention—this is the second moral obligation of management.

Management Fairness

Management also has an obligation to be concerned about employee theft and to make that concern known in the organization. If management is perceived as not caring about the problem, does not have a clear policy on employee theft, and does not enforce that policy or applies it more leniently to managers, the spirit of fairness necessary to deter employee theft will be eroded. Management must be concerned about employee theft and treat all employees similarly when dealing with the problem.

Management-Instilled Ethics

Management has a moral obligation to instill ethics in the organization. This means that management must nurture ethics in the company and create an open environment for discussion of ethics. A code of ethics should be in place in every company; it should be widely promulgated and discussed with each employee. Meetings and seminars on ethics should be regularly conducted, and ethics and employee theft should be a point of discussion in an employee's annual review with management. Procedures for bringing questions of ethics or of employee theft to management should be established. And violators of the code of ethics should be treated fairly and swiftly. In essence, management must lead by example.

CONCLUSION

Employee theft is a problem of people—a problem of managers and their employees. Both managers and employees have an obligation to deter employee theft. Instilling ethics in an organization is an important process in deterring employee theft. Ethics enhances an individual and an organization. As people and their organizations are enhanced—as the culture becomes one of pride and honesty—employee theft will be deterred.

NOTES

1. "Light-fingered Work Ethics," *Time,* June 23, 1986, p. 64.
2. James D. Walls, Jr., "The Workplace: America's Hot Bed of Crime," *Vital Speeches of the Day,* April 1988, pp. 381–84.
3. "Notice Anything Missing Lately?" *Venture,* November 1988, p. 16.
4. Richard T. DeGeorge, *Business Ethics* (New York: Macmillan, 1986), p. 15.
5. Kenneth E. Goodpaster, "Some Avenues for Ethical Analysis in General Management," *Harvard Business School Note 383–007,* p. 6.
6. DeGeorge, *Business Ethics,* p. 32.
7. Immanuel Kant, *The Metaphysical Element of Justice* (New York: Library of Liberal Arts, 1965).
8. William J. Kehoe, "Ethics for Banking," *VBA Banking News,* December 1985, pp. 10–11.
9. John Stewart Mill, *Utilitarianism* (1863; reprint, Indianapolis: Bobbs-Merrill, 1957).
10. T. L. Beauchamp and N. E. Bowie, *Ethical Theory and Business* (Englewood Cliffs, N.J.: Prentice-Hall, 1988), p. 18.
11. Ibid. p. 19.
12. Harry Bacas, "To Stop a Thief," *Nation's Business,* 75 (June 1987), p. 17.
13. "Honestly, Can We Trust You?" *Time,* January 23, 1989, p. 44.
14. "How to Keep 'em Honest," *Psychology Today,* November 1981, p. 53.
15. Charles R. Carson, *Managing Employee Honesty* (Los Angeles: Security World Publishing Company, 1977), p. 19.

CRIME AND PUNISHMENT:
A HARD LOOK AT WHITE-COLLAR CRIME

In an era marked by more severe federal sentencing guidelines for white-collar criminals, most American corporations still don't have a clue about effectively deterring this type of misconduct.

BARBARA ETTORRE

It is one of the ironies of doing business today that, while companies are being asked to do more with less, they are also being told to do so under stricter legal and ethical guidelines. In a time of tighter rules, the days of tolerance for cutting corners, looking-the-other-way and one-hand-washing-the-other are rapidly fading. But the experts say that most companies haven't yet learned how to cope with changing paradigms.

Just being "within the law" doesn't cut it in this ever-more-complicated world. To the beleaguered manager, it may seem that standards are constantly changing and that their organizations must scramble to adhere to new norms—even as they are subject to new regulations that require even more rigorous conformity and self-examination.

"There was a time in our country when white-collar crime was tolerated," says Jeffrey

M. Kaplan, an attorney with the New York firm of Arkin Schaffer & Supino, and an expert in business ethics and legal compliance. "Now, in a time of diminishing resources, both the costs of crime and the costs of punishment—including the impact on shareholders, consumers and employees—have become too great for society to bear."

In support, a new set of far-reaching guidelines came into effect in November 1991. Called the Federal Sentencing Guidelines—directives for federal judges to follow in white-collar crime sentencings—they mandate much stricter punishments, among them enormous financial settlements up to and exceeding $500 million, depending on the crime. Slaps on the corporate wrist? Hardly.

But the more interesting part of the guidelines stresses prevention of these kinds of crime, putting the responsibility squarely on corporations to do so. In fact, for the first time in modern statutory law, the federal government is telling American business that a serious, proactive effort to prevent white-collar crime in the workplace can mitigate a judgment against a company.

These guidelines have accelerated an already strong movement in some corporations to create ethics and whistle-blowing procedures, to hire ombudspeople, to inaugurate ethics statements and internal hotlines and to educate employees and define ethical behavior. In fact, the "business" of business ethics is, arguably, a billiondollar industry, considering the consultants' fees and the videos, training programs, interactive psychodramas and other tools used by companies today.

Some of these organizations are in the vanguard. But professionals glumly delineate two contradicting attitudes that coexist in American business today. First, any company that professes to be unaware of the importance of ethics in doing business now is, quite simply, lying or ignorant. And, second, most companies are giving insufficient attention to ethics—until they get into trouble and learn the lesson the hard way.

A Little History

To be sure, American corporations have done their fair share of malfeasance. Similar white-collar crimes seemed to run in decade-long cycles. In the '60s, there was a spate of bid-rigging by electrical companies. In the '70s, it was ille-

---

BRIEFCASE

There's a general feeling out there that the world has become a less ethical place. That feeling may be difficult to quantify, but in corporate America, are ethical standards higher? Are people being allowed to get away with less?

---

gal payments overseas by giant government contractors. The '80s saw pervasive insider trading, banking abuses and illegal practices by defense contractors.

The '90s? Well, there have been some brokerage scandals, a corporate finagle here and there, and one big bond scandal at Salomon Brothers for illegal bidding at U.S. Treasury auctions. But no defining set of white-collar

crimes has yet emerged to shape this decade. There are no major cases under the Federal Sentencing Guidelines yet, either. Legal specialists say it will take several years for a test case to surface. This is not for lack of intense government interest; the 1993 Federal Bureau of Investigation budget, for example, included $200 million earmarked for 20,000 new investigations, most of them in white-collar areas.

The wheels of law grind exceedingly slow—which is why the guidelines themselves are an extraordinary instrument for compliance. They came to pass during the long Reagan-Bush tenure—administrations noted for getting regulation off the back of business. The rules mandated, in effect, that in exchange for that business-friendly climate, corporations would have to do their own policing.

The government got ahead of the curve for once, say the professionals, and defined what an ethics program might include. At the heart of the guidelines are seven fundamental points spelling out in detail the ideal ethical compliance policy. "In theory, these are tremendous strides, creating an organization that is ethically state-of-the-art," says attorney Kaplan.

In brief, the guidelines call for a company to create powerful internal constituencies with a mandate to ensure an ethical climate. These could consist of committees of top officers who must meet regularly, receive information, act and report to the board. Moreover, what these entities do must be disseminated to the entire organization, and there must be a public report within the company, involving the CFO, the corporate legal officer and division heads, as one example.

"To a greater degree, employees, shareholders and officers feel ethical issues are the issues for them," says Kaplan. "We are seeing the beginning of solutions. That's where we're at."

But a host of experts might take issue with those statements. Darlene Orlov, president of Orlov Resources for Business, a human resources consulting and training company based in New York, maintains that when people look to the law alone as the arbiter of what is right and wrong, they frequently get into trouble. "A corporation could say, 'If it's legal, it's okay,' and exempt moral judgements," she says.

Spirit vs. Letter of the Law

Orlov goes on to say that not only are there morally incorrect laws—slavery is an historical example—but also that laws themselves occur because of changes in what people think is

"A corporation could say, 'If it's legal, it's okay,' and exempt moral judgments."

—Darlene Orlov, HR professional

right and wrong. These changes come from "internal mechanisms for recognizing ethical dilemmas."

"People are compartmentalized in their ethics," Orlov continues. "Someone who cheats on her spouse would never steal a dress. A man who cheats on his taxes would never cheat a friend at cards."

Another specialist contends that corporate codes of ethics focus too much on the negative "thou shalt not," what employees should not do. "Employees can always find an exception,"

says Craig Dreilinger, president of The Dreiford Group, a management consulting firm in Bethesda, Md. "[Corporations] must go beyond the negative particulars and get their people to see the spirit of the law."

As elusive as the understanding of law and behavior can be, certainly there is no lack of corporate interest in finding a workable solution to ethical dilemmas. In the past six to 12 months, Dreilinger alone has seen "at least double" the number of serious inquiries for assistance in setting up ethics programs—introduc-

---

"I'M NOT JUST A COP"

Thomas A. Russo winces at the world "cop." What he is trying to do goes beyond the description of police work. He is, he says, "not just a cop."

Russo, managing director and an officer at Lehman Brothers, is one of a new breed on Wall Street: the proactive senior-level compliance officer, with far-reaching responsibilities and clout. He has counterparts at such well-known concerns as Goldman, Sachs & Company, Salomon Brothers, Morgan Stanley and Paine Webber Group Inc.

"Just three to four years ago, [Wall Street] wouldn't have put the emphasis on preventative steps," says Russo. "The emphasis was on revenue generation." Early last year, Russo began his tenure at Lehman as head of the corporate advisory division. Reporting to him are, among other areas, the firm's general counsel and its credit and corporate audit departments.

"We are putting a system in place to prevent problems," says Russo, who brings heavy credentials to his position:

15 years as partner at a leading Wall Street law firm, former deputy general counsel of the Commodity Futures Trading Commission and author of numerous textbooks and articles on securities law and financial regulation.

But even Russo admits that he can't remember the complex maze of rules governing financial transactions. How should a trader be expected to? So, Russo is at Lehman to monitor the firm's compliance, educate its employees before problems occur and get the firm's lawyers out onto the trading desks to see how the business works.

Under Russo's direction, compliance has become part of the planning process. In February, he surprised the firm's senior operating committee with a 60-page summary of his division's 1994 business plan, the first time in memory that compliance goals were set out in detail. Preemptive in nature, they are intended to reduce Lehman's regulatory exposure, limit litigation costs and avoid adverse publicity and erosion of client confidence--the pragmatic stuff of an ethics strategy.

Russo also co-chairs a new committee, in which new financial products are investigated thoroughly for compliance before they are actively marketed. "This is a signal to the firm that compliance is part of everything we do," Russo says, adding that only select, seasoned traders will deal with sophisticated products, and only to institutions, not to the general public.

"We are geared very much to developing an [ongoing] relationship with [Lehman's] businesses," he continues. "They should feel comfortable telling us their problems during the quiet times. They should know we've thought it through and should have confidence in us."

Can one create ethical behavior from outside the individual? "You can tweak it," says Russo. "If leaders at the top say with clarity, 'I don't want an atmosphere where unethical behavior is acceptable,' then the entire organization can get it. Sure, people will have unethical thoughts—but maybe they'll think twice."

—B.E.

tion and implementation from companies who haven't had them before, or the need to "drill deep into the issues" from those who have.

Clearly, American managers have focused on ethical compliance programs as the way to fulfill their responsibilities and to avert white-collar crime in their workplace. Even Winthrop M. Swenson, deputy general counsel of the U.S. Sentencing Commission—and chairman of the staff unit that developed the corporate guidelines—says, "If [corporations] have done everything reasonably necessary to implement a rigorous compliance program, it doesn't make sense to hit them over the head, because we really can't ask them to do more than that."

Swenson's statement quite rightly applies to the sentencing aspect of the guidelines—the "letter" of the law. But many experts maintain that most corporate compliance programs fall short of the guidelines, or, worse, that these programs do not prompt more ethical behavior, the "spirit" of the law.

"I personally don't think [the guidelines] have changed the landscape," says Robert J. McGuire, former New York City Police Commissioner and president of Kroll Associates, the New York-based white-collar crime investigative firm. McGuire says the guidelines have been, "a blip on the radar screen" producing only "modestly more enlightened" corporations.

Roger J. Magnuson, a partner at the Minneapolis law firm of Dorsey & Whitney and head of its white-collar and corporate compliance practice groups, concurs. "A surprising number of compliance programs at companies are not well benchmarked and probably would not pass guidelines' muster," he says.

If we assume that ethics programs at some American companies—programs executed from the top down and with the best of intentions—are ineffectual, we must also assume that these strategies haven't made that much of

"NOBODY PUT ME IN PRISON BUT MYSELF"

Edward P. "Ted" Wolfram Jr., is an unlikely white-collar criminal. He is a 63-year-old grandfather, a former stockbroker, a public speaker at major corporations—and, a convicted felon.

In 1983, the government charged Wolfram, a managing partner at a Toledo, Ohio, brokerage firm, with four counts of mail and wire fraud, saying that he swindled $47 million from the firm, which subsequently went bust. Sentenced to 25 years, Wolfram served, "exactly 10 years, minus one hour," at several federal prison installations, and eventually was released on parole last October 3.

"No one aided me in what I did, and nobody put me in prison but myself," Wolfram says in a telephone interview from his Las Vegas home. "Because of what I did, 7,000 clients were injured. I stole, and I defrauded my clients, my partners, my friends and my family."

He says the fraud amounted to less than $47 million—but he does not criticize the sentence or the judge. "If it's $2, it's too much," he asserts.

Wolfram's 89-year-old father (Edward Sr.), as well as Wolfram's wife and four children, stood by him during those years, actions that he says "speak of them, not me." ("The chances of a family staying together if someone is in prison for three years are minuscule," he points out.)

Wolfram began lecturing on white-collar crime to MBA students from Pepperdine College who visited the jail as part of Professor James Martinoff's classes. Wolfram now lectures organizations for Martinoff's Ethical Management Con-

sultants group, providing his listeners with a voice of experience and sometimes leaving them in tears.

For each out-of-state lecture, Wolfram must get written permission from his probation officer and must call in within 24 hours of his return. He also must file a monthly financial report.

Wolfram pays no restitution to those he wronged; he voluntarily gave up his assets—including his home, a collection of European racing cars and his wife's engagement ring—before he was sentenced, and the proceeds were distributed then. His monthly pay at the consultancy is $1,500 (plus $299 for healthcare insurance), which is supplemented by his wife's earnings.

Of his current career, Wolfram says, "This is not something I enjoy doing, but I'm compelled. There are no reasons for ethical misconduct—just a lot of excuses. I loved myself too much and others too little. There were consequences to people who really matter."

A telling consequence was driven home to him while Wolfram was in a Tallahassee prison. During a telephone conversation, his son told him that Wolfram's young grandson (Edward IV) had burst into tears in class when his teacher asked students to talk about their grandfathers. "He didn't want to say his granddad was in jail," says Wolfram, quietly. "How much time would a man have to spend in prison for the misery he's caused his family?"

—B.E.

"If [corporations] have done everything reasonably necessary to implement a rigorous compliance program...we really can't ask them to do more than that."
—*Winthrop M. Swenson, U.S. Sentencing Commission*

a difference in the way companies operate. This is a conclusion both depressing and frightening.

The Ethics Resource Center, a well-known nonprofit Washington consultancy that has worked with more than 100 companies on ethics, recently surveyed 10,000 employees from its client companies in aerospace, telecommunications, healthcare and consumer products. The survey indicated that ethics programs "failed to penetrate the [corporate] culture." Fifty-five percent of the respondents said they "never" or "only occasionally" found their company's standards of conduct "useful in guiding their business decisions and actions." And, 8 percent had not read the standards.

It has become standard practice to point out that business is becoming ever more complicated. Enterprises will have to make increasingly sophisticated decisions in less time, with intangible intellectual property issues and murky technological distinctions. Face-to-face contact has waned; companies these days often don't fully know who they are doing business with and what is the source of capital in a deal.

In addition to the federal guidelines, corporations can find themselves subject to other avenues of punishment. The Sentencing Commission's Swenson points out that a corporation that has honored the letter of the guidelines could still be subject to antitrust, interstate trade, the False Claims Act, and other considerations. "The guidelines control criminal penalties," he says, "but they don't control penalties from other quarters, such as state laws and corporate liability laws."

So, what is a good-citizen company to do if compliance programs alone don't promise —or, even foster—ethical behavior? Can ethics be imposed on an organization? How can a corporation truly raise the level of its ethical behavior?

Attorney Magnuson, author of *The White-Collar Crime Explosion* (McGraw-Hill, 1992), suggests crossover—temporary job postings, internships and the like—between the specialists in public policy (i.e., the regulators and think tank people) and those in corporate law or private practice. "Let everyone see the body of regulations that has an actual impact in day-to-day corporate life," he exhorts. "Even the good-faith employee has to have his or her consciousness raised."

Some companies have been aggressively policing themselves beyond ethics compliance strategies. They have become mini-prosecutors, setting up stringent internal guidelines for employee compliance and disciplinary action. If any malfeasance occurs, they punish swiftly, then preemptively take the results to the authorities.

"These companies want to forestall major litigation—multimillion-dollars in attorneys' fees alone," says Magnuson. "As a mark of good faith, they are hoping that the federal authorities will say, 'Go, and sin no more.' It works."

Depending on the crime, such corporations use various punishments toward the employee wrongdoer: forfeiture of bonuses, suspensions with or without pay, letters of reprimand in permanent files, downward job reclassification for those on management tracks, various probationary tasks, as well as outright dismissal. Of course, the danger in this "terrible swift sword" school of policing is that a corporation can become too aggressive in its search for compliance. The employee can be accused, judged and punished out of hand.

No Law Breaking Here

The Sentencing Commission's Swenson acknowledges that the guidelines give "a strong incentive" for companies to "disclose and cooperate with authorities," increasing the likeli-

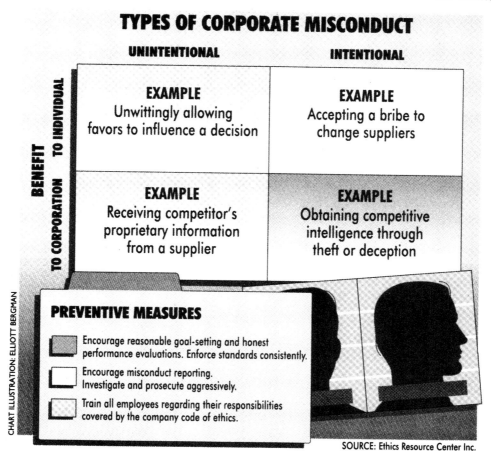

TYPES OF CORPORATE MISCONDUCT

	UNINTENTIONAL	INTENTIONAL
BENEFIT TO INDIVIDUAL	**EXAMPLE** Unwittingly allowing favors to influence a decision	**EXAMPLE** Accepting a bribe to change suppliers
BENEFIT TO CORPORATION	**EXAMPLE** Receiving competitor's proprietary information from a supplier	**EXAMPLE** Obtaining competitive intelligence through theft or deception

PREVENTIVE MEASURES

- Encourage reasonable goal-setting and honest performance evaluations. Enforce standards consistently.
- Encourage misconduct reporting. Investigate and prosecute aggressively.
- Train all employees regarding their responsibilities covered by the company code of ethics.

CHART ILLUSTRATION: ELLIOTT BERGMAN

SOURCE: Ethics Resource Center Inc.

hood that individuals will be held accountable. "The concern is about getting the right balance here," he says carefully. "We want to send the message that lawbreaking won't be tolerated. Yet, we don't want employees to be scapegoats. It may be a problem [with the guidelines]. I don't know that it's a weakness."

Employee training is one small step for companies. HR specialist Orlov says that workers bring to their workplace their ethical makeup, derived from many factors including society, past experiences, upbringing, role models and institutions, and media attention. Sometimes, the level of corporate ethics clashes with their own.

"There must be a framework for recognizing ethical dilemmas, and a process for resolving them and thinking about them proactively before problems arise," Orlov says. "People have to be trained within the context of work." To this, she advocates ethical training using relevant examples appropriate to an employee's job, level and industry. For example, training an entry-level worker how not to take a bribe doesn't make sense. What does is training him

WORKBOOK

Unlike a standard financial audit, an ethics audit is a useful tool to sweep your company and retrieve important findings to be acted upon. These tips come from W. Michael Hoffman, director of the Center for Business Ethics at Bentley College and professor of philosophy there.

☑ Survey employees on sensitive questions (How are we living up to our ethical criteria? Do you feel safe calling into the hotline?). Conduct skip-level interviews, in which a manager meets with an employee two levels below. This keeps immediate supervisors on their toes.

☑ Conduct detailed opinion surveys after every employee training session on ethics programs.

☑ Analyze the pattern of calls made to the hotline. Are calls indicating trouble increasing? Is there a particular complaint or family of complaints?

☑ Conduct random interviews with employees—but only after your compliance efforts (hence, your corporate credibility) have received high marks over time.

or her to recognize pilfering and providing clear-cut steps to report it, protect confidentiality, and ensure no retribution.

Here we come to the true heart of the matter. Are all the guidelines, programs and training inadequate because—unless there is a culture change from the skin, bones and very fiber of America's companies—corporate ethical behavior is just about impossible?

Gary Edwards, president of the Ethics Resource Center, maintains that goal-setting in today's businesses hampers ethical performance. Goals, he says, are typically set at the top, with no input from lower levels. Managers exhort workers to exceed goals, and they empower them to act on their own—all while worker resources are shrinking. Hence, he says true ethical behavior must examine motivation.

For the Good of the Company

Edwards says the overwhelming number of white-collar crimes arises from the intentional employee misconduct designed to benefit a company. "The paradigm of improper conduct," he calls it. The kind of wrongdoing that puts a corporation on the front page and ruins its reputation. He says these white-collar criminals think they are different from and above the common criminal, because they did it "for the good of the company."

"They believe the objectives have overriding importance over legalities and ethics," he says, adding that this is the basic ethical flaw, especially as employees see goal achievement rewarded by promotions and bonuses. This tacit approval sends strong signals to employees to cut corners ethically.

Without a cataclysmic change in corporate culture and values and in reward systems and goal-setting, "the guidelines are inadequate," Edwards says. "It is likely that a company and its attorney can look at the [guidelines'] seven factors and infer from them that meeting those requirements would reduce substantially the likelihood of misconduct.

"That would be a wrong assumption," he states. "False comfort. The company would be impaled on the guidelines."

Six Myths of Sexual Harassment

Recognizing that sexual harassment may be alive in your company is the first step to ridding the workplace of this potentially devastating plague.

Jan Bohren

Jan Bohren is the director of human resources at the Argonne National Laboratory. He has held senior executive positions in the health insurance industry, with the U.S. Office of Personnel Management, the Department of the Navy, and the Federal Labor Relations Authority.

he Anita Hill-Clarence Thomas hearings and the Navy's "Tailhook" scandal were eye-openers for many people in this country—not necessarily for those employers that have worked for years to rid the workplace of outmoded male attitudes, but for all the other employers that had ignored the problem for years.

Enlightened companies recognize that their employees, and especially their manage-ment teams, need explanations and education about this relatively new subject, and they have moved quickly to fill the gap in information. Others remain skeptical, chalking up sexual harassment as the latest liberal fad and convincing themselves that "this too shall pass."

But it won't—and the stakes are too high to continue to ignore it. Sexual harassment transgressions will continue to be serious liabilities, and those that are overlooked can bring a corporation to its knees, even cause shareholders to question management's ability to manage. And the liabilities are not just careers, but financial. Managers, especially CEOs, who want to avoid these liabilities, need to understand more about sexual harassment than what they may have seen on television, and they need to recognize and dispel the myths surrounding sexual harassment. Here are six of them:

MYTH #1:
IT'S NOT A PROBLEM HERE

Several years ago, a senior executive made a comment in a room of senior executives, including one woman, "Well, this kind of thing isn't happening at the top management level, but we need to make sure that it's not occurring at the worker level." The woman executive remained silent. The top executive of that organization had recently resigned over a sexual harassment scandal.

Flash! Sexual harassment is alive (if not rampant) in every organization that isn't paying attention to the issue. Remember, most sexual harassment complaints are lodged against people who have power over employees' careers. They're called supervisors, managers, vice presidents and, yes, even CEOs! The courts are not blind to managerial hierarchy, by the way. Juries generally hold higher-level managers to higher-level standards. Translation: the higher the level of the harasser, the higher the costs for the company.

MYTH #2:
IT'S HUMAN NATURE. THEY'LL WORK IT OUT

It's not human nature, but it is prevalent. If you're a woman who has worked for five years or more, it is almost certain that you have been harassed in the workplace. If you're a man, it's just as likely that someone has harassed your spouse, your mother, your sister or your daughter in the workplace.

The employee who complains and is not heard will either quit or fight. If she quits, the harasser will continue to harass other employees—and the company loses a valuable person in whom time and money has been invested. In either event, the employer loses.

Sexual harassment is not human nature. It is unacceptable behavior, it's learned, it's illegal and, contrary to what many companies would like to believe, by merely leaving it alone, the problem will not disappear.

MYTH #3:
WOMEN HARASS MEN AS MUCH AS MEN HARASS WOMEN

Yes, women can and do harass men. Remember the Biblical story about Joseph, who was taken captive, sent to Egypt and assigned to Potiphar, the captain of Pharaoh's guard? Potiphar's wife harassed Joseph, but she claimed it was Joseph who harassed her and presented her husband with a piece of Joseph's clothing as evidence.

Based on this circumstantial evidence, Potiphar would not even listen to Joseph's side of the story. There was no trial. Innocent as he was, Joseph went to jail. But even if there had been an investigation, Potiphar's wife and her "evidence" might have prevailed.

Of course, women can be the harassers. However, the vast majority of sexual harassment cases involve men harassing women. But you will often hear men counter charges of sexual harassment with, "She was the one who harassed me." This is a feeble defense. If he has no documentation, it won't hold up in court. If a man truly is harassed, he can't treat it lightly. He needs to document and report the occurrence immediately.

Some men also counter that the woman dressed or acted provocatively or "came on" to them. That, again, is no defense of the men's behavior.

MYTH #4:
IF THERE'S NO INTENT TO HARASS, YOU'RE NOT LIABLE

This is one of the most common misconceptions and mistakes. Most sexual harassment involves no intended sexual misconduct or activity. Most men accused of sexual harassment will admit to the behavior, but claim they did not *intend* to harass the employee alleging the conduct.

The law, however, does not address intent, but focuses on whether the sexually oriented activity occurred. If it did, and it was unwelcome, there was harassment. If it occurred repeatedly or if it was explicitly objected to and occurred again, some very strong action can be expected. If management was aware of the conduct, you and your general counsel will be spending a great deal of time together.

MYTH #5:
IT'S HARD TO DETERMINE GUILT; IT'S ONE PERSON'S WORD AGAINST ANOTHER'S

If the Hill-Thomas hearings supported or created support for one myth, it's the one that presupposes that most sexual harassment is one-on-one, secret or hard to determine. The truth is, even where there are no witnesses, most men accused of harassment *admit* the conduct, claim no intent, and/or claim ignorance of the law. The bottom line is, when properly investigated, sexual harassment cases rarely end up as "judgment calls." And, while there are cases in which sexual harassment charges have been totally fabricated, these are rare.

ual advances and had sexual encounters with her. One piece of evidence presented to the jury before the out-of-court settlement was the trousers of her supervisor, which she had taken when he was harassing her.

Preventative Steps

If you have responsibility for employees, you need to talk to them, especially the women, and find out how prevalent sexual harassment is in your workplace. If you have employees with "locker-room mentalities," you are at risk.

How do you make sure the myths surrounding sexual harassment don't prevail in your office or workplace?

• First of all, continue the educational process launched by the Hill-Thomas hearings and "Tailhook"—make sure that your company has a clear written policy prohibiting sexual harassment and that it is included in mandatory supervisory training programs.

• Talk to your managers and your employees, including women—personally. Don't leave this to your human resources people or your EEO manager. Employees need to know that concern about this issue is coming from the top. If you have subordinate managers, it is essential that they know where you stand on this important subject—tell them.

• Walk around. You may be surprised with what you see—like nude calendars, sexually oriented cartoons and offensive or pornographic magazines and literature.

• Make sure that your human resources staff is equally committed to your policies, that it understands its role in overseeing the program, and that it knows what steps to take when sexual harassment complaints are received.

• Insist on being kept informed of all sexual harassment complaints in the company, and the outcomes of investigations, including any corrective action or disciplinary action taken (or not taken).

You can't eliminate sexual harassment from your workplace until you first recognize that you are not immune from it. Once you dispel these myths, you are that much closer to eliminating the inappropriate behavior from your workplace. Your employees will appreciate the sensitivity and demonstrated awareness of management, and stockholders will appreciate the money saved by a strongly enforced policy. Besides, it's the right thing to do.

Here's what you can do to help keep your workplace harassment-free:

 Have a clear written policy prohibiting sexual harassment.

 Have mandatory supervisory training programs.

 Ensure that the workplace is free of offensive materials.

 Implement a program for steps to take when a complaint of harassment is received.

 Keep informed of all complaints and steps taken.

 Make sure the commitment is at every level.

MYTH #6:
THERE'S NOT MUCH
THEY CAN DO TO US

Oh yeah? Ask the automaker that was ordered to pay $185,000 in back pay to a woman whose supervisor told her she was in a male-dominated field and had better get used to her coworkers discussing sex.

Ask the food company that had a manager who commented daily about an employee's breasts, buttocks and physical appearance, who suggested to women that they show him a "good time," and who imposed a dress code designed to show off women's legs. What would they have paid to avoid the court award of $625,000?

Ask the publishing company that was told by the court to pay $800,000 in punitive damages and $85,000 in compensatory damages to an employee who proved that she was subjected to lascivious remarks made by a supervisor about women and passed over twice for promotion in favor of younger men, despite demonstrating exemplary qualifications for the particular promotion.

Ask the grocery chain that settled out of court in a $14 million suit by an employee who charged that her supervisor made constant sex-

Ten steps to follow when investigating a sexual harassment complaint

Stuart H. Brody and Wm. Lee Kinnally, Jr.

Stuart H. Brody is Senior Counsel to the Labor and Employment Group at Gibney, Anthony & Flaherty, a New York law firm. Wm. Lee Kinnally, Jr. heads Gibney, Anthony & Flaherty's litigation department.

Although sexual harassment has become one of the most contentious issues of the modern workplace, employers need not be helpless bystanders to the problem. For instance, a well publicized policy and periodic employee training can do much to minimize both the occurrence of sexual harassment and an employer's liability.

But what happens when you get a complaint? Responding to a sexual harassment charge by an employee is loaded with pitfalls. Here are ten rules to guide you.

1. Make a prompt investigation.

Case law has not defined "prompt" in terms of time, but courts have left no doubt that it means as soon as practicable. Prompt means days, not weeks. The key is to leave no room for the complaining party to believe, or a judge to conclude, that there was foot-dragging. An investigator needs to be appointed quickly. Therefore, someone should be designated, in advance of a complaint, to conduct an investigation if called for.

2. The investigator should be a person with the experience, temperament and stature to conduct the investigation.

This means someone whose job normally entails interviewing employees, most frequently a personnel officer, and who is somewhat independent of the day-to-day operations of the department involved. Having an investigator of the same sex as the complaining party (or two available investigators—one male and one female) facilitates the difficult process of obtaining reliable and complete evidence.

If a personnel officer is viewed as too close to the situation, or otherwise incapable of creating trust by the parties, consider asking someone outside the normal chain of command, such as the head of an unrelated department. But remember, do not delay in commencing the investigation.

You should discuss with your attorney whether he or she should perform the investigation. An investigation conducted by an attorney may be shielded from discovery or subpoena in subsequent agency or court proceedings. This may be a significant consideration. For instance, if the investigation yields a finding of sexual harassment and the complaining party sues because she is unsatisfied with the action, if any, taken by the employer against the harasser, she will surely seek to have the investigation report introduced as an admission against the employer. An admission that sexual harassment occurred does not automatically establish liability. However, admissions can have a powerful effect on propelling complaining employees to litigation and influencing juries. At the very least, the investigator's report should be reviewed by a lawyer specializing in employment law, not only to minimize the problem of damaging admissions, but also to correct poor drafting and eliminate unnecessary findings.

Witnesses must be assured of confidentiality and must understand there will be no retaliation against them by anyone.

3. Provide all witnesses with assurances of confidentiality and freedom from retaliation.

Such assurances are given to witnesses to encourage their cooperation with the investigation. But the investigator must also be mindful that breaches of confidentiality

 From *Ethikos*, January/February 1994, pp. 9, 11-12. © 1994 by Ethikos, Inc. Reprinted by permission.

can expose the employer to suit for defamation by the alleged harasser.

Obviously, in the course of the investigation it will be necessary for the investigator to communicate to witnesses the substance of the charges involved. An investigator has a "privilege" to communicate such obviously derogatory material, but only to the extent necessary to legitimately further the investigation.

4. Make a complete record of every aspect of the investigation.

This means not only recording the time, date, location and duration of witness interviews, but also what questions were asked and answered and those that were not answered. A complete record of responses is essential. Witness responses, especially quotes, should be repeated to witnesses to ensure accuracy.

Although it is often thought useful to have a witness sign his or her statement to protect against subsequent variation, we do not recommend this. A request for signature injects an intimidating element into the investigation and is invariably accompanied by a counter request for a copy of the statement, which increases the possibility that defamatory statements will be disseminated.

5. Conduct the interview in a private place away from the normal flow of business, and off-duty if the complaining party is concerned about a supervisor noticing his or her absence.

Witnesses must be assured of confidentiality and must understand there will be no retaliation against them by anyone. They should be encouraged to submit any further information that occurs to them and should be assured that opportunities exist to update information at any time.

6. In communicating the charges to the alleged harasser and other witnesses, be only as specific as necessary to get his version.

You need to protect against unnecessary dissemination of the charges.

Skill is required to strike a balance between offering too much detail and not enough. If the sexual harassment charges are given verbatim, the risk is that the alleged harasser will simply deny the accusations. If they are too sketchy (such as, "Can you think of anything you ever said that was offensive?"), a blanket denial is also likely. A middle course will result in more specific responses, such as identifying the time, date, and location of an alleged remark and referencing it to the context of conversation that surrounded it.

But remember, witnesses should be afforded only so much information as they need to give their account of an occurrence. You need to protect against unnecessary dissemination of the charges.

7. When the investigation is completed, issue a report that is clearly written with specific findings and recommendations of remedial steps.

This is the most difficult part of the investigator's job. It is no secret that one key purpose of the investigator's report is to show a court that the employer kept its own house in order. An effective report can avoid liability; a poor one can assure it. An employer may avoid liability for a supervisor's conduct, even if it imposes inappropriately light discipline or no discipline at all, provided that the investigation was conducted in good faith and that the harassment does not recur. To be in good faith, however, there must be a reasonable attempt to resolve credibility disputes and to determine whether the conduct was unwelcome and sufficiently serious to constitute sexual harassment.

Conclusions must be carefully framed. As indicated earlier, the investigator must be aware that the report may be subsequently disclosed, and that the admissions in the report will be brought to light. If the alleged harasser is to be discharged or suspended for his or her behavior, then an admission that such conduct was committed is appropriate and expected. The difficulty for the investigator occurs when sexual harassment is found, but remedial action short of discharge is recommended. For instance, a finding of sexual harassment with a recommendation for written warning of the harasser leaves the employer open to the charge that the penalty was inappropriate and the investigation was not in good faith. Accordingly, in cases where less severe discipline is imposed, it is useful to avoid stating a legal conclusion that sexual harassment occurred. Rather, the behavior should be characterized as "inappropriate," "improper," "disparaging," "having no place in a work environment," and so forth.

Even if an attorney does not conduct the investigation, the preparation of the report should be under the attorney's supervision. At the very least, the attorney should approve the final document.

8. If you find sexual harassment was committed, you must take some action.

Although oral warnings may be appropriate in minor cases, you cannot simply tell the harasser to refrain from the behavior. Oral warnings tend to be associated with a lack of resolve on the employer's part. It must be made clear through written warnings, suspension, transfer, demotion, delays in salary increases or other adverse action that the behavior will not be tolerated, and that any further occurrences may lead to termination. In a serious case, particularly one where conduct is repeated despite timely warnings, discharge must be considered.

9. Communicate results to both parties.

Both the complaining party and the alleged harasser must be told whether the investigation reached a conclusion that sexual harassment occurred (although it may be desirable to characterize the behavior in other terms—see item seven above). They should also be told what discipline or other steps will be taken against the harasser, if any, and what steps generally are planned to ensure that occurrences of sexual harassment do not recur.

There is no reason, however, to show the investigator's report to the complaining party and the alleged harasser. The report is an internal document and should only be viewed by those responsible for imposing discipline and implementing recommendations of the report. Nor is the investigator obligated to explain the thought processes leading to the decision or the specific credibility findings made. Although there may be a natural tendency to submit to such questions, the investigator, or other party explaining the results, should avoid doing so to minimize unnecessary dissemination (or distortion) of the investigative work product.

10. Monitor effectiveness of discipline imposed and other ameliorative steps taken.

Once sexual harassment has been charged, an employer must be especially sensitive to its recurrence, not only with respect to the workplace as a whole, but especially between the complaining party and the harasser. Courts will take a dim view of the effectiveness of the employer's response to the initial allegations if the harassment recurs. For some courts, recurrence is proof of the inadequacy of the employer's response and hence the basis of liability for the sexual harassment. Mediation or counseling should be considered to reestablish a working relationship between the two parties. And, if not already conducted, training should be done so that all employees will have a better appreciation of the right to work in an environment free from harassment.

In some cases, the complaining party may be so dispirited that the alleged harasser was not discharged that she cannot effectively continue her work, or may actually refuse to work, thus raising the prospect of insubordination. Taking action in such cases is a very delicate matter and should not be done without the benefit of employment counsel.

Sexual harassment can be a pernicious element in any workplace. "Can be" is the key phrase. With the appropriate sensitivity and adherence to the type of sexual harassment policy we have outlined here, the potentially devastating effects of sexual harassment can be forestalled and remedial steps toward repairing damage implemented.

The Waiting Game
Women Make Strides, But Men Stay Firmly in Top Company Jobs

Female Management Gains Are Impeded by Culture Still Dominated by Males

From Ford Motor to Sara Lee

Rochelle Sharpe

Staff Reporter of The Wall Street Journal

Thirty years after the Civil Rights Act barred sex discrimination in the workplace, the debate over women's progress in corporate America boils down to this:

You've come a long way—maybe.

Women have moved into nonclerical white-collar jobs in droves. They held 46% of all such positions at the companies reporting to the U.S. Equal Employment Opportunity Commission in 1992, up from 22% in the late 1960s.

But women aren't matching these gains in management. A Wall Street Journal analysis shows that women still held less than a third of the managerial jobs in the 38,059 companies that reported to the EEOC in 1992, the latest year for which data are available. And among 200 of the nation's biggest companies analyzed by the Journal, they held just one-fourth of the jobs classified by the EEOC as "officials and managers"— a broad category that includes a wide variety of supervisory posts, from the manager of the janitorial service to the CEO of the company.

At the vice presidential level, women make up an even smaller percentage— less than 5% in 1990 according to Catalyst, a nonprofit research group in New York that studies women in business.

The issue of women's progress in management is especially sensitive in these days of corporate streamlining, when many men, in particular, are losing jobs. Between 1982 and 1992, men lost a net 93,000 management jobs and women gained a net 520,000, according to the Journal study. Some men, facing unemployment or reduced status and power, feel beleaguered by what seems like the constant push of women behind them, asking for more and more. "As a proportion of the managerial work force, women have gained fairly considerably," says Howard Hayghe, economist at the U.S. Bureau of Labor Statistics. The Journal's analysis shows that women held 30.5% of managerial jobs in 1992, up from 21.7% in 1982. (In 1992 at Dow Jones & Co., publisher of the Journal, 26.0% of managers were women.)

Yet in spite of men's losses and women's gains, men continue to hold the bulk of management jobs and, unless growth rates change considerably, will continue to hold them for a long time. At the current pace, women will not achieve parity with male managers for another 20 to 30 years.

This wasn't supposed to be the path of women's progress. For years, the argument has been that once more women entered the pipeline and earned solid business credentials, their numbers in the management ranks would rise rapidly. Women are in the pipeline; they have earned credentials; their educational levels are almost on a par with men. But they aren't even close to closing the managerial gap.

MOSTLY MALE

Many women say that the Catch-22 to greater representation lies in the simple fact that 15.1% of all male employees in the work force are managers and only 7.5% of all women are managers. As long as the percentages of male managers remain high, the culture remains mostly male and, women say, indifferent or hostile to their advancement. Women say they are ignored, not taken seriously and shunted into support jobs far from the company's core business, where there is little chance of breaking through the glass ceiling.

Many companies just shrug their corporate shoulders, wondering what they should do about women—if anything. But even those that make extraordinary efforts to recruit and promote women, or institute family-friendly policies, often fail to make the culture hospitable to women.

"The culture is more important than policy," says Rose Jonas, a consultant who formerly worked as a personnel manager for Monsanto Co. "If the culture doesn't change, nothing will change for women."

Consider Ford Motor Co., which has a male/female management ratio of 22 to 1: 4.4% of its officials and managers are women, according to the Journal's analysis. Jack Hall, vice president of employee relations, says that Ford's challenges are much greater than other firms because of its history as a blue-collar, male-dominated company in the Midwest. This makes it difficult to compete with newer, more glamorous companies for the highly sought-after women with technical degrees. "We're not Microsoft. We're not the high-tech Silicon Valley," he says.

But Ford isn't General Motors Corp., either. GM, just across town, had 11.7% female managers in 1992, according to the Journal's analysis, and Chrysler Corp. had 7.8%. (Ford questions whether it is fair to compare the three companies, since each may report differently to the EEOC. But looking only at their manufacturing units, Ford comes out at 4.0%, GM at 9.9% and Chrysler at 5.9%.)

At Ford, where until last summer the women's bathroom doors were painted pink, some male executives still treat women as though they are invisible, says 46-year-old Renee Lerche, manager of employee and education planning. Ms. Lerche wasn't initially included in the company's new committee to review their recruiting strategy, she says, even though she is in charge of all diversity work.

"I used to worry that they didn't like me or they felt competitive," Ms. Lerche says. "But now I've reached the conclusion that they wouldn't even see it as competition." Rather than be offended by such oversights, she says she now asks to be included in important meetings, and her colleagues are happy to oblige.

Many women who succeed at companies discover they can't simply wait for the culture to accept them. "Women need to change themselves to fit the corporation, and then figure out how to change the corporate culture," says Ms. Jonas, the consultant.

Linda Miller, 43, who became Ford's first female plant manager last November, is a good example of the kind of woman that gets ahead at the company. She shares with her male colleagues a fanaticism about cars, even dismantling engines in her spare bedroom.

Now manager of Ford's engine and fuel-tank plant in Dearborn, Mich., and married to a Ford plant manager in Cleveland, Ms. Miller has lived in a different city from her husband for half of their 10-year marriage—sometimes, in a different country. She speaks of her need to be flexible to pursue her career: "If being in the same house with your husband is critical, that's a barrier."

SURVIVAL TACTICS

Ms. Miller believes Ford has fewer women managers than GM and Chrysler be-

cause of the company's hiring freeze in the early 1980s, which she calls "one of our biggest mistakes." It was a time, she says, when many women were getting jobs at car companies, yet at Ford, two of her female supervisors were laid off.

Lately, the auto maker has launched an aggressive recruitment campaign for women and is developing a corporate strategy that will focus on training as well as changing the company culture to accommodate women. "If we don't change the culture, we're not going to survive," says Jack Hall.

DuPont Co., on the other hand, is often cited as being one of the nation's friendliest companies for female workers with families and one that has made real efforts, on the policy level, to recruit women. The company set stiff recruiting goals in 1979, which it has met or exceeded every year since. It launched a diversity sensitivity training program in 1982, so far ahead of other companies that it became a national model. It started a special succession planning program, where individual women's careers are analyzed for gaps in experience. It has a sexual-harassment policy, a rape-prevention program, a daycare center, flextime, flexplace, even an executive whose job title is "Director of Upward Mobility."

Still, in 1992 women made up only 9.3% of managers at DuPont, or 925 of the 9,975 management jobs. Though the percentage has increased from 4.5% in 1982, DuPont has one of the lowest percentages of female managers in the basic-materials industry, according to the Journal's analysis.

Partly, the company says, this is due to cutbacks. DuPont slashed its senior management by 50% since 1985; seven layers of management have been eliminated between the CEO and the plant. This often means that as women get more and more eligible for promotion, there is simply no job for them. "In many ways, the track has disappeared" for women, says Faith Wohl, who until recently was DuPont director of human-resource initiatives. "It is a painful irony that we got everybody all dressed up, but we have nowhere to go."

GOING FOR RESPECT

DuPont's family-friendly policies clearly haven't made huge inroads into bringing women into management or changing the culture. Some ambitious women

don't use them, feeling that it puts them on the "mommy track." Others don't need them. And many female DuPont employees believe that while Chairman Edgar Woolard Jr. is firmly committed to diversity, there is a whole level of managers beneath him who aren't comfortable working with women.

Mary Lou Arey left DuPont two years ago and launched a diversity consulting firm called Respect Inc. after she became convinced she would never move higher in the company. Ms. Arey, 53, who devised the sensitivity training programs that brought DuPont acclaim, says she was perceived as too vocal on women's issue. She noticed that male colleagues had a hard time adjusting to her expressive personal style, which she characterizes as the opposite of the unemotional demeanor of most DuPont men.

Ms. Wohl, 57, who now works for the federal government, agrees that the subtle, cultural attitudes that pervade DuPont can derail careers. "We've been the ultimate example of a hierarchical, male-dominated corporate culture," she says. By instituting progressive, women-friendly programs, she says, "We ruled out everything except something which is the most elusive of all—culture."

The upside to bright, aggressive women leaving corporations is that they are starting their own businesses and creating environments that reflect their own management styles. Women owned 32.3% of all sole proprietorships as of 1990, compared with 23% in 1977, according to the Small Business Administration. In fact, some women now look upon corporations as a place to get experience before moving on.

THE SARA LEE EXPERIENCE

But while this may be good for some women, it doesn't help companies that want to increase their female ranks—and it helps perpetuate the male-dominated culture that many women find daunting.

Rather than wait for women to climb the rungs of power (the trickle-up approach), Sara Lee Corp. started hiring women into high-level jobs during the 1980s and watched the cultural changes trickle down. "The more women in top management jobs, the more women are attracted to them," says Gary Grom, senior vice president of human resources.

Suddenly, women lower in the company had solid proof they could make it to the top, he says. When Judy Sprieser, 40, president and CEO of the Sara Lee bakery division, tours the plants, she says, "Invariably, a woman on the plant line will pull me aside and say, 'We're so excited you're up there.' "

When executives want to hire more female managers, they can turn to their top females, who have wide networks of qualified candidates. At 36.2%, the company has one of the highest percentages of women in the consumer noncyclical industry group, according to the Journal's analysis.

These changes took a solid commitment from Chairman John Bryan, a former civil-rights activist who became Sara Lee's CEO in 1976. "We decided to apply the same techniques we do with everything else. We set targets," says Mr. Bryan.

Some Sara Lee targets for the year 2000: 20% of the company's 55 division presidents will be female, up from 11% last year, and 30% of its top 500 managers will be women, up from 1993's 17%. The CEO tied executives' bonuses to the plan, too, giving managers a chance to earn as much as 7%—at least $7,000—of their base salaries for reaching the objectives.

"We are the largest company in the world named for a woman, a distinction we are proud of," says Mr. Bryan. "It gives us a little bit of responsibility to be ahead of the curve on women's issues." Since many of Sara Lee's products, such as its Hanes panty hose, are designed for women, Mr. Bryan says it didn't make sense to have "a bunch of old men sitting around trying to figure out the business."

Mr. Bryan thinks diverse management improves a company's creativity, a view he suspects other CEOs may not share. "There's a secret belief this is not worth the effort," he says. And this, he believes, is the main reason the companies have so few female executives. "They think it's sort of dangerous for the business."

—David Mulholland contributed to this article.

Many Minorities Feel Torn by Experience of Affirmative Action

While Program Opens Doors, It Can Attach a Stigma That Affects Self-Esteem

---

Firefighter: 'I'll Stick to Merit'

Sonia L. Nazario
Staff Reporter of The Wall Street Journal

At first, Roland Lee was thrilled to be the newest lieutenant in the San Francisco Fire Department. Then he learned he had beaten out a close friend in the department for the promotion. Then he discovered that his friend had scored higher on the qualifying exam. Then his friend quit.

The son of Chinese immigrants, Mr. Lee welcomed being hired and promoted under affirmative action quotas at the department. Without them, he believes, minorities would have been barred from the fire station's doors. But he also says he is "disgusted" that race denied his white friend the promotion.

Mr. Lee is plagued by the stigma he feels is attached to affirmative action: white co-workers questioning his abilities and assuming he's not as qualified as they. He says that this has forced him "to work twice as hard" to prove others wrong, and that at times, his own self-esteem has been battered. "If I had to do it over again," he says with regret, "I would get my promotion" without using affirmative action preferences. "That would give me back my credibility."

Ambivalent Beneficiaries

Such an overt rejection of affirmative action by one of its beneficiaries is uncommon. But as minorities look at the effects of affirmative action nearly a quarter-century after its inception, many feel torn by the policy's outcome.

Minorities say it has opened doors that would have remained shut, forced companies to look to employment groups they had ignored, and decreased racism by prodding workplace integration. But it has also brought unwelcome baggage: assumptions that minorities were hired only because of race, and what may be unwarranted skepticism about their abilities. This makes some minorities fear that even promotions and accomplishments they earn by working harder than their peers won't be respected.

Some minority employees believe racism—on the part of co-workers or employers—has a lot to do with their ambivalence. Others believe companies and government agencies approach affirmative action too much as a burden to be met as painlessly as possible rather than as something that can truly benefit the workplace. Still others, like Mr. Lee, believe the problem is inherent in affirmative action, part and parcel of a process that gives preference to people for reasons other than strictly merit.

"I don't know if promoting someone because they are Chinese is the way to do it," he says.

The High Court

Several recent Supreme Court decisions have sparked a renewed debate over the legitimacy of affirmative action. Many now see an increasingly conservative court turning against the concept of setting quotas for hiring minorities.

First, the high court in January toughened the criteria under which a court could impose an affirmative action program on a business or municipality. Then earlier this month, the court made it easier for white workers to challenge affirmative action plans in court, and it also raised the difficulty for a plaintiff alleging racial discrimination in hiring.

Buoyed by the high court's recent decisions, conservatives are hoping they soon will be able to lessen what they see as "reverse" discrimination, while civil-rights activists are appalled at what they see as a chilling threat to years of progress in integrating the workplace.

Rarely heard in the debate, however, are the voices of those who actually have been hired or promoted under an affirmative action plan. In the workplace itself, lines that divide liberals and conservatives are blurred by the intrusion of a more complex reality. "I'm reluctantly appreciative of the affirmative action jobs I've had," says Migdia Chinea-Varela, a Hispanic Hollywood scriptwriter. "But at the same time, they made me really depressed."

Employees Are Heard

The personal responses to affirmative action are diverse, as are the difficulties minorities have experienced using such programs. Mary Whitmore, a carpenter in Los Angeles who pried her way into the male-dominated construction business with the help of affirmative action, says her experience has been a wholly positive one. Co-workers "treat me equal. They let me use the saw. They give me the nails. They let me work."

Many minorities agree with William Mays, a black who now owns his own Indianapolis-based chemical-distribution company, and who got a graduate fellowship and several jobs through affirmative action. "I had to deal with the grief [affirmative action] brought," he says, "but it was well worth it."

Others argue that the emphasis of government-sponsored integration plans must change toward encouraging equal educational and hiring opportunities rather than setting numerical goals and timetables. And a small number believe affirmative action should be abolished. "Affirmative action robs us of our dignity. It says that somehow color, not our hard work, can bring us advancements," says Shelby Steele, a black associate professor of English at San Jose State University who says he no longer applies for affirmative-action-related research grants so he can shake the stigma that he somehow isn't as talented as a white professor.

All employers must by law provide equal hiring opportunities to people of all races, but affirmative action requires much more: specific goals and timetables for hiring and promoting underrepresented women and minorities. Since a 1965 executive order by President Johnson, all companies that do more than $50,000 in annual business with the federal government and have more than 50 employees have been required to institute affirmative action plans. Companies and government agencies are bound to more rigid quotas when they are sued for discrimination under the 1964 Civil Rights Act and either agree to or are ordered by the court to remedy it through hiring and promotions.

The Need for Action

Interviews with scores of affirmative action employees reveal that despite their individual impressions of specific programs, all cite a strong need for some effort to combat racism and purposefully open jobs to minorities that they might have held, absent past discrimination. Louis Winston, a black who is the affirmative action officer for Stockham Valves & Fittings Inc. in Birmingham, Ala., recalls the days when that company had two entry gates—one for whites, one for blacks—and a divided cafeteria. When he began in the 1960s, blacks were forced to work in the sweltering heat of the foundry, while only whites could qualify for training programs to become machinists or electricians.

In part because of a 1969 lawsuit he helped initiate that then led to an affirmative action plan, he became the first black electrician trained at Stockham in 1975; now there are many, and blacks hold 60% of Stockham's jobs. Affirmative action, he says, has "put some blacks in higher jobs, and shown the company that we aren't ignorant. We can do the job, if given the chance."

It has also helped reduce racial tensions by forcing blacks and whites to work together, he says. "Without affirmative action, Stockham may have come around, but I wouldn't swear on it," he says. More important, he says, there are still no blacks among the company's 35 managers.

Breaking the Ranks

Diane Joyce believes that without affirmative action, she couldn't have advanced in the male-dominated Santa Clara County, Calif., road-maintenance department. A road worker for six years, she took an oral test to become a dispatcher in 1980 and was ranked fourth of those who took the test.

County rules allowed the supervisors to give the job to any one of the seven highest-scoring candidates, and she knew that one wouldn't be her; she claims the men who administered her test told her they didn't like her. So she phoned the county affirmative action officer, and got the job. A man who scored second on the test and was about to get the job sued the county in a case that went all the way to the Supreme Court. He lost.

Three years later, Ms. Joyce scored first in a written and oral test to become a road foreman. A man who ranked fifth got the job. This time, she didn't challenge it, even though she again felt unfairly treated. "I'm tired of fighting," she says.

One reason she and some others weary of the fight is the way their accelerated promotions or even their hiring are received by co-workers. Take, for example, the Birmingham, Ala., fire department.

Problems in Birmingham

When Carl Cook applied to be a firefighter in 1964, a city clerk took one look at his face and refused to even hand over an application to the young black man, he says. In 1976, two years after Mr. Cook finally was hired, only 1.4% of firefighters were black. Attorney Susan Reeves, who helped file a suit for blacks against the city, says a Birmingham official once explained that "blacks congenitally don't like to fight fires."

Now the department is divided by a court-imposed affirmative action plan: Some white and black firefighters don't even speak to each other. Some whites refer to promoted minorities as "welfare captains." In a highly publicized case, the Supreme Court last month gave Birmingham's white firefighters the right to challenge the affirmative action plan initiated by the lower court.

Mr. Cook, who was both hired and promoted under affirmative action, says, "I feel I am under a microscope." He won't ask white supervisors for advice or information for fear they are looking for an excuse to label him incompetent, he says. Battalion chief Tony Jackson, the city's highest-ranking black firefighter, says a white colleague once approached him and said, "Well, it sure is nice to be black. If I were black, I could have been promoted."

A white firefighter in Birmingham, David Morton, believes such suspicions will continue as long as some minorities are given special treatment—promoted over whites who rank higher in the test scores and experience. "If you take an airplane, do you want a pilot who was ranked No. 1, or one who is ranked No. 50 but is black?" he asks.

Ms. Chinea-Varela, the scriptwriter, says she has participated in four programs to encourage ethnic writers at four different production companies. No show she worked on was ever produced, she says. In one of the programs, sponsored by CBS Inc., a secretary explained to Ms. Chinea-Varela that she was just part of the network's minority headcount, the scriptwriter says.

As part of the CBS program, Ms. Chinea-Varela says she developed a situation comedy involving a young Hispanic woman who, trying to make ends meet after the death of her husband, takes in a white male boarder. "Because I came through the affirmative action door," she says, "there was no seriousness to the project."

A CBS spokeswoman says that this specific minority program no longer exists, and that the company has a strong commitment to affirmative action.

Regardless of the reaction of employers and co-workers, the mere fact that affirmative action involves special treatment has the potential to damage one's self-confidence, some minorities say. "Sometimes I wonder: Did I get this job because of my abilities, or because they needed to fill a quota?" says Caridad Dominguez, a Hispanic who is director of special studies for Bank of America, and who nonetheless says her own self-esteem carries her through such situations. "I consider myself a good contributor," she says.

Questioning Quotas

The perception that affirmative-action hires sometimes aren't as good as other workers is perpetuated in some respects by employers so bound by court-ordered quotas that the measurable qualifications of minorities hired fall far below white counterparts. "We hire 60% Hispanics here, regardless of qualifications," says Freddie Hernandez, a Hispanic lieutenant in the Miami fire department. "The fire department doesn't go to schools in other cities to recruit for minorities. They just have people take a test, and they pick minorities [even] from the bottom of the list." Fire Chief C.H. Duke says that a city ordinance requires his hires to be 80% women and minorities, and that this does require passing up whites with higher test scores for minorities, although anyone considered must pass the test.

Theodore Edwards, a black division manager at Ameritech Corp.'s Illinois Bell Telephone and an affirmative-action hire, says, "I think affirmative action is necessary, but I don't think it should be administered so that we say we have to have X number of minorities regardless of qualifications." He sees a need for more active recruiting so that firms can find minorities who are as qualified as other workers.

Whether they blame bosses, co-workers or simply human nature for their dissatisfaction with affirmative action, some minorities have been led by years of experience to call for major changes in government's approach to integrating the workplace.

The scriptwriter, Ms. Chinea-Varela, argues that hiring based on quotas should be done only in entry-level jobs, and that thereafter, a pure merit system should be used. She and others note that any hiring may at times be based less on merit than such factors as whom you know, ties to the appropriate Ivy League college, or nepotism. Still, she says that "there's a point where affirmative action should stop: I'd like to by now be considered on my own merits," having been in the business 10 years.

A Hispanic scriptwriter friend of hers, Julio Vera, is opposed to affirmative action altogether and will no longer apply for minority writing programs. "Martin Luther King's dream was to erase color lines; affirmative action hasn't done that," he says. Mr. Vera advocates spending more to redress the legacy of unequal education for minorities so they have a better chance of being equally qualified when they apply for a job. Affirmative action, he says, "is a handout."

Mr. Hernandez, the 34-year-old Hispanic firefighter from Miami, agrees. He turned down an affirmative-action promotion to lieutenant six years ago, waiting three years until he had the seniority and test scores to qualify for the promotion under normal procedures.

By doing so, he passed up $4,500 a year in extra pay and had to undergo 900 hours of extra study time. But "it was a self-pride thing," he says. "I knew I could make it on my own." Mr. Hernandez plans to take the exam for fire chief soon, but says he'll accept the job only if he wins it on paper. "I will stick to merit," he says.

WHITE, MALE, AND WORRIED

Last April, Doug Tennant lost his job as a long-term contract employee for Pacific Gas & Electric Co. in Tracy, Calif. He says he was the first one in his three-person unit to be laid off. He claims the others—a black woman and a man of Indian descent—were kept on even though he was more qualified. Tennant, who is white, blames PG&E's push for a more diverse workplace. "I feel like I'm losing out," he says. PG&E says his race and sex had nothing to do with his departure.

Marilyn Moats Kennedy, a Chicago-based career counselor, recently got a plaintive letter from a white male who wanted a job hauling baggage for United Airlines Co. It seemed that all the candidates who were having any luck were women and minorities. "How am I going to get on with the airlines?" the man wrote. "Wrong pigment, wrong plumbing."

He hasn't selected any colleges yet, but Curt Harms is concerned about the impact of diversity on his chances for acceptance. "I'm worried," says Harms, a

15-year-old sophomore from Lake Bluff, Ill., who is white. "If there's a candidate who has grades and credentials exactly the same as mine, these days it's more likely they'll take that person over me, if the person is a minority or a woman. There's nothing I can do."

Peek inside any corporate boardroom, or take a look at the senior managers of most top corporations, and it's hard to see what Harms, Tennant, and others like

---

As companies hire and promote more women and minorities, they feel a backlash from some white males

---

them are complaining about: It's still a white man's world.

But in a growing minority of com-

panies—especially those aggressively pushing diversity programs—some white males are coming to a different conclusion. They're feeling frustrated, resentful, and most of all, afraid. There's a sense that, be it on the job or at home, the rules are changing faster than they can keep up. "Race and gender have become factors for white men, much the way they have been for other groups," says Thomas Kochman, a professor at the University of Illinois-Chicago who consults with companies on white male issues. "The worm is turning, and they don't like it."

The phenomenon Kochman and others are talking about is far from universal in Corporate America. In fact, most white males don't feel particularly threatened or haven't noticed such changes where they work. But then, the impact of diversity programs, even in the companies that have them, is still limited. "Sadly, we find a lot of these diversity programs hang out there by themselves and don't loop back into a coherent management development program," says Jeffrey A.

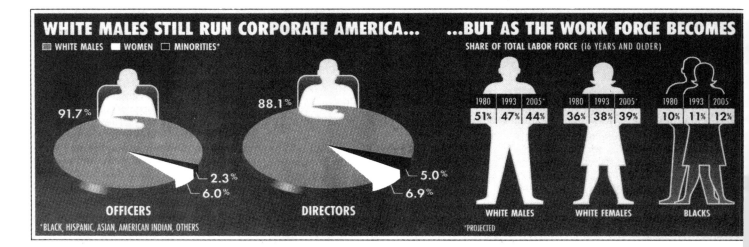

WHITE MALES STILL RUN CORPORATE AMERICA...

▨ WHITE MALES ■ WOMEN ☐ MINORITIES*

91.7% 2.3% 6.0%
OFFICERS
*BLACK, HISPANIC, ASIAN, AMERICAN INDIAN, OTHERS

88.1% 5.0% 6.9%
DIRECTORS

...BUT AS THE WORK FORCE BECOMES

SHARE OF TOTAL LABOR FORCE (16 YEARS AND OLDER)

	1980	1993	2005*
WHITE MALES	51%	47%	44%
WHITE FEMALES	36%	38%	39%
BLACKS	10%	11%	12%

*PROJECTED

From *Business Week*, January 31, 1994, pp. 50-55. © 1994 by McGraw-Hill, Inc. Reprinted by special permission.

Sonnenfeld, director of the Center for Leadership & Career Studies at Emory University. "The programs often are window-dressing."

Open Season. But in such companies as AT&T, DuPont, and Motorola, where diversity is becoming more than just a buzzword, the emotional landscape for white males is changing. There, white men must compete against people they may not have taken all that seriously as rivals—mainly women, blacks, Hispanics, and Asians. White males also say that the diversity programs often make them feel threatened or attacked. "In the diversity group I was in, there were some understandable reprisals against white males and, implicitly, the company," says John L. Mason, vice-president for recruiting and equal employment at Monsanto Co. The reprisals "discounted all the good things white males have done."

Even in companies where diversity programs are new or haven't made much impact, white males are feeling pressure. Often for the first time in their lives, they're worrying about their future opportunities because of widespread layoffs and corporate restructurings. Outside the corporation, white men are feeling threatened because of racial and gender tensions that have been intensifying in recent years. " 'White male' is what I call the newest swear word in America," says Harris Sussman, president of Workways, a strategic consulting firm in Cambridge, Mass. "We all know that's not a compliment."

No matter what company they're in, white males must face a sobering new reality: With a more diverse population entering the work force, white men are slowly becoming a minority. From 1983 to 1993, the percentage of white, male professionals and managers in the work force dropped from 55% to 47%, while the same group of white women jumped from 37% to 42%. The diversification of the workplace will only pick up. Through the year 2005, the Labor Dept. estimates that half of all labor force entrants will be women, and more than one-third will be Hispanics, African Americans, and those of other races.

All this is driving what some diversity experts and executives call a white, male backlash. So far, it has occurred mostly in companies experiencing the greatest flux, where some men blame their stalled careers on racial or gender differences. "When everybody is working and happy, diversity is just talk over the water cooler," says one laid-off, white, male executive who attributes his 18-month job hunt to employers who "earmark" jobs for female and minority candidates. "But when it impacts you directly, you become kind of angry."

Quandary. At the heart of the issue for many white males is the question of merit—that in the rush for a more diverse workplace, they will lose out to less qualified workers. Most white men claim they have no problem with promoting or hiring women and minorities if they are the best people for the job. It's another story when two candidates are of equal merit. In that case, if the company picks a woman or minority, some white men are quick to cry reverse discrimination—even though the law lets companies take race into account in employment decisions to remedy past discrimination.

The shifting dynamics of the work force have placed managers, many of whom are white males themselves, in a moral quandary. In their efforts to make their companies more diverse, they are certain to hire or promote women and minorities over other white males. That is sure to lead to anger from those who are passed over. In the extreme, productivity could suffer as white males flee to more old-line competitors. Yet if these managers fail to embrace diversity, they not only perpetuate past injustices but risk leaving their companies less globally competitive.

Many white, male managers say that those pressures become even harder to bear when they, rather than senior executives, are blamed for a litany of past wrongs committed by white men. "I'm certainly not part of the power structure," says James Gault, a systems engineer with American Telephone & Telegraph Co. in New Jersey. "But compared to blacks and women, I am."

Complicating such issues is the split between what many white men say they believe and what they actually feel: They recognize intellectually that they're still calling the shots and getting most of the promotions. But that does little to assuage fears that the pendulum will swing too far. "White males are like the first-born in the family, the ones who have had the best love of both parents and never quite forgave the second child for being born," says Kochman, the University of Illinois professor. "We're dealing here with a sense of entitlements."

For companies committed to a corporate culture that embraces groups besides white males, all this raises two dilemmas: First, how to ensure a diverse work force without antagonizing either white males, whose support is critical for

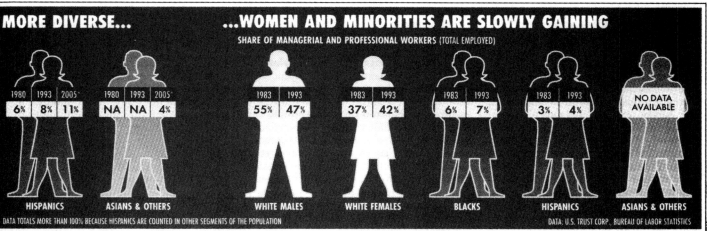

MORE DIVERSE... ...WOMEN AND MINORITIES ARE SLOWLY GAINING

SHARE OF MANAGERIAL AND PROFESSIONAL WORKERS (TOTAL EMPLOYED)

	1980	1993	2005*	1980	1993	2005*	1983	1993	1983	1993	1983	1993	1983	1993	
HISPANICS	6%	8%	11%												
ASIANS & OTHERS				NA	NA	4%									
WHITE MALES							55%	47%							
WHITE FEMALES									37%	42%					
BLACKS											6%	7%			
HISPANICS													3%	4%	
ASIANS & OTHERS															NO DATA AVAILABLE

DATA TOTALS MORE THAN 100% BECAUSE HISPANICS ARE COUNTED IN OTHER SEGMENTS OF THE POPULATION

DATA: U.S. TRUST CORP., BUREAU OF LABOR STATISTICS

GRAPHIC BY RAY VELLA/BW

change, or women and minorities, who may resent efforts to win over white males; and second, how to reverse historical discrimination without creating new forms of it.

The experience at Rochester Telephone Corp. shows how tough those tasks can be. Until recently, white males criticized the company's diversity efforts as affirmative action under a different name—something they say doesn't affect them. The predominately white unions refused to support the initiative. "It was very divisive," says Robert Flavin, president of Local 11709 of the Communications Workers of America. "The minorities had an open door to the president."

Now, Michael O. Thomas, who is black, is trying to change all that. Hired last summer as Rochester's corporate director of staffing and diversity, Thomas expanded the definition of diversity to cover job sharing, career planning, and other employee concerns as well as race and gender. To oversee those efforts, he and members of an internal Diversity Council, already comprising a cross section of the company, hired a diversity manager—who happened to be a white female—and eliminated the minority-run diversity department. He also refocused the council's mission to make it more inclusive and help set an agenda. Thomas says his efforts have drawn mixed reactions from minorities, some of whom worry he's ignoring their problems. Thomas is determined to prove them wrong. His approach is already winning over labor. "The old program didn't have anything to do with our members. Now it does," says Flavin.

Tokenism Charges. While Rochester's diversity program isn't focusing on white males, some of the most aggressive employers on the diversity front are realizing that winning over white male employees requires special efforts—and is crucial to their programs' success. AT&T and Motorola Inc. are hiring consultants to lead seminars that help white males handle anxieties over their changing status. CoreStates Financial Corp. is forming a white men's support group similar to those in place for people of color as well as gays, lesbians, and bisexuals. For all male employees, DuPont Co. is creating a "Men's Forum." "White males are feeling left out," says Bernard Scales, DuPont's manager of diversity, who is black. "They are questioning from the sidelines: What is going on? What is the company doing? What is it that women and people of color are trying to tell them?'"

Managers who ignore such issues risk

WHAT COMPANIES SHOULD DO

ADOPT a broad definition of diversity in the workplace covering all kinds of differences among employees, including race, gender, age, work, and family issues. Have senior management emphasize that diversity is an issue that affects everyone.

STRESS that managing diversity is more than just sensitivity or awareness training on race or gender issues that impact the work force but is a competitive weapon that helps the company capitalize on its talent pool and compete in the global marketplace.

SECURE a visible commitment from top executives to address employees directly and often about why diversity is important to the company's bottom line and global competitiveness. Carefully monitor programs, and hold managers accountable for meeting diversity goals.

TAKING ADVERSITY OUT

In the long history of the American workplace, the notion of fostering diversity is a recent phenomenon. In 1987, the Hudson Institute, an Indianapolis think tank, released a study called *Workforce 2000: Work and Workers for the 21st Century,* which has set the agenda ever since. By the year 2000, the study projected, only 15% of the people entering the work force would be American-born white males, compared with 47% in 1987. The statistic struck fear in executive suites. Companies rushed to put together diversity courses or hire consultants to sensitize employees to racial and gender differences. But such programs often did more harm than good: They stereotyped groups or pitted one against another. Or they blamed white males for all workplace inequities.

For some companies, diversity simply means affirmative action. But at others such as IBM, Corning, and Honeywell, it's part of a broader effort to change the corporate culture. Instead of just focusing on race or gender, they're expanding the definition of diversity to cover everything from age to physical disabilities to concerns such as flex time and job-sharing.

Dollars and Cents. More important, companies are linking diversity more closely to business objectives—and holding managers accountable for meeting them. The goal: to create a culture that enables all employees to contribute their full potential to the company's success.

Says Barbara Coull Williams, vice-president for human resources at Pacific Gas & Electric Co.: "The diversity of ideas is important, not that you've got a certain ethnicity or sexual preference." For PG&E, that means moving its focus beyond sensitivity training for employees on race and gender issues to better meeting the needs of a diversifying customer base. One way is to groom more qualified women and minorities through active succession planning. From senior executives down to low-level managers, PG&E identifies candidates with potential and makes sure they have the skills they need to compete. Then the company picks the most qualified person for the position. A mentor program links potential high achievers with higher-ups who share insights into the way PG&E operates.

Other companies with diversity initiatives are taking more of a dollars-and-cents approach. At NutraSweet, the diversity program is focused on "making things happen in the global marketplace and measuring how well we're doing based on profits," says CEO Robert E. Flynn. The company is using the same approach to develop untapped U.S. markets. For example, it's creating a "diverse markets" initiative. One goal is to sell more of the company's Aspartame sugar substitute to blacks and Hispanics, whose incidence of diabetes is higher than that of the general population.

inflaming dissension and hurting morale and productivity. At some companies, white middle managers are filing internal complaints about unfair treatment. At NutraSweet Co., CEO Robert E. Flynn says evidence of white, male resistance surfaced in two similar incidents in recent months: White men picked white males for key positions—without posting the jobs for females, minorities, and others. Both jobs were reopened so that a broad range of candidates could apply. In one case, the initial candidate got the job, but some of the women and minorities who were interviewed got promoted as well. The other case is pending. "There is a backlash," Flynn says. "There is some uneasiness about how aggressive we are in terms of diversity."

OF DIVERSITY

Besides using the diversity of ideas as a competitive weapon, companies are embracing a broad definition of diversity that includes white men. Part of their motivation is legal. Civil-rights laws cover white males as well as women and minorities, though companies can take race into account in employment decisions to remedy past discrimination.

At Honeywell Inc., Curtis White, vice-president for corporate diversity, has made a special effort to reach out to white males and gain their support. In 1992, Honeywell established a 20-member Diversity Council, made up of the chairs of key employee groups, such as the Honeywell Women's Council and the Black Employee Network. It also includes a white, male middle manager, who represents the Minneapolis Technical Operations Council. White says he chose the operations director for one reason: "It was a totally Caucasian council. I couldn't find a graceful way to encourage Caucasian males to form a group, so I seized this opportunity to practice our inclusiveness concept."

Whether White's maneuver will pay off is still unknown. But given the changing demographics, companies that support all kinds of groups will likely be the first to prosper from a diverse talent pool.

By Michele Galen, with Ann Therese Palmer in Chicago

All too often, say many women and minorities, that uneasiness is expressed in the kind of behavior they have long had to put up with from white men. Women complain that some white, male managers try to undermine their credibility by doing such things as attributing their rise to tokenism. "When a female or minority or some combination is appointed to a particularly prestigious job, there's always the comment that the reason they were selected is that they were a woman or minority. That's one of the statements white males still aren't afraid to make in public," says Sara Kelsey, vice-president and assistant general counsel at Chemical Bank in New York. "I find those remarks very irritating because the men make it sound like that's the only reason."

Orgy of Blame. Rather than address such behavior, white males say too many diversity programs just encourage women and minorities to vent their anger. Ken E. Richardson, a white male, attended a week-long diversity program in the spring of 1992. An administrator

WHAT COMPANIES SHOULD AVOID

STEREOTYPING groups of employees such as white males to explain cultural or ethnic differences. Instead, stress respect for individual differences and characteristics that all employees have in common.

AGITATING employees with one-shot sensitivity workshops and seminars that stir up emotions by pitting different groups against each other. Favor ongoing training programs that seek not only to educate workers about ethnic, racial, and cultural differences but also seek to change the company's culture.

BLAMING white males or others for the company's problems or inequities in society. Instead, find trainers with experience in diversity who are not divisive in their approach, emphasize similarities among groups, and stress the connection between managing diversity and competitiveness.

with the Licking County (Ohio) Sheriff's office, he was one of five white males in a racially and sexually diverse group of 30. Having lived in a mixed neighborhood and abroad, Richardson says he has always respected cultural and racial differences. But in the training session, he says he was blamed "for everything from slavery to the glass ceiling." The instructors—a white female and two black males—seemed to "feed into the white-male-bashing," he says. "I became bitter and remain so."

Despite the risk that some programs will alienate men like Richardson, even such white, male bastions as the oil industry are pushing diversity initiatives. For Amoco CEO H. Laurance Fuller, managing diversity is a "business imperative." He says women and minorities account for 40% of his work force, though they remain disproportionately in lower-ranked jobs; one of every six employees is not a U.S. citizen. Last fall, Fuller established a Diversity Advisory Council, which he chairs. Its mission is to create an environment in which Amoco Corp.'s increasingly diverse work force can reach its full potential.

The council is finalizing a long-term action plan, but some white, male middle managers are already worried. From time to time, they've questioned Fuller—himself white—about the consequences of diversity on their careers. "I reply that they have nothing to fear but more and better competition, which can only enhance Amoco's prosperity and their own," Fuller says.

For now, such reassurance is all the attention some white males at Amoco seem to want. Last summer, the company accepted a consultant's suggestion to hold a focus group solely for white, male middle managers. It was intended to get them to express their concerns, says Jim Fair, Amoco's director of media relations who attended the workshop. But some men didn't think they needed the seminar. "Are you trying to get me to be upset?" Fair reports one manager asked the moderator. Others objected to being singled out. Fair said the men agreed that a more valuable experience would be sessions with different people together.

Surprising Conclusions. AT&T has embraced just such an approach, partly through a course called "White Males: The Label, the Dilemma." Led by consultant Sussman, the course presents the future work force, then asks white men how they feel about being labeled a minority. The women and minorities in the class react to the white males' views or challenge their conclusions. Beate Sykes, an AT&T diversity counselor, sought out the course in response to requests by white men "to do something for them."

The intensity of the one-day seminar surprised some of the white men who attended. "I didn't realize how much other white men felt attacked and how oblivious" they were to the benefits that their race and gender bestowed, says James Gault, the systems engineer. "They felt everything was equal now." Other attendees say the seminar changed their self-image. "I never thought of myself as a white male," says Lee Arpin, a development manager. "In a lot of cases, we have privileges we don't appreciate."

Minorities left the seminar with insights into white men. David Clanton, a software designer who is black, says the class made him "more empathetic" to white males because it showed how deeply felt their concerns were, just like other groups. He learned that white men don't like being lumped together or blamed for "something their fathers and grandfathers might have done." The class also helped him feel more comfortable with white male colleagues who seemed to be "more to my way of thinking than I would have expected."

Not all AT&T employees view the company's attention to white men favorably. On Nov. 5, Sussman was the key speaker at a mandatory, all-day confer-ence sponsored by an affirmative action committee at an AT&T division in northern New Jersey. The occasion drew some complaints from women and minorities, who wanted to know why an affirmative action workshop should devote any time at all to white men. One minority employee was so incensed that the worker didn't attend.

Other companies with diversity programs are reaching out to white males. Corning Inc. has made a big diversity push since 1987 and, among other things, now requires all employees to attend race and gender sensitivity training. The result, says Gail O. Baity, manager of strategic corporate education, is that "white males are asking questions like, 'The demographics show there will be fewer white males entering the work force. Will we be in the minority?' Or they're asking about parity. 'You have all these programs focused on women and color. What about me?' "

Core Requirements. In response, Corning has made a special effort to share employment statistics to correct a misperception of trends. "White males still predominate within the company and still hold the predominant positions of authority," Baity says. Corning also is trying to make the advancement process more objective by identifying core competencies for various jobs. When an employee gets a certain post, Corning can then point to the fulfillment of the core competencies as a valid reason why he or she deserved it. Ultimately, Corning expects managers to assemble a diverse talent pool for any opening, then select the best person.

That's an approach more companies are likely to take as women and minorities continue to make strides. Companies will also find that diversity programs to encourage those trends are in their interest. The programs are in their customers' interests as well: They help to promote employees who, given their rich backgrounds, are not only qualified but more sensitive to the diverse cultures of the markets they serve. "There's not too many white faces in Indonesia," says NutraSweet's Flynn, who is pushing to raise the company's foreign revenues.

But companies must walk a fine line: If they pay only lip service to diversity, they risk losing or alienating women and minorities, an increasingly important sector of the talent pool. If they push diversity too hard without taking stock of the fears of their white, male employees, they risk losing white males or their backing. To be sure, the transition from a corporate culture dominated by white males to one that embraces all employees equally will not take place without a degree of tension. But if companies are to compete in the changing marketplace, and if they are to treat all employees with equal respect, diversity is essential. And so, too, is the proper training for all involved.

Michele Galen in New York,
with Ann Therese Palmer in Chicago
and bureau reports

AGEISM:

The New Diversity Issue

GENEVIEVE CAPOWSKI

It's no secret that America's workforce is rapidly graying. Workers 55 and older are the fastest growing segment of the workforce, with the median age of the workforce projected to reach 40 by 2010. The Baby-Boomer blip continues: In fact, the number of people age 50 to 65 will increase at more than twice the rate of the overall population by the end of the century.

What remains a well-kept secret is how businesses intend to deal with this phenomenon because there's little indication that many companies are taking much action now. And as the bulk of the labor force approaches its golden years, the outlook for this group of workers is less than glowing.

Face it. We're a youth-oriented—youth-*obsessed*, really—culture. And corporate America represents just an extension of those values. The largest segment of the workforce for some time to come will be the part historically valued the least—older workers, otherwise known as old "fogies," "geezers" and "coots." Witness the plethora of "50-plusers" scanning the want ads and pounding on search firm doors. They are the group most targeted by the corporate bloodletting of the '90s. In fact, the number of over-50s who were unemployed jumped 68.1 percent compared with a 40.6 percent increase for people under 50 from 1989 to 1992, according to *Business Week*.

On the surface, the corporate rationale for instituting early retirement programs, rather than adhering to the "last hired, first fired" philosophy for slimming down the payroll, appears to be pure economics. Get rid of the older, more expensive workers and find younger, cheaper replacements. But many see the rationale for this option running deeper.

They point to an underlying, insidious element that's becoming more and more apparent in our business practices—ageism. Unlike its counterparts racism and sexism, ageism is a much more subtle bias and, therefore, often goes unrecognized. "Age is the forgotten diversity issue," says Denise Loftus, manager of workforce education, Workforce Programs, at the American Association of Retired Persons (AARP). Indeed, "The age piece [of diversity] is so subtle, people aren't even aware that they're doing it," adds Helen Dennis, a lecturer at the Andrus Gerontology Center at the University of

Southern California, and author of *Fourteen Steps in Managing an Aging Workforce* (Lexington Books, 1987).

Why Now?

Yet, the workforce has always included a mix of old and young. Why are we just hearing about ageism now? Blame it on those incorrigible Baby Boomers now pushing the big five-oh, who are increasingly faced with justifying their existence in a world where youth and vitality are often prized more than wisdom and experience. This is the generation that "never trusted anyone over 30." But when discrimination hits home, "it's amazing how your perspective changes," says Cathy Fyock, author of *Unretirement* (AMA-COM, 1994) and president of Innovative Management Concepts, Louisville, Ky.

"The Boomers have always gotten what they wanted," explains Fyock, who specializes in providing solutions for the aging workforce. "They've long influenced the direction of this country"—from fashion and entertainment to business, she says. "By their sheer numbers they've been able to yell the loudest." And right now, as the first wave approaches 50, what they want is to change traditional perceptions about aging. They don't look old. They don't feel old. So they certainly don't want to be treated as old. But when 2001 rolls around, the Baby Boomers start turning 55, which classifies them as "older workers," according to the Bureau of Labor Statistics standards.

Dennis agrees that ageism strikes a chord of fear in people of all ages, so everyone has a vested interest to change their way of thinking. "I think it's because we have a personal stake in it," she says. Eventually, most everyone will become an "older worker." "People are saying, 'Wait a minute, this could be me. If I'm lucky, I'm going to be working while I get older,'" Dennis points out.

In fact, Don Davis, vice president of senior community services employment at the National Council on the Aging, predicts that "age discrimination will be the civil rights issue of the next decade," mostly because an increasing number of the people who fought for civil rights in the 1960s are now middle aged. "Age transcends color: We all will grow old despite our color," says Davis.

The deck is clearly stacked in favor of younger employees. Although most of us don't like to admit it, we have some culturally ingrained stereotypes working against older workers. Top that off with the widespread belief that older workers cost companies more due to perceived higher healthcare costs. But even that argument has been widely refuted by contrary evidence. If older workers cost more in terms of healthcare, then early retirement programs wouldn't include healthcare benefits, points out Phoebe Liebig, assistant professor at the Andrus Gerontology Center. In fact, she says, studies have shown that employees with school-age children are likely to cost more. In addition, keeping an employee on payroll longer saves companies money because they don't have to pay out pensions until later.

The fact is, however, that as the workforce ages, employers must confront their own prejudices through education and training and learn how to manage older employees effectively, to keep them motivated and encourage them to stay on the job. Not only for the obvious reason that they increasingly will need older workers as the replacement workforce diminishes in size, but also because studies confirm that older workers are more often motivated, more committed, more loyal, less apt to call in sick, less prone to accidents on the job—plus, more experienced and sometimes more highly skilled. With that in mind, experts predict that companies that focus on managing this issue will see quick returns on their investment.

Myths and Myopia

Working against companies are corporate policies that don't have the flexibility to accommodate a changing, diverse workforce, especially one with older workers. "There is enough research that says older workers are dependable, they can change, they can learn. What we haven't come to grips with is that research and management practice are not always related," says Dennis. A study by the International Foundation of Employee Benefit Plans found that while almost 86 percent of Fortune 2000 companies consider older workers to be a valuable resource, only 23 percent actually have corporate policies in place that encourage hiring older employees.

Why? For starters, there's the aphorism "You can't teach an old dog new tricks." As Fyock points out, however, while it may be true that you can't teach an old *dog* new tricks, you can teach older *people.* Studies continuously show that the capacity to learn continues well into the 70s and beyond for most people. What's more, a life-long process of learning is probably the way most people continue to feel young and vibrant.

McDonald's, one of the most publicized

companies in terms of its commitment to the retirement age workforce, still serves as a good example of how formal corporate policies that value and encourage the older worker can also be beneficial to companies. Almost a decade ago, McDonald's recognized that there would be a shortage of young workers—a bad demographic trend for the fast-food industry. So it took a proactive approach to the situation. In 1986 it instituted the McMasters program, a formal recruitment and training program for older workers. Although the program is no longer officially in place, today there are more than 40,000 seniors at work in McDonald's around the world, according to Malesia Webb-Dunn, a McDonald's spokesperson. Overall, the company has found that "seniors are very dependable, committed employees," says Webb-Dunn. In addition, she says, seniors and young employees work extremely well together, the older workers acting as mentors to their younger counterparts.

The hardest thing to overcome, however, are people's own experiences, says Dennis. "You can't deny someone's experience; if a manager has a tough time with a worker who happens to be older, who is rigid and unwilling to change or

to learn, you can't say, 'Well, that's not true.' And as human beings our tendency is to generalize. 'I'm never going to hire one of *them* again.'" This is why it's so important for companies to provide ongoing education on aging. Companies need to attack biased corporate attitudes and then work them into actual policy; otherwise those biases can be poisonous, she points out.

"It's often unintentional, so it can be a very subtle kind of discrimination," Dennis says. Even the AARP's Loftus, who is in her 60s, admits to falling into this kind of thinking occasionally. "I see someone with gray hair who does something stupid behind the wheel of a car, and I say, 'Oh my God, why is that old person…' and then I catch myself. But it just sort of comes out."

"There's a myth that older workers can't adapt to use computers, that they aren't receptive to learning new ways of doing work," says the National Council on the Aging's Davis. "It's one of the most disabling myths. They are. You just have to take your time. All people are unreceptive to change. No one is comfortable with it."

We also perpetuate the myth that once employees reach a certain age, they are no longer motivated, that they are interested only in re-

OLDER AND WISER

It started with a simple concept: Many retirees aren't ready to stop working. Out of that premise has grown the National Retiree Volunteer Coalition (NRVC), a grass-roots organization based in Minneapolis that is mobilizing corporate retirees into community assets nationwide. The NRVC provides training and resources to corporations that are interested in developing a re-

tiree volunteer workforce. In exchange, organizations must make a two-year commitment to the program, provide an on-site office (staffed by retiree volunteers) and pay a $25,000 training fee.

Through the program, management and blue-collar retirees alike have found volunteer work

that builds on both their work skills and their vocational interests—from bicycle repair to tutoring children (shown here). In 1994, through 56 corporate

programs, nearly 11,000 retirees contributed in excess of 2.3 million hours of service to their communities. To learn how to set up a National Retiree Volunteer Coalition network in your corporation, call 1-800-833-NRVC.

—Martha H. Peak

tirement. Yet, most older workers do want to continue working—even beyond the traditional retirement age. Many want to continue working because much of their self-esteem is tied to their jobs; others, because it increasingly is becoming an economic necessity. In fact, studies indicate that people often become severely depressed when they are forced to retire, says Cathy Ventrell-Monsees, an attorney and manager of worker equity at the AARP.

All too often, older employees are overlooked when it comes to training and career development, and hence become disillusioned and, as a result, unmotivated. "In many cases, older people were passed over for training because it was assumed that they couldn't learn—this gets reinforced and it just becomes a self-fulfilling prophesy," Loftus says. "It's sad, because the ability to learn continues."

"Assuming that everyone will retire at age 65 is still a predominant mind-set for corporate America today," says Fyock. Hence, the push by organizations for employee training often wanes after employees hit their mid-40s. "If you make the assumption that people are going to retire at age 65, then you also go on to assume that they don't need to be enrolled in ongoing training, they don't need to be involved in educational programs, and so on," adds Fyock. "If you don't invest in individuals, if you don't have them going through additional training and education,

then obviously they're not going to be equipped to stay on the job," she says.

Know Your Responsibility

Whose responsibility is it, then, to ensure that employees of every age are properly trained? Since it takes longer to change a corporate culture, employees need to change their own thinking, many say. They need to take responsibility for their own careers—which includes training and career planning. "There's been a death of corporate paternalism in this country," says Loftus of the AARP. "We have always tried to stress to people that it is their responsibility; nobody is going to take care of you."

She adds that companies do have an obligation to ensure that all employees are given the opportunity to receive training and to encourage them to take it. But, too often, companies just dismiss their older employees, saying, "Oh, they're just going to retire in a few years." In fact, a study by the AARP found that only three out of 10 companies include older adults in their training programs. Another study by the Society for Human Resource Management showed that 59 percent of businesses claim that older employees show resistance to training.

"All of us need to keep learning new skills, whether it's computer skills or people skills," says USC's Liebig. "When people hear about retrain-

---

WHEN COST-CUTTING DOESN'T PAY

Employees 40 years and older are protected under the Age Discrimination in Employment Act (ADEA). Especially in this climate of downsizing, reengineering and streamlining, companies need to be extra cautious that their efforts to stay lean do not discriminate against older workers and land companies in court.

Although most employers are getting smarter about it, many companies use reengineering or downsizing as an excuse to get rid of their older, higher-paid employees. This trend hasn't gone unnoticed. The American Association of Retired Persons (AARP) has found a link between downsizing and charges of age discrimination. "We looked at downsizing and early retirement incentive (ERI)

programs and found a correlation in how they have both gone up and down over the past 10 or more years," admits attorney Cathy Ventrell-Monsees, manager of worker equity at the AARP. "When downsizings and ERI programs leveled off, and they remained almost constant in the late '80s, we saw that charges also leveled off and remained constant. Now in the early '90s, we're seeing an upsurge in charges."

"The disturbing trend is that employers have become more callous. They are more willing to risk age discrimination lawsuits because the courts have become more conservative over the past dozen years," says Ventrell-Monsees. And it's true that age discrimination suits are difficult to prove. In fact, employees win only

about 60 percent of the cases, and those are the ones that even make it to trial.

The flip side, however, is that jury awards tend to be much higher in age discrimination suits than in other types of discrimination cases. A recent survey by Jury Verdict Research showed that successful age bias claims resulted in average awards of $302,914, compared with $255,734 for sex discrimination, $176,578 for race bias and $151,421 for disability discrimination. The reason the awards are typically higher, according to Ventrell-Monsees, is that victims tend to be employees who are higher paid because they have been with the company longer, and damages are based on the amount of lost income.

—G.C.

ing they tend to think, 'Oh God, I've got to go learn about computers.' But there are also new kinds of management skills that people need to learn. Because obviously, an employee who has good solid skills and a fairly good range of skills is going to be useful, if not to their current employer, than to their next one. It's essential for people to continue to prove their worth."

Then there's the cost factor. It's a common assumption that older workers cost more. These days, the short-term, bottom-line mentality of a lot of businesses tricks them into getting rid of older workers. "They need to get what they perceive as the best for the least cost," explains Dennis. "It plays out initially as economics—you need to cut X percent of your overhead, you need to increase profits, you need to reduce costs, and so your long-term employees who happen to get the higher salaries leave."

"Businesses believe that they're going to get less for their money by hiring older workers," adds Fyock. "They see older individuals as a depreciating asset instead of an appreciating asset, and so they tend to see the older worker as having less value."

But Fyock and others see this as a deadly failing on the part of employers. "This is a real short-sightedness," points out attorney Ventrell-Monsees. "It's just looking at the bottom line for today really, and not seeing even five years from now. Companies keep cutting and cutting, supposedly to save cost, and then they find that they cannot replace the experience and skill of those older workers."

In fact, she points out, losing your older, experienced workforce often ends up being more expensive. "When we've done research on cost cutting, we find there are all types of costs that companies neglect to look at," says Ventrell-Monses." Some of these include replacement costs, retraining costs and downtime following the layoffs. In addition, organizations forfeit the experience, the expertise, the commitment, the loyalty, the maturity and the productivity of this growing group of workers. "It's very problematic for employers because in this massive exit it is very likely that they are losing some of their best and brightest," concurs Dennis. And, with them out the door often goes knowledge of the corporate history.

A Positive Outlook

Is it all bad news for the aging workforce? Not necessarily. "There *are* companies out there

that acknowledge the value [of older workers]," says Dennis, they're just not in the majority. "I said there was good news; I just didn't say the incidence of the good news," she laughs.

Fyock is equally tentative in her optimism. "There are a few companies that are waking up," she says. "They've said, 'Oh, yes, here's a resource that's wonderful and that can offer a lot to our business,' and they are making a concerted effort to keep [those older workers] on board."

Flexibility is one of the keys to helping the older workforce stay motivated and productive. "We are starting to hear more about sabbaticals, something we haven't heard about in a long while," says Fyock. Companies are realizing that as "we work longer, maybe we need time to recharge our batteries, retool or revitalize before we come back to work." So many organizations are encouraging interspersing periods of education and leisure throughout their employees' work lives.

Polaroid, for one, has developed a "flexible work alternative" program to help its older workers make decisions about retirement—and help them ease into the process. "We're convinced that people shouldn't retire precipitously," says Michael Muther, senior human resources administrator at the Cambridge, Mass.-based company. "People shouldn't jump from full-time work to full-time leisure. We try to ease that transition." To do so, the firm offers several options designed for its 55-plus employees. One is called "rehearsal retirement," which allows employees to take a leave of absence for three months (it can be extended up to six months). "They're entitled to come back to the same job, no questions asked," says Muther.

The other program, "tapering off," enables older workers to reduce their hours, from a 40-hour work week to, say, a 32-hour work week, down to a minimum of 20 hours a week. In addition, the company offers one-on-one retirement counseling sessions and "life planning seminars," which cover retirement, pensions, profit sharing, employee stock options, etc., and are open to employees of all ages, as well as classes on women in transition and eldercare.

The programs are more than just altruistic for Polaroid. The bottom-line result is increased morale and worker productivity, says Muther. "These are valued workers and there's something to be said for retaining them."

Other companies have developed internal advocacy organizations, such as the Older Workers League (OWL) at Honeywell. The

14 STEPS TO MAXIMIZING YOUR OLDER WORKFORCE

1. Understand the changing workforce.
2. Implement the Age Discrimination in Employment Act and recognize its implication for management policy and practice.
3. Know the facts about the normal aging process.
4. Take steps to slow work-induced stress, detrimental to older workers, and encourage effective stress management.
5. Know the health-related cost benefits issues of older workers and use cost management strategies to get the most bang for your healthcare buck.
6. Use objective performance appraisals.
7. Offer well-designed retraining programs and encourage older workers to participate.
8. Implement alternative work schedules.
9. Use knowledge of life stages for job assignment and team building.
10. Conduct management training on the subject of aging to prevent age discrimination and to encourage effective use of older workers.
11. Use community resources for future employment and career development opportunities.
12. Examine labor's history, policies, needs and services regarding older union workers.
13. Capitalize on older workers' desires and abilities to extend their working careers.
14. Offer comprehensive retirement programs.

Source: "14 Steps in Managing an Aging Workforce," by Helen Dennis (Lexington Books, 1987)

thrust of OWL is dealing with generic issues that affect the older workforce and providing a perspective to management that will help it design benefits and policies with this group in mind, explains Ralph Johnson, a finance systems coordinator for the home and building control and chair of OWL for the Minnesota area. Among its educational thrusts, it publishes a quarterly newsletter, *The Owl's Nest*, which provides general information of interest to its older workers, including articles on Social Security, finance and dealing with retirement, and acts as a communication vehicle for top management. "Life is a constant transition process," says Johnson, "and we're concerned about that and helping people cope. Our emphasis has been how do we plant the seeds and help people get ready for retirement. We've taken a holistic view of the process."

More Than Lip Service

What more can business do? The most important vehicle for change is education, says USC's Dennis. "That's increasing awareness, increasing knowledge, increasing problem solving, and that's moving in a proactive way. And that's all very business-like; it's not academic pie-in-the-sky," she says. "To believe it will get done out of the goodness of people's hearts is naive; it has to be declared a priority [by management]."

"Managers need to treat their older workforce as they would a younger one. They have to look at them as individuals, not as 'older' but just as any staff, and manage them based on their capabilities and their performance, regardless of their age," says Loftus.

Just as corporations try to be racial and gender blind, organizations need to focus now on becoming age blind. "I'm not saying that all older workers should be hired or retained," says Dennis. "The point is, age should be irrelevant."

"The buzzword for the '90s is diversity," Dennis continues. How companies deal with diversity, after all, will make all the difference in the world in how well they can compete in an increasingly competitive environment. And that means that organizations must do more than just pay lip service to these issues.

"We manage diversity, we commit to diversity, we value diversity," Dennis says. But companies have ignored the age part of the equation. One reason, she says, may be that "there are just other competing issues that are screaming louder." Yet she is optimistic that as the Boomers advance further into decision-making positions, they won't tolerate age discrimination. "I think they will scream. And Boomers get what they want. They always have. That may be our hope for the future," she says. "But we still have a long way to go."

BURNED-OUT BOSSES

Lee Smith

BECAUSE WE believe in you, we are raising your sales quota 20%. But your relationship with customers is already strong, so we're trimming your travel budget. Also, would you mind sharing your secretary with several other managers? Finally, over the next few months we want you to reduce your staff by a third. Oh, one more thing . . .

As corporations restructure, they are forcing managers through one of the most harrowing stress tests in business history. It is more than just the searing pace of change that makes bosses feel pressed—it's what's happening where their business touches their lives every day. The sales and production quotas they have to meet go up relentlessly, but everything else about their careers seems headed down: operating budgets, travel allowances, expense accounts, salary increases, and opportunities for promotion.

Most painful of all, managers who were trained to build are now being paid to tear down. They don't hire; they fire. They don't like the new mandate, but most have come to understand that it's not going to change. That realization makes the daily routine different: Work no longer energizes; it drains.

If this is something you see in others—or feel yourself—you're not alone. A growing number of line managers, senior staff, and

REPORTER ASSOCIATE *Rosalind Klein Berlin*

other executives suffer some stage of burnout. Though not a precisely defined medical condition, burnout has recognizable symptoms and is a result of prolonged stress, says Dr. Donald E. Rosen, a psychiatrist who directs the Professionals in Crisis program at the Menninger Clinic, the celebrated psychiatric hospital in Topeka. "Victims are lethargic, feel empty, no longer able to take satisfaction in what they once enjoyed," says Rosen. "They have a deep questioning of the value of the tasks they perform." In everyday parlance, they hate to go to work, not just on an occasional morning but on most mornings.

Companies devote vast resources to dealing with the trauma of downsizing, but most of that goes to the most obvious victims—those let go. Outplacement firms that help the displaced find new jobs collected $700 million in fees last year. But over time, many *survivors* may suffer more psychological damage than the departed. The dismissed sales manager who goes to work for a small but growing fish may settle for less income and fewer benefits at the new company but be more content than the colleague who remains behind with a whale struggling to turn itself into a shark.

Observes Daniel Yankelovich, the public opinion scholar whose organization recently completed a survey of top executives on the tactics of reorganization: "Most managements don't have as firm a hand on the human aspects of restructuring as they do on finance and technology." That shortcoming can wind up costing em-

ployers greatly in lost talent and lower sales.

David Noer, an expert in organizational behavior at the Center for Creative Leadership in Greensboro, North Carolina, calls the misery of those left clinging to the big fish "survivor sickness." No one knows for sure how many executives suffer from it. Companies that are aware of the problem in their midst are not eager to talk about it. But a striking increase in the number of disability claims for mental and nervous illness may be an indicator. UNUM Life Insurance, which writes more private disability policies than any other U.S. insurer, says the number of such claims it processed rose from 7.8% of its total in 1989 to 10.2% in 1993.

Survivors, says Noer, go through a process of psychic numbing that is similar in many ways—although certainly far less shattering—to that of those who have lived through plane crashes or similar disasters where other people perished. Even though there may be a rationale to the reorganization, survivors often feel guilty because from their perspective it is arbitrary; they are no worthier than those who were fired, only luckier.

Under the circumstances it seems almost immoral to take much joy in work. So they become morose and cautious, worrying that they will be washed away in the next wave of discharges. Meanwhile, they work harder and longer to make up for the toil of those who have left. Fatigue and resentment begin to build.

A director of marketing reflects with

contempt and exhaustion on the reorganization that the television station she works for has gone through. When she joined the company in 1985, she respected her employer and enjoyed managing her staff of eight. Two years ago a handful of senior executives unexpectedly revealed plans for a top-to-bottom restructuring. "We down in the trenches had no voice," she says. The effect on her department was paralyzing: She lost half her staff to layoffs. "Things that once happened as automatically as breathing ceased to work," she says. "I walked in one day last summer and discovered I had three full-time jobs. With a load that size, I hate them all. As a result, my employer is getting 10% of my former creativity and maybe 50% of my energy. I'm the classic employee who quit but still shows up to pick up her paycheck."

BUT NOTHING—not overwork, not confusion, not lost perks, not apprehension—is as deadening to a manager's morale as firing subordinates. To do it once is traumatic enough, but subsequent dismissals wear down one's resilience. The American Management Association's most recent survey of employment practices at 870 companies found that almost half had reduced their work forces from mid-1992 to mid-1993. For two-thirds of those companies, this was at least their second year of downsizing in a row.

Unlike most other duties executives undertake, cutting staff is not something they get better at; they often get worse. More precisely, it gets worse for them. David Sokol sprinted onto his fast-track career at the age of 27, ten years ago. He built a garbage-to-electricity co-generation business from scratch to 1,100 employees and $350 million a year in revenues. Three years ago Sokol and a partner made a major investment in California Energy, which sells power to utilities, and gained management control. The previous managers had so burdened the company with unneeded staff that earnings on revenues of $90 million were only $5 million, a profit margin far below the industry average. The new management decided to let 150 people go. Sokol fired 15 personally. "It made me angry because it wasn't the employees' fault," he says. His stomach twisted into a knot before each dismissal.

One year later Sokol left California Energy to become president of a much larger company and discovered to his dismay that it had even more serious financial problems. There he had to fire half a dozen senior people and supervise the dismissals of several hundred other employees. "You get through firing people the first time around, accepting it as part of business," says So-

kol. "The second time I began wondering, 'How many miscarriages is this causing? How many divorces, how many suicides?' I worked harder so that I wouldn't have to think about it."

Adam Zak, an executive recruiter in Chicago, in the course of a search visited a prospect he had known before as an assertive, powerful executive. Since their last encounter, Mr. Take Charge had gone through several rounds of firing subordinates. Zak describes him: "He was smoking, had lost weight, had trouble looking me in the eye, was extremely nervous. It seemed to me that a few months of telling people they were out the door had gone a long way in destroying his personality."

In another case, a rapidly rising executive in a major communications company had been required to eliminate several thousand jobs a couple of years ago. It bothered him, but he soldiered on, putting in more hours at work. Last year he was promoted, and a month later he was asked to oversee the elimination of several thousand more positions. Within weeks of that new assignment he began losing his appetite and had trouble sleeping. Although he had never had difficulty making decisions before, he started to second-guess himself. Was he cutting the wrong jobs? Occasionally he began to cry spontaneously. One day he couldn't get out of bed.

With the help of medication and psychotherapy, this executive is back on the job. But the incident helped illuminate for his employer the depth of the crisis among the senior staff. Hundreds of managers have had to tell waves of subordinates they were finished. And they see no end to it. "People there don't know when the rain is going to stop," says one of the company's retired executives. The toll on managers rises: The human resources department reports an increase in absenteeism and alcoholism among managers. The medical department has called in consulting psychologists.

In the course of continuing restructurings, IBM has eliminated more than 100,000 jobs over the past four years. Listen to a former marketing vice president who spent 20 years with the now struggling computer maker. "Through most of the years, I loved that company so much I would get excited on Sunday night about going to work on Monday," she says. But beginning in 1986 and every year since, IBM has been shrinking. "Every year we'd call it something different—early retirement, reorganization, re-engineering," she recalls. "It was slow water torture."

At first she could tell subordinates that they could have jobs if they were willing to be mobile. Moving from Armonk to Oklahoma was unrealistic for most IBMers, tied

down by spouses with other jobs, houses, schools, and commitments. Still, she wasn't actually firing anyone. As those faraway opportunities began to vanish, the executive spent days on the telephone trying to find "catchers," colleagues who might be able to scoop up the talented people she had to let go. "I came home every night worried how this one or that one was going to support himself. I snapped at my husband. I had trouble sleeping." At Christmastime in 1992, she promised herself that the next time a decent retirement package was offered, she would take it. So in the middle of the following year she left IBM. "Reorganization had been five years out of my life," she says, "and when I quit, I felt the biggest load in the world had been lifted from my shoulders." As she circulated her résumé elsewhere, one prospective employer was attracted by her experience in downsizing. He had the same thing in mind for his company. She fled the prospect.

Some managers are able to cope easily with successive dismissals—employees call them the "hatchets." But many more executives loathe it. For 15 years Nolan Brohaugh, a senior associate at the Menninger Clinic, has helped conduct weeklong seminars in which managers take a break from their routine and reflect on their work. "I've never met one of those caricature executives with blood dripping from his teeth," says Brohaugh. "In my experience, they have a lot of trouble even firing people who deserve to get canned."

Dismissal is clearly an attack on the ego of the person being fired, but in ways that are less obvious it also assaults the ego of the person wielding the ax. Dr. Gerald Kraines, a Harvard psychiatrist and CEO of the Levinson Institute, which advises companies on organizational strategies, explains how. "We all carry around internal aspirations, generally ideals from our childhood," he says. "Anything that increases the gap between what we think we ought to be and what we are actually doing drives down our self-esteem."

OVERWORK DOESN'T do that. Toiling 70 hours a week may be exhausting, but it's consistent with the American ethic. Taking the redeye overnight flight from Los Angeles to New York so as not to miss a day's work is as much an occasion for boast as complaint. Firing is something else. Its underlying principles are un-American—authoritarian and classist. Like nothing else in a manager's repertoire, it accentuates I'm-the-boss-and-you're-not. Also, from kindergarten through business school, Americans are taught to expand and build to the horizon. Firing has the smell of defeat and retreat.

As the manager's self-esteem is threatened, he is inclined to work harder—beyond what is required by the reduction in staff—to feel good about himself again. The reason for that response, says Kraines, has to do with a physiological defense mechanism: "When there's a threat—whether it's to our bodies or to our self-esteem—the mind ratchets up a few notches." For short spurts, that can help prepare an effective response to the threat. But if the brain stays in racing gear for too long, mental and physical reserves run down, and burnout begins to set in.

One of the first things to go as the flame flickers is creative spirit. Managers undergoing prolonged threats react in one of several ways, says Kraines. They become hostile toward those around them or toward themselves—depression—or they try to impose strict control on everything within their jurisdiction. "All of those postures discourage the easy flow of ideas, which is the basis of creative output," Kraines observes. Once this syndrome takes hold in an organization, the result can be a cadre of uptight managers with little energy or imagination.

What makes the waves of dismissals in recent years especially damaging is that so often workers have been fired not for cause but because their skills were no longer needed. They were accountants, perhaps, when the times cried out for salespeople. Consider the torment of a 49-year-old controller of a Midwestern utility. He is active in his church and not long ago led a major fundraising drive on behalf of a paralyzed girl. He has generally found business compatible with his faith and generous nature. Even when he occasionally had to dismiss a misfit, someone not cut out to be an accountant, he felt okay about it. "One young man started a string of quality photo shops, and we became customers," he recalls.

But late last year the controller had to fire 18 accountants because the utility had sold off some of its properties and no longer needed so large a staff. "That was very different," he says. "I no longer had the crutch of being able to say this was the best thing that could happen to them. It wasn't. One woman had been with the company for 15 years. She told me her father had just died, and her mother was sick. I felt as if *I* was the one being fired."

CEOs don't enjoy handing out pink slips any more than lower executives do, but at least the CEO gets some balancing psychological benefits out of a downsizing. The company's outside directors and security analysts, to whom the layoffs spell higher profits, applaud his courage for doing what has to be done—excellent salve for the self-esteem. Subordinate managers don't receive that applause. Muses Levinson's Kraines: "Misery flows downhill."

A NOTHER REASON for managerial angst is that midlevel bosses face two incompatible assignments: Be a cold-blooded cost cutter, and be liked. Notes the Menninger Clinic's Dr. Rosen: "He has been told that the new management style of the Nineties is to think of himself and his people as teammates." But in front of his subordinates the manager has to play contradictory roles: He is their friend; he may also be their executioner. The strain of reconciling these personas fans the flames of stress and resentment.

In firing longtime employees, managers feel that they have violated a trust. "You joined AT&T knowing you would never own the biggest house in the neighborhood," says Chuck Taylor, 56, a former division controller there. "But in exchange for lower income, you got an implicit guarantee of lifetime employment." Or did until the mid-Eighties, when Taylor and hundreds of other managers began to dismiss what eventually amounted to 140,000 workers. Typically, those whom Taylor fired were men between 45 and 55 with a child or two in college and a wife who stayed home. One of the men broke down and shouted abuse at him. Security came and escorted the distressed employee out of the building.

Taylor's morale sank. "When I was in high school trying out for football, there was a guy who put a slip of paper in your locker if you were cut from the team," he says. "We called him the Turk. Nobody wanted to get near him. We looked the other way when he came by. At AT&T, I began to feel like the Turk." So in 1989, after participating in three rounds of downsizings, Taylor accepted a generous retirement package and left.

What can companies do to help thousands of other valuable, experienced managers before they burn out and leave? The Levinson Institute's Kraines insists that the first thing top management must do is walk managers below them through all the steps that led to the decision to restructure the company. What was happening in the marketplace that made it necessary? Why did they have to reorganize in this way and not in some other? Were there mistakes made at the top? This kind of information can lessen the guilt and enhance the performance of the managers who stay behind.

AT&T may be getting the message. When James Smith, 47, a division manager in Indianapolis, had to fire 20 of his 80 subordinates in 1988, he fretted that if he had led his troops better he might have prevented the downsizing. His guilt grew into a sense of personal failure. "I would characterize my reaction as depression," he says, "waking up at 2 A.M., crying at times, feeling out of control of things." Unlike Taylor, Smith stayed on. He is still cutting staff, but AT&T has made the anguish of his assignment more bearable. The company has taken great pains to explain how changes in the global marketplace and not managerial failures forced the restructuring. The financial benefits for those who are leaving have improved as well.

T OP EXECUTIVES also need to spell out which of the company's traditional values will be preserved, says Kraines. Lifetime loyalty to employees is gone. What else is out the window? Will prestigious products be junked if their profit margins erode a bit? "People join companies for more than paychecks," Kraines points out. "You don't want people signing a new psychological contract they can't live with."

Sound advice, no doubt, but it doesn't do much to relieve the anguish of layoffs. Top management ought to acknowledge the pain. "A restructuring is always presented in nothing but a positive way, as an opportunity to get lean and mean or whatever," observes one psychologist who counsels senior executives on relations with colleagues. "That may be true, but it creates a taboo against talking about the other side of the restructuring. It doesn't give people permission to say, 'This is hell.'"

Constant restructuring has become a fact of business life in this era of change. Well and good, but companies that don't acknowledge the stress that survivors undergo and support those who are in danger of burning out may find that their glistening, reengineered enterprises end up being run by charred wrecks.

THE PAIN OF DOWNSIZING

What it's really like to live through the struggle to remake a company

John A. Byrne

The bombshell fell last summer in the guise of a videotape. It was one of those slick, corporate "news" programs for employees, the kind that typically delivers some feel-good message.

Not this one. It featured a fidgeting Nynex Corp. executive who insisted that the profitable company needed to slash its operating budget by up to 40% to remain competitive. The upshot: another downsizing that would eliminate 15,000 to 25,000 people from the payroll. That meant more than one in five employees would lose their jobs. The survivors of earlier cutbacks cried foul, while management soberly tried to justify the employee meltdown.

This is the tale of what has been happening at Nynex in the wake of that shattering announcement. It's the story of a flabby company in the midst of a gargantuan effort to remake itself, reduce costs, improve customer service, and prepare for an onslaught of more aggressive competition in the years ahead. But it is also a wrenching human drama. The players: a dynamic, steely executive leading the effort; an outside consultant whose firm is billing the company $1 million a month to help with the downsizing; a thoughtful survivor; and a resentful victim. In unusually revealing, introspective interviews, they offer an inside look at what it's really like to live through the painful process that has become a central fact of corporate life in the 1990s.

ANGRY AND BITTER. Like many big corporations, Nynex has been shrinking for years. Since 1990, the company has rid itself of 19,200 employees out of a total of 95,400, including 13,000 managers. In pure percentage terms, this latest cutback is one of the largest ever reported by a major corporation. The company made its plans official on Jan. 24 by taking a $1.6 billion charge to earnings to cut 16,800 employees, or 22% of its workforce, over the next three years. Two months later, Nynex acknowledged the cutbacks would cost an additional $1.3 billion in charges for severance terms more acceptable to union leaders.

Even though the company hopes to avoid forced layoffs by enticing employees to accept buyout offers, many Nynex managers are angry and bitter. "Two months ago, I would have said that morale was low and it couldn't go any lower," says one executive. "But I'd have to say it's even lower today." Adds a former manager: "The top executives are willing to sacrifice people to make their bottom line on a quarterly basis. In the long term, they are selling the corporation out."

The drama now playing out at Nynex is being enacted at many other corporations. Despite the economic recovery, massive downsizings continue at one brand-name behemoth after another. Rarely a week passes without the announcement of yet more cutbacks, in what has become the most unsettling and disruptive event in Corporate America. In a quest for efficiency, companies have been charging billions of dollars off their earnings to lay off hundreds of thousands of workers. The current euphemism is "reengineering"—a bloodless term for corporate bloodletting on an unprecedented scale. In the year's first quarter, employers announced an average of 3,106 cutbacks per day.

The sight of so many bodies on the corporate scrap heap is sparking a complex debate—about profits and loyalty, and about the benefits and unforeseen consequences of layoffs. Critics, including some prominent executives, believe massive downsizing has become a fad, a bone to throw Wall Street when investors begin baying for cost-cuts. Others maintain that large-scale staff reductions, even at profitable companies such as Procter & Gamble Co. and Xerox Corp., are necessary to maintain competitiveness in a fast-changing global marketplace.

HARD CHOICES. Few observers expect an end to the spate of downsizing announcements. "In many large companies, we still see tremendous fat," says Noel M. Tichy, a management professor at the University of Michigan. "Yet there still remains this naive view that as the economy continues to take off, these jobs will come back. That's nonsense."

Tichy and others believe that recent gains in productivity—which rose at a 4% rate in the last half of 1993—are largely the result of these employee meltdowns. What the statistics of efficiency don't measure, of course, is the costs in emotional trauma to laid-off workers and their families, to the executives who often carry out the orders, or to the less secure survivors in dramatically changed organizations.

Today's corporation is no longer a secure or stable place. It's an uncertain, turbulent environment where managers often find their compassion and humanity in conflict with the pressures of competition and ambition. Fear is almost palpable in the corridors of the reengineered workplace, where loyalty takes a backseat to survival and personal advancement.

The events unfolding at Nynex are unique, colored by the company's own culture, traditions, personalities, and politics. But they're also universal: They exemplify the challenges and the pain

JOB DEATH: 25 LARGE DOWNSIZINGS

In a quest for efficiency and survival, many of America's corporate behemoths have been shedding employees at unprecedented rates. Here are 25 of the largest announced staff reductions since early 1991:

Company	Staff cutbacks
IBM	85,000
AT&T	83,500
GENERAL MOTORS	74,000
U.S. POSTAL SERVICE	55,000
SEARS	50,000
BOEING	30,000
NYNEX	22,000
HUGHES AIRCRAFT	21,000
GTE	17,000
MARTIN-MARIETTA	15,000
DUPONT	14,800
EASTMAN KODAK	14,000
PHILIP MORRIS	14,000
PROCTER & GAMBLE	13,000
PHAR MOR	13,000
BANK OF AMERICA	12,000
AETNA	11,800
GE AIRCRAFT ENGINES	10,250
McDONNELL DOUGLAS	10,200
BELLSOUTH	10,200
FORD MOTOR	10,000
XEROX	10,000
PACIFIC TELESIS	10,000
HONEYWELL	9,000
U S WEST	9,000

DATA: PEOPLE TRENDS

that face both healthy and troubled organizations everywhere.

THE COST-CUTTER

HE'S GUTSY, BRILLIANT, AND CARRIES AN AX

Behind every major downsizing there is a person who leads the effort, and in so doing becomes both leader and scapegoat. At Nynex, it's Robert J. Thrasher. He's a tough-minded, 51-year-old executive vice-president with a history of breaking the rules.

At 5 feet, 3 inches, Bob Thrasher is a compact, muscular bundle of frantic en-

ergy—"a bionic gerbil," he jokes. Thrasher is always pacing, always talking at high-decibel level. And he's completely committed to the company: Divorced from his physician wife, he typically arrives at his office at 6:45 a.m. and leaves at 7 p.m. He can't remember a Sunday in the past 20 years when he hasn't worked at home or in the office.

Thrasher would surely prefer to be known as the "agent of change." Instead, the executive who nervously announced the impending layoffs on that in-house video has been branded the "corporate assassin"—the person responsible for the plan to eliminate 16,800 jobs. His critics—and there are many of them—would say that he has ice water in his veins and a pocket calculator for a heart.

Since Nynex announced its downsizing, he has had to disconnect the answering machine at his Stamford (Conn.) home because every evening it was filled with obscene messages and threats from anonymous employees. Colleagues dub him "Thrasher the Slasher." In that same employee video, an interviewer wryly noted that he was running "unopposed as the top management SOB."

A former Air Force captain in a tactical fighter group, Thrasher insists that the tough choices he's now making are inevitable. "I know this is the right thing to do," he says. "Today, we have a virtual monopoly, but the states are in the process of opening up their markets. We have to improve service and reduce costs to stay competitive."

That realization, says Thrasher, came in mid-1992, during long-range planning discussions when he was chief operating officer of Nynex' New York Telephone unit. Top management concluded that if

it continued to run the business the same way, the company's costs per access line would keep increasing even as revenues steadily declined.

Thrasher was relieved of his COO job to head the effort to reinvent Nynex. Why him? Many companies, from IBM to Westinghouse Electric Corp., have sought outsiders to lead their attempts at transforming themselves. Thrasher, by contrast, is the consummate insider. He joined the company as a construction foreman in 1965, fresh out of Massachusetts Institute of Technology, where he earned a graduate degree in structural engineering. The job was in his blood: His late father was a foreman for the Niagara Mohawk Power Corp. And what would he have thought of what his son is doing now? "My dad would have thought I'm breaking a social contract we have with our employees," Thrasher says—but then dismisses the notion. "That's the monopoly mind-set."

"This is tough, ugly work. The stress is palpable. I'm vilified throughout the company. . . . That's a tough thing to carry around." Robert J. Thrasher, Exec. V-P, Nynex

No one would ever accuse Thrasher of being a Bell-head, the sort of cautious bureaucrat who found shelter in the highly regulated embrace of the mother

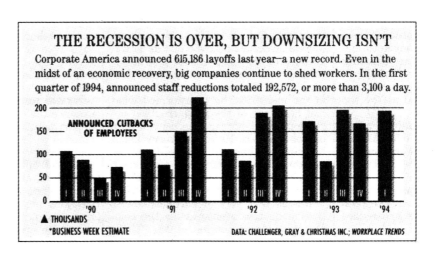

THE RECESSION IS OVER, BUT DOWNSIZING ISN'T

Corporate America announced 615,186 layoffs last year—a new record. Even in the midst of an economic recovery, big companies continue to shed workers. In the first quarter of 1994, announced staff reductions totaled 192,572, or more than 3,100 a day.

ANNOUNCED CUTBACKS OF EMPLOYEES

▲ THOUSANDS
*BUSINESS WEEK ESTIMATE

DATA: CHALLENGER, GRAY & CHRISTMAS INC.; WORKPLACE TRENDS

of all utilities. If anything several associates describe him as "crazy" because of his gutsy candor and his irreverence for authority. As general manager of the company's Long Island unit in the mid-1980s, he transformed what had been one of the most troubled operations with horrendous service into one of the best. He didn't worry about bruising feelings. "In the first six months," boasts Thrasher, "I reassigned, furloughed, and forced-retired half of the senior management team there."

It was that sort of hardheadedness that made him a natural for the companywide reengineering effort. "There was no other choice than Bob Thrasher," says Ivan G. Seidenberg, president of Nynex. "He has enormous energy, commitment, and passion for the company. He's relentless."

WEEKEND HUDDLE. Thrasher wanted to examine the company not by division, or department, or function. Instead, he planned to analyze the company by its four core processes, which cut across the $13.4 billion corporation: customer operations, customer support, customer contact—i.e., sales and marketing—and customer provisioning, that is, the planning, design, and building of Nynex' network. He created four teams, with a handpicked captain for each. After spending three days at GTE Corp. to get an inside look at its reengineering effort, he hired GTE's consultants, Boston Consulting Group Inc. (BCG), to help with the process at Nynex.

By late March, 1993, at a weekend meeting at the Stouffer Westchester Hotel in White Plains, N.Y., he put his teams together with the consultants and told his incredulous audience what he wanted: a 35% to 40% reduction in operating expenses. The teams, with 80 Nynex insiders and some 20 BCG consultants in total, dispersed and rushed through the bureaucracy observing all its key operations. They visited 152 "best practice" companies, from Avis Inc. to Virginia Power & Light, looking for useful ideas.

Back home, the inefficiencies they discovered shocked all of them—most of all Thrasher. Among many things, he learned that Nynex bought 83 brands of personal computers a year; that dozens of New York Telephone Co. employees spent their time repainting newly purchased trucks a different shade of white at a cost of $500 a truck; that Nynex spent $4.5 million to find and bill only $900,000 in

previously unbillable telephone calls. There was plenty more. "Think of how embarrassed I was," says Thrasher. "I ask myself how I could have presided for two and one-half years over an operation that has been that screwed up."

His teams first came up with a list of 85 "quick wins"—easy fixes to make. By printing on both sides of customer bills, for example, the company will save $7 million a year on postage costs alone. By standardizing on only two personal computers, Nynex could save $25 million in annual capital outlays. And then, in November, came the more substantive recommendations that would lead to the massive layoffs.

All told, the four teams compiled more than 300 specific changes, from consolidating work centers to simplifying procedures for approving customer service. Change doesn't come free, however. Thrasher initially estimated the moves would cost $700 million in expenses and $400 million in capital. But by 1997, the changes will cut $1.5 billion to $1.7 billion from the company's $6 billion in operating expenses.

HUGE RETURN. On three consecutive days last December—"the most excruciating days of my life"—he made presentations to the directors of three boards at Nynex and its operating subsidiaries, New York Telephone and New England Telephone. He did something that would make any executive cringe: He asked the directors to swallow a record $1.6 billion charge against earnings and to make wholesale cuts from the payroll.

The slide that cinched the decision contained the prediction that all of Thrasher's fixes, if implemented, would generate an internal return of 1,025% and a payback on investment in two years. Thrasher told directors that if his teams could achieve only 25% of their goals, they would see a 226% return and a three-year payback. But those estimates didn't reflect the sharp increase in the actual cost of cutbacks, which has grown from $700 million in January to $2 billion two months later as a result of union negotiations.

Although he got approval to move forward—some 950 people are working to implement the changes—Thrasher still meets resistance. "Some of our senior management still don't get it," he says. "What we've got to do is find them and get them out of the business."

That's tough talk. "This is tough, ugly work," says Thrasher. "The stress is palpable. I'm vilified throughout the company. People look upon me as the principal to the downsizing. That's a tough thing to carry around. Hell, I'd like not to downsize a single employee. But that would not be a prudent decision to make."

THE CONSULTANT
A DENTIST WHO ONLY DOES ROOT CANALS

For Phillip B. Catchings, the Nynex assignment has been the most challenging and difficult of his consulting career. As a partner at Boston Consulting Group, Catchings is the day-to-day leader of the consulting project that is costing Nynex $1 million a month. If BCG stays at Nynex until the job is done, the total bill could reach nearly $40 million.

Like Thrasher, he's hardly a popular figure at Nynex these days. For one thing, employees have seen their share of high-priced consultants come and go. "Nynex is a champion at spending millions of dollars on consultants and doing nothing with the results," grouses one manager.

Besides, every time Catchings begins a consulting assignment—and he has done about 45 so far—he is typically met with cynicism. "There is some natural resentment when we come in," he says. People ask, 'What makes you guys so smart?' and 'Why doesn't top management trust us to do this ourselves?'

His job, he says, is to allay such fears—but he can't do so by pretending that his remedies will be painless. "A dentist who claims a root canal is not going to hurt will lose his credibility," he says. "I am here to do the best possible job for the organization."

Above all, of course, Catchings' presence provokes shudders because he is a *memento mori* in pinstripes. His arrival at Nynex or anywhere else usually means layoffs ahead. In half of his past 10 assignments, he has been part of a retrenchment effort. Yet his background hardly seemed to have prepared him for his role as the hardheaded, coldhearted consultant. After graduating from Dartmouth College in 1973 with a degree in psychology, Catchings ran a foster home for delinquent teenagers. He grew a beard and long hair, bicycled across the country, and studied pottery in Washington state. The wanderlust out of his system, he spent five years in human resources with AT&T, then headed to Harvard B-school. He graduated with his MBA in 1982 and went straight to BCG.

Like most consultants, he's afflicted with jargon. Catchings, 42, speaks of

---

"People ask: What makes you guys so smart? Why doesn't top management trust us . . ." Phillip Catchings, partner, BCG

"crafting process platforms" and "de-averaging costs," of "optimum solutions" and "phase-one diagnostics." He concedes that his family is often disappointed with his inability to tell an anecdote about his work. "I must have a confidentiality filter on my brain," he says.

Along with partner Jeffrey A. Bowden, Catchings first consulted for Nynex and Chairman William C. Ferguson in 1989. That established a relationship that led to the current assignment. Catchings, whose expertise is mainly in "change management," has spent 80% of his 55-hour workweeks at Nynex since late 1992. Bowden, a telecom expert, was already spearheading a similar effort at GTE that will claim 17,000 jobs.

SCRIPTWRITING. The consulting pair huddled with Thrasher and other top executives once a week for four months, mapping out the project. By early March, Thrasher had picked his captains for the teams; Catchings and Bowden assembled two-dozen BCG consultants. Their role: write the script for the reengineering exercise and guide the effort.

A "compendium" of several hundred pages detailed the project's five major phases, from "direct process observation" in the first four months to "broad scale implementation," which is now under way. Catchings and Bowden helped to select the companies that teams visited for inspiration and ideas. After each trip, teams engaged in so-called clay-modeling sessions in which lessons from the visits were molded into recommendations.

Now, Catchings must get on with the painful task of building the new structure and helping to make the staff reductions

that will entail. How does he reconcile himself to the job of helping others wield an ax to people, their careers, and families? "I try not to focus on that aspect of it," he says. "I'm also part of taking a frustrated, comparatively unsuccessful 70,000 employees and transforming their environment so they can be more productive. I think I'm involved in saving lots of jobs, not destroying them."

THE SURVIVOR

STAYING POWER HAS REWARDS—AND A PRICE TAG

Nancy P. Karen, 46, is pretty sure her job won't be destroyed. In her 24 years with the company, she has been an energetic workaholic in the critical area of information systems. As director of the company's personal-computer network, Karen is facing new and tougher demands as a result of Thrasher's efforts.

She joined New York Telephone in 1969 during the company's big bulge in hiring, often referred to as "the service glut." To meet explosive growth, the company hired tens of thousands of people in the late 1960s and early 1970s. Karen, a Vassar College graduate with a degree in math, was one of 103,000 employees at New York Telephone in 1971. Today, NYT has about 40,220 people. Working in a regulated monopoly, she felt a sense of comfort and security that now seems a distant memory. "Downsizing was totally unheard of," she says. "Just about everybody here started with the company at a young age and retired off the payroll."

Thrasher's plan—and Nynex' earlier efforts to slash the payroll—have changed all that. Of the 79 people who report directly to Karen, 59 have already seen colleagues forced off the payroll in previous rounds of cutbacks. Her department is likely to suffer a 30% reduction in staffing. "When they started talking about another round of downsizing, people were a little more anxious because they feel they're already stretched thin. Now we'll have to learn to work smarter and completely change the way we do things.

Working smarter also means working harder—much harder. She once directly supervised 26 people, instead of 79, and she used to work more normal hours as well. No longer. Karen now puts in 50 to

60 hours a week, from 8 a.m. to 7 p.m. every weekday, at Nynex' White Plains (N.Y.) office. Wherever she goes these days, she carries a beeper and a cellular phone and checks her voice mail every hour. "It's a different mentality," she says. "My weekends and holidays are not reserved." On a recent biking vacation through California's wine country,

---

"Now we'll have to learn to work smarter and completely change the way we do things" Nancy Karen, Dir., Nynex PC network

---

she called the office at least once a day from "every little town." Since Karen is single, "nobody complains about my work hours," she says.

Nynex didn't push Karen into her new and grueling pace completely unprepared. The company dispatched her to the local Holiday Inn in early 1993 for a workshop on culture change put together by Senn-Delaney Leadership, a Long Beach (Calif.) consulting firm. She was skeptical at first. "To me, it was yet another program," she says.

Surprisingly, Karen left a believer. The sessions—dubbed Winning Ways—are an effort to inculcate the new values and skills that Nynex believes it needs to make Thrasher's reengineering changes take hold. It's a quick-and-dirty roundup of today's managerial commandments, stressing teamwork, accountability, open communications, respect for diversity, and coaching over managing.

Although impressed by how the sessions encouraged employees to speak more freely to each other, Karen saw her share of nonconverts at the initial two-and-one-half-day meeting. "Some people come back to work unchanged," she says. "But there's a big middle section that seems willing to change, and then there's a small percentage at the top that's very enthusiastic about it."

BRAIN DRAIN? Not that Karen, who earned an MBA from Columbia University on the company's tab in 1981, doesn't have some big worries about the change effort. One of them is that the downsizing will get ahead of the company's ability to figure out ways to get the work done more efficiently. She's also worried that the company will lose

Commentary/by John A. Byrne

THERE IS AN UPSIDE TO DOWNSIZING

Next to the death of a relative or friend, there's nothing more traumatic than losing a job. Corporate cutbacks threaten the security and self-esteem of survivors and victims alike. Layoffs disrupt careers and families. They cause turmoil and shatter the morale inside organizations. And they confirm the public's view that profits always come before people.

So it comes as no surprise that when consulting firms survey human resource executives about recent downsizings, they find some negative results. Indeed, study after study appears to prove that the downside of downsizing often outweighs any savings the cutbacks produce. Management underestimates the costs to slash workers and the impact cutbacks have on the morale of survivors. "People become preoccupied with layoffs," says John J. Parkington, a consultant with Wyatt Co., which published a downsizing study last year. "People spend more time on internal politics. They become less productive."

BAD PRESS. In truth, downsizing has gotten something of a bum rap. Parkington's own study shows that 77% of the executives Wyatt surveyed believe that restructuring had a positive impact on productivity. Only 13% considered the impact adverse. Sure, morale suffered in the short term. But the mood does pick up, especially when cutbacks are combined with efforts to bust up bureaucracy. Other benefits from downsizing cited by the survey's respondents: enhanced quality and customer service and greater willingness among survivors to take risks, perhaps because of accompanying efforts to encourage them to be more venturesome.

Yet another survey by the American Management Assn. last year claimed that downsizing's "goals of increased profits and greater productivity continue to prove elusive." The survey gathered these views, however, from human resource managers, who are far more likely to view cutbacks in a highly negative light. And even the human resource managers said profits declined at only one in five companies downsized since early 1988.

Another study by three professors at the University of Wisconsin also generated bad press for layoffs. The report contends that a company's financial performance worsens two years after the announcement of a downsizing. Although there's often a short-term advantage to layoffs, any gains in profit margins and return on equity disappear two years after the announcement.

THE REAL PICTURE

Study after study contends that companies commonly underestimate the costs of downsizing and often fail to gain the expected efficiencies. But the studies have their faults, too.

CRITICISM	REALITY
▶ Financial performance worsens two years after a company announces a massive layoff, according to a 1993 study by three academics at the University of Wisconsin. Though there is often a short-term advantage to downsizing, any gains in profit margins and return on equity soon disappear.	▶ This limited study of only 17 companies that announced layoffs in 1989 is hardly definitive. The authors reviewed 1991 financial results which were adversely affected by the recession. Many of these troubled companies would have been even worse off if they hadn't reduced costs through cutbacks.
▶ Fewer than half the companies that downsize meet the financial and operational goals they set for themselves, according to a 1993 study by Wyatt Co. Morale was hurt in 56% of the 531 surveyed.	▶ The report also found that downsizing led to such positive changes as improved productivity, enhanced quality and customer service, and a greater willingness among survivors to take risks.

Dig behind these headline-grabbing conclusions, however, and you find some remarkable information. The study is based on only 17 companies that announced layoffs in 1989. Because the authors chose to study companies immediately after they announced cutbacks, rather than after the layoffs took place, they give a distorted view.

Dig further, and you find that the authors' list of companies includes Digital Equipment, General Motors, IBM, and Unisys—troubled giants that are hardly candidates for quick turnarounds. "A lot of these companies are poorly managed concerns that got in trouble," says Noel M. Tichy, a management professor at the University of Michigan. "If they refused to lay off people, they would report bigger losses or go bankrupt." Concedes Kenneth P. De Meuse, one author of the study: "There may be a chicken-and-egg thing here."

In other words, there's no telling whether the deteriorating results are the consequence of the layoffs, or—as is more likely—merely the further playing out of the business woes that sparked the downsizing in the first place. Two years may not be long enough to see results. Indeed, if De Meuse and his colleagues had extended their period of review, they also would have found sizable rises in net income and profit margins at other companies in the study, including Boeing, Chrysler, Hewlett-Packard, Motorola, and Texas Instruments.

These companies are among those that have aggressively cut costs and changed the way work is done. When John F. Welch became chief executive of General Electric Co. in 1981, the company employed nearly 420,000 people. Today, some 222,000 are on the GE payroll, yet the company has tripled its net profits and more than doubled its revenues. "I know that GE made a bundle of money out of downsizing," adds Tichy, co-author of a book on Welch. "If you figure that each person with salary and benefits costs about $60,000 a year, that means GE has taken $18 billion out of its cost structure."

Make no mistake: Downsizing is hardly a quick fix. It is not a strategy, and it is not a panacea for poor management. Healthy companies that slash payrolls instead of devising new game plans for growth are sending a demoralizing message to employees. Massive layoffs should be avoided when possible through shorter workweeks, wage and hiring freezes, and cutbacks in executive perks. But the idea that downsizing can't sometimes be an effective way for bloated, uncompetitive companies to cut costs is pure nonsense.

Byrne is a senior writer covering management for BUSINESS WEEK.

expertise and talent. That would mean that she and other managers won't have enough of the right people to accomplish the tasks placed before them. "It's not going to work perfectly," she says. "There will be cases when the downsizing occurs before the reengineering."

Despite the increased workload and her concern over employee morale, Karen considers herself lucky. "This is a wonderful challenge," she says. "I'm looking at a task of building a new organization in the next six months to a year. I have the chance to test myself as I've never been tested before.

THE VICTIM

THE LIVING HELL OF LIFE ON THE FIRING LINE

Not everyone shares Karen's optimistic view of life at Nynex. Uncertainty and fear loom over many. Only two weeks ago, Nynex began sending out details of the buyout packages to some workers in New England. Employees know that if enough people refuse the package, the company will be forced to push them out.

Many are understandably bitter. They feel as if they are victims of some abstract management exercise beyond their control or even their capacity to understand. One of them, an urbane manager with more than 20 years of experience, expects to pounce on an early-retirement package, to walk out, and start a new phase of life. "This company's values have changed," the manager says. "There are now right people and wrong people here, and I don't believe in that."

Fearful of retribution, this employee doesn't want to be identified. But Pat, as we'll call this middle manager in a staff

position, is remarkably candid about the turmoil inside the company. Pat has made presentations before Bob Thrasher and thinks he's a "brilliant, if ruthless, executive. As an officer of the company, he's very focused and clearly sees the possibilities." But this Nynex veteran doesn't see Thrasher and other top managers sharing the pain. "The officers all have golden parachutes. They're in charge of their own fates. We're not involved. We're just affected."

"The officers . . . are in charge of their own fates. We're not involved. We're just affected" Pat, a middle manager in jeopardy

---

Looking at the fate of the managers and employees who lost their jobs in Nynex' earlier cutbacks, Pat can see the profound changes that may lie ahead. Many are still without work. More than 150 of them have joined a class action against the company, alleging that they were selected for dismissal because of age discrimination.

Although the company formally announced its latest round of cutbacks three months ago, not a single employee has yet lost a job. Details of buyout offers, including accelerated pensions, are being sent to employees in selected business units. Thrasher says the buyout offer "removes the anxiety and angst in the workforce."

Not to this middle manager, who believes offering incentives to quit isn't that

much different from terminating employees outright with severance pay. "Even if people won't be fired this time, they're still frightened of the future. It affects their self-esteem and their pocketbook. And most people aren't going from something to something. They have no place to go."

VALUE LOST. Sure, Pat fears for a job that may be lost. But mostly, Pat claims to fear that the company to which this middle manager's professional life has been devoted will never recover from the bloodletting. Pat recalls taking hours to walk to work in the aftermath of a major snowstorm—a degree of commitment employees won't be likely to feel in the future. This manager wonders if the repairmen who now rush to set up emergency communications lines at the scene of incidents such as the bombing of the World Trade Center will move less urgently because of Nynex' perceived lack of loyalty to its employees. Corporate values that not long ago focused on caring for employees have been rewritten so that now employees come last, Pat says, after shareholders and customers.

The Draconian downsizing, Pat believes, is really a kneejerk response to a complex set of problems that might be addressed more subtly. "Other companies, like Hewlett-Packard, have refocused their strategy, cleaned up their product and service lines, and for the most part retrained their folks without massive layoffs, and they're doing exceptionally well."

Such humane options, however, may be for executives and companies that don't have to cut as deeply or as thoroughly as Nynex. As everyone involved would concede, the pain of this massive downsizing isn't likely to go away anytime soon.

"You're Fired."

It was over. Steve had been forced out of the company with little warning, and no one had helped him. What was worse, he suspected the firing might have been because of an ethical stance he had once taken.

DOUG WALLACE

Doug Wallace does frequent consulting work on corporate ethics, and was formerly the vice president for social policy at Norwest Bank in Minneapolis.

THE CASE

Staring numbly at his glistening kitchen table, Steve swirled his spoon in his coffee. He thought about his afternoon—his last hours at the company he had served faithfully for over ten years.

"I'm reorganizing the department, and you aren't a candidate for any position in it," Jeanette Rigley, his thirty-two-year-old boss, had told him. "I've prepared two memos: one describing your severance agreement, and one describing our reorganization and decision to let you go . . . because of a performance problem."

He had quickly scanned the memos. "Can't we discuss this?" he asked.

"There's nothing to discuss," she snapped. "The decision is final."

Steve's mind drifted back to just five days ago when Allied Tech CEO Bruce Ship had introduced him to some 600 managers at the "heads up" session. He had felt confident standing before his colleagues, describing the dynamic plans his public affairs group had devised. It had gone well, Steve thought. But apparently, not well enough, for days later Jeanette had given him the boot.

He stood slouching near the stove, remembering last year's merger and Jeanette's arrival on the scene. Steve remembered the scuttlebutt in the office before Jeanette was hired—women in the office were putting tremendous pressure on Bruce, the CEO, to hire a woman for one of the few remaining executive positions. Steve had thought at the time that Bruce was responding hastily by hiring her, especially since her experience was with a financial services company, not with a technical firm like Allied. Now, look-

In the middle of a recession, Steve found himself unemployed at fifty-two, with only ten weeks severance pay.

ing back, he had probably been right. Steve remembered feeling uneasy when he had first met Jeanette. He had been puzzled by her style, but had made up his mind not to let his feelings hinder their working relationship.

Within six months, though, trouble began. It had started last spring, when Jeanette abruptly handed Steve a performance review as he was on his way out the door to the state capitol. It had been the first negative review of his long career. She ended up changing that evaluation, but only after he sent a documented, follow-up memo. Then, three months later, she had surprised him with another performance memo. Again, Steve documented the inaccuracies in her review. But this time, he also requested the human resources department's assistance with Jeanette. Despite its promise to mediate, no one had ever followed through.

"I should have seen this coming," Steve thought. "There must have been a turning point." And then he remembered. His mind shot back to a meeting last fall. He had questioned the company's proposed international sales policy, at the time thinking others would also recognize the serious ethical implications of the proposal. "I was only doing my job," Steve thought. Members familiar with his work had invited his "thoughtful perspective," because of the potentially volatile public exposure to the company.

As he recalled the reaction he got—blank stares and silence—Steve's stomach sank. He recalled the queasy feeling he had leaving the conference room that day. And he knew why he was fired. "Bruce must have authorized Jeanette's action," Steve thought. "Maybe she was just being a good soldier."

For whatever reason, he hadn't been treated fairly. And almost every ethical principle he held dear had been violated. His dismissal was demeaning. And it left him at risk of joining the unemployed, at fifty-two, in the middle of a recession, with only ten weeks severance pay.

"Should I seek legal help?" he wondered. "Should I protest the decision? What can I do?"

SARA PICARD
Assistant Vice President, U.S. Health Care, Blue Bell, Pennsylvania.

I DO BELIEVE THAT, ethically, Steve wasn't treated fairly, and I would probably be as angry or as shocked as he was. His record shows that he was a fine employee. If I was in his place, I would have confronted Jeanette after the first performance review. I would have taken copies of my previous reviews and sat down with her and had a heart-to-heart. The ten-week severance seemed particularly harsh. If the company was trying to terminate an employee with Steve's background and tenure, I don't understand why some type of retirement package wasn't offered.

Would I leave quietly? Yes. I would not make a large stink about it. Would I seek legal help? If I were in his shoes, I would definitely pursue legal counseling. At Steve's age, I think he has a good case. Would I protest the decision and ask for reconsideration? Yes, I would present some sort of retirement package request to them, in view of the time I had been with the company and my past record of performance. What responsibility do I have? If Steve pursued legal counseling, he might be advised to bring in other employees who were similarly affected, but I wouldn't pursue that on my own. I would try to come up with alternatives to litigation. However, if I didn't get anywhere, I would pursue the legal point and take it as far as I had to.

BERNIE VITTI
Associate Director of Sales Training and Development, Sandoz Pharmaceuticals, East Hanover, New Jersey.

I RECOMMEND SIX STEPS. First, I would ask the human resources and legal departments to help me with Jeanette. In most cases today, HR will get involved with cases like this. Second, Jeanette as a manager must have a sit-down performance appraisal with Steve. That is a must. The role of the enlightened manager today is to get subordinates to work better, to show them how to do the job rather than saying, "What you've done is not acceptable." It's Jeanette's job to show Steve what is not acceptable and to teach him how to do it better. Third, I would develop objectives and projects so that Steve can best do that job. Fourth, Jeanette must agree to set appropriate deadlines, and define what is expected of Steve, so that both parties agree on what the finished projects will look like. Fifth, checkpoints along the way should be determined. Steve's success or failure could be documented at these checkpoints, which would also provide Jeanette every opportunity to help Steve, instead of just approaching him on the end

---

Workers shouldn't acquiesce to an unfair firing. Autocratic managers count on that happening.

---

dates with, "You didn't do your job, so your evaluation is unsatisfactory." Steve has to be given every benefit of the doubt.

Sixth, Jeanette should discuss all options with Steve. A summary of his job should be presented, and if he hasn't met the requirements of the job, Jeanette should recommend another position. But not until Steve has been given every opportunity to become more proficient.

DOUG WALLACE'S COMMENTS

A RECURRING THEME in this column is avoiding Lone Ranger ethics in organizations. Most ethical conflicts are communal in nature. They often involve a variety of persons and groups within the company. Sometimes they erupt because mixed messages about priorities have been sent. But in almost all cases, an ethical conflict is not the result of one person's independent action, and it cannot be understood or successfully resolved without the engagement of those who contributed to the conflict and those who will be affected by its resolution. The art of doing ethics in organizations entails learning how to effectively put an issue on the table, bring together the people who contributed to it (even if they did so unknowingly), and work the conflict through to a good end.

What happens, however, when the one who recognizes the problem no longer has standing in the organization? Steve, a good, productive employee, has been fired. I suspect that the reason Steve was pushed out has more to do with his ethical questions than his performance or his difficulties with Jeanette. But Steve is on the outside looking in. How can he affect anything now?

There are a lot of Steves, or Stephanies, if you will, in this tightening economy, people whose bosses tolerate no debate, and who often find themselves the first to go when an organization restructures. And they aren't necessarily troublemakers. What should, and can, they do?

For starters, people should not simply acquiesce and accept what's occurring. Autocratic managers count on that happening. Both of our guest commentators presume that Steve should take responsibility not only to protect himself, but also to attempt to get the organization to take another look at what it is doing. To do that will invariably involve the assistance of others who still belong to the company or who have access to powerful players within it. This should not be confused with hammering the organization or

individuals in it. Rather, seeking inside assistance aims at encouraging a company to re-examine and improve the way employees are treated—blending caring and fairness into the way people manage.

And if those initiatives fail, there is always the option of litigating the matter.

WHAT ACTUALLY HAPPENED?

STEVE CONCLUDED that the ethical principles of fairness and respect for dignity had been breached. The next day he wrote a memo to the human resources department requesting copies of all policies on layoffs, termination, and supervisor dispute resolution. He knew such policies existed. Since it was a newly merged company, he wanted confirmation that the company was at least temporarily operating under policies from one of the former organizations.

He then wrote a detailed response to Jeanette's performance evaluation, proposing an alternative severance agreement or a way for him to continue employment with a different reporting relationship. Rather than citing a general statement of unfair treatment, he detailed the history of his relationship with Jeanette and his performance. He sent this memo to the vice president of human resources, with copies to the CEO, chief operating officer, general counsel, and the attorney for human resources.

To get proof of his strong performance, Steve contacted Walt Haverford, a retired executive from the original organization. After explaining his situation, and asking for advice and a letter of reference, Steve leveraged Walt's personal relationship with the COO of Allied to request a meeting. Since Allied's COO was the person at the highest level who hadn't been directly involved in the situation, Steve thought he would be an influential, impartial witness. The COO did write a letter of reference for him, citing Steve's contributions, which in turn helped get human resources to develop a fair and balanced view of the situation.

Finally, Steve solicited legal help to assess whether or not he had a case that could be litigated.

The case is still going forward. As we go to press, the company has not taken action to resolve the issue any differently than where Jeanette originally left it.

Changing Unethical Organizational Behavior

Richard P. Nielsen
Boston College

Richard P. Nielsen is an associate professor in the Department of Organizational Studies, School of Management, Boston College. He has been a faculty member at Boston College since 1980. He has served as a speaker and taught seminars and management development courses in France, Germany, Holland, Indonesia, Mexico, Pakistan, and Switzerland. He has also served as a consultant and presented management development progams to such organizations as Citicorp, GSX/Genstar, IBM, Arthur D. Little, the Society of Friends and the American Friends Service Committee, the United Nations, the U.S. Agency for International Development, the U.S. Office of Education, and the WGBH Educational Foundation.

His research, teaching, and consulting interests are in the areas of ethics practice and cooperative change management. He serves as an editorial board member and referee for the Journal of Business Ethics. *Some of his related recent publications include "Limitations of Reasoning as an Ethics Action Strategy" (*Journal of Business Ethics, *1988), "Arendt's Action Philosophy and the Manager as Eichmann, Richard III, Faust or Institution Citizen (*California Management Review, *1984), and "Cooperative Strategy" (*Strategic Management Journal, *1988).*

> *"To be, or not to be: that is the question:*
> *Whether 'tis nobler in the mind to suffer*
> *The slings and arrows of outrageous fortune,*
> *Or to take arms against a sea of troubles,*
> *And by opposing end them?"*
>
> William Shakespeare, *Hamlet*

What are the implications of Hamlet's question in the context of organizational ethics? What does it mean to be ethical in an organizational context? Should one suffer the slings and arrows of unethical organizational behavior? Should one try to take arms against unethical behaviors and by opposing, end them?

The consequences of addressing organizational ethics issues can be unpleasant. One can be punished or fired; one's career can suffer, or one can be disliked, considered an outsider. It may take courage to oppose unethical and lead ethical organizational behavior.

How can one address organizational ethics issues? Paul Tillich, in his book *The Courage to Be*, recognized, as

Hamlet did, that dire consequences can result from standing up to and opposing unethical behavior. Tillich identified two approaches: *being* as an individual and *being* as a part of a group.[1]

In an organizational context, these two approaches can be interpreted as follows: (1) Being as an individual can mean intervening to end unethical organizational behaviors by working against others and the organizations performing the unethical behaviors; and (2) being as a part can mean leading an ethical organizational change by working with others and the organization. These approaches are not mutually exclusive; rather, depending on the individual, the organization, the relationships, and the situation, one or both of these approaches may be appropriate for addressing ethical issues.

Being as an Individual

According to Tillich, the courage to be as an individual is the courage to follow one's conscience and defy unethical and/or unreasonable authority. It can even mean staging a revolutionary attack on that authority. Such an act can entail great risk and require great courage. As Tillich explains, "The anxiety conquered in the courage to be . . . in the productive process is considerable, because the threat of being excluded from such a participation by unemployment or the loss of an economic basis is what, above all, fate means today. . . ."[2]

According to David Ewing, retired executive editor of the *Harvard Business Review*, this type of anxiety is not without foundation.

> *"There is very little protection in industry for employees who object to carrying out immoral, unethical or illegal orders from their superiors. If the employee doesn't like what he or she is asked to do, the remedy is to pack up and leave. This remedy seems to presuppose an ideal economy, where there is another company down the street with openings for jobs just like the one the employee left."*[3]

How can one *be* as an individual, intervening against unethical organizational behavior? Intervention strategies an individual can use to change unethical behavior include: (1) secretly blowing the whistle within the organization; (2) quietly blowing the whistle, informing a responsible higher-level manager; (3) secretly threatening the offender with blowing the whistle; (4) secretly threatening a responsible manager with blowing the whistle outside the organiza-

From *The Executive*, May 1989, pp. 123-130. © 1989 by the Academy of Management. Reprinted by permission.

tion; (5) publicly threatening a responsible manager with blowing the whistle; (6) sabotaging the implementation of the unethical behavior; (7) quietly refraining from implementing an unethical order or policy; (8) publicly blowing the whistle within the organization; (9) conscientiously objecting to an unethical policy or refusing to implement the policy; (10) indicating uncertainty about or refusing to support a cover-up in the event that the individual and/or organization gets caught; (11) secretly blowing the whistle outside the organization; or (12) publicly blowing the whistle outside the organization. Cases of each strategy are considered below.

Cases

1. Secretly blowing the whistle within the organization. A purchasing manager for General Electric secretly wrote a letter to an upper-level manager about his boss, who was soliciting and accepting bribes from subcontractors. The boss was investigated and eventually fired. He was also sentenced to six months' imprisonment for taking $100,000 in bribes, in exchange for which he granted favorable treatment on defense contracts.[4]

2. Quietly blowing the whistle to a responsible higher-level manager. When Evelyn Grant was first hired by the company with which she is now a personnel manager, her job included administering a battery of tests that, in part, determined which employees were promoted to supervisory positions. Grant explained:

> "There have been cases where people will do something wrong because they think they have no choice. Their boss tells them to do it, and so they do it, knowing it's wrong. They don't realize there are ways around the boss.... When I went over his [the chief psychologist's] data and analysis, I found errors in assumptions as well as actual errors of computation.... I had two choices: I could do nothing or I could report my findings to my supervisor. If I did nothing, the only persons probably hurt were the ones who 'failed' the test. To report my findings, on the other hand, could hurt several people, possibly myself."

She quietly spoke to her boss, who quietly arranged for a meeting to discuss the discrepancies with the chief psychologist. The chief psychologist did not show up for the meeting; however, the test battery was dropped.[5]

3. Secretly threatening the offender with blowing the whistle. A salesman for a Boston-area insurance company attended a weekly sales meeting during which the sales manager instructed the salespeople, both verbally and in writing, to use a sales technique that the salesman considered unethical. The salesman anonymously wrote the sales manager a letter threatening to send a copy of the unethical sales instructions to the Massachusetts insurance commissioner and the *Boston Globe* newspaper unless the sales manager retracted his instructions at the next sales meeting. The sales manager did retract the instructions. The salesman still works for the insurance company.[6]

4. Secretly threatening a responsible manager with blowing the whistle outside the organization. A recently hired manager with a San Francisco Real Estate Development Company found that the construction company his firm had contracted with was systematically not giving minorities opportunities to learn construction management. This new manager wrote an anonymous letter to a higher-level real estate manager threatening to blow the whistle to the press and local government about the contractor unless the company corrected the situation. The real estate manager intervened, and the contractor began to hire minorities for foremen-training positions.[7]

5. Publicly threatening a responsible manager with blowing the whistle. A woman in the business office of a large Boston-area university observed that one middle-level male manager was sexually harassing several women in the office. She tried to reason with the office manager to do something about the offensive behavior, but the manager would not do anything. She then told the manager and several other people in the office that if the manager did not do something about the behavior, she would blow the whistle to the personnel office. The manager then told the offender that if he did not stop the harassment, the personnel office would be brought in. He did stop the behavior, but he and several other employees refused to talk to the woman who initiated the actions. She eventually left the university.[8]

6. Sabotaging the implementation of the unethical behavior. A program manager for a Boston-area local social welfare organization was told by her superior to replace a significant percentage of her clients who received disability benefits with refugee Soviet Jews. She wanted to help both the refugees and her current clients; however, she thought it was unethical to drop current clients, in part because she believed such an action could result in unnecessary deaths. Previously, a person who had lost benefits because of what the program manager considered unethical "bumping" had committed suicide: He had not wanted to force his family to sell their home in order to pay for the medical care he needed and qualify for poverty programs. After her attempts to reason with her boss failed, she instituted a paperwork chain with a partially funded federal agency that prevented her own agency from dropping clients for nine months, after which time they would be eligible for a different funding program. Her old clients received benefits and the new refugees also received benefits. In discussions with her boss, she blamed the federal agency for making it impossible to drop people quickly. Her boss, a political appointee who did not understand the system, also blamed the federal agency office.[9]

7. Publicly blowing the whistle within the organization. John W. Young, the chief of NASA's astronaut office, wrote a 12-page internal memorandum to 97 people after the Challenger explosion that killed seven crew members. The memo listed a large number of safety-related problems that Young said had endangered crews since October 1984. According to Young, "If the management system is not big enough to stop the space shuttle program whenever necessary to make flight safety corrections, it will not survive and neither will our three space shuttles or their flight crews." The memo was instrumental in the decision to broaden safety investigations throughout the total NASA system.[10]

8. Quietly refraining from implementing an unethical order/policy. Frank Ladwig was a top salesman and branch manager with a large computer company for more than 40 years. At times, he had trouble balancing his responsibilities. For instance, he was trained to sell solutions to customer problems, yet he had order and revenue quotas that sometimes made it difficult for him to concentrate on solving problems. He was responsible for signing and keeping important customers with annual revenues of between $250,000 and $500,000 and for aggressively and conscientiously representing new products that had required large R&D investments. He was required to sell the full line of products and services, and sometimes he had sales quotas for products that he believed were not a good match for the customer or appeared to perform marginally. Ladwig would quietly not sell those products, concentrating on selling the products he believed in. He would quietly explain the characteristics of the questionable products to his knowledgeable customers and get their reactions, rather than making an all-out sales effort. When he was asked by his sales manager why a certain product was not moving, he explained what the customers objected to and why. However, Ladwig thought that a salesman or manager with an average or poor performance record would have a difficult time getting away with this type of solution to an ethical dilemma.[11]

9. *Conscientiously objecting to an unethical policy or refusing to implement it.* Francis O'Brien was a research director for the pharmaceutical company Searle & Co. O'Brien conscientiously objected to what he believed were exaggerated claims for the Searle Copper 7 intrauterine contraceptive. When reasoning with upper-level management failed, O'Brien wrote them the following:

> "Their continued use, in my opinion, is both misleading and a thinly disguised attempt to make claims which are not FDA approved. . . . Because of personal reasons I do not consent to have my name used in any press release or in connection with any press release. In addition, I will not participate in any press conferences."

O'Brien left the company ten years later. Currently, several lawsuits are pending against Searle, charging that its IUD caused infection and sterility.[12]

10. *Indicating uncertainty about or refusing to support a cover-up in the event that the individual and/or organization gets caught.* In the Boston office of Bear Stearns, four brokers informally work together as a group. One of the brokers had been successfully trading on insider information, and he invited the other three to do the same. One of the three told the others that such trading was not worth the risk of getting caught, and if an investigation ever occurred, he was not sure he would be able to participate in a cover-up. The other two brokers decided not to trade on the insider information, and the first broker stopped at least that type of insider trading.

11. *Secretly blowing the whistle outside the corporation.* William Schwartzkopf of the Commonwealth Electric Company secretly and anonymously wrote a letter to the Justice Department alleging large-scale, long-time bid rigging among many of the largest U.S. electrical contractors. The secret letter accused the contractors of raising bids and conspiring to divide billions of dollars of contracts. Companies in the industry have already paid more than $20 million in fines to the government in part as a result of this letter, and they face millions of dollars more in losses when the victims sue.[14]

12. *Publicly blowing the whistle outside the organization.* A. Earnest Fitzgerald, a former high-level manager in the U.S. Air Force and Lockheed CEO, revealed to Congress and the press that the Air Force and Lockheed systematically practiced a strategy of underbidding in order to gain Air Force contracts for Lockheed, which then billed the Air Force and received payments for cost overruns on the contracts. Fitzgerald was fired for his trouble, but eventually received his job back. The underbidding/cost overruns, on at least the C-5/A cargo plane, were stopped.[15]

Limitations of Intervention

The intervention strategies described above can be very effective, but they also have some important limitations.

1. *The individual can be wrong about the organization's actions.* Lower-level employees commonly do not have as much or as good information about ethical situations and issues as higher-level managers. Similarly, they may not be as experienced as higher-level managers in dealing with specific ethical issues. The quality of experience and information an individual has can influence the quality of his or her ethical judgments. To the extent that this is true in any given situation, the use of intervention may or may not be warranted. In Case 9, for example, if Frank Ladwig had had limited computer experience, he could have been wrong about some of the products he thought would not produce the promised results.

2. *Relationships can be damaged.* Suppose that instead of identifying with the individuals who want an organization to change its ethical behavior, we look at these situations from another perspective. How do we feel when we are forced to change our behavior? Further, how would we feel if we were forced by a subordinate to change, even though we thought that we had the position, quality of information, and/or quality of experience to make the correct decisions? Relationships would probably be, at the least, strained, particularly if we made an ethical decision and were nevertheless forced to change. If we are wrong, it may be that we do not recognize it at the time. If we know we are wrong, we still may not like being forced to change. However, it is possible that the individual forcing us to change may justify his or her behavior to us, and our relationship may actually be strengthened.

3. *The organization can be hurt unnecessarily.* If an individual is wrong in believing that the organization is unethical, the organization can be hurt unnecessarily by his or her actions. Even if the individual is right, the organization can still be unnecessarily hurt by intervention strategies.

4. *Intervention strategies can encourage "might makes right" climates.* If we want "wrong" people, who might be more powerful now or in the future than we are, to exercise self-restraint, then we may need to exercise self-restraint even when we are "right." A problem with using force is that the other side may use more powerful or effective force now or later. Many people have been punished for trying to act ethically both when they were right and when they were wrong. By using force, one may also contribute to the belief that the only way to get things done in a particular organization is through force. People who are wrong can and do use force, and win. Do we want to build an organization culture in which force plays an important role? Gandhi's

response to "an eye for an eye" was that if we all followed that principle, eventually everyone would be blind.

Being as a Part

While the intervention strategies discussed above can be very effective, they can also be destructive. Therefore, it may be appropriate to consider the advantages of leading an ethical change effort (being as a part) as well as intervening against unethical behaviors (being as an individual).

Tillich maintains that the courage to be as a part is the courage to affirm one's own being through participation with others. He writes,

> "The self affirms itself as participant in the power of a group, of a movement . . . . Self-affirmation within a group includes the courage to accept guilt and its consequences as public guilt, whether one is oneself responsible or whether somebody else is. It is a problem of the group which has to be expiated for the sake of the group, and the methods of punishment and satisfaction . . . are accepted by the individual . . . . In every human community, there are outstanding members, the bearers of the traditions and leaders of the future. They must have sufficient distance in order to judge and to change. They must take responsibility and ask questions. This unavoidably produces individual doubt and personal guilt. Nevertheless, the predominant pattern is the courage to be a part in all members of the . . . group . . . . The difference between the genuine Stoic and the neocollectivist is that the latter is bound in the first place to the collective and in the second place to the universe, while the Stoic was first of all related to the universal Logos and secondly to possible human groups. . . . The democratic-conformist type of the courage to be as a part was in an outspoken way tied up with the idea of progress. The courage to be as a part in the progress of the group to which one belongs . . . ."[16]

Leading Ethical Change

A good cross-cultural conceptualization of leadership is offered by Yoshino and Lifson: "The essence of leadership is the influential increment over and above mechanical compliance with routine directives of the organization."[17] This definition permits comparisons between and facilitates an understanding of different leadership styles through its use of a single variable: created incremental performance. Of course, different types of leadership may be more or less effective in different types of situations; yet, it is helpful to understand the "essence" of leadership in its many different cultural forms as the creation of incremental change beyond the routine.

For example, Yoshino and Lifson compare generalizations (actually overgeneralizations) about Japanese and American leadership styles:

> "In the United States, a leader is often thought of as one who blazes new trails, a virtuoso whose example inspires awe, respect, and emulation. If any individual characterizes this pattern, it is surely John Wayne, whose image reached epic proportions in his own lifetime as an embodiment of something uniquely American. A Japanese leader, rather than being an authority, is more of a communications channel, a mediator, a facilitator, and most of all, a symbol and embodiment of group unity. Consensus building is necessary in decision making, and this requires patience and an ability to use carefully cultivated relationships to get all to agree for the good of the unit. A John Wayne in this situation might succeed temporarily by virtue of charisma, but eventually the inability to build strong emotion-laden relationships and use these as a tool of motivation and consensus building would prove fatal."[18]

A charismatic, "John Wayne type" leader can inspire and/or frighten people into diverting from the routine. A consensus-building, Japanese-style leader can get people to agree to divert from the routine. In both cases, the leader creates incremental behavior change beyond the routine. How does leadership (being as a part) in its various cultural forms differ from the various intervention (being as an individual) strategies and cases discussed above? Some case data may be revealing.

Cases

1. Roger Boisjoly and the Challenger launch.[19] In January 1985, after the postflight hardware inspection of Flight 52C, Roger Boisjoly strongly suspected that unusually low temperatures had compromised the performance effectiveness of the O-ring seals on two field joints. Such a performance compromise could cause an explosion. In March 1985, laboratory tests confirmed that low temperatures did negatively affect the ability of the O-rings to perform this sealing function. In June 1985, the postflight inspection of Flight 51B revealed serious erosion of both primary and backup seals that, had it continued, could have caused an explosion.

These events convinced Boisjoly that a serious and very dangerous problem existed with the O-rings. Instead of acting as an individual against his supervisors and the organization, for example, by blowing the whistle to the press, he tried to lead a change to stop the launching of flights with unsafe O-rings. He worked with his immediate supervisor, the director of engineering, and the organization in leading this change. He wrote a draft of a memo to Bob Lund, vice-president of engineering, which he first showed and discussed with his immediate supervisor to "maintain good relationships." Boisjoly and others developed potential win-win solutions, such as investigating remedies to fix the O-rings and refraining from launching flights at too-low temperatures. He effectively established a team to study the matter, and participated in a teleconference with 130 technical experts.

On the day before the Challenger launch, Boisjoly and other team members were successful in leading company executives to reverse their tentative recommendation to launch because the overnight temperatures were predicted to be too low. The company recommendation was to launch only when temperatures were above 53 degrees. To this point, Boisjoly was very effective in leading a change toward what he and other engineering and management people believed was a safe and ethical decision.

However, according to testimony from Boisjoly and others to Congress, the top managers of Morton Thiokol, under pressure from NASA, reversed their earlier recommendation not to launch. The next day, Challenger was launched and exploded, causing the deaths of all the crew members. While Boisjoly was very effective in leading a change within his own organization, he was not able to counteract subsequent pressure from the customer, NASA.

2. Dan Phillips and Genco, Inc.[20] Dan Phillips was a paper products group division manager for Genco, whose upper-level management adopted a strategy whereby several mills, including the Elkhorn Mill, would either have to reduce costs or close down. Phillips was concerned that cost cutting at Elkhorn would prevent the mill from meeting government pollution-control requirements, and that closing the mill could seriously hurt the local community. If he reduced costs, he would not meet pollution-control requirements; if he did not reduce costs, the mill would close and the community would suffer.

Phillips did not secretly or publicly blow the whistle, nor did he sabotage, conscientiously object, quietly refrain from implementing the plan, or quit; however, he did lead a change in the organization's ethical behavior. He asked research and development people in his division to investigate how the plant could both become more cost efficient and create less pollution. He then asked operations people in his division to estimate how long it would take to put such a new plant design on line, and how much it would cost. He asked cost accounting and financial people within his division to estimate when such a new operation would achieve a breakeven payback. Once he found a plan that would work, he negotiated a win-win solution with upper-level management: in exchange for not closing the plant and increasing its investment in his division, the organization would over time benefit from lower costs and higher profitability. Phillips thus worked with others and the organization to lead an inquiry and adopt an alternative ethical and cost-effective plan.

3. Lotus and Brazilian Software Importing.[21] Lotus, a software manufacturer, found that in spite of restrictions on the importing of much of its software to Brazil, many people there were buying and using Lotus software. On further investigation, the company discovered that Brazilian businessmen, in alliance with a Brazilian general, were violating the law by buying Lotus software in Cambridge, Massachusetts and bringing it into Brazil.

Instead of blowing the whistle on the illegal behavior, sabotaging it, or leaving Brazil, Lotus negotiated a solution: In exchange for the Brazilians' agreement to stop illegal importing, Lotus helped set them up as legitimate licensed manufacturers and distributors of Lotus products in Brazil. Instead of working against them and the Lotus salespeople supplying them, the Lotus managers worked with these people to develop an ethical, legal, and economically sound solution to the importing problem.

And in at least a limited sense, the importers may have been transformed into ethical managers and business peo-

ple. This case may remind you of the legendary "Old West," where government officials sometimes negotiated win-win solutions with "outlaw gunfighters," who agreed to become somewhat more ethical as appointed sheriffs. The gunfighters needed to make a living, and many were not interested in or qualified for such other professions as farming or shopkeeping. In some cases, ethical behavior may take place before ethical beliefs are assumed.

4. Insurance company office/sales manager and discrimination.[22] The sales-office manager of a very large Boston-area insurance company tried to hire female salespeople several times, but his boss refused to permit the hires. The manager could have acted against his boss and the organization by secretly threatening to blow the whistle or actually blowing the whistle, publicly or secretly. Instead, he decided to try to lead a change in the implicit hiring policy of the organization.

The manager asked his boss why he was not permitted to hire a woman. He learned that his boss did not believe women made good salespeople and had never worked with a female salesperson. He found that reasoning with his boss about the capabilities of women and the ethics and legality of refusing to hire women was ineffective.

He inquired within the company about whether being a woman could be an advantage in any insurance sales areas. He negotiated with his boss a six-month experiment whereby he hired on a trial basis one woman to sell life insurance to married women who contributed large portions of their salaries to their home mortgages. The woman he hired was not only very successful in selling this type of life insurance, but became one of the office's top salespeople. After this experience, the boss reversed his policy of not hiring female salespeople.

Limitations to Leading Ethical Organizational Change

In the four cases described above, the individuals did not attack the organization or people within the organization, nor did they intervene against individuals and/or the organization to stop an unethical practice. Instead, they worked with people in the organization to build a more ethical organization. As a result of their leadership, the organizations used more ethical behaviors. The strategy of leading an organization toward more ethical behavior, however, does have some limitations. These are described below.

1. In some organizational situations, ethical win-win solutions or compromises may not be possible. For example, in 1975 a pharmaceutical company in Raritan, New Jersey decided to enter a new market with a new product.[23] Grace Pierce, who was then in charge of medical testing of new products, refused to test a new diarrhea drug product on infants and elderly consumers because it contained high levels of saccharin, which was feared by many at the time to be a carcinogen. When Pierce was transferred, she resigned. The drug was tested on infant and elderly consumers. In this case, Pierce may have been faced with an either-or situation that left her little room to lead a change in organizational behavior.

Similarly, Errol Marshall, with Hydraulic Parts and Components, Inc.,[24] helped negotiate the sale of a subcontract to sell heavy equipment to the U.S. Navy while giving $70,000 in kickbacks to two materials managers of Brown &

Root, Inc., the project's prime contractor. According to Marshall, the prime contractor "demanded the kickbacks. . . . It was cut and dried. We would not get the business otherwise." While Marshall was not charged with any crime, one of the upper-level Brown & Root managers, William Callan, was convicted in 1985 of extorting kickbacks, and another manager, Frank DiDomenico, pleaded guilty to extorting kickbacks from Hydraulic Parts & Components, Inc. Marshall has left the company. In this case, it seems that Marshall had no win-win alternative to paying the bribe. In some situations it may not be possible to lead a win-win ethical change.

2. Some people do not understand how leadership can be applied to situations that involve organizational-ethics issues. Also, some people — particularly those in analytical or technical professions, which may not offer much opportunity for gaining leadership experience — may not know how to lead very well in any situation. Some people may be good leaders in the course of their normal work lives, but do not try to lead or do not lead very well when ethical issues are involved. Some people avoid discussing ethical, religious, and political issues at work.

For example, John Geary was a salesman for U.S. Steel when the company decided to enter a new market with what he and others considered an unsafe new product.[25] As a leading salesman for U.S. Steel, Geary normally was very good at leading the way toward changes that satisfied customer and organizational needs. A good salesman frequently needs to coordinate and spearhead modifications in operations, engineering, logistics, product design, financing, and billing/payment that are necessary for a company to maintain good customer relationships and sales. Apparently, however, he did not try to lead the organization in developing a win-win solution, such as soliciting current orders for a later delivery of a corrected product. He tried only reasoning against selling the unsafe product and protested its sale to several groups of upper-level engineers and managers. He noted that he believed the product had a failure rate of 3.6% and was therefore both unsafe and potentially damaging to U.S. Steel's longer-term strategy of entering higher technology/profit margin businesses. According to Geary, even though many upper-level managers, engineers, and salesmen understood and believed him, "the only desire of everyone associated with the project was to satisfy the instructions of Henry Wallace [the sales vice-president]. No one was about to buck this man for fear of his job."[26] The sales vice-president fired Geary, apparently because he continued to protest against sale of the product.

Similarly, William Schwartzkopf of Commonwealth Electric Co.[27] did not think he could either ethically reason against or lead an end to the large-scale, long-time bid rigging between his own company and many of the largest U.S. electrical contractors. Even though he was an attorney and had extensive experience in leading organizational changes, he did not try to lead his company toward an ethical solution. He waited until he retired from the company, then wrote a secret letter to the Justice Department accusing the contractors of raising bids and conspiring to divide billions of dollars of contracts among themselves.

Many people — both experienced and inexperienced in leadership — do not try to lead their companies toward developing solutions to ethical problems. Often, they do not understand that it is possible to lead such a

change; therefore, they do not try to do so — even though, as the cases here show, many succeed when they do try.

3. Some organizational environments — in both consensus-building and authoritarian types of cultures — discourage leadership that is nonconforming. For example, as Robert E. Wood, former CEO of the giant international retailer Sears, Roebuck, has observed, "We stress the advantages of the free enterprise system, we complain about the totalitarian state, but in our individual organizations we have created more or less a totalitarian system in industry, particularly in large industry."[28] Similarly, Charles W. Summers, in a *Harvard Business Review* article, observes, "Corporate executives may argue that . . . they recognize and protect . . . against arbitrary termination through their own internal procedures. The simple fact is that most companies have not recognized and protected that right."[29]

David Ewing concludes that "It [the pressure to obey unethical and illegal orders] is probably most dangerous, however, as a low-level infection. When it slowly bleeds the individual conscience dry and metastasizes insidiously, it is most difficult to defend against. There are no spectacular firings or purges in the ranks. There are no epic blunders. Under constant and insistent pressure, employees simply give in and conform. They become good 'organization people.' "[30]

Similar pressures can exist in participative, consensus-building types of cultures. For example, as mentioned above, Yoshino and Lifson write, "A Japanese leader, rather than being an authority, is more of a communications channel, a mediator, a facilitator, and most of all, a symbol and embodiment of group unity. Consensus building is necessary to decision making, and this requires patience and an ability to use carefully cultivated relationships to get all to agree for the good of the unit."[31]

The importance of the group and the position of the group leaders as a symbol of the group are revealed in the very popular true story, "Tale of the Forty-Seven Ronin." The tale is about 47 warriors whose lord is unjustly killed. The Ronin spend years sacrificing everything, including their families, in order to kill the person responsible for their leader's death. Then all those who survive the assault killed themselves.

Just as authoritarian top-down organizational cultures can produce unethical behaviors, so can participative, consensus-building cultures. The Japanese novelist Shusaku Endo, in his *The Sea and Poison*, describes the true story of such a problem.[32] It concerns an experiment cooperatively performed by the Japanese Army, a medical hospital, and a consensus-building team of doctors on American prisoners of war. The purpose of the experiment was to determine scientifically how much blood people can lose before they die.

Endo describes the reasoning and feelings of one of the doctors as he looked back at this behavior:

> "At the time nothing could be done. . . . If I were caught in the same way, I might, I might just do the same thing again. . . . We feel that getting on good terms ourselves with the Western Command medical people, with whom Second [section] is so cosy, wouldn't be a bad idea at all. Therefore we feel there's no need to ill-temperedly refuse their friendly proposal and

hurt their feelings. . . . Five doctors from Kando's section most likely will be glad to get the chance. . . . For me the pangs of conscience . . . were from childhood equivalent to the fear of disapproval in the eyes of others — fear of the punishment which society would bring to bear. . . . To put it quite bluntly, I am able to remain quite undisturbed in the face of someone else's terrible suffering and death. . . . I am not writing about these experiences as one driven to do so by his conscience . . . all these memories are distasteful to me. But looking upon them as distasteful and suffering because of them are two different matters. Then why do I bother writing? Because I'm strangely ill at ease. I, who fear only the eyes of others and the punishment of society, and whose fears disappear when I am secure from these, am now disturbed. . . . I have no conscience, I suppose. Not just me, though. None of them feel anything at all about what they did here.' The only emotion in his heart was a sense of having fallen as low as one can fall."[33]

What to Do and How to Be

In light of the discussion of the two approaches to addressing organizational ethics issues and their limitations, what should we do as individuals and members of organizations? To some extent that depends on the circumstances and our own abilities. If we know how to lead, if there's time for it, if the key people in authority are reasonable, and if a win-win solution is possible, one should probably try leading an organizational change.

If, on the other hand, one does not know how to lead, time is limited, the authority figures are unreasonable, a culture of strong conformity exists, and the situation is not likely to produce a win-win outcome, then the chances of success with a leadership approach are much lower. This may leave one with only the choice of using one of the intervention strategies discussed above. If an individual wishes to remain an effective member of the organization, then one of the more secretive strategies may be safer.

But what about the more common, middle range of problems? Here there is no easy prescription. The more win-win potential the situation has, the more time there is, the more leadership skills one has, and the more reasonable the authority figures and organizational cultures are, the more likely a leadership approach is to succeed. If the opposite conditions exist, then forcing change in the organization is the likely alternative.

To a large extent, the choice depends on an individual's courage. In my opinion, in all but the most extreme and unusual circumstances, one should first try to lead a change toward ethical behavior. If that does not succeed, then mustering the courage to act against others and the organization may be necessary. For example, the course of action that might have saved the Challenger crew was for Boisjoly or someone else to act against Morton Thiokol, its top managers, and NASA by blowing the whistle to the press.

If there is an implicitly characteristic American ontology, perhaps it is some version of William James' 1907 *Pragmatism*, which, for better or worse, sees through a lens of interactions the ontologies of being as an individual and being as a part. James explains our situation as follows:

"What we were discussing was the idea of a world growing not integrally but piecemeal by the contributions of its several parts. Take the hypothesis seriously and as a live one. Suppose that the world's author put the case to you before creation, saying: 'If I am going to make a world not certain to be saved, a world the perfection of which shall be conditional merely, the condition being that each several agent does its own 'level best.' I offer you the chance of taking part in such a world. Its safety, you see, is unwarranted. It is a real adventure, with real danger, yet it may win through. It is a social scheme of co-operative work genuinely to be done. Will you join the procession? Will you trust yourself and trust the other agents enough to face the risk? . . . Then it is perfectly possible to accept sincerely a drastic kind of a universe from which the element of 'seriousness' is not to be expelled. Who so does so is, it seems to me, a genuine pragmatist. He is willing to live on a scheme of uncertified possibilities which he trusts; willing to pay with his own person, if need be, for the realization of the ideals which he frames. What now actually are the other forces which he trusts to co-operate with him, in a universe of such a type? They are at least his fellow men, in the stage of being which our actual universe has reached."[34]

In conclusion, there are realistic ethics leadership and intervention action strategies. We can act effectively concerning organizational ethics issues. Depending upon the circumstances including our own courage, we can choose to act and be ethical both as individuals and as leaders. Being as a part and leading ethical change is the more constructive approach generally. However, being as an individual intervening against others and organizations can sometimes be the only short or medium term effective approach.

Acknowledgements

I would like to acknowledge and thank the following people for their help with ideas presented in this article: the members of the Works in Progress Seminar of Boston College particularly Dalmar Fisher, James Gips, John Neuhauser, William Torbert, and the late James Waters; Kenneth Boulding of the University of Colorado; Robert Greenleaf; and, Douglas Steere of Haverford College.

Endnotes

1. Paul Tillich, *The Courage to Be.* New Haven, CT: Yale University Press, 1950.
2. See Endnote 1, page 159.
3. David Ewing, *Freedom Inside the Organization.* New York: McGraw-Hill, 1977.
4. The person blowing the whistle in this case wishes to remain anonymous. See also Elizabeth Neuffer, "GE Managers Sentenced for Bribery," *The Boston Globe*, July 26, 1988, p. 67.
5. Barbara Ley Toffler, *Tough Choices: Managers Talk Ethics.* New York: John Wiley, 1986, pp. 153-169.

6. Richard P. Nielsen, "What Can Managers Do About Unethical Management?" *Journal of Business Ethics*, 6, 1987, 153-161. See also Nielsen's "Limitations of Ethical Reasoning as an Action Strategy," *Journal of Business Ethics*, 7, 1988, pp. 725-733, and "Arendt's Action Philosophy and the Manager as Eichmann, Richard III, Faust or Institution Citizen," *California Management Review*, 26, 3, Spring 1984, pp. 191-201.

7. The person involved wishes to remain anonymous.

8. The person involved wishes to remain anonymous.

9. See Endnote 6.

10. R. Reinhold, "Astronauts Chief Says NASA Risked Life for Schedule," *The New York Times*, 36, 1986, p. 1.

11. Personal conversation and letter with Frank Ladwig,1986. See also Frank Ladwig and Associates' *Advanced Consultative Selling for Professionals*. Stonington, CT.

12. W. G. Glaberson, "Did Searle Lose Its Eyes to a Health Hazard?" *Business Week*, October 14, 1985, pp. 120-122.

13. The person involved wishes to remain anonymous.

14. Andy Pasztor, "Electrical Contractors Reel Under Charges that They Rigged Bids," *The Wall Street Journal*, November 29, 1985, pp. 1, 14.

15. A. Ernest Fitzgerald, *The High Priests of Waste*. New York: McGraw-Hill, 1977.

16. See Endnote 1, pp. 89, 93.

17. M. Y. Yoshino and T. B. Lifson, *The Invisible Link: Japan's Saga Shosha and the Organization of Trade*. Cambridge, MA: MIT Press, 1986.

18. See Endnote 17, p. 178.

19. Roger Boisjoly, address given at Massachusetts Institute of Technology on January 7, 1987. Reprinted in *Books and Religion*, March/April 1987, 3-4, 12-13. See also Caroline Whitbeck, "Moral Responsibility and the Working Engineer," *Books and Religion*, March/April 1987, 3, 22-23.

20. Personal conversation with Ray Bauer, Harvard Business School, 1975. See also R. Ackerman and Ray Bauer, *Corporate Social Responsiveness*. Reston, VA: Reston Publishing, 1976.

21. The person involved wishes to remain anonymous.

22. The person involved wishes to remain anonymous.

23. David Ewing, *Do It My Way or You're Fired*. New York: John Wiley, 1983.

24. E. T. Pound, "Investigators Detect Pattern of Kickbacks for Defense Business," *The Wall Street Journal*, November 14, 1985, pp. 1, 25.

25. See also Geary vs. U.S. Steel Corporation, 319 A. 2nd 174, Supreme Court of Pa.

26. See Endnote 23, p. 86.

27. See Endnote 14.

28. See Endnote 3, p. 21.

29. C. W. Summers, "Protecting All Employees Against Unjust Dismissal," *Harvard Business Review*, 58, 1980, pp. 132-139.

30. See Endnote 3, pp. 216-217.

31. See Endnote 17, p. 187.

32. Shusaku Endo, *The Sea and Poison*. New York: Taplinger Publishing Company, 1972. See also Y. Yasuda, *Old Tales of Japan*. Tokyo: Charles Tuttle Company, 1947.

33. See Endnote 32.

34. William James, *Pragmatism: A New Name for Some Old Ways of Thinking*. New York: Longmans, Green and Co., 1907, p. 290, 297-298.

WHISTLEBLOWERS:
Who's the Real Bad Guy?

JOHN HOLM

BARBARA ETTORRE

The popular notion persists that whistleblowers are crazy and vengeful malcontents.

This goes against overwhelming statistics that show they are well-educated, well-liked and committed employees, generally in middle-to-senior-level posts. Yet, with all too few exceptions, whistleblowers continue to be ostracized and humiliated by the companies they hope to improve. Worse, in more than half of whistleblowing instances, the charges are ignored.

When an employee steps forward and legitimately accuses an organization of wrongdoing, it can bring out the worst in everyone. The hierarchy—right up the line to the CEO and the board, if the allegations are serious enough—may enact one of several scenarios: The company may instigate a cover-up. It could make the whistleblower (instead of the allegations) the issue by trying to discredit the individual. It could retaliate against the whistleblower. Or, in perhaps the most insidious of the lot, the company could pretend to listen, appoint the whistleblower to solve the problem, deny access to needed information—and make the whistleblower the scapegoat when the wrongdoing persists.

Fear of bad publicity, expensive litigation and loss of business can make a company hostile and defensive, usually at the expense of the

Call them tattletales, sneaks, troublemakers. Messengers who bring bad news have traditionally been badly treated by society. Today, most American businesses handle whistleblowers only marginally better.

whistleblower's personal or professional reputation. The individual's coworkers get suspicious and angry because their expertise or ethics may be suspect. The whistleblower's family becomes anxious and insecure: "If we lose that paycheck, what happens to us?"

Then, of course, there is the whistleblower, who has stepped forward to tell the truth, despite a jumble of contradictory emotions and fears. Feelings of disloyalty are at war with those of obligation and, possibly, outrage at something very wrong in the company and frustration that no one seems to want to listen.

If that employee has blown the whistle not only on his or her boss but also on the company by taking the case outside to other authorities or to the media, the harsh truth is that this represents a failure on everybody's part. It means the business had not allowed the normal use of communications from the bottom up and that reporting procedures had not worked—or that the whistleblower had not found them to be receptive.

The sad fact is that in today's supposedly enlightened business world, corporate America continues to treat its whistleblowers poorly. The notion persists that it is disloyal and irresponsible to criticize one's employer, notwithstanding the fact that the company has done wrong. Making matters worse is the thicket of often contradictory state and federal laws and procedures. These can help or hinder the whistleblower in the recovery of damages, in reinstating his or her job—even in addressing the company's wrongdoing itself.

Consider a few whistleblowing cases, some ending more happily than others:

➤ Chester Walsh, a former employee at GE Aircraft Engine, a division of General Electric Company, gathered information for four years to expose a defense contract fraud at the company. Senior company executives and an Israeli general were accused of a scheme to divert U.S. funds in connection with a contract involving Israel's purchase of GE jet engines. Last year, a federal judge awarded Walsh $11.5 million un-der provisions of the False Claims Act, a federal statute permitting employees to sue their employers on behalf of the government and to collect as much as a quarter of the assessments and fines. During the tortuous legal process, Walsh was vilified as an employee just out for the money.

➤ Allan McDonald and Roger Boisjoly, engineers at Morton Thiokol Inc., testified before the Rogers Commission investigating the 1986 Challenger shuttle disaster that there had been ongoing problems with the rocket's O-rings and that they had urged their supervisors and NASA officials to postpone the fatal launch. Following their testimony, the engineers were demoted to menial jobs. Only the intervention of the Commission members got them reinstated.

➤ Billie Garde, a Census Bureau employee in Oklahoma in 1980 and a single mother of two, was ordered by her supervisor to misrepresent civil-service test scores so he could hire incompetents. Garde, a former schoolteacher, also was directed to recruit female ex-students as sex partners for visiting political officials. When she refused and blew the whistle, her manager fired her and helped her ex-husband win custody of the children. Garde eventually regained custody with the help of whistleblower advocates. She attended law school and now, as a Houston attorney, represents whistleblowers.

➤ Last year, an administrative law judge for the U.S. Labor Department found that managers at the Oak Ridge National Laboratory had retaliated against a technician who had expressed concern about radiation exposure there. The worker, Charles D. Varnadore, had undergone colon cancer surgery in 1989 and had subsequently appeared on television to voice distress about the prevalence of cancer among his colleagues and the lax protection against radiation. His supervisors transferred Varnadore to a room full of toxic and radioactive substances and gave him useless work. Martin Marietta Energy Systems, which runs

2. ETHICAL ISSUES AND DILEMMAS: Whistle-Blowing in the Organization

The good news is, there are methods in place at a growing number of corporations for employees to report wrongdoing. The bad news is, businesses usually establish these procedures after someone has blown the whistle—and they continue to mismanage whistleblowing.

the lab for the U.S. Department of Energy, was ordered to pay Varnadore damages, the amount to be set by Labor Secretary Robert B. Reich.

➤ A. Ernest Fitzgerald, an Air Force financial analyst, battled the military because of its wasteful practices during several administrations. President Nixon fired Fitzgerald in 1969 after he exposed a $2 billion overrun in an Air Force contract. (Fitzgerald was reinstated by court order, but it took him until 1982 to be restored to his old job.) He was the kind of civil servant the Pentagon loved to hate: He testified before Congress about $7 claw hammers costing $436 and 25-cent washers purchased for $693 each.

Resentful coworkers christened Fitzgerald and his staff "attic fanatics" because of their cramped upper-floor Pentagon offices.

A Problem, You Say? You're Fired.

Discussions with experts, advocates, human resource professionals and public interest groups about how organizations treat employee whistleblowers illuminate a dismal picture. Other than outright dismissal, retaliation can and does include demotion, false complaints about job performance, reassignment and relocation, assignment of unsympathetic coworkers or supervisors and otherwise making the job difficult, withholding of pension, orders to undergo psychological examination, investigation of finances and personal life, and harassment of family and friends.

"The menu of reprisals is limited only to the imagination," says Thomas Devine, legal director of the Government Accountability Project (GAP), a Washington-based public-interest watchdog group that assists and represents both government and corporate whistleblowers.

Donald R. Soeken, who has been counseling whistleblowers since 1978, puts it directly: "If you blow the whistle on somebody below

you, you'll get a pat on the back. Above you? You'll be fired."

Soeken was a therapist at a public service health clinic when he realized that federal agencies were using fitness-for-duty psychiatric examinations to weed out whistleblowers. The strategy, he found, was to find the individuals eligible for disability discharges, ending their whistleblowing claims. The object was to discredit their testimony and to make them appear crazy. Soeken's subsequent testimony before Congress helped abolish these examinations from some of the federal system, although the practice persists.

While retaliation is still business-as-usual, a surprisingly large number of whistleblowing charges die from benign neglect. "As a proportion, retaliation isn't done in even half the instances," says Marcia P. Miceli, associate dean for academic programs and professor of human resources at Ohio State University. She and a colleague, Indiana University Professor Janet P. Near, have written extensively on whistleblowing, including *Blowing the Whistle* (Lexington Books, 1992).

"The typical response is to ignore the charges," Miceli continues. "Corporations will say there is no merit in them, but corporations need to communicate and explain their actions—even when they do find no merit."

In the midst of such unremitting negatives, surely there must be some ray of hope, some enlightened companies that not only foster communication among employees who are compelled to report problems, but also encourage them to come forward. After all, the past few years have seen a meteoric rise in ethics programs and all the trappings of compliance systems that go into them, including confidential hotlines and employee surveys, ombudspersons and neutral-party inspector generals. Then, why is whistleblowing still treated as it was in the Dark Ages?

To answer this, we need to ponder some of the larger ideas that motivate ethical behavior in America.

The United States has been weaned on the notion that there are no moral absolutes, that whatever works is true or right, say the philosophers. We have been conditioned to think that what may be right for one person may not necessarily be right for another. Human beings, say the behaviorists, are products of genetics and environment, with little or no self-determination. The only thing meaningful is what you can measure.

"Put this all together and you have a picture that leaves out the immeasurables of ethics,

"WOULD I DO IT AGAIN? YOU BET"

When Robert A. Bugai realized that he would have to blow the whistle in the early '80s, he made a "premeditated and deliberate" decision to learn about what he was getting into. "I took the time to find out," says Bugai, 37. "I researched whistleblowing at the library. I sat down and considered the cost—mentally, financially, physically, emotionally and spiritually."

When Bugai decided to go ahead, he blew the whistle on college marketers, which he figures is currently a $140 million market. These are firms hired by advertising agencies to get their clients' products and services (credit cards, car rentals, periodicals, grooming aids, dorm room supplies, apparel) to college students.

Beginning as a student in 1974, Bugai worked on a commission basis for various college marketing firms, supplying placards, posters, product samples, magazines, stand-up card displays and other ad tools to be placed on college campuses. Trouble was, Bugai had found the products and ad messages weren't reaching the intended audience.

Bugai found that campus representatives were filling out job completion forms—while posters and other sales materials and samples languished undistributed in campus storage closets and basements and empty vandalized merchandise racks went unrepaired and unfilled. Posters were ripped off bulletin boards and were not replaced. College newspaper organizations, which had payment contracts with marketers for inserting their clients' ads in newspapers, were not being paid.

Bugai went back to the library, taught himself investigative techniques and went to the clients, documenting his charges with photographs and legitimately retrieved samples, many of them bearing original wrappings and shipping documents. Twice he was taken to court by the marketers, but both cases were settled before trial. When threatened with a court action, Bugai would write a polite thank-you letter saying how honored he was to have such a formidable opponent. "I wasn't going to be nasty," he says. "I wanted to give positive reinforcement to other whistleblowers."

In 1985, Bugai made his expertise formal by founding College Marketing Intelligence, based in North Arlington, N.J., offering advice, competitive intelligence and marketing programs on his own. "I would encourage people who are thinking of being whistleblowers to think about the real cost involved," he says. "Would I do it again? You bet."

—B.E.

religion and aesthetics," says W. Michael Hoffman, director of the Center for Business Ethics at Bentley College and a professor of philosophy. "Ethics are a matter of personal, rather than community, choice. A lot of society works on the myth that 'telling on someone is bad.'"

Professor Hoffman goes on to say that shared accountability and responsibility as part of an organization are not valued today. The American corporation has operated on the basis of goals set from the top, with little input from below. Employees have been encouraged to put their shoulders to the wheel and not to complain. There are signs that this mentality is slowly changing: increased corporate interest in participatory management, flattened hierarchies, work teams and shared goals. But it will be decades before these elements shape and define the typical organization.

Meanwhile, a whistleblower persists as someone who tattles and who presumes to judge the whole organization, causing resentment of supervisors and coworkers alike. In fact, a whistleblower's colleagues often can be the biggest problem—stonewalling any investigation of the charges, for example, or shunning the whistleblower and spreading rumors about the individual's professional or personal life. It is not without irony that in some companies, employees have taken to calling the ethics hotline "1-800-RAT-FINK."

Hero or Tattletale?

"We need to begin to turn tattletales into moral heroes," Professor Hoffman declares.

The epithets of "rat fink," "tattletale" and "snitch" notwithstanding, it would certainly seem that the concept of shared responsibility moves enough people to come forward and blow the whistle when they see something wrong in their workplace. Statistics aren't reliable, but there are arguably at least several hundred thousand whistleblowing incidents annually, in all walks of organizational life—ranging from the "I think my coworker is stealing office supplies" calls to the ethics hotline, to full-blown charges of widespread fraud with documentation quietly accumulated over several years.

Understandably, most lesser whistleblowing charges do not reach the media because they are not grievous and, in the best cases, are handled by companies' ethical compliance programs. But serious whistleblowing can go unreported because, under pressure, whistleblowers recant their allegations, for instance, or because they become too discouraged or intimidated.

Clearly, whistleblowing presents knotty problems for the manager. If, however, an organization really wants to encourage its employees to come forward with critical disclosures, there are ways to make the process easier, say the experts. Companies must begin to set up a climate conducive to responsible whistleblowing. One big step, suggested by Miceli, is to select an arbiter who is highly trusted by all and who is visible.

Additionally, what steps to take when reporting wrongdoing and what evidence is needed should be laid out for every employee to know—preferably in writing, with input from all levels. If issues arise, they should be resolved in a timely way. Companies should communicate to all workers the actions they took and why. When appropriate, whistleblowers should be praised and rewarded for their actions. In turn, employees need to be apprised of their rights and ethical responsibilities as members of an organization.

"I'm an optimistic person," says Professor Miceli. "If an organization really wants to encourage whistleblowing, there are ways. But, I'm pessimistic, too. I wish I could really see companies doing so."

Legal Aid

Mistreated employees have legal avenues for redress, although many of these laws are enforced by the same systems in which the charges originated. Nevertheless, there are signs that whistleblowers will be afforded some protection from employer reprisals. One of the biggest stumbling blocks has been that whistleblower protection laws have evolved inconsistently. There is no coherent body of law that protects all whistleblowers—state, municipal, federal and corporate (both public and private companies), says GAP's Devine. And, some laws protect better than others. As Devine says, "With or without legal changes, it is a fact of life that when you bite the hand that feeds you, it tends to slap you, at the least."

This may be alleviated by a bill expected to be introduced by Representative Patsy T. Mink (D-Hawaii) this spring. The proposal attempts to be a comprehensive whistleblowing code for corporate, municipal, federal and state employees who are alleging violations of federal law. Some 200 companies and public policy groups have petitioned Congress to extend whistleblowing protection.

Mink's proposal stipulates a due process hearing by a U.S. Department of Labor administrator. Also, the case must be adjudicated by legal standards of the Whistleblower Protection Act of 1989. In part, it says that if an employee alleges he or she was discriminated against because of whistleblowing as a contributing factor, the employer has to prove legitimate independent grounds for its actions. Additionally, when a whistleblower files a reprisal complaint, the allegations of wrongdoing will simultaneously be forwarded to law enforcement and federal agencies for investigation.

IF YOU ARE BLOWING THE WHISTLE

There is a wealth of advice available from ex-whistleblowers, counsellors and advocates. The following strategies are from the Government Accountability Project:

➤ Talk everything over first with your family or loved ones.

➤ In a non-accusatory manner, first try to work within the system, involving several layers of management, before going outside the organization. Be aware that sounding the alarm may trigger a cover-up.

➤ Develop a specific record—keep a factual log, documenting both wrongdoing and any harassment you receive.

➤ Make a detailed memorandum for the record, when you need a permanent record of an important event or conversation. Sign it, date it, and, if possible, have someone witness it. If you believe your word will be challenged, you can apply the "poor person's copyright": mail a copy to yourself, and keep it, unopened, until it is needed.

➤ Pinpoint and copy key records before drawing attention to your allegations. You may be denied access later.

➤ Create a larger support circle, a constituency of those outside the organization who would benefit from the exposure of your allegations.

➤ Seek the help of specialists, organizations that assist whistleblowers.

Congress is slowly showing some muscle. Last year it refused to re-authorize the U.S. Office of Special Counsel. It was created in 1978, ostensibly to assist federal employee whistleblowers, but the OSC had been widely criticized for hampering and intimidating them over the years.

Yet, the False Claims Act has been criticized as counterproductive because it provides monetary incentives to employees to bypass internal reporting systems, while the Federal Sentencing Guidelines require corporations to set up these systems. In addition, recent amendments to the act have stipulated that if wrongdoing isn't reported immediately, the whistleblower has less of a right to share in eventual damages.

Here's What You Get

What happens to whistleblowers after the fact? It is like getting a divorce, says Mary Louise Cohen, a partner at Washington-based Phillips, Cohen & Goldstein, and an advocate for whistleblowers in false claims cases. "They may have had 25 years at the company. They give up their identities and fulfilling relationships."

Counsellor Soeken and other experts advise whistleblowers to leave their careers and to start fresh in other lines of work—because their actions have effectively blacklisted them. Most whistleblowers, while avowing they would sound the alarm again under the same circumstances, would rather never have gone

through the turmoil, even if they were vindicated and if they received millions of dollars in settlement. They wish the occasion to blow the whistle—the wrongdoing—had never occurred.

But at least one whistleblower says he wouldn't do it again. In 1975, William C. Bush, then a 50-year-old aerospace engineer in the National Aeronautics and Space Administration (NASA), challenged agency policies that kept workers inactive. Threatened with dismissal, Bush saw his grade level reduced and his salary cut by $10,000. He was eventually given a clerical job. It took more than three years for him to be reinstated.

Bush also blew the whistle on a private NASA directive (later rescinded) disallowing executive leadership training programs for employees after age 40. Eventually, the Supreme Court ruled 9-0 against Bush, saying that federal employees did not have the constitutional right to blow the whistle.

Bush retired from NASA in 1986 and now suffers from several stress-related illnesses he says were brought on by continual harassment. One of the country's best-known former whistleblowers, he has maintained a support network for others and has pleaded their causes to members of Congress, the press and concerned organizations. Although less active now, Bush says he still receives a couple calls a week from whistleblowers.

"Hell, no, I wouldn't do it again," Bush asserts. "I ruined my life, my wife's life. And, I wouldn't do it anonymously, either. There is no protection whatsoever."

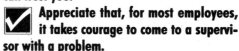

WORKBOOK

Few managers are ever comfortable hearing from their subordinates that a problem exists in the company. As a manager, how can you develop an atmosphere in which it would be likely your people will come to you if they know of wrongdoing? Here are a few timeless suggestions:

 Don't play favorites, above or below you.

 Keep an open-door policy so that your staff knows you are available and accessible. Ivory towers have fallen; you should already be listening to your people every day.

 Maintain confidentiality on unimportant matters; when important matters come along, your employees will know they can trust you.

Appreciate that, for most employees, it takes courage to come to a supervisor with a problem.

Investigate all allegations, and if appropriate, act on them. Document what you do and communicate your actions to the employee.

Show by example that you believe ethics are paramount.

Implementing Business Ethics

Patrick E. Murphy

Patrick E. Murphy is an Associate Professor of Marketing in the College of Business Administration at the University of Notre Dame. He is coeditor of Marketing Ethics: Guidelines for Managers, *Lexington Books, 1985 (with G. R. Laczniak). His articles on ethics have appeared in* Journal of Marketing, Review of Marketing *and* Advances in Marketing and Public Policy. *Professor Murphy currently serves as editor of the* Journal of Public Policy and Marketing.

ABSTRACT. This article outlines an approach for *implementing* business ethics. A company should both organize for ethical business policies and execute them. The organizational dimension refers to structural components including codes of ethics, conferences and training programs and an ethical audit. The corporate culture must support these structural elements with top management playing a central role in implementing ethics.

The execution of ethical business policies includes implementation responsibilities and tasks. These responsibilities are leadership in ethics, delegation, communication and motivation of the company's ethical position to employees. Execution tasks are delineated for the marketing function. Although many company examples are provided, a program in place at McDonnell Douglas is highlighted as a model of ethics implementation.

Introduction

Most organizations have learned that it is not enough to have a well designed corporate strategy in place. Equally important is to be able to *implement* this strategy. In fact, one projection is that only about ten percent of all strategies are effectively implemented. If implementation is to succeed, the entire organization must be committed to the strategy and even the smallest detail should not be overlooked. The same is true with ethics. Implementing ethics is not just a concern of managers setting the firm's overall strategic direction, but should pervade all levels of the business.

Recent events concerning unethical business practices not only on Wall Street, but also in many other places, appear to highlight the lack of attention to implementation of ethical policies. The existence of a carefully defined ethical code does not guarantee ethical behavior. A good example is General Electric (GE). The company has long had a formal, written code of conduct that is communicated to employees and perceives itself as a leader in subscribing to ethical business practices. Yet, GE ran into trouble in 1985 for having time cards forged at a Pennsylvania defense plant. This situation caused a suspension of new defense contracts for a time and much embarrassment for the firm. More recently, their Kidder Peabody subsidiary was implicated in the insider trading scandal even though GE was assured before their June, 1986 acquisition of Kidder that the firm faced no major problems with the SEC or Justice Department. These events lead to a management shake-up at Kidder. GE found that it is quite difficult to implement ethics in their far flung range of businesses.

What can be done to make sure that ethical policies are implemented and that the firm will steer clear of wrongdoings that result in legal problems and/or bad press? The answer is not an easy one. This article outlines steps that companies might use in carrying out ethical business practices. Implementing business ethics involves organizing for and executing ethical policies.[1] The organizational aspects of implementation are covered initially and then we will turn our attention to executing ethical strategies.

This paper takes a pragmatic, rather than a philosophical, approach to examining ethics. The manager is pulled from several directions — personal, organizational and market — in reconciling ethical dilemmas.[2] Making good moral judgments requires frank discussions and ethical sensitivity. This point was well articulated by B. H. McCoy (1983): "In contrast to philosophy, business involves action and implementation — getting things done. Managers must come up with answers to problems based on what they see and what they allow to influence their decision making process."

Organizing for ethical business policies

Figure 1 lists the organizational dimensions of business ethics and procedures that will bring about the implementation of ethical company practices. *Structure* refers to formal organizational mechanisms that foster ethical decisions. *Culture* pertains to the informal organizational climate.

Structure

Corporate codes have long been viewed as the major organizational structure in which to implement ethical policy. Research indicates that approximately 90 percent of *Fortune 500* firms and almost half of all companies have codes in place (Center for Business Ethics, 1986; Murphy, 1986). Several writers, the first being the late Ted Purcell, S. J. (1978), have viewed ethical codes as the cornerstone to "institutionalizing" ethics. However, codes of conduct continue to be criticized as being too general, containing too many platitudes, serving purely as public relations ploys or being designed strictly to avoid legal problems (Berenbeim, 1987; Wartzman, 1987). Cressey and

---

Organizing for Ethical Business Policies

Structure: the formal organization

  Corporate codes
    Specific
    Public documents
    Blunt and realistic
    Revised periodically

  Committees, conferences
  and training

  Ethical audit
  questions

Culture: the informal organization

  Open and candid

  Management role

- -

Executing Ethical Business Policies

Implementation responsibilities

  Leadership
  Delegation
  Communication
  Motivation

Implementation tasks

  Product alteration
  Price negotiation
  Place determination
  Promotion presentation

Fig. 1. Implementing business ethics.

Moore (1983) found that codes give more attention to unethical conduct likely to decrease firm's profits than to conduct that might increase profits. After closely examining over 50 corporate codes of ethics, several observations can be offered.

If codes, are to serve as a foundation for implementation, they should possess the characteristics listed in the Figure 1. Corporate codes should be *specific*. Employees need guidance in interpreting their actions. Motorola gives specific examples (i.e., A Motorolan traveling on Motorola business may accept the courtesy of free lodging in a customer facility so long as properly noted on the Motorolan's expense records) after each of the sections of its code. IBM lists three types of activities — mandatory, acceptable and unacceptable — in its Business Conduct Guidelines.

An area needing specificity is gifts and entertainment. Several companies state that employees can give or receive gifts of "nominal," "token" or "modest" value. However, it is very difficult to determine what is nominal or token and when a gift becomes a bribe. A number of companies have made their codes more specific in this area. Ford and GM stipulate that employees cannot give or receive gifts exceeding $25. Waste Management defines nominal value as "not exceeding $100 in aggregate annual value." Donnelly Mirrors gives the following guidelines: "If you can't eat it, drink it or use it up in one day, don't give it or anything else of greater value."

Second, codes should be *public documents*. Some corporate codes are exclusively for internal corporate use. If a code is worth developing, it should demonstrate to customers, suppliers, stockholders and others interested in the company the organization's commitment to fair and ethical practice.

Corporate codes should also be *blunt and realistic about violations*. For example, Baxter's code states that violators will be terminated. Gellerman (1986) indicated that the most effective deterrent is not to increase the severity of the punishment, but to "heighten the perceived probability of being caught." Therefore, active enforcement of existing codes should enhance compliance. Firms also need to consider how employees should react when confronted with violations of the code. Several codes instruct them to talk to their supervisor. Difficulties arise when the supervisor is the violator. Marriott tells employees to "see your manager or department head" if the issue cannot be resolved with the immediate supervisor.

Finally, codes should be *revised periodically*. That is, they should be living documents and updated to reflect current ethical problems. Caterpillar has revised its code three times since 1974. Investment banking firms likely would want to revise their codes in light of recent events. Specifically, Goldman Sachs now lists fourteen business principles and the last one states: "Integrity and honesty are at the heart of our business. We expect our people to maintain high ethical standards in everything they do, both at work for the firm and in their personal lives." This point probably should be placed much higher on the list and given greater emphasis in future revisions.

Ethics committees, training and conferences are a second structural method for implementing ethical business policies (see Figure 1). Only 15 percent of firms have ethics modules in their training programs and about 30 percent discuss ethics in management or policy sessions (Murphy, 1986). Motorola has a Business Ethics Compliance Committee that is charged with interpreting, clarifying, communicating and ajudicating the company's code. Some firms have used ethical consultants or speakers at dealer meetings on ethics. Cummins Engine for a time had an in-house ethicist. Polaroid held day long in-house conferences on ethics in '83 and '84 as part of a major ethics program.[3]

The Drackett Company, a subsidiary of Bristol Myers, recently implemented an ethics module in their 1987 Market Research Conference. Attendees at the meeting submitted in advance their responses to sixteen ethical scenarios. During the meeting small groups met to discuss three of the eleven scenarios where there was the greatest disagreement. According to the manager who led this activity, it was enthusiastically received. Many of the participants were surprised by their colleagues' judgments, but enjoyed the interchange in analyzing these issues.

Another structural suggestion for implementing business ethics listed in Figure 1 is an ethical audit. Just as financial and marketing audits seek to gain information about these functions, an ethical audit would pose questions about manufacturing practices, personnel policies, dealings with suppliers, financial reporting and sales techniques to find out if ethical abuses may be occurring. It might be argued that the answers to such questions are less important than raising and grappling with the issues.

Dow Corning instituted a face-to-face audit in their firm over ten years ago at company locations throughout the world. The agenda has shifted over the years from a standard one of 8—10 items for each site to a tailored discussion of specific questions about functional areas. At sales offices, issues such as kickbacks, unusual requests from customers and special pricing terms are examined. John Swanson, who heads this effort as Manager of the Corporate Internal and Management Communications Division, explained that the benefit of their innovative audit approach is "to make it virtually impossible for employees to consciously make an unethical decision."[4] Swanson (1987) indicated that twenty-one meetings were led by one of the four Business Conduct Committee members in '86—'87 and a report was prepared for the Audit Committee of the Board. He emphasized that there are no shortcuts to implementing this program and it requires time and extensive interaction of the people involved.

Culture

The informal organization or corporate culture is the second component of the organizational dimension of ethics implementation (see Figure 1). Some commentators have indicated that the informal organization is much more important in the development of the firm's ethical posture than the formal organization. The informal organization creates the culture and formal policies are then a reflection of that culture. It works well at Hewlett-Packard, where the firm follows policies of liberal health benefits and no layoffs, because Bill Hewlett and David Packard want to remain true to the ideals on which the firm was founded. On the negative side, the recent revelations of nepotism and bribe taking by executives at Anheuser Busch was at least partially explained by observers who criticized the Busch family for perpetuating a corporate culture that condoned these activities. Therefore, the informal organization must reward ethical activities and give signals to managers that the company is committed to integrity in all business dealings.

A candid and ethical culture is one where communication freely flows within the organization (Serpa, 1985). This type of culture can help to reduce "moral stress" (Waters and Bird, 1987) and achieve "moral excellence" (Hoffman, 1986). A number of individuals including a CEO of a Big Eight accounting firm have advocated this approach to dealing with ethical problems. A climate where ethical issues can be openly discussed can lead to this type of culture. Spending time in management meetings is one avenue that has been used effectively. This sort of ethical training should ideally occur before problems arise and not after the fact such as the instance of E. F. Hutton and General Dynamics

contracting with the Ethics Resource Center for ethics training after running into serious problems.

The role of top management is crucial in creating the culture of an organization. The tone starts at the top. The CEO and other Vice-President level executives are extremely important in setting the ethical tenor of the firm.

Executing ethical business policies

Figure 1 also shows the two components of the executing phase of business ethics implementation. It is not enough to have the structure and culture that support ethical decision making. These organizational dimensions must be combined with implementation responsibilities and tasks so that a firm is ethical in its execution of strategies.

Implementation responsibilities

Although there are four execution responsibilities listed in the Figure, the over-arching one is leadership. As Bennis and Nanus (1986) have stated: American corporations are over-managed and under-led. Leadership is important in all aspects of the business, but it is critical in the ethics area.[5] Horton (1986) examined characteristics of CEOs and listed integrity as an "indispensible ingredient." A good example is James Burke of Johnson & Johnson who had managers evaluate the J & J Credo (which is often given as the reason for the swift and ethical reaction to the Tylenol poisonings). Basically, they reaffirmed the company's longstanding commitment to ethical business practice. A recent illustration is Lee Iacocca's stance regarding Chrysler's questionable practice of disconnecting odometers during testing by executives. He admitted that the company made mistakes in judgment and set forth a program to rectify them and promised that they would not happen again in a two page national ad. Mr. Iacocca did not view this as a product recall, but added "the only thing we're recalling here is our integrity."

Delegation follows from leadership, but is an essential responsibility for effective implementation to occur. Middle and lower level managers are sometimes placed in difficult ethical situations because high level executives are unclear in their delegation of ethical responsibilities. Statements such as "I don't care how you do it, just meet or beat your quota" or "Ship more to that customer this month than you did last" or "Find a way to fire that person" often give subordinates the impression that any tactic can be used to reach organizational objectives. Several years ago managers in a truck plant installed a secret control box to override the speed of the assembly line because they felt it was the only way to achieve production objectives set by upper management. If the delegation responsibility is to be dispatched properly, executives must be more explicit about what are acceptable and ethical practices.

Communication is an essential responsibility if ethical policies are to be executed in any organization. Formally, this communication can happen in many ways through the ethical code and seminars/training programs that deal with ethical issues. New employees of most companies are asked to read and sign the ethical code upon their employment. In many instances, however, little communication follows the initial exposure. To overcome this potential problem, Caterpillar requires its managers to report annually about its implementation of the code within the division/department. Similarly, Michigan National Bank requires that employees sign off on the ethical code every year.

Informal communication is also a potentially effective implementation responsibility. The grapevine can disseminate information that formal vehicles cannot. For instance, the fact that a salesperson lost his/her commission for padding the expense account may not lend itself to discussion in the company newsletter. However, the word can get through informal channels and consequently influence future behavior.

The last, but certainly the not the least important, implementation responsibility is motivation. If companies are to be successful in executing ethical marketing policies, individuals must be motivated to do the right thing. This means that higher level executives must look closely at how performance is measured. Managers who engage in exorbitant entertaining of clients or informally practice discrimination should not be rewarded for these activities. One of the problems with the Wall Street scandal was that top managers did not look closely at the large profits their firms were earning. How did these large returns happen? Unfortunately, we know the answer in many cases. Employees are motivated by higher level executives and their expectations regarding ethical business practices.

Implementation tasks

Implementation tasks relate to specific functional areas within the firm. One area that has received

much attention in the academic and popular press is marketing implementation (Bonoma, 1984; Enis and Murphy, 1987; Peters and Waterman, 1982). Since marketing is charged with external relations with customers where many ethical issues arise, it will serve as the focal point for this discussion. Other functional areas could be treated similarly. For example, if human resources were the focus, tasks relating to hiring, training and promoting employees would be relevant.

Figure 1 lists the relevant implementation tasks for the marketing mix variables of product, price, channel and promotion. Product alteration is intended to get the consumer to make the intended exchange. Ethical issues result when minor adjustments are promoted as being significant changes to the product. Furthermore, the development of me-too products could be questioned from an ethical standpoint. One other product alteration issue relates to the product manager. Does this person, who is usually on the fast-track, make needed modifications to a brand to insure its long-term marketplace staying power or only perform cosmetic changes to improve next quarter's market share or profit picture?

Price negotiation is often at the heart of marketing implementation. Those sales executives and marketing managers who can effectively negotiate on price win many contracts. An ethical problem occurs in this process when one of the participants has much more power than the other. An example is a large Midwestern department store chain which dealt with a small candy producer and told the company that they would pay 70 percent of the negotiated price and the small firm could keep the account or pay 100 percent and they would lose the account. These types of practices are unethical, but not illegal. They possibly might be curbed by the small firm taking its case to the top echelon of the larger company.

Place determination refers to getting the product to the place it is demanded in an expeditious manner. Here marketers often promise more than they can deliver. It becomes an ethical issue when there is economic or psychological harm to the client/consumer. In health care or other life threatening situations, execution of place determination is critical. Greater emphasis on marketing by these organizations may heighten the ethical problems they face. Furthermore, large retailers may coerce other members of the channel to achieve their objectives in getting products to the market.

Promotion presentation is often viewed as a

crucial function of marketing. Both selling and advertising have persuasive, informative and reminding components. The persuasive area is most often associated with ethical abuses. In selling, ethical problems often arise when persuasion is too intense or competitors are unscrupulous in their appeals. What the ethical salesperson should do is to insure that the buyers are making decisions on what he/she believes are the most important evaluative criteria. If the unethical marketer cannot deliver on their promises, the ethical firm has a good chance to gain the business. Even if the business is lost once, there is sometimes an opportunity to gain it later. For example, a communications firm sought a contract with a defense contractor, but found the defense company only wanted entree to newspaper editors. The consultant indicated that he could not meet these unrealistic goals and ". . . walked out. Several months later he got a $50,000 contract" (Davidson, 1986).

Some companies even identify the types of sales tactics that are acceptable in their firm's code of ethics. For instance, ADP, a computer software company, states: "Aggressive selling should not include defamation of competition, malicious rumors or unsupportable promises." IBM's code makes a similar point: "It has long been the company's policy to provide customers the best possible products and services. Sell them on their merits, not by disparaging competitors."

The advertising area is one where persuasion is often criticized for being unethical. If the message includes puffery, but not deception (which is illegal), then it falls into an ethical gray area. One type of advertising that is receiving growing criticism is advertising to children, especially for war toys and highly sugared products. Furthermore, the current debate about advertising beer and wine on television centers on free speech vs. potential negative effects of product usage on consumers, especially teenagers who find the lifestyles portrayed in these commercials to be rather desirable.

In examining a number of codes of conduct, it was surprising to find that very few list a specific posture with respect to advertising. An exception is Ford which provides explicit policies for the use of comparative advertising. This might be an area where consumer products marketers consider developing explicit guidelines. Some have ad hoc policies regarding sponsorship of shows dealing with sensitive subjects or containing large amounts of sex/violence. It appears that thought should be given to appropriate advertising messages and possibly even

media in implementing the ethical policies of the firm.

An illustration of business ethics implementation

In 1987 one firm, McDonnell Douglas, has engaged in an extensive business ethics implementation program.[6] Their effort even has a theme — "Always take the high road." The corporate code has been revised for the third time in the 1980s. A series of three ethics books were distributed to all employees at their home address in June. The "Code of Ethics" book features ethical decision making guidelines, a short version of their code and the ethical decision making checklist. The latter two are also available in pocket size cards and are shown in Figure 2.

The "Standards of Business Conduct" book lists five overriding standards and several areas pertaining to each of them. Discussion of these standards is treated in three sections — *In General* (states the overall principle), *Specifically* (contains specific rules, laws and requirements applicable to each standard) and *Where to Go* (where to turn to for help). This book concludes with a section on procedures for reporting possible violations including employees' obligation to report, confidentiality and absence of reprisals.

The third book, "Questions and Answers," shows how selected standards apply in potentially difficult work situations through a question and detailed answer format. This publication is written in layman's terms and cross referenced to the longer standards book. The company also has a corporation-wide ethics training program that all management and blue collar employees attend. A seven person ethics committee is formally charged with implementing all facets of the program.

The informal organization is involved in several ways. An extensive ombudsman program is operational as well as a number of instructions to employees to openly discuss and air ethical abuses they see occurring. At the end of the "Questions and Answers" book, employees are asked for their comments or questions on ethical issues. These informal responses are to be returned directly to the Corporate Ethics Committee. Another alternative for responding about ethical problems and violations is a hotline number used exclusively for reports to this committee.

The role of top management is instrumental in making the program work. S. N. "Sandy" McDonnell,

McDONNELL DOUGLAS CODE OF ETHICS

Integrity and ethics exist in the individual or they do not exist at all. They must be upheld by individuals or they are not upheld at all. In order for integrity and ethics to be characteristics of McDonnell Douglas, we who make up the Corporation must strive to be:

- *Honest and trustworthy in all our relationships;*

- *Reliable in carrying out assignments and responsibilities;*

- *Truthful and accurate in what we say and write;*

- *Cooperative and constructive in all work undertaken;*

- *Fair and considerate in our treatment of fellow employees, customers, and all other persons;*

- *Law abiding in all our activities;*

- *Committed to accomplishing all tasks in a superior way;*

- *Economical in utilizing company resources; and*

- *Dedicated in service to our company and to improvement of the quality of life in the world in which we live.*

Integrity and high standards of ethics require hard work, courage, and difficult choices. Consultation among employees, top management, and the Board of Directors will sometimes be necessary to determine a proper course of action. Integrity and ethics may sometimes require us to forgo business opportunities. In the long run, however, we will be better served by doing what is right rather than what is expedient. (From MDC Policy 2, *MDC Policy Manual*).

ETHICAL DECISION MAKING CHECKLIST

Analysis

- *What are the facts?*

- *Who is responsible to act?*

- *What are the consequences of action? (Benefit-Harm Analysis)*

- *What and whose rights are involved? (Rights/Principles Analysis)*

- *What is fair treatment in this case? (Social Justice Analysis)*

Solution development

- *What solutions are available to me?*

- *Have I considered all of the creative solutions which might permit me to reduce harm, maximize benefits, respect more rights, or be fair to more parties?*

Select the optimum solution

- *What are the potential consequences of my solutions?*

- *Which of the options I have considered does the most to maximize benefits, reduce harm, respect rights and increase fairness?*

- *Are all parties treated fairly in my proposed decision?*

Implementation

- *Who should be consulted and informed?*

- *What actions will assure that my decision achieves its intended outcome?*

- *Implement.*

Follow up

- *Was the decision implemented correctly?*

- *Did the decision maximize benefits, reduce harm, respect rights and treat all parties fairly?*

Fig. 2. McDonnell Douglas ethical code and check list.

the former CEO, has been on the forefront in advocating ethical practices in the aerospace industry. He has taken a leadership role as evidenced by the following comment made in 1984:

A company has to go beyond just tacking an ethics code up on the wall. You have to make sure that everyone knows and understands it — from the chairman on down through supervision (Miller 1984);

and this statement which appeared in a 1987 company publication describing his commitment to the current ethics program:

What I hope all this will lead to is a business environment in which the issue of ethics remains in the forefront of everything we do. If we always make the ethical choice, if we always take the high road, we will be doing not only what is right, but also what is best for McDonnell Douglas and ourselves as individuals.

A procedure is delegated and communicated throughout the organization in the form of the company's "ethical decision making" check list in Figure 2. The steps outlined are analysis, solution development, selection of the optimum solution, implementation and follow-up parallel closely those advocated by Nash (1981) several years ago. These mechanisms have motivated employees to become more active in providing comments and suggestions on how ethics can be improved in the firm. This complete ethics implementation program can serve as a model for other companies.[7]

Conclusion

The major premise articulated here is that firms can ethically implement their business strategies. Several conclusions can be drawn.

1. Codes of ethics must be more than legal or public relations documents. They must provide specific and useful guidance to employees. Firms are urged to rethink their codes to make them more viable by including specific practices, examples or answers to often asked ethical questions.

2. Visible signs must exist that ethics matters to the firm. This can be accomplished by spending time in formal meetings discussing ethical issues and working through the corporate culture. Both the carrot and stick methods should be used. Employees should be rewarded for making ethical choices and at the same time the code must be enforced. These actions must be communicated throughout the firm, so that the commitment is understood.

3. Top management must pay attention to detail on how results are accomplished. The same scrutiny should be employed when examining profits as costs. Similarly, management should not give vague or unrealistic goals to subordinates without some explanation of how they are to be attained.

4. Ethics implementation needs a champion. Someone must make it happen. It is essential that the CEO be in support of it, but in companies like McDonnell Douglas and Polaroid the ethics cause had a champion. This is likely most effective if the job title in not solely related to this task.

In implementing business ethics, attention must be paid to both the organizing and executing components (see Figure 1). Only if managers and top executives are consciously committed to carrying out ethical policies will implementation actually occur. Tough questions must be asked and appropriate answers should be given at all levels of the organization. We can improve the ethical posture of business, but everyone must be committed to it.

Notes

The author would like to thank Gerald Cavanagh, S. J., Stephen Greyser, Gene Laczniak, Lee Tavis, Clarence Walton and Oliver Williams, C. S. C. for their helpful comments on an earlier version of this article.

[1] This definition and format of the article are partially adapted from "Marketing Implementation," in Murphy and Enis (1985).
[2] The following discussion of implementing business ethics relies primarily on structural or organization procedures. An alternative approach which focuses on individual responsibilities is outlined by Nielsen (1986).
[3] For a discussion of Polaroid's program, see Godfrey (1987) and Godfrey and Williams (1985).
[4] For more detail on this program, see Swanson (1984) and ("Dow Corning" . . . 1986).
[5] A recent in-depth examination of the ethical leadership issue appeared in Enderle (1987).
[6] McDonnell Douglas is a participant in the eighteen point voluntary industry agreement, "The Defense Industry Initiatives on Business Ethics and Conduct." The company's commitment to ethics is the driving force for this program, not industry or governmental pressure.
[7] Although McDonnell Douglas was implicated in recent U.S. Defense Department contract problems, the company feels that its policies are sound and set up a high level task force to determine whether additional guidelines are needed. The CEO stated: "We want to leave no doubt that McDonnell Douglas believes in and acts in accordance with the highest ethical standards" (Schachter 1988).

References

Bennis, Warren and Bert Nanus: 1985, *Leaders*, New York: Harper & Row.

Berenbeim, Ronald E.: 1987, *Corporate Ethics*, New York: The Conference Board.

Bonoma, Thomas V.: 1984, 'Making Your Marketing Strategy Work', *Harvard Business Review* (March—April), 69—76.

Center for Business Ethics: 1986, 'Are Corporations Institutionalizing Ethics?', *Journal of Business Ethics* 5, 85—91.

Cressey, Donald R. and Charles A. Moore: (1983), 'Managerial Values and Corporate Codes of Ethics', *California Management Review* (Summer), 53—77.

Davidson, Jeffrey P.: 1986, 'The Elusive Nature of Integrity', *Marketing News* (November 7), 24.

'Dow Corning Corporation: Ethics, "Face-to-Face" ': 1986, *Ethics Resource Center Report* (Winter), 4—7.

Enderle, Georges: 1987, 'Some Perspectives of Managerial Ethical Leadership', *Journal of Business Ethics* **6**, 657—663.

Enis, Ben M. and Patrick E. Murphy: 1987, 'Marketing Strategy Implementation', in G. L. Frazier and J. N. Sheth (eds.), *Contemporary Views on Marketing Practice*, Lexington, MA: Lexington Books, pp. 159—173.

Gellerman, Saul W.: 1986, 'Why "Good" Managers Make Bad Ethical Choices', *Harvard Business Review* (July—August), 85—90.

Godfrey, Joline: 1987, 'Ethics as an Entrepreneurial Venture', *Training News* (June).

Godfrey, Joline and R. Williams: 1985, 'Leadership and Values at Polaroid Corporation', unpublished paper.

Hoffman, W. Michael: 1986, 'What Is Necessary for Corporate Moral Excellence?', *Journal of Business Ethics* **5**, 233—242.

Horton, Thomas R.: 1986, *What Works for Me: 16 CEOs Talk About Their Careers and Commitments*, New York: Random House.

McCoy, Bowen H.: 1983, 'The Parable of the Sadhu', *Harvard Business Review* (September—October), 103—108.

Miller, William H.: 1984, 'Business' New Link: Ethics and the Bottom Line', *Industry Week* (October 29), 49—53.

Murphy, Patrick E.: 1986, 'Marketing VPs Views Toward Marketing Ethics', Working Paper, University of Notre Dame.

Murphy, Patrick E. and Ben M. Enis: 1985, *Marketing*, Glenview, IL: Scott-Foresman.

Nash, Laura: 1981, 'Ethics Without the Sermon', *Harvard Business Review*, (November—December), 79—90.

Nielsen, Richard P.: 1987, 'What Can Managers Do about Unethical Management?', *Journal of Business Ethics* **6**, 309—320.

Peters, Thomas J. and Robert H. Waterman, Jr.: 1982, *In Search of Excellence*, New York: Harper & Row.

Purcell, Theodore V., Jr.: 1978, 'Institutionalizing Ethics on Corporate Boards', *Review of Social Economy*, December, 41—53.

Schachter, Jim: 1988, 'McDonnell Douglas to Probe Use of Defense Officials as Consultants', *Los Angeles Times* (August 5, 1988), Part IV, 3.

Serpa, Roy: 1985, 'Creating a Candid Corporate Culture', *Journal of Business Ethics* **4**, 425—430.

Swanson, John E.: 1984, 'Developing a Workable Corporate Ethic', in W. M. Hoffman, J. M. Moore, and D. A. Fedo (eds.), *Corporate Governance and Institutionalizing Ethics*, Lexington, MA: Lexington Books, pp. 209—215.

Swanson, John E.: 1987, Personal communication with the author, June 21.

Wartzman, Rick: 1987, 'Nature or Nurture? Study Blames Ethical Lapses on Corporate Goals', *The Wall Street Journal* (October 9), 21.

Waters, James A. and Frederick Bird: 1987, 'The Moral Dimension of Organizational Culture', *Journal of Business Ethics* **6**, 15—22.

Right vs. wrong

Taking a stand about misconduct at the office isn't easy for newly hired recent graduates

Lori A. Tansey

Ms. Tansey is director of advisory services and a consultant with the Ethics Resource Center Inc. in Washington, D.C.

Dilemma #1: *Degree in hand, you've just landed a dream job in finance and accounting with a Fortune 500 company. But because of several quarters of poor financial results, your boss asks you to make improper changes in the accounting records "to help the company look a little better." Nobody will get hurt, he assures you. "You're just keeping the stockholders happy—and protecting employees' jobs." What should you do?*

* * *

Dilemma #2: *Your friends are envious of your new job as an assistant buyer for a major retail chain. While the salary isn't quite what you'd hoped for, the company gives employees significant discounts on purchases. Suddenly, friends and family members are inundating you with requests to buy things for them using your employee discount. Company policy states, however, that the discounts are for employees only. You think, "Everybody else in the store does this. Besides, who really gets hurt?" But what should you do?*

* * *

Sooner or later, ethical dilemmas like these will confront you at work. Has your college education prepared you to make the right decisions—and accept the consequences?

Many experts don't think so. New grads may have textbook knowledge, but most lack training, in the types of interpersonal interactions that lead to ethical dilemmas.

"Students come into the workplace without knowing what to expect as far as ethics," says Dan Hall, vice president for legal affairs and general counsel for Cordis Corp., a Miami medical device manufacturer.

The majority student view about ethics is perhaps best expressed by Becky Groen, a junior at the University of Utah in Salt Lake City. "I've never really thought about business ethics because I've never been faced with it," she says. "I've never been asked to do something wrong."

For most students, ethics in the workplace takes a back seat to job hunting. "People aren't prepared because you're more worried about getting a job than being ethical on the job," says Dan Dodd, who landed a systems engineering position at Farradyne Systems Inc., a Rockville, Md., engineering firm, after graduating last year from Princeton University in New Jersey.

Although he held several part-time jobs while working his way through school, he says he never had to deal with a major ethical issue, "just minor stuff like [unauthorized] copying of software on someone else's computer."

Ethics at the office

Many new graduates will confront ethics issues at work, however, according to a forthcoming study by the Ethics Resource Center Inc., a nonprofit organization in Washington, D.C. Of 4,000 employees surveyed, 30% admit to feeling pressured to compromise their company's ethical standards because of deadlines, overly aggressive objectives, concerns about the company's survival and other factors.

Additionally, 30% say they personally observed conduct that violated the law or their company's standards in the past year. Frequently mentioned types of misconduct include lying to supervisors, falsifying reports or records, theft and sexual harassment. However, less than half the respondents say they attempted to report their observations to others in the company. Lack of confidentiality in the reporting process and fears of retribution were the main reasons for not reporting.

Ethical issues are particularly difficult for new grads to deal with. Young employees often feel too insecure to risk questioning current practices or reporting their concerns. Thus, they're likely to follow a supervisor's instructions—regardless of the ethical implications. Lack of experience also can make new hires susceptible to such rationalizations as, "That's the way things are done in the real world," or "Everybody does it."

Yet some believe new employees may be more inclined to challenge the status quo. "Younger people are more likely to question practices than older employees," says Hall. "Long-time employees don't take as much time to analyze things."

Others say new hires' reactions can't be generalized. "Ultimately, it depends on the person," says Dodd. "New grads are certainly untrained and naive. But that means their reactions could go either way—to ignore things or to make a fuss about them."

He cites the case of a recent grad who knew a colleague had falsified a time sheet. Her family and friends told her to ignore the problem because the person would eventually get caught. Why should she stick her neck out by reporting her concerns—especially when she had nothing to gain from the situation, they asked. She eventually did nothing, Dodd says.

Is this how companies want employees to handle ethical violations? "No way," says Graydon Wood, vice president of business ethics for NYNEX Corp. in White Plains, N.Y.

His company's code of ethics is based on employees reporting their knowledge and suspicions of unethical activities, Wood says. "If the organization says you have an obligation to report and you don't, then you become a party to the misconduct," he says. "Companies can best protect themselves if ethics issues are analyzed fully and promptly."

Why do ethics matter?

"Businesses increasingly view ethics as an investment vs. a cost—not as an afterthought or a frill, but fundamental to the organization," says Lynn Sharp Paine, associate professor at Harvard Business School in Cambridge, Mass., who has monitored business interest in ethics for a decade. "Concern for ethics and integrity is now

more accepted. Young people should figure out why this has happened and how it affects them, and not write it off."

Indeed, ethics play an important role in developing and maintaining good relationships with customers, stockholders, employees and suppliers. Companies also want to avoid such costs of misconduct as fines, penalties and loss of reputation. Moreover, when corporations regulate themselves, government intervention—which typically results in more regulation, bureaucracy and red tape—is less likely.

The current business environment also is propelling ethics concerns. For instance, downsizing is driving key business decisions lower within organizations. Therefore, companies must have trustworthy employees at all levels who can uphold business standards, says Wood.

"We need people with a strong ethical grounding," he says. "That's even more important in tomorrow's world, particularly in the international environment when you bump up against divergent cultures."

As evidence of this, many companies are factoring ethics into employees' annual performance evaluations and salary reviews, says Paine. Future leaders also are judged for their integrity. "If you do something inappropriate that winds up hurting the company, you can be sure you won't be rewarded, and you can get into a lot of trouble," she says.

Many professional associations also require members to maintain standards that exceed corporate policies or the law. For example, failure to adhere to the International Association of Certified Public Accountants' Code of Ethics can result in a loss of certification.

Teaching ethics

An increasing number of colleges, universities and business schools offer ethics courses designed to prepare students for real-world challenges. Some schools require the courses for graduation, while others are integrating ethics into such functional disciplines as marketing or accounting. And many colleges are proud of their long-established honor codes, under which students are obligated to report unethical behavior.

But the problem with such courses and codes is that they don't address every situation students may encounter at work, says Bruce Barry, assistant professor of management at Vanderbilt University's Owen School of Graduate Management in Nashville, Tenn. "A lot of ethical issues don't have salience to students until they experience them firsthand," he says. "It's very difficult to prepare people for that."

Emphasizing broad-scale business policy issues, rather than day-to-day challenges new hires are likely to face (such as being asked to do something wrong by a supervisor), is another problem with current ethics instruction. For instance, few case studies deal with the situations described at the beginning of this article.

The correct responses appear straightforward: You shouldn't manipulate financial statements or violate company policy. But doing what's right while being pressured to do the contrary is what makes business ethics so difficult.

"Students aren't prepared for the difficulties with what appear to be simple ethics issues," Paine says. "It seems an easy matter to tell the truth, but sometimes actually doing it requires great capabilities. The stakes are so much higher than they've ever had to deal with."

Corporate ethics initiatives

Corporations also are seeking ways to improve employees' responses to ethics issues, either by instituting ethics codes or offering training programs. By 1988, almost all major U.S. corporations had established codes of conduct, while 47% had ethics training programs, according to the Ethics Resource Center.

Employers also are creating ethics offices to help employees with questions about potential misconduct and to provide confidential, sometimes anonymous, channels for reporting it. This safety valve is essential to helping "people come forward—anonymously, confidentially and without fear of reprisals," says Wood at NYNEX.

These offices can serve as sounding boards for new grads to discuss issues they may be embarrassed to bring up with their supervisors, perhaps because they're afraid of looking stupid or causing a commotion.

Handling ethics issues

Before accepting any job, investigate the employer's reputation and financial statements. Working for a company that has a history of poor leadership increases your chances of encountering serious problems. During interviews, don't be afraid to ask questions about the company's values and whether it has an ethics program. Most interviewers will be impressed by your concerns. However, if they seem uncomfortable or unreceptive, it's a clear signal to proceed with caution.

Once you're on the job, if an action or decision doesn't "feel" right, take a second look. The best early warning signals often come from "gut" instincts. To clarify whether an issue is an ethics problem, ask yourself the following:

* **Are my actions fair?** Have I considered how my decision will affect others? Would I be comfortable with my decision if I were an affected party (i.e., customers, stockholders, etc.)?

* **Would I be comfortable reading about this decision in the newspaper?** How would I feel if the action appeared on the front page of The Wall Street Journal or my local paper? Could I explain my decision to my friends, family or the company's senior management?

* **Is it legal?** Many industries are highly regulated and an action may seem acceptable from an ethics perspective, yet be illegal.

If any of your answers to the above questions is "no" or "I don't know," talk to your supervisor. But what if your supervisor is the problem? If your company encourages open communication, talk to your supervisor's manager and continue up the management chain until the problem is satisfactorily resolved.

However, at many firms, it's intimidating for new grads to go over their bosses' heads. In such cases, talk to officials in security, legal, human resources or the ethics office.

Unfortunately, many grads rely on counsel from family and friends who may not have the technical understanding or knowledge of a company's culture to accurately gauge a situation. For instance, the new grad who knew an employee was falsifying time cards was advised by friends to ignore the problem. However, depending on the industry, misreporting time can violate regulations and have serious repercussions.

For many new grads, ethics decisions ultimately are a question of character. Groen at the University of Utah says she couldn't live with herself if she ignored an ethical concern. "If the problem wasn't solved, I'd ultimately quit," she says.

Moreover, "blowing the whistle" doesn't carry the same stigma it once did, says Hall, who recommends that new hires always report or correct unethical conduct within their companies. "Refuse to do the unethical thing," he says. "If that doesn't work, go above your supervisor. Doing the right thing isn't career limiting like it may have been. Business today is really attuned to ethics."

Signs and Signals of Unethical Behavior

John Paul Fraedrich

JOHN PAUL FRAEDRICH, Ph.D., is an assistant professor of marketing at Southern Illinois University, Carbondale, Illinois. His areas of interest include ethical decision making and international marketing. He has published articles in the Journal of Macromarketing, Journal of Business Ethics, Journal of Education for Business, Journal of Value Based Management, *and the* Journal of International Consumer Marketing. *Dr. Fraedrich has also recently co-authored the book* Business Ethics: Ethical Decision Making and Cases, *(Houghton Mifflin, 1991).*

When certain factors in the work place combine, an environment develops which increases the probability of an unethical decision. This author argues if managers and CEOs recognize the symptoms, they can take steps to release some of the pressure before unethical behavior results.

What causes people, and ultimately companies, to make unethical decisions? Why did Jose L. Gomez, a former managing partner of the Grant Thornton accounting firm commit fraud at the age of 39? A bright, energetic family man and one of the youngest employees ever to be made a partner, why did he commit an act that cost investors at least $320 million?[1] Why did Barry J. Minkow, CEO of the now defunct ZZZZ Best firm, cost investors more than $70 million?[2] On a grander scale, what were the pressures that caused Yoshihisa Tabuchi of Nomura Securities Company to pay a total of more than 33 billion yen ($237.6 million) to compensate large clients for their losses in Japan's 1990 stock market plunge?[3] Why are friendly foreign countries increasing their efforts to spy on U.S. corporations?[4]

The answer is not simple, especially for those in the business community. Much has been said about the supposed lack of moral fiber by those who work in business.[5] Most of the criticism is unfounded. The majority of business people are honest and hard working with the same high value structure as those in other forms of work. Yet, why do business people get into these ethical dilemmas?

I believe, in many instances, unethical decisions are the result of a combination of factors which interact simultaneously and make an unethical decision easier to choose.

The Factor of Competition

One of the first major factors that contribute to increased pressure on people and companies is the dimension of competition.[6] Competition is one of the driving forces behind business and the ultimate factor in providing quality goods and services to the consumer. Competition helps companies strive for higher quality at lower prices. In general, competition helps a business to improve by forcing it to seek new customers, new ways to satisfy customers, and to develop new technologies that increase business. However, when competition becomes so intense that business survival is threatened, then those within a company may begin to see once unacceptable alternatives as acceptable.[7] This can cause employees to engage in unethical practices in order to save the company. Although no empirical research has been done, there is much anecdotal evidence which points to this causal link. Examples can be found in such intense industries as advertising, airlines, banking, commodities, and stock or bond markets.[8]

There are several ways that employees and companies deal with pyrrhic competition. One is through corporate espionage. One example involved the acquisition of information on General Electric's turbine parts by a small manufacturing firm. GE employees were offered money in exchange for drawings. The acquisition of these documents would have saved millions of dollars in research and development costs and could have enabled the small firm to capture a significant share of the more than $495 million turbine parts market.[9] As this illustrates, some firms believe that corporate espionage is acceptable if it saves the company from failure. Unfortunately, society deems such actions as unethical and illegal.

In other cases, society may judge certain actions as unethical in a post hoc fashion. When Frank Lorenzo used the bankruptcy laws to reduce Continental's operating costs, Congress reacted by developing new rules that precluded such practices. Although what Mr. Lorenzo did was legal, society deemed it unethical.

As competition becomes more intense, profit margins become smaller and business personnel may start substituting lower-quality materials for higher-quality ones in order to reduce costs. This practice is commonly known as value exchange.

Beech-Nut Nutrition Corporation took this concept to an extreme when it changed the contents of its apple juice product. Instead of selling a product made from apples, the company substituted a chemical concoction which had the same taste, smell, and look of apple juice. However, the company continued to label and promote its product as being 100 percent apple juice. In fact, experts found it difficult to distinguish from pure

From *Business Forum*, Spring 1992, pp. 13-17. © 1992 by the School of Business and Economics, California State University, Los Angeles. Reprinted by permission.

apple juice. However, Beech-Nut failed to inform consumers that its apple juice no longer was made from apples.[10] In many cases, companies do not inform consumers that components of their products no longer have the same quality they had in previous years.

When a firm is in a highly competitive industry other questionable practices often occur such as those which produce increased Environmental Protection Agency violations, use of bait-and-switch techniques, bribery, and mechanical devices installed to periodically increase assembly line speeds. These measures are used because of the fear of company extinction.

The Firm is a Factor

A second major factor that puts pressure on personnel is the company itself. Three facets of the company have been proven to be important in the ethical equation: corporate culture, a person's superiors, and opportunity.[11]

Corporate culture is the patterns and rules, the shared values and beliefs, and the traditions that govern the behavior of the organization and its employees. The informal organization creates the culture that determines how people must behave to be successful. For example, if developing deceptive sales presentations and offering bribes is generally accepted by superiors, then it perpetuates a corporate

"I believe, in many instances, unethical decisions are the result of a combination of factors which interact simultaneously and make an unethical decision easier to choose."

culture that condones such activities. Therefore, the informal organization rewards these activities and signals managers that the company is willing to accept these questionable practices.

The roles of top management and superiors are extremely important in developing the culture of an organization. Many agree that the chief executive officer and vice president level executives set the ethical tone for the entire organization. For example, when Chrysler Corporation President Lee Iacocca learned that several executives of his company had driven new Chryslers with the odometers disconnected which were later sold as new, he admitted the company's unethical behavior in a national press conference and developed a program to compensate customers who had bought the pre-driven cars. Iacocca took out two-page advertisements in *USA Today, The Wall Street Journal,* and *The New York Times* to apologize for the ethical mistake and added, "The only thing we are recalling here is our integrity." Messages like this send a strong signal to all employees in the organization concerning corporate ethics.[12] Lower level superiors obtain their cues from high ranking individuals, yet they too exert some of their personal value system on the company. This interplay between corporate culture and executive values helps determine the ethical direction of the firm.

In addition to corporate culture and superiors, opportunity plays an important part in the decision process. Opportunity is a set of conditions that limit or reward behavior. Salespeople, buyers, managers, accountants, and CEOs all have the opportunity to act in an unethical way.

If an individual uses the opportunity afforded him or her to act unethically and is either rewarded or no penalty is ascribed as a result, that person becomes more likely to repeat such acts as the opportunity arises. For example, an accountant who receives a raise for preparing financial documents that he or she knows are not completely accurate is being rewarded for that behavior and, therefore, will probably continue to use such tactics in the future. Opportunity to engage in unethical behavior can be another indicator of whether or not a person will behave unethically. Several elements within the business environment help to create opportunities, including knowledge and an individual's status within an organization.

Personal Moral Values

The personal dimension of ethics relates to an individual's moral values or phi-

losophy. These values are made up of attitudes and beliefs learned from family, religion, school, and business experiences. Values are generally assumed to stay constant unless a cathartic experience has occurred, but doubt was first cast upon this generalization by Albert Carr.[13] He argued that business people have two sets of ethics—one for the home and one for business. Recently, an empirical study tested Carr's argument and found that people may actually have several sets of ethical values.[14] This may partly explain why people such as Mr. Gomez appear to have strong moral commitments but later become embroiled in unethical activities.

The personal dimension also interacts with the corporate culture. In one study concerning the values of corporate managers and their critics, personal values were found to be involved in ethical decisions but were not the central component that guides the decisions, actions, and policies of the organization.[15] The burden of ethical behavior within the organization appears to relate in part to the organization's values and traditions rather than solely to individuals who actually make the decisions and carry them out.

Others have developed a "bad apple," "bad barrel" argument.[16] The bad apple argument is that people are basically evil and will do things in their own self interest. In order to eliminate unethical behavior one gets rid of the bad apples within the corporation. The bad barrel argument is that corporate cultures become unethical not because individuals are bad, but because pressures create such a state.

Steps to Take

As these three dimensions interact they cause pressure on the company and individuals to "cut corners." Invariably these corner-cutting practices produce ethical dilemmas. To avoid making unethical decisions, steps can be taken both by the firm and its personnel.

It is impossible to regulate the competitive environment that a firm is in, however, steps can be taken at the corporate level to relieve some of the pressure that can arise from it. An initial step that a business can take is to establish industry guidelines that all companies can adhere to. This can help create a level playing field which is defined by high standards of conduct.

A second step is to develop corporate codes of ethics, with both an external and internal orientation. Codes of ethics are important for both line and staff personnel in that both are exposed to ethical dilemmas. An external code of ethics deals with such individuals as clients, competitors, the community, and society as a whole. This code establishes guidelines in interacting with each of these groups or domains. It is important that within the code, perspective is considered. For example, former U.S. Secretary of State Henry Kissinger, who writes a newspaper column for the Los Angeles Times Syndicate, devoted one of his recent articles to praising Chinese leader Ding Xiao Ping's economic reforms. Most individuals didn't realize that Mr. Kissinger is engaged in joint business dealings with an industry of the Chinese government. The arrangement is legal and in itself, proper; however, it has elicited criticism because many people perceive the situation as a conflict of interest, hence the ethics of using Mr. Kissinger as a credible source of information on the Chinese situation becomes suspect.

An internal code of ethics should also be established. This code of ethics should have specific language in it to help new hires, low, mid, and senior level managers deal with ethical situations or dilemmas that occur in day-to-day operations. The CEO should also incorporate details within this internal code of ethics for himself or herself to be able to use as guidelines in establishing prudent behavior. Both codes of ethics should be worded in such a manner that they are general in scope but with specific ways of use. This is not to say that the code of ethics that a corporation establishes should be so detailed that it takes into account every situation, rather it should have general guidelines which operationalize the main goals and objectives that the code has suggested.

Codes of ethics should also incorporate penalties. Sanctions or penalties against those individuals who are caught in unethical behavior are important if a company is to maintain ethical standards. Increasing ethical behavior is a business goal no different than increasing profits. If the number of employees making ethical decisions on a regular basis is not increasing, then the company needs to determine why and take corrective action through stronger enforcement. If these codes are window dressing and do not relate to what is expected or what is rewarded in the corporate culture, then the codes serve no purpose other than to give the illusion that there is concern for ethical behavior.

Another way of relieving the pressure of committing unethical acts is for leadership to take a proactive stance with employees. One step is to incorporate an ethics test at the pre-hire stage. An ethics test compares home and work values to determine whether or not an individual is likely to commit unethical acts within the company. For example, James Rest created a moral content test which is based on Lawrence Kohlberg's cognitive moral development theory that can show managers the moral values of employees.[17] Work has also been done by William Boyce and Larry Jensen which ties moral philosophy to Kohlberg's

---

"It is impossible to regulate the competitive environment that a firm is in, however, steps can be taken at the corporate level to relieve some of the pressure that can arise from it."

---

theory.[18] In addition, others have developed or suggested values tests which can be used to identify an employee's values both from a process and content perspective.[19]

A second way to screen personnel is through cultural acceptability tests (CAT). Cultural acceptability tests are qualitative measures that help the company determine whether or not the new hire is congruent with the corporate values system. In essence, a CAT measures and delineates the corporate culture through an extensive appraisal of the company's rules, procedures, history, and implicit codes of conduct. Value analyses are done on key corporate personnel and integrated to determine the type of culture a company has. This culture-type is then compared to the employee's value system for congruency. Although it is unwise for an enterprise to have employee clones, key deviations from significant value points can suggest that an employee may have different values from those of the company. Such conflict can result in poor performance, rapid turnover, and disgruntled employees.

Another step in helping new employees to become more aware of ethics is through periodic ethical reviews of trainers, managers, and new hires. This can be done through the use of vignettes, cases, role playing, and personnel moral values tests. These methods can help sensitize employees within the organization to the ethical decision making process.

In addition to these steps, a periodic review of the enforcement procedures should also be done. All too often businesses have codes of conduct but do not test their employees on the knowledge of such codes. What may occur is that every year employees are only required to read and sign a code of ethics manual or pamphlet without taking into account what they may have learned from such codes. It is important to realize that in order for ethics codes to be effective, employees must feel such codes are an integral part of the corporate culture. Although knowledge of an ethical code or a review of enforcement procedures doesn't guarantee ethical behavior, it can send a message to the employee that deviation from such codes can result in negative consequences.

The formation of focus groups emphasizing potential ethical problems with markets, products, and services can also help in relieving some of the potential ethical pressure that can arise in business. In addition, periodic evaluations of industry and corporate cultures can also help the firm develop standards of ethics.

A quick checklist for determining whether a company is at risk of unethical behavior would include the following factors:

1. The competitiveness of the environment, industry, and company itself.
2. Implicit and explicit company or corporate culture that promotes questionable societal or industry behavior.
3. Superiors who condone or do not punish unethical or illegal behavior.
4. Industries where the opportunity for unethical behavior is great.

5. A significant percentage of employees whose value analysis shows a high self interest rating.

From this checklist companies can help reduce unethical behavior by incorporating the following suggestions:

1. Help develop ethical guidelines for your industry.
2. Develop codes of ethics which have internal and external perspectives.
3. Incorporate penalties for the violation of such codes.
4. Use ethics tests in the prehire stage.
5. Do periodic ethical reviews of key personnel.
6. Establish a periodic review of enforcement procedures.
7. Establish focus groups using personnel to identify potential ethical problems and devise ways of dealing with them.

Sensitizing the entire corporate culture to the need for high ethical standards can eliminate or defuse some of the pressures that occur in day to day business activities.

Whether one believes in the bad apple or bad barrel approach, both arguments can be solved through the steps that have been outlined. To continue to have an ethically aware and sensitive organization is to continually review those potential problems that may occur in the future. Doing so eliminates the risk of employees making unethical decisions.

Notes

1 Brannigan, Martha, "Auditor's Downfall Shows a Man Caught in Trap of His Own Making," *The Wall Street Journal*, March 4, 1987, 31.
2 "Trial of ZZZZ Best's Founder Will Offer Inside Look at Workings of a Bold Scam," *The Wall Street Journal*, August 23, 1988, 25.

3 "Nomura's President Resigns Amid Scandal," *The Wall Street Journal*, June 24, 1991, C1, C19.
4 "Corporate Targets: As Cold War Fades, Some Nations' Spies Seek Industrial Secrets, "*The Wall Street Journal*, June 17, 1991, A1, A4.
5 Fraedrich, John P., "Philosophy Type Interaction in the Ethical Decision Making Process of Retailers," dissertation, Texas A&M University, College Station, TX, 1988.
McNichols, Charles W. and Thomas W. Zimmerer, "Situational Ethics: an Empirical Study of Differentiators of Student Attitudes," *Journal of Business Ethics*, 4, 1985, 175-180.
6 Ferrell, O.C., Larry Gresham, and John Fraedrich, "A Synthesis of Ethical Decision Models for Marketing," *Journal of Macromarketing*, Fall, 1989, 9(2), 55-64.
Ferrell, O.C. and John Fraedrich, "Understanding Pressures that Cause Unethical Behavior in Business," *Business Insights*, Spring/Summer, 1990, 1-4. Also reprinted in *Business Ethics* 91/92, 3rd Edition, John E. Richardson, editor, 26-29.
7 Theoretical research on this construct can be found in Ferrell and Gresham 1985, Ferrell, Gresham and Fraedrich 1989 and Ferrell, O.C. and Steven Skinner 1988, "Ethical Behavior and Bureaucratic Structure in Marketing Research Organizations," *Journal of Marketing Research*, February, (25), 103-109.
8 Carroll, Archie B., *Business and Society: Ethics and Stakeholder Management*. South-Western Publishing Co., Cincinnati, OH, 1989, 230-249.
"Fare Game: Airlines May Be Using A Price-Data Network to Lessen Competition," *The Wall Street Journal*, June 28, 1990, A1, A6.
"Former Owner of Western Savings Indicted in Failure of Texas Thrift," *The Wall Street Journal*, October 26, 1990, B4.
"Tracing the Billions: Just What Happened To All That Money Savings & Loan Lost?" *The Wall Street Journal*, November 5, 1990, A1, A10.
"SEC Charges Ex-Moran Brokers With Bilking Investors," *The Wall Street Journal*. December 14, 1990, B6.
"Vernon Savings' Former Owner Gets Conviction," *The Wall Street Journal*. December 21, 1990, B4.
"Banker Seems to Thrive By Promising Funding and Not Delivering," *The Wall Street Journal*, March 26, 1991, A1, A12.
"Commodities Abuses Have Long Continued Despite NFA Scrutiny," *The Wall Street Journal*, October 16, 1990, A1, A16.
"Penny-Stock Scams Still Aren't Penny Ante," *The Wall Street Journal*, November 30, 1990, C1, C6.
"Is Insider Trading Widespread in Junk Market?" *The Wall Street Journal*, January 31, 1991, C1, C14.
"FBI Agent Plays a Smooth Hand in Penny-Stock Sting," *The Wall Street Journal*, April 8, 1991, C1, C6.
9 Carley, William M., "Secrets War: GE Presses Campaign to Halt Rivals' Misuse of Turbine Parts Data," *The Wall Street Journal*, August 16, 1988, 1, 10.

10 Hall, Mini, "O. J. Wasn't 100% Pure, FDA Says," *USA Today*, July 26, 1989, A1.
11 Ferrell, O. C. and Larry Greshman, "A Contingency Framework for Understanding Ethical Decision Making in Marketing," *Journal of Marketing*, Summer, 1985, 87-96.
Ferrell, O. C., Larry Greshman and John Fraedrich, "A Synthesis of Ethical Decision Models for Marketing," *Journal of MacroMarketing*, Winter, 1989.
12 Schlesinger, Jacob, "Chrysler Finds A Way to Settle Odometer Issue," *The Wall Street Journal*, December 10, 1987, 7.
13 Carr, Albert Z., "Is Business Bluffing Ethical?" *Harvard Business Review*, (January-February 1968), 145.
14 Fraedrich, John P., "Philosophy Type Interaction in the Ethical Decision Making Process of Retailers," *Ph.D. Dissertation*, Texas A&M University, College Station, TX, 1988.
15 Frederick, William C. and James Weber, "The Value of Corporate Managers and Their Critics: An Empirical Description and Normative Implications," *Research in Corporate Social Performance and Social Responsibility* (9), William C. Frederick, ed., Greenwich, CT, 1987, 149-50.
16 Trevino, Linda K. and Stuart Youngblood, "Bad Apples in Bad Barrels: A Causal Analysis of Ethical Decision Making Behavior," *Journal of Applied Psychology*, 1990, forthcoming.
17 Rest, James R., *Moral Development: Advances in Research and Theory*, New York: Praeger Publications, 1986.
Kohlberg, Lawrence, "Stage and Sequence: The Cognitive Developmental Approach to Socialization," in D. A. Goslin (ed.) *Handbook of Socialization Theory and Research*, Chicago: Rand McNally, 1969, 347-480.
Kohlberg, Lawrence, "Moralization: The Cognitive Developmental Approach," in *Morality: Theory Research and Social Issues*, New York: Holt, Rinehart & Winston, 1976.
18 Boyce, William D. and Larry C. Jensen, *Moral Reasoning: A Psychological-Philosophical Integration*, Lincoln: University of Nebraska Press, 1978.
Jensen, Larry, Andrew Taylor and John Burton, "A Factorial Study of the Moral Components Test," *Educational and Psychological Measurement*. 1981, 613-623.
19 Bales, R. and A. Couch, "Value Profile," *Sociological Inquiry* 39, 1969, 3-17, in Robinson, John P. and Phillip R. Shaver's, *Measures of Social Psychological Attitudes*, Survey Research Center Institute for Social Research, University of Michigan, Ann Arbor, 1985, 528-33.
Reidenbach, R. E. and D. P. Robin, "Toward the Development of a Multidimensional Scale for Improving Evaluations of Business Ethics," *Journal of Business Ethics*. August, 1990, 9(8), 639-654.
Ferrell, O. C. and John Fraedrich, *Business Ethics: Ethical Decision Making and Cases*, Houghton Mifflin Co., Pub.: Boston, 1991, 244-266.

WHAT WOULD YOU DO?

A Twisted Arm

*Jack had nothing against making a donation to this cause,
but to be threatened into giving was another matter.*

DOUG WALLACE

Doug Wallace does frequent consulting work on corporate ethics, and was formerly the vice president for social policy at Norwest Bank in Minneapolis.

All cases used in What Would You Do? *depict actual events, although individual and company names are changed to protect privacy. Please contact Margaret Kaeter at the* Business Ethics *office if you have a case to suggest or if you would like to become a guest commentator.*

O N A SNOW-SWEPT MONDAY morning, Jack Smilich glanced away from the memo he had been reading, finding himself languishing somewhere between anger and frustration. He stared toward a photo of his children and absent-mindedly wondered whether any of them would turn up someday within the walls of a large corporate office like this one. When he thought back to the corporate politics represented in the memo he'd just read, he fleetingly wondered if he wanted any of his children to live this life.

Jack was an executive vice president for Farrot Corporation, a Fortune 500 company that specialized in various tools used by major manufacturers. Farrot had been built by Sandy Erickson, whose high esteem within the company was only matched by what was close to reverence from a knowing public. In a state whose high expectations were rarely met when measured by its demanding citizens, Sandy had become an important figure. Years before his retirement, Sandy had contributed to important social causes in his community, and few had forgotten the footprints of respect that he'd left behind.

As a lasting tribute, the trustees from Sandy's alma mater had approached Farrot

Corporation, suggesting that a distinguished lecture series be established in his honor. The response was predictable. Within a short time, the development office of the college moved into action and so did Farrot. The college tapped its foundation, but, of course, it didn't

> **"Here's the contribution we expect," the memo said. "What you give will have a bearing on your future compensation."**

stop there, for there were several around the state who owed a great deal to Sandy, and they would certainly be approached.

Likewise, many of Farrot's employees wanted to contribute; Sandy had created a large, successful company with a strong family culture. Jack was planning to make a sizable contribution himself. But then something happened that took Farrot's executive row by surprise, like getting poked in the eye with a sharp stick. The memo was the stick.

It was soliciting money from the top ten officers of the company. As Jack got to the details of the stiff business prose, the hairs bristled on the back of his neck. "Here is the figure (in thousands of dollars) that we are setting for your contribution. Please send your check to our audit company. They will be submitting a report to me of the names and amounts each executive is contributing." It was signed by Jed Harris, a close friend of Farrot's current CEO and an outside board member.

This wasn't a letter soliciting a voluntary contribution. Jack was well aware that it had come from the chair of the board's compensation committee, which annually reviewed and set the compensation levels for the top officers of the company. This memo was a summons that said, in effect, "Here is what you will give; I will know what you contribute and that will have a bearing on your future compensation."

"This is not only unfair, it violates my right to determine my own level of giving as it fits within the larger picture of many other causes that I support," Jack mused to himself. "It also undermines the confidentiality policies of this company. There is something wrong about such an implied threat."

What struck Jack as most ironic is that Jed, the memo's author, was also the chair of the board's audit committee. This committee played a major role in reviewing and supporting the company's ethical practices policy, a policy that placed a strong emphasis on confidentiality of employee records. And Jack had line reponsibility for the policy.

Clasping his hands behind his head, Jack sat back in his chair and stared at the walnut-framed photo of his children's smiling faces. He wondered whether he should just let the matter go and simply write the check, or try to face the issue head on.

What would you do?

TOMMY CHISHOLM
Vice President, Secretary, and house counsel, Southern Company Services, Atlanta, Georgia

I REALLY THINK that Jack has two issues. From one perspective, he received the letter as a senior officer of the company. But from another perspective, he also received the letter as one who is responsible for the administration of the company's ethics policy. He's got to treat these responsibilities separately.

His immediate concern centered on how the action in the memo infringed upon a personal right of his, and whether it was appropriate for the director, who also chaired the Compensation and Audit committee, to infringe on his personal right. Jack also thought that if he elected not to give the amount (designated by the director) it might potentially impact his compensation in the future and, in that sense, be considered a threat. I certainly think that in terms of his career, it puts a cloud on how he might view his future if he does not participate.

The bigger question, however, centers upon his role in administering the ethics policy. The policy probably includes a section regarding the treatment of employees, including something about not coercing employees. If the policy indeed addresses that matter, Jack has a very important member of that company who would appear to be in violation of the ethics policy.

He might consider talking with another senior officer (who also received the memo) and see if he or she thought the language was as tilted toward the necessity of giving a specified amount as Jack thought it was. It might be that Jack misread it, although it certainly did seem to be rather strong. If the other officer agrees with Jack's assessment, then, as the administrator of the ethics policy, Jack should go to top management, in this case, the CEO, and express to him his concerns and let it play from there.

In either case, he is potentially putting himself in jeopardy regarding job security. But, having major responsibility for implementing the ethics policy, that's the way it is. That goes with the territory. You cannot put yourself in a position to prostitute your policy just because it's contrary to the wishes of top management at that particular time.

DON CONNELLY
Secretary and ethics officer,
Delmarva Power, Willmington, Delaware

I think Jack has more opportunities to resolve the situation beyond simply sending the check or facing the issue head on. If I were in his position I would probably feel the director out. I would use the "contribution" as a mechanism to get some dialogue going. I think my approach would be to say, "You caught me at a time that is a little bit inconvenient; I really don't have that amount of money available for a contribution. Is there a chance that I could give a lesser amount?" When you've got personal stakes involved, you really are increasing the

> **Sometimes the rules are a little different for the ten top executives in a company than they are for the rest of the workforce.**

possibility of not being able to make an objective decision. But Jack may be reading some things into this that are not really there. The director may be trying to make himself look good, by getting a certain amount collected.

Then I think Jack has to play the scenario of "What ifs?" If the director does come back and say, "No, this is what I'm expecting of you, and if you don't come through, you'll pay the consequences down the road," then I think we have a much more serious situation. At that point Jack has to make a personal decision. First of all, I would focus on the amount of money, and ask, "How much does it really hurt me?" before I decide to take it to the wall or not. Sometimes the rules are a little different for the top ten people in a company than they are for the masses. And it may be expected that the top ten participate in this sort of thing; it may be one of the prices of being in that position. On the other hand, there may be a need to take it to the wall.

DOUG WALLACE'S COMMENTS

I THINK TOMMY CHISHOLM is right when he assumes that the company's ethics policy includes expectations on how employees are to be treated, which would imply that they should not be intimidated on the job. Most ethics policies that I know of do address that issue. The principles of autonomy (the freedom to act in concert with one's own ethical beliefs) is dangerously close to being violated here, unless there was a previous understanding that the top officers of the company would be expected to set aside a certain percentage of their salary for various giving programs (which Don Connelly pointed out).

But, putting aside the personal situation, our guest commentators' point that there is another issue at stake — the integrity of the ethics policy — is right on the

mark, from my point of view. If, in learning more about the facts of the matter, this action conflicts with a company standard, then there is much more at stake than violating one person's autonomy. It symbolizes a willingness to jettison fair treatment when it suits someone in power to do so. That kind of management behavior has a way of coming back and haunting you down the road, because, as anyone with experience knows, there is no such thing as keeping a secret in an organization. As author Harlan Cleveland is fond of saying, "Information leaks." This activity will eventually hit the street among folks in the company, and when it does, it will erode confidence in the integrity of the ethics program. And once trust is eroded, it is very difficult to restore.

Once Jack has checked out his perceptions, if he verifies his suspicions through further consultation, then he does have a personal decision to make that carries some risks with it. When working in one corporation, I went through a different, but still challenging dilemma with the top executive. I know the anxious feeling of realizing that bringing forward an issue and a point of view that stands on principles may personally cost you something. It turned out that it did cost me some of the relationship and support that I once had enjoyed. But looking back on it now I wouldn't have done it any other way; at the time it was the right thing to put on top of the table for discussion. Sometimes we have to be willing to let the chips fall where they may. Some call that courage. Others call it harmony.

WHAT ACTUALLY HAPPENED?
After talking with another senior officer, Jack laid out his concerns, in strict confidence, to Bob Smith, the manager of corporate responsibility (who took care of some of the ethics program) regarding the ethical issues it raised. Bob worked with Jed, the board member who wrote the memo. Soon after that meeting, Jed called Jack, repeating the general sense of what Jack had said, without acknowledging that he was aware of Jack's conversation with Bob. When Jack asked him about the propriety of the manner in which the contribution was being solicited, Jed said, "You know the way the world turns is that you raise money by leveraging a little bit, and I think that's appropriate; I want to make sure that we raise sufficient funds" for this chair.

Jack was surprised by Jed's defense of his original action. He felt that it "violated the general tenor of all of our ethical statements," but knowing the CEO as he did, he saw no sense in taking it any further.

Business and Society: Contemporary Ethical, Social, and Environmental Issues

- Changing Perspectives in Business and Society (Articles 28–32)
- Major Contemporary Dilemmas (Articles 33–35)
- Global Ethics (Articles 36–39)

Both at home and abroad there are social and environmental issues that have potential ethical consequences for management. Incidents of insider trading, deaths resulting from unsafe products or work environments, AIDS in the workplace, and the adoption of policies for involvement in the global market are a few of the issues that need to be seriously addressed by management.

This unit will investigate the nature and ramifications of some of the prominent ethical, social, and environmental issues facing management today. The unit articles are grouped into three subsections. "The New Crisis in Business Ethics," the first article in the first subsection, describes how, during tough economic times, managers are being tempted to put more pressure on subordinates and to cut ethical corners. "The New World of Work" discloses how vast changes in the economy, technology, and the workforce have altered work itself. "Family Friendliness" reveals the importance of organizations' helping employees balance work and family. The last two articles in this subsection explain how "the green movement" is increasing in many organizations as the working world learns that recycling makes both dollars and sense and why, for the first time in years, environmentalists are on the defensive.

The second subsection addresses some of the major dilemmas facing contemporary business today. The first article in this subsection considers the impact of drugs in the workplace and suggests ways to establish sensitive policies and ongoing programs to help deal with this problem. The last two articles in this subsection scrutinize

the importance of embracing diversity and family-related issues in the workplace.

The last subsection, on *Global Ethics,* includes four articles that provide helpful insight on ethical issues and dilemmas inherent in multinational operations. They describe adapting ethical decisions to a global marketplace and offer guidelines for helping management deal with ethical issues in international markets. How one company in particular—Levi Strauss—practices ethics globally is discussed in the last two subsection articles.

Looking Ahead: Challenge Questions

How well do you feel organizations are responding to issues of work and family—for example, via flexible schedules, day care, job sharing, telecommuting? Explain your assessments.

What do you believe will be the hottest issue (such as sexism, racism, ageism) in the next decade? Why?

Is it fair to bring criminal charges against corporations and executives for unsafe products, dangerous working conditions, or industrial pollution? Why or why not?

How do you feel management should deal with illicit drugs in the workplace? Should management deal with alcohol-related problems in the same way? Why or why not?

What types of ethical dilemmas are management likely to face when conducting business in foreign environments? How can management best deal with these dilemmas?

THE NEW CRISIS IN BUSINESS ETHICS

To meet goals in these tough times, more managers are cutting ethical corners. The trend hurts both the culprits and their companies, even if they don't get caught.

Kenneth Labich

As this economic slowdown lingers like some stubborn low-grade infection, managers are putting the heat on subordinates. Many of the old rules no longer seem to apply. Says Gary Edwards, president of the Ethics Resource Center, a consulting firm in Washington: "The message out there is, Reaching objectives is what matters and how you get there isn't that important."

The result has been an eruption of questionable and sometimes plainly criminal behavior throughout corporate America. We are not dealing here so much with the personal greed that propelled Wall Street operators of the Eighties into federal prisons. Today's miscreants are more often motivated by the most basic of instincts—fear of losing their jobs or the necessity to eke out some benefit for their companies. If that means fudging a few sales figures, abusing a competitor, or shortchanging the occasional customer, so be it.

People lower down on the corporate food chain are telling the boss what they think he wants to hear, and outright lying has become a commonplace at many companies. Michael Josephson, a prominent Los Angeles ethicist who consults for some of America's largest public corporations, says his polls reveal that between 20% and 30% of middle managers have written deceptive internal reports.

At least part of this is relatively harmless—managers inflating budget proposals in the hope of ultimately getting what they really need, for example. But a good share of it will almost surely hurt the people and the companies involved, in some cases grievously. The U.S. press, broadcast and print, has become increasingly adept at uncovering corporate misdeeds. Witness the frenzy of reports raising questions about Dow Corning's breast implants. The stock of Corning Inc., one of the two corporate parents of Dow Corning, has declined by about 15% since the scandal erupted, even though the implants represented only around 1% of Dow Corning's revenues and its insurance coverage seems adequate to cover potential litigation.

The Justice Department has become far keener on catching and punishing white-collar criminals since the S&L crisis and the BCCI scandal. Last November tough new sentencing guidelines for corporate crimes went into effect. Warns Josephson: "We are going to see a phenomenal number of business scandals during the 1990s. We are swimming in enough lies to keep the lawyers busy for the next ten years."

The faint sign of good news is that many big U.S. companies have begun to respond to the crisis. According to a survey of FORTUNE 1,000 companies conducted by Bentley College in Boston, over 40% of the respondents are holding ethics workshops and seminars, and about one-third have set up an ethics committee. Some 200 major U.S. corporations have recently appointed ethics officers, usually senior managers of long experience, to serve as ombudsmen and encourage whistleblowing.

Regrettably, such actions won't put an end to ethical dilemmas—or to the current spree of shoddy practices. Dow Corning had a substantial ethics program in place for 18 years before the breast-implant scandal, but no questions about safety or testing of the implant materials were ever raised to the ethics committee.

The problem, says Kirk Hanson, a Stanford management professor and president of an ethics research group called the Business Enterprise Trust, is extreme pressure to perform. "Quite simply," he says, "the individual who isn't perceived as a top achiever is a candidate for a layoff." Under such circumstances, flirtations with impropriety are hardly surprising.

Virtually every day we read about the hapless folks who get caught. Citicorp fires the president and senior executives of a credit-card-processing division for allegedly overstating revenues. American Express cans several executives for failing to write off accounts of customers who had filed for bankruptcy, as required by company policy. Alamo Rent A Car agrees to refund $3 million to customers who were overcharged for repair costs to damaged vehicles.

There is clearly quite a bit more iceberg down there. No one knows how many top managers are intentionally overlooking questionable acts because they are paying off. Josephson tells of a bank whose executives one day discovered that a large number of customers had been overbilled for mortgage payments. "There's no doubt what you ought to do in a case like that," says Josephson. "You come clean and you take your hit." That's what the bank

REPORTER ASSOCIATE *Temma Ehrenfeld*

eventually did—but only after regulators discovered the error.

Some practices born of competitive excess fall into a kind of gray area. Last autumn Toys "R" Us managers sent employees to rival Child World stores around the country to buy up large quantities of heavily discounted items, which were then resold in their own stores. Misrepresentation? Other acts now taking place clearly cross the line. Gary Edwards tells of one struggling company that recently placed fake want ads in the hope of luring competitors' employees to job interviews where they might reveal trade secrets. Stanford's Hanson reports that three of his returning students were asked by summer employers to call up competitors and seek information under the guise of doing academic research.

Many top managers desperate for profits have turned to emerging markets overseas, a trend that presents a fresh set of ethical dilemmas. Far too often, a company will send off its team with no directive other than finding new business. Bribery and sloppy accounting may be a fact of business life over there, the customer base may be riddled with questionable characters, and yet the sales force is supposed to find its way with no ethical compass. Mark Pastin, an Arizona State University management professor who has consulted with many companies seeking to go global, suggests that the confusion overseas could later lead to problems at home. Says Pastin: "Don't forget that you eventually are going to re-import those managers. Once they've come back, do you think they're going to put on their old ethics like a new suit?"

As Pastin notes, ethics begin at home, in the nexus between employer and employee. The recent layoffs at many big companies carry a slew of ethical implications. Many job reductions have clearly been necessary, the result of lousy business. But at least some top managers have axed employees to pump up profits for the short term or impress Wall Street. Says Hanson: "Unfortunately, layoffs have sometimes become a way to buy a multiple." At such companies much of the work load may still be there, while many of the bodies are not. Middle managers end up pressuring the remaining employees to work unconscionable amounts of overtime. What are the ethics of that?

Compensation for top executives has become a hot-button ethical issue during this recession as well, especially at those companies where workers are being fired and the big guy's salaries appear excessive or unrelated to job performance. In such cases the old argument that companies need to bestow grand wealth on chief executives to prevent them from fleeing to a more beneficent competitor seems especially flimsy. The market for the overpaid chiefs of losing or minimally profitable enterprises is not a large one. In effect, the top dogs are isolating themselves—but not their employees—from the brutal realities of the marketplace. The basic injustice involved is obvious.

In tough times it's all the more important to remember that ethics pay off in the end, and the bottom line. Ten years ago James Burke, chief executive of Johnson & Johnson, put together a list of major companies that paid a lot of attention to ethical standards. The market value of the group, which included J&J, Coca-Cola, Gerber, IBM, Deere, Kodak, 3M, Xerox, J.C. Penney, and Pitney Bowes, grew at 11.3% annually from 1950 to 1990. The growth rate for Dow Jones industrials as a whole was 6.2% a year over the same period.

The case is probably easier to make in the negative: Doing the wrong thing can be costly. Under the new federal sentencing guidelines, corporations face mandatory fines that reach into the hundreds of millions for a broad range of crimes—antitrust violations, breaking securities and contract law, fraud, bribery, kickbacks, money laundering, you name it. And that's if just one employee gets caught.

Even if you don't land in court, you might find yourself on the front page or the evening news, which could be worse. In the past few years, most media have given much more coverage to business. Newspapers and magazines all over the U.S. now employ investigative reporters with MBAs and business experience to dig into the affairs of companies. The old advice is still the best: Don't do anything on the job you wouldn't want your mother to read about with her morning coffee.

Even if a company's slippery practices go undetected, there is still a price to pay. Successful enterprises are inevitably based on a network of trust binding management, employees, shareholders, lenders, suppliers, and customers—akin to the network that Japanese call keiretsu. When companies slip into shoddy practices, these crucial relationships start to deteriorate. Says Barbara Ley Toffler, senior partner of a Boston ethics-consulting firm called Resources for Responsible Management: "The effects aren't obvious at first. People may feel bad about what they're doing, but they rationalize it somehow." Eventually a kind of moral rot can set in, turning off employees with higher personal standards and stifling innovation throughout the company. She adds: "People in these situations feel frightened, constrained. They are not in the proper frame of mind to take prudent risks."

Companies that depend heavily on customer service are especially vulnerable. A company that jacks up prices unfairly, skimps on quality, or beats up on employees can hardly expect its salespeople to treat customers properly. Says Arizona State's Pastin: "You can put on a happy face for only so long before reality intrudes. I don't believe employees can deliver superior service if they don't think their company is treating customers with respect." Ultimately, many of the most effective managers and most productive workers will find a way to work somewhere else. When the economy turns up again, companies with a sorry reputation for ethical behavior will have a harder time attracting top-quality people.

Among the scariest aspects of the current situation, ethicists say, is how unaware many top managers are of what is going on. Michael Josephson, who is usually called in after a company has landed in the headlines, begins by circulating questionnaires among top and middle managers to determine what's happening. More often than not, the CEO expresses shock and disbelief at the results of the anonymous survey. Adds Josephson: "There's very often a sort of 'kill the messenger' attitude, which may have led to some of the problems in the first place."

Once the scope of the problem is clear, the next step is to communicate in no uncertain terms what is expected of managers and other employees. Hewlett-Packard, for example, works hard to ensure that all employees are familiar with its extensive standards for business conduct, which cover everything from conflicts of interest and accounting practices to handling confidential information and accepting gratuities. The standards are high; salespeople are instructed to avoid commenting on a competitor's character or business practices, even to refrain from mentioning the fact that a competitor might be facing a lawsuit or government investigation.

A little innovation helps in getting the message across. Citicorp has developed an ethics board game, which teams of employees use to solve hypothetical quandaries. General Electric employees can tap into specially designed interactive software on their personal computers to get answers to ethical questions. At Texas Instruments, employees are treated to a weekly column on ethics over an international electronic news service. One popular feature: a kind of Dear Abby mailbag, answers provided by the company's ethics officer, Carl Skoogland, that deals with the troublesome issues employees face most often. Managers at Northrop are rated on their ethical behavior by peers and subordinates through anonymous questionnaires.

More and more companies are appointing full-time ethics officers, generally on the corporate vice-presidential level, who report directly to the chairman or an ethics committee of top officers. One of the most effective tools these ethics specialists employ is a hot line through which workers on all levels can register complaints or ask about questionable behavior. At Raytheon Corp., Paul Pullen receives some 100 calls a month. Around 80% involve minor issues that he can resolve on the spot or refer to the human resources department. Another 10% of callers are simply looking for a bit of advise. But about ten times a month, a caller reports some serious ethical lapse that Pullen

must address with senior management. Says he: "Most people have high standards, and they want to work in an atmosphere that is ethical. The complaints come from all levels, and they are typical of what you would find in any business: possible conflicts of interest, cheating on timecards, cheating on expense reports."

Some companies have been motivated to set up an ethics office after a spate of unfavorable publicity. Nynex took the step in 1990 following a series of scandals, including revelations of lewd parties in Florida thrown for suppliers by a Nynex executive. Later 56 middle managers were disciplined or discharged for allegedly receiving kickbacks, and the SEC accused a former unit president of insider trading. The company has since been beating the drum about ethics, but Graydon Wood, Nynex's newly appointed ethics officer, says the job requires a realistic view of human behavior. Says he: "You have to recognize that even with all the best programs, some employees do go wrong. Last year some marketing people didn't report properly, resulting in unjustified commissions. We fired them."

In the current crunch much deception and unethical conduct can be avoided if top managers make sure that the performance goals they set are realistic. Ethicists often cite a classic case that occurred at a GM light-truck plant several years ago. The plant manager got caught with a device in his office that periodically speeded up the line beyond the rate designated in union contracts. Confronted with the evidence, he pointed

out that the company's production specifications were based on the line running at maximum allowable speed 100% of the time. He was simply trying to make up for inevitable down time.

Managers must be sure that what they actually do fosters rather than impedes ethical conduct. One sure way to send the word is by rewarding admirable behavior. No code of ethics and no amount of cajolery by the chief executive will have much effect if promotions regularly go to the people who pile up big numbers by cutting corners. Says Kirk Hanson: "Senior management has got to find a way to create heroes, people who serve the company's competitive values—and also its social and ethical values."

These role models could be especially important for younger employees who are trying to survive in what seems to be an increasingly hostile business environment. Michael Josephson reports some dispiriting news about the start that the new generation are off to. He cites surveys of Americans 18 to 30 years old that show between 70% and 80% cheated in high school and between 40% and 50% cheated in college. And—are you ready for this?—between 12% and 24% say they included false information on their résumés.

Commenting on Americans' ethical standards in the 19th century, Alexis de Tocqueville declared that the nation had become great because it was good. He may have overstated a bit, but in pursuit of profits today we may indeed be losing an element vital to our long-term success tomorrow.

THE NEW WORLD OF WORK

Beyond the buzzwords is a radical redefinition of labor

It's 9 a.m., and the workplace of the future is . . . awfully quiet. On one side of the converted warehouse, beneath orange girders and massive yellow ducts, perhaps 50 of 220 desks are occupied. Employees tap at laptop computers, or whisper into phones; some meet in small groups or venture across "Main Street" to confer with administrators and managers. A low roar from the air conditioning blankets the cavernous space in antiseptic stillness.

Beneath the remarkable austerity at IBM's new Cranford (N.J.) sales office, though, is something of a revolution. The 600 representatives based here have no offices; a day each week, or less, they come in to pick up mail and see associates, and are computer-assigned a spot with little accoutrement save one chair, a telephone, and a jack for a laptop.

Most of the time, they're on the road. Software marketer Lynn M. Fox gets most administrative work done by modem, from home or spare offices at customer sites. Her time with customers is better spent: Because all the product, pricing, and technical data she needs are available via her laptop, a bid takes minutes, not days, to work up. No approvals are needed from the office bureaucracy. She's home by 6 p.m., allowing her a few hours with Matthew, her three-year-old, before she checks in again for electronic messages. It's still a 10-to-12-hour workday, "but a lot more productive, and I have more control," she says.

Duke Mitchell directs all this from a steel desk, just like the others, at one windowless corner of the room. His lieutenants, who work in similar spaces, are few: In moving five sales offices to Cranford, Mitchell cut out two layers of middle management. He also halved the number of sales and service reps. Pan-

eled offices? Gone. Fancy art? No more. Except for the carpeting, all the furnishings are used. "This isn't about importance, about epaulets," says Mitchell. "It's about what you get done."

My dad worked here for 38 years. He retired here. Now, if the company can make a product cheaper, or serve the customer better, it's going to leave. You can't blame them. Everyone has to work for themselves. Individuals have to be as flexible as companies are in the '90s. — Kevin Whalen, 33, laid off when Procter & Gamble Co. shut its Quincy (Mass.) factory.

Mobility. Empowerment. Teams. Cross-training. Virtual offices. Telecommuting. Reengineering. Restructuring. Delayering. Outsourcing. Contingency. If the buzzwords don't sound familiar, they should: They are changing your life. The last decade, perhaps more than any other time since the advent of mass production, has witnessed a profound redefinition of the way we work.

The job, certainly, is not dead. There's still a robust need for relationships between employer and employed that rely on stability, security, and shared economic interests. "Man has always sought the company of people, and that will continue to be the driving force of organization," says CEO Robert J. Saldich of Raychem Corp., one employer that is creatively confronting workplace changes.

The relationship isn't what it was. The new compact between company and worker dismisses paternalism and embraces self-reliance. Bid farewell to unconditional lifetime employment, even at the bluest of blue-chip companies that once implicitly turned on such an ethic. "That clearly is no longer the name of

the game," says Kevin Becraft, director of employee relations and resources at IBM, which has cut 171,000 jobs since 1986. "Instead, it's lifelong employability." The key difference: shared responsibility. Employers have an obligation to provide opportunity for self-improvement; employees have to take charge of their own careers.

If your company hasn't laid that out, you could probably guess. More than likely, you are working longer and harder, and making less money than did someone in comparable work a decade ago. Constantly in training, you must acquire new skills to keep up with new technologies. The corporate terrain is shaky, with near-continuous downsizing and reorganization reminders that anything can change; shared, too, is the risk of business itself.

A global economy, rousting American employers from business-as-usual management, demands such change; rapidly evolving technology allows it. "Almost every employment relationship is contingent on the employer being able to continue in the same business with the same product and the same technology with the same quiescent competition," says Audrey Freedman, a former Labor Dept. economist. "Now, who's in that position?"

ELEGANT RESULT. Essentially, no one is: We confront a workplace that will evolve year after year. Many will find the result both enervating and rewarding. In companies that are flattening hierarchies and, bit by bit, decentralizing decision-making, workers are gaining greater control over what they do; self-direction has superseded the doctrine that workers do only what they're told. High performers are rewarded with higher pay. And flexible human resource strategies can free workers to pursue more fulfilling combinations of varied work, family life, and other interests.

The resulting business can be as elegant as European Collision Center, a tiny auto body shop in Cambridge, Mass. There, worker empowerment and autonomy drive customer service. Bodymen take "ownership" of a car while it's in the shop, staying with it start to finish. No one looks over their shoulders: "There are a set of parameters, then they have to be responsible," says owner Wayne Stevenson. Workers are cross-trained to take on new tasks and sent back to school yearly to keep skills up to date. Customers love what they get, and Stevenson's traffic has doubled every year for five years.

The question: How many losers will there be? Not every-one, certainly, will be empowered. For many workers, part-time jobs and temping will mean less money, not more freedom. Low-skill employees will be marginalized in a labor market that rewards education and training. In companies that cut jobs without redesigning processes and structures, the remaining employees simply will take on more work.

Here's one clue to the future: The Bureau of Labor Statistics' occupational forecast for the year 2005 (chart). Notice which jobs are gaining: professional, managerial, and technical—high wages, high skills. What's losing: crafts and operators and laborers, the domain of low-skill union jobs. Then there's that jolting bar to the right: Service workers—that low-pay catch-all for everyone from burger-flippers to home health aides—will gain 6.4 million jobs.

Any forecast for a decade down the road is open to question, of course. Statistical noise, though, shouldn't obscure the essential challenge: Everywhere, workers and their employers will have to rethink traditional roles and relationships. Even as both sides warily look each other up and down, they'll be confronted with the need to act fast, to transform new competitive pressures into mutual gains.

Years ago, we had one guy who told us what to do and we did it. He made all the decisions. We never really had any input. Now, you have to listen to your men. They have empowered us so much that we don't have to do a job if we think it's unsafe. If I tell one of the men to do a job and he thinks it's unsafe, we sit down and talk about it.—Joseph Stiffarm, Burlington Northern Inc. track foreman, Havre, Mont.

Plant 12, Pulaski Furniture Corp.'s new $20 million factory in Pulaski, Va., is a gleaming testament to technology's capacity for reordering work. Computerized equipment shapes wood with spurts of laser beams; an automated machine instantaneously cuts eight pieces. Each would take a craftsman 30 minutes by hand.

This is labor-eliminating automation at its most severe: Plant 12's 125 workers manufacture more furniture than five times as many people at Pulaski's much larger Dublin (Va.) operation. The tech-

nology lowers costs, keeping Pulaski ahead of competitors. It also leaves 60-year-old Howard Frazier strangely out of place. Having fashioned furniture by hand for 40 years, he now advises a new breed of machine operators, 90% of them computer-literate. "They have good educations and they know about computers, but they don't know a lot about building furniture," Frazier says.

Technology's starkest feature is its inexorability: Today, the power of a personal-computer microchip doubles every 18 months. Our ability, as a nation, to maintain and build wealth depends in large part on the speed and effectiveness with which we invent and adopt machines that lift productivity.

Such a relationship has been a given throughout the Industrial Age, as has the job loss that automation normally produces. In the last decade, though, technology and concomitant restructuring have had a disconcerting effect on the U.S. workforce, dramatically widening the divide between those with more skills and those with fewer. Although pay, adjusted for inflation, has dropped across the board, it has fallen far more for those without college degrees (chart).

It's no cyclical oddity. "We are in the midst of a major polarization of work," says consultant Michael Hammer, America's high priest of reengineering. "Organizations need fewer and fewer of better and better people. The jobs organizations are going to have are going to be better jobs."

Visit Cyprus Amax Mineral Co.'s Twentymile Mine near Oak Creek,

PERCENT CHANGE IN SHARE OF TOTAL EMPLOYMENT, 1992-2005

OCCUPATION ▶	PROFESSIONAL	MANAGERIAL	TECHNICAL	CRAFT	SALES & MARKETING	ADMINISTRATIVE SUPPORT	OPERATORS & LABORERS	SERVICE	FARM & FORESTRY
% change	12.4%	3.0%	8.3%	-7.1%	-0.9%	-6.5%	-10.4%	9.4%	-13.8%
EARNINGS* ▶	$682	$664	$528	$501	$457	$392	$365	$293	$269

PROMISE AND PERIL IN A POLARIZED JOB MARKET

High-wage occupations will grow, creating more opportunities for those with skills and education. But low-paying service jobs will also be on the rise.

*WEEKLY MEDIAN 1993 EARNINGS, FULL-TIME WORKERS

DATA: LABOR DEPT.

Colo., where workers with push-button controls walk alongside massive machines that shear 30-inch slices from an 850-foot coal wall. Laptop computers help miners track equipment breakdowns and water quality. "Down on the longwall, you don't feel any less of a man when the day is over," says Charles J. Kistler, 38, who walks six miles on a good day, carrying 25 pounds of gear. But these aren't the illiterate laborers of mining's past. The average Twentymile employee has two years of college; an executive says the company looks for people with "high math skills, more technical background, more comfort with electronics."

Better technology, better processes, and fewer, better workers. The ideal: Technology that actually helps workers make decisions, in organizations that encourage them to do so. That's the promise of computers, just now starting to be realized. "Free access to information across an organization eliminates the need for hierarchical management systems that existed before," says James K. Sims, CEO of consultant Cambridge Technology Partners Inc. People can think for themselves. Decisions can be made faster, by those closest to the customer.

Such is the intent of Southland Corp. as it expands the autonomy of its 7-Eleven store managers. In a Texas pilot project, managers track daily orders and leftovers of fresh sandwiches and pastries on handheld computers; a headquarters computer processes the data and generates a report on sales and profits the next morning.

Bob Price, a store manager in The Colony, Tex., a Dallas suburb, makes use of such data to map out future orders, figuring in weather reports, special events in the area, and other factors that could affect demand. He decides what and how much to order. "Before this, we had no say about what we needed in our store," Price says. "Either you had a field consultant come in and say we need to have more of something, or else they'd just automatically ship stuff. Now, we have to make decisions."

Empowerment, of course, is a fixture on manufacturing floors, pioneered in the U.S. by carmakers and the United Auto Workers. Now, a decade or so behind, service industries are discovering effective work redesign as well. In all, says Massachusetts Institute of Technology professor Paul Osterman, nearly

80% of employers across industries have adopted quality circles, total quality management, team-based systems, or some combination.

The results, though, have been mixed. Too many such efforts lack commitment from the top, or fail to secure worker support from the beginning. Resources—time, money, managerial expertise—go wanting. The sense of urgency fades. And the workplace returns to the status quo—or worse.

This year, I had to downsize my area by 25%. Nothing has changed in terms of the workload. It's very emotionally draining. I find myself not wanting to go in to work, because I'm going to have to push people to do more, and I look at their eyes and they're sinking into the back of their heads. [People] numbing. But they're not going to complain, because they don't want to be the next 25%.—Middle manager at a large high-tech company undergoing reengineering

Is America burning out? The great risk of downsizing and restructuring is that they'll do nothing to change the way we work. Fewer of us simply will work harder.

Reengineering proponents say that shouldn't happen. Raymond L. Manganelli, president of Gateway Management Consulting, recalls an assignment at his own first job—securing signatures of 17 managers who had to authorize a computer requisition. It took three months. New technology, delayering, and fewer people, he says, should cut out that sort of fat: "People don't do more work. They do more valuable work."

Insurer USF&G Corp., for example, has cut staffing by 48% in five years—but instituted a matrix organization to replace hierarchy. Melissa K. Wilcox, a marketing manager assigned work originally designed for three people, says she "would have hit the wall a year ago," but has managed to share old tasks far more effectively with more people in the matrix.

Yet many managers report that, between mass firings and coping with the mound of work still remaining, job stress is pervasive. And an annual survey of managers by the American Management Assn. finds widespread erosion of morale at companies with job cuts. Says Jerome M. Rosow, president of the Work in America Institute: "Where the focus has been on downsizing, getting lean and

mean, the effect on managers has been very severe."

This is the bleak underside of the new workplace: For every empowered employee, there's at least another cowering in his office, putting in longer hours to keep up with a job that used to keep two people busy. For every highly skilled worker moving up the ladder, there's another, marginalized, struggling to make ends meet.

TEMP FUGIT. A quarter of those employed today do so on a temporary, part-time, or contract basis (chart). The number of Americans working part-time has grown by 2.2 million since 1973—entirely a function, according to the Economic Policy Institute, of more "involuntary" part-timers who would rather work full-time. Hundreds of big companies, moreover, have outsourced noncore operations: Continental Bank Corp. has contracted its legal, audit, cafeteria, and mailroom operations to outside companies. In September, American Airlines Inc. announced it would do the same with customer-service jobs at 30 airports.

Outsourcing can work wonders for the bottom line: So-called contingent workers get pay comparable to full-time staff's, but without benefits that typically add 40% to labor costs. A contingent workforce, too, is more flexible: When business sags, the temps go first. Blue Cross/Blue Shield of Rhode Island cut its work-

THE NEW CONTINGENT WORKER

Employers are pushing more people than ever into the organizational fringes. Part-time, contract, and self-employed workers are rising as a percent of total employment.

PART-TIME
CONTRACT
SELF-EMPLOYED

1973   1993

▲ PERCENT   DATA: ECONOMIC POLICY INSTITUTE

CHART BY LISA KNOUSE BRAIMAN/BW

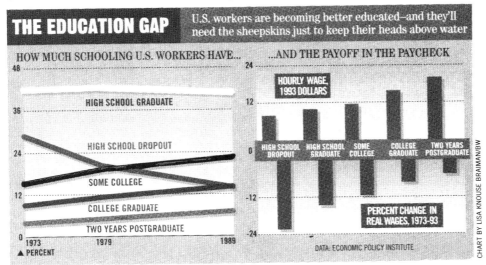

THE EDUCATION GAP | U.S. workers are becoming better educated—and they'll need the sheepskins just to keep their heads above water

HOW MUCH SCHOOLING U.S. WORKERS HAVE...

...AND THE PAYOFF IN THE PAYCHECK

HOURLY WAGE, 1993 DOLLARS

HIGH SCHOOL GRADUATE

HIGH SCHOOL DROPOUT

SOME COLLEGE

COLLEGE GRADUATE

TWO YEARS POSTGRADUATE

1973   1979   1989
▲ PERCENT

HIGH SCHOOL DROPOUT · HIGH SCHOOL GRADUATE · SOME COLLEGE · COLLEGE GRADUATE · TWO YEARS POSTGRADUATE

PERCENT CHANGE IN REAL WAGES, 1973-93

DATA: ECONOMIC POLICY INSTITUTE

CHART BY LISA KNOUSE BRAIMAN/BW

force by 40% over five years without laying off a single full-timer.

Such dislocation, though, has its price. In her 1992 book, *The Overworked American,* Harvard University economist Juliet B. Schor estimated that, in attempting to maintain their standard of living in the face of declining compensation, workers spent the equivalent of four weeks more a year on the job in 1989 than they had two decades earlier. A large part of the increase came from the flood of women into the labor force in that time: Their participation rate shot to 57.4% from 42.7%. In many families, that has more than compensated for a decline in hourly earnings. But the addition, clearly, has brought its own pressures.

For the most part, recent studies indicate, the two-income family hasn't figured out yet how best to balance jobs with kids and housework. And despite efforts by many employers to provide child care and eldercare, employees voice frustration with the juggling act. "Unfortunately, the reality and logistics of being a working mother—or involved father, for that matter—have not become any easier," complains Aimee B. McCrory, president of an investment management firm in Houston and mother of two. "I mean, most parents work, and yet the P. T. A. meetings are still at 10 a.m."

I'm grateful to have work, and I'm happy with what I'm doing. I do a good job for them because I feel an obligation as a contractor. But I don't feel loyalty, not the old-fashioned sense of loyalty we used to have. It's the realization that it's just not going to be the same ever again.—Joan Young, Catonsville, Md.,

laid off from her job as a bankruptcy collection agent, then taken on again as a contractor

Henry B. Schacht, chairman of Cummins Engine Co., is worried. Two years ago, his company reopened a factory in Columbus, Ind., to build midrange truck engines. Workers at Cummins' other Columbus factory, which produces heavy-duty engines, make $17.60 an hour under union contract; those at the new plant average $8.75. They're trained in statistical process control and engine technology and maintenance, and tested for math ability and communications skills. Pay increases are predicated on completing coursework.

Schacht wonders whether it will fly. He turned Cummins around with a combination of hard-nosed cost-cutting and progressive high-performance work systems. Now, "we have fewer people doing much more work, much of which is knowledge-based, and we're paying people less," he says. How will Cummins reward employees enough to keep them committed? How will it create promotion paths, now that many middle management jobs have been eliminated? What's going to give?

How, in short, will the new compact work? Schacht expects that companies will have to expand use of employee stock ownership and profit sharing plans. Raychem Corp. has another answer—the "career-resilient workforce," as consultant Robert H. Waterman Jr. describes it. The strategy acknowledges that job skills, like businesses, are ephemeral, and that employees themselves must be continually reinvented. It recognizes, too, that it has a responsibility to help workers sharpen existing skills or take

on new ones—even if such programs eventually lead employees to other companies.

No one at Raychem has a job for life. Nothing is guaranteed except the opportunity for self-improvement and the promise that breadth of skills and experience are valued. An in-house career center offers training in interviewing and resume' writing and assists employees looking for new posts within the Menlo Park (Calif.) industrial-products maker. The payback, says CEO Saldich: "We get a person who is fully engaged, who is excited about what he or she is doing—a much more productive, dedicated employee."

Certainly, education forms a foundation for the new workplace: The continuing growth in professional and technical occupations will demand ever-higher capabilities of Americans. Says Joe Lo Galbo, a Ford Motor Co. machinery repairman-turned-trainer: "The auto worker is almost a scientist in a technical way. He's required to know so many trades, he's required to know so much." Ford offers workers up to $3,100 a year toward tuition for approved courses. AlliedSignal Corp. sent all 86,000 employees through a four-day course on total quality and is gearing up for a second session.

Even so, at 1.4% of payroll, U.S. employers are spending relatively little on training. *Training* magazine says formal staff development spending by U.S. companies with more than 100 employees, at $50.6 billion this year, will be up just 11% from 1990—less than inflation.

Economists and executives worry, too, whether all the training, reengineering, and empowerment are sustainable. We increasingly demand that our workers take on responsibility and risk, yet their pay is falling. Will $8-an-hour machinists do high-performance work? "The real answer is, we don't know yet," says MIT's Osterman. "But you can't expect workers to keep contributing their ideas when they don't get rewarded for them."

The new compact still binds employer and employee in a web of loyalty and mutual responsibility—a blend of community and autonomy. But it no longer protects from the reality of competition. Perform, it demands, and we shall see. Share in the risks. No guarantees.

By Keith H. Hammonds in New York, with Kevin Kelly in Chicago, Karen Thurston in Atlanta, and bureau reports

Family friendliness

What workplace revolution? At most companies, families still rank low

When her son, Colin, was born seven years ago, Denise Searfass considered herself lucky. The new mother's employer was ISI, a database publisher in Philadelphia that had been hailed by child-care experts and the media as a corporate pioneer when it opened its on-site center a few years earlier. Searfass figured she'd keep working as an administrative assistant and snatch peeks at her son on the playground.

The center's $150-a-week fee was barely affordable, but Searfass scraped by for a year, trading in vacation leave time to reduce the cost. When her daughter, Corey, was born, however, Searfass, who is now single, could no longer justify spending half her annual income — then $18,000 — on day care. She placed the children in a cheaper center a half-hour drive from her office. "It was extremely frustrating," says Searfass. "Here was this wonderful, convenient day-care center, but I couldn't afford to use it." Neither could most other ISI employees. When the facility closed in June 1991 under a pile of debt, the 150 children being cared for included just seven offspring of ISI employees. Most of the other 143 came from affluent professional families in the surrounding community.

Oft-told tale. The story of Denise Searfass and ISI is a small metaphor for the obstacles that confront even well-intentioned employers who try to make themselves more "family friendly." It is also the story of a putative workplace revolution exaggerated by companies looking for quick fixes and image makeovers, hyped by the media and miscast by a handful of well-publicized surveys from business-research groups and employee benefits consulting firms. In an age when child-care problems can undermine first Zoë Baird's and then Kimba Wood's bids to become the next U.S. attorney gener-

al, the struggle faced by the average working parent has never seemed more acute. The first federal attempt to lend a hand — President Clinton's February 5 signing of the long-awaited Family and Medical Leave Act — is a half-way measure. Its key provision of 12 weeks of unpaid leave following childbirth or adoption, to care for a seriously ill child, spouse or parent or for an employee's own serious illness is clearly unaffordable for many wage earners. And the law covers only firms with 50 or more employees, leaving more than a third of U.S. workers unaffected. On the plus side, the law does continue health benefits, and it guarantees the same or a comparable job upon return.

Gray-flannel ghost. Beyond a doubt, companies today play a larger role in family life than they did a decade ago. Flextime, job sharing, telecommuting and elder care have moved off the pages of human-resources journals onto board-room agendas. Given a 46 percent female work force corporate America now acknowledges that the once sacred separation of work and family is as outdated as the organized man of the '50s.

The change isn't just workplace demographics. Evidence is mounting that companies whose family friendliness is real can make shareholders happy, too. The Conference Board, a business-research group in New York, documents lower turnover and absenteeism and increased productivity at such companies. Firms with broad work and family benefits also attract a higher-quality work force. Fel-Pro, an automotive-parts maker with 2,000 employees in Skokie, Ill., that offers benefits like a subsidized on-site day-care center and a summer camp, has a waiting list of 5,000 would-be workers and hasn't had an unprofitable quarter in 30 years. "We are *not* a charity," stresses Fel-Pro Cochairman David

Weinberg. "We are enhancing profits by keeping employees satisfied."

Doing good, however, can be confused in the popular mind with looking good. Take chemical manufacturer Du Pont, frequently cited as a model of family friendliness. Since 1985, Du Pont has publicized its in-house surveys showing increased interest among male employees in family leave. The most recent, released in 1991, stated that 35 percent of men favored time off to care for their newborns, up from 15 percent five years before. The study did not note that in the previous four years only 54 men out of 41,000 actually took family leave. "Having an image that is ahead of reality has given us something to strive for," Faith Wohl, director of work-family programs, says in Du Pont's defense.

Check-in-the-box. Even the most committed companies also discover that putting policies on paper is just the first step; management has to get the message. Michelle Carpenter, manager of work/family strategies for Aetna Life & Casualty Co. in Hartford, Conn. — Zoë Baird's employer and named by *Working Mother* magazine last fall as among the 10 family-friendliest companies in America — estimates that no more than 3 in 10 supervisors at the company fully support employees who want to take advantage of Aetna's programs. "Getting managers to buy into them is extremely difficult," she says, citing the stubborn persistence of some in scheduling meetings for early morning and late afternoon. That sabotages day-care arrangements and signals that truly committed employees let nothing interfere with work.

Flawed measures of employee benefits have perpetuated the impression that a genuine revolution is at hand. Surveys of work and family policies by business-research groups and benefits consulting firms generally ignore small businesses, few of which can afford family services. The "check-the-box" mentality of many surveys often lumps together virtually useless programs with truly innovative efforts. A new survey by Hewitt Associates, a giant benefits consulting firm in Lincolnshire, Ill., is an example. The study shows that 74 percent of large companies offer some type of child-care assistance. But the bulk of that assistance turns out to be "resource and referral services" (translation: a list of potential child-care providers), offered by 41 percent of the companies, and dependent-care spending accounts, provided by 93 percent. These tax-free spending accounts permit employees to set aside up to $5,000 of their pretax salaries annually to pay for child care. Notwithstanding the tax advantage, the accounts have attracted little employee interest. At American Express, about 4 percent of an estimated 10,000 eligible employees participated in a dependent-care account during the 6½ years before the program was expanded in 1991 to include direct reimbursement of child-care costs. Hewitt spokesperson Christine Seltz admits that the company could play down the hype. "It was necessary early on to get people talking, but now it may be time for a more sober assessment," she says.

Since few surveys dig deep enough to reflect even gross distortions, highly informal programs often are given more weight than they deserve. A 1991 study by the Families and Work Institute, a New York research group, counted John Hancock Insurance Co. among the 35 percent of *Fortune* 1,000 companies that offer "flexplace" or telecommuting, both of which permit working at home during all or part of the workweek. Although John Hancock has no formal telecommuting policy and does not encourage such arrangements, by the survey's methodology the company was justified in its response because a few workers at the company do telecommute on an informal basis. "If it goes on it is very low-key," says Diane Smigel, vice president of corporate information services.

The appetite for trendy human-interest stories has made the media a too-willing partner in promoting overzealous corporate claims. Television reports and newspaper and magazine articles routinely herald the introduction of "model" programs like on-site day-care centers and elder-care services that cover few employees and often don't perform as hoped. Three years ago, the opening of Stride Rite Corp.'s "intergenerational day-care center" for children and the elderly was proclaimed with major articles in, among other places, the *New York Times,* the

Washington Post, the *Los Angeles Times* and the *Chicago Tribune.* To date, however, just two employees of the Cambridge, Mass., shoe manufacturer—long a supporter of family programs—have enrolled elderly relatives in the center, and none of the 20 current elderly participants is related to a company worker. "We need to do a better job of educating employees about what the center is and why they should use it," says Karen Leibold, director of work and family programs.

The problem may go beyond employee education, however; programs like on-site day care need a large and diverse work force from which to draw. The pool of employees who place their relatives in centers like Stride Rite's is generally limited, says Michael Creedon, a national elder-care consultant, since many elderly people don't live near their children and may be too frail to use day care. Demographics have also played a role in Stride Rite's child-care efforts. Employees' children make up 60 percent of the enrollment in the day-care center at the company's Cambridge headquarters, where the work force is relatively large and young. The work force in the Boston distribution center is much smaller and tends to be older; few employees' kids use the day-care center there.

The Stride Rite example shows the need for more than good intentions.

THE SITTER TAX

Now, Social in-Security

As if finding a family-friendly company weren't challenge enough, consider the tax bullets you must dodge when hiring someone to help around the house. The flap in Washington over paying a domestic worker's Social Security tax shows the maze you enter when hiring someone to clean, baby-sit, do repairs, mow the lawn—or whatever.

Suddenly you must determine whether someone is self-employed, and thus handles his or her own taxes, or is your employee. If the latter, and you pay wages of $50 or more in a calendar quarter, you must report the wages to the Internal Revenue Service and pay Social Security tax. When quarterly wages top $1,000, you must pay federal

unemployment tax. (A worker employed by a firm, say by a home-cleaning service, isn't your responsibility.)

Householders who fail to pay employment taxes don't even make a blip on the IRS's radar screen. But if an unreported employee later seeks Social Security benefits, a taxpayer could be nailed for back tax, interest and penalties.

The rub is that rules to determine whether someone is your employee are vague. Here are the key factors:

■ **Work for others?** The greater the number of people someone works for, the likelier the odds the IRS would consider the worker to be self-employed. A person who works solely for you, even once a week or less, probably is your employee.

■ **Behave self-employed?** People who have business cards, send invoices, solicit customers and claim to be self-employed if asked have a good chance of being treated as such by the IRS, especially if they pay their taxes.

■ **How is payment made?** Paying someone by the hour intimates status as an employee. Paying a flat amount in response to a bill carries weight in proving someone is self-employed.

■ **Degree of control.** Telling someone when to show up, how long to stay and how to do his job are signs of status as an employee. The more discretion you allow, the stronger the case for self-employment.

■ **Whose tools?** The kid who cuts your lawn and brings his own lawn mower might be self-employed. A kid who uses your mower is more likely an employee.

So what about a teenager who baby-sits on occasion for you and seems to be an employee? Does anyone *really* pay Social Security in such cases? Responds Jack Porter, national director of tax practice at the accounting firm of BDO Seidman: "Only if you want to be attorney general."

LEONARD WIENER

Even innovative work and family policies are frequently undone by seemingly immutable factors. For example:

■ **Supervisors balk.** In a 1990 survey of 521 large companies by the Conference Board, 90 percent of employers claimed to offer part-time schedules and 50 percent said they had flextime. In general, however, such arrangements are made at the whim of individual supervisors, even when the concept is formal company policy. That makes it difficult for most workers to break out of the 9-to-5 routine. A study last year by Federally Employed Women Inc., a nonprofit membership organization in Washington, D.C., found that 20 years after flexible schedules were introduced in the federal government, 60 percent of employees did not feel they could use them. Based on a sampling of 700 fed-

Reading between the lines

A guide to spotting family-loving firms

Cutting through the corporate haze to determine a company's real record on family issues calls for attention to key signs—and posing strategic questions. Intangibles can be more important than detailed written policies, since many businesses without formal programs will bend to accommodate individual employees.

One sign of a company's degree of family support is that top executives push the benefits. Laura Whitley, an international account manager with NationsBank in Dallas, felt she could look into a new flexible-scheduling program in 1991 after Chairman Hugh McColl circulated memos announcing training sessions for managers and urging them to pay attention to workers' family needs. When Whitley asked about working just four days a week, her boss didn't have the details. So she asked the personnel department to supply them, unworried that he would resent it. "When you know the head of the company is committed, it gives you confidence," says Whitley, who began spending most Fridays at home with her daughter in October 1991 and was promoted to senior vice president a year later.

No special favorites. Work-family programs promoted equally to all employees, not just executives or hard-to-replace creative types, signal genuine commitment. Fel-Pro, an automotive-parts manufacturer in Skokie, Ill., could be the model. Frank and Lupe Castro, for instance, started taking their 3-year-old daughter, Elizabeth, with them to work last month, dropping her off at Fel-Pro's $80-a-week day-care center. Frank then goes to the factory floor, where he runs an automatic punch press, and Lupe heads for the benefits office, where she is an assistant supervisor. They try to have lunch with Elizabeth once a week. In the summer their three older children, ages 7 to 13, go to work as well, boarding a bus at the factory that takes them to the company's $20-a-week Triple R day camp.

What mommy track? It doesn't always take flashy benefits to signal a company's family support; there are more subtle signs, too. If part-time workers or those taking parental leave still get promotions, for example, your career is less apt to get derailed because you take advantage of a family benefit. Companies that promote a team approach make it easier for co-workers to fill in for someone home with a sick child. And just looking around can reveal if employees are harried or can get home on time when they have to.

Job hunters who are less privy to company dynamics have to be more creative. Some key questions:

■ **Do many men use family leave or job-sharing programs?** It's a sign that family concerns aren't culturally taboo.

■ **Are there flexible arrangements for staying home with a sick child?** If such days are deducted from vacation time, the company probably won't respond enthusiastically to other family needs.

■ **Can I interview future co-workers?** (You wouldn't want to ask this until a job offer materialized, of course.) "If the company says no," says consultant Lyn Christiansen of Argos Executive Group near Boston, "they're hiding something." If the company agrees, talking to other employees can give you a good sense of corporate priorities. Nervous job seekers might call the company's personnel office and ask about turnover rates and participation in work-family programs, identifying themselves only as possible applicants.

How a boss or recruiter answers questions about family benefits can be more telling than the answer itself, says Fran Rodgers, head of the Boston consulting firm Work/Family Directions. "The best answer is not glib," she says. "You want to see a company that is struggling with the issue"—that openly states, for instance, it is constantly reworking its policies. Many companies, for example, may quickly point to formal flextime policies but allow only a one-hour twist on the normal schedule.

Creative compromises. An employer interested more in the results of your work than in how you get there is more prone to cut some slack for workers even in the absence of a formal policy. Plante & Moran, a 600-person Michigan accounting firm, encourages workers to perform their work on flexible schedules if they need to, although it has only loose guidelines. Accountant Colleen Rose decided she wanted to work part time after having her first baby 5½ years ago and approached her boss with a plan to scale back from a full workweek to three 10-hour days. Her boss agreed—and a year later offered her a promotion to manager of her seven-person department, even though Plante & Moran had never had a part-time manager. The two worked out a compromise: Rose would handle fewer clients than her predecessor but would make herself available whenever a client or an employee needed her, even on her days off. She still works 40 hours occasionally, earning additional pay, but she says her own flexibility is worth the extra time at home with her children.

Employees might even recommend companywide programs to bosses who have similar family concerns. Carol Bowles, who runs a 15-person engineering firm with her husband in North Ferrisburg, Vt., didn't think much about child-care benefits until she had a baby in 1986. She began taking her child to work, and employees with their own kids asked about splitting the cost of a baby sitter. Bowles eventually hired two day-care providers and spent $2,500 to buy a used mobile home and convert it to a small on-site day-care center that's now used by five employees. Having their kids nearby provides peace of mind, says Bowles, although "part of the issue was selfish at first." America's 33 million other working parents with no spouse at home wish their bosses were so selfish.

RICHARD J. NEWMAN

eral workers, the study concluded that flexible arrangements are "granted to favorites but denied to others."

The experience of Mary Maguire is typical. For three years until last June, the secretary at a U.S. Department of Defense office in Owego, N.Y., tried to work a part-time schedule of 8:30 a.m. to 3 p.m. so she could be home to meet her young son after school. During that period she had four different managers, only one of whom approved of the arrangement. "Whether I was able to work the schedule was completely dependent on who my supervisor was," says Maguire, a 46-year-old single mother. She ultimately went back to work full time and hired an after-school baby sitter.

The lower employees sit on the organizational chart, the less pull they have with managers and the more often they are shut out of family-friendly programs. In a recent survey by the U.S. Department of Labor on flexible schedules, 22.1 percent of managers and professionals but only 7.6 percent of blue-collar workers had such flexibility. A study by the Employee Benefits Research Institute, a public-policy research firm in Washington, D.C., found that women in professional occupations were most likely to be offered some kind of child-care program; women in service, production and agricultural jobs were the least likely.

■ **The culture is gridlocked.** Like any institution, a corporation has a culture, and that can be the biggest obstacle. "A company that calls itself family friendly but still gives awards to those macho 'heroes' who go 60 hours without sleep and work every weekend is clearly sending mixed messages," says Fran Rodgers, president of Work/Family Directions, a Boston consulting firm.

With downsizing the order of the day, few employees want to send a signal that they are less than 100 percent devoted to their jobs. In a Conference Board survey last year of 152 companies that claimed to have work and family programs, 69 percent said they believed employees were inhibited from using flexible schedules because of a concern that commitment is still measured by hours spent at the office. It's a concern well taken. "Employees who take advantage of flexible schedules experience significant damage to their careers," says a human-resources manager at Xerox Corp., which regularly shows up on family-friendly lists.

Even with the added security of the Family and Medical Leave Act, many employees, especially men, may be reluctant to take time off for fear of derailing their careers. So far, paternity leave has been a hard sell. Corning Inc., named one of the four most family-friendly companies in the country by the Families and Work Institute along with Aetna, IBM and Johnson & Johnson, estimates that no more than 10 men have taken paternity leave in the past two years. At Aetna, the number was nine in 1991 and five last year. Says Aetna's Michelle Carpenter: "The company still isn't sending men the message that it's OK to take time off. Most wouldn't even consider it." Quizzing small groups of men who have taken the leave, she says, might help the company understand why others won't participate. But with limited resources, she adds, it isn't an Aetna priority.

■ **Hopes run too high.** Imagination and vision cannot substitute for resources and reality. Database publisher ISI's day-care center was then CEO Eugene Garfield's dream fulfilled when it opened in 1982. A onetime single father who had struggled to find care for his child, Garfield was sensitized to working parents' plight and wanted ISI's center to be a model for other companies. But quality costs money. By the time the center closed, weekly fees for infant care approached $200—on the high side for the area and all but out of reach for the company's primarily middle-income, 550-person work force. What's more, by focusing on keeping the day-care center afloat, ISI ignored cheaper programs that might have proved more useful, like helping employees locate other, more affordable child care.

■ **Leaping, then looking.** A tendency to jump on the fad benefit of the moment without researching employees' needs has hampered many an attempt at family friendliness. During the three years Remington Products Co. offered its respite-care program, just four people used it, and it was scrapped in 1990. The service subsidized employees who wanted to hire a health-care aide to be with an elderly parent during nonwork hours and on weekends. Michael Duda, vice president of human resources for Remington, admits the company was anxious to be out in front with a family program and failed to adequately research the plan. As it turned out, Remington's primarily blue-collar work force relied on family and friends to care for elderly relatives and saw little need to pay for help.

"Family life rarely conforms to the neat boxes of the 9-to-5 world," says Rodgers of Work/Family Directions. Diane Graham, president of Stratco Inc., a chemical-engineering firm in Leawood, Kan., seemed to recognize that when she instituted a policy that allows employees to bring their babies to work whenever they want to. Few employees actually take advantage of the program on a regular basis, but, says Graham, they know it's there when they need it. For employees, that kind of flexibility is priceless.

AMY SALTZMAN

Business rethinks, refines, recycles, and recoups

Ted J. Rakstis

"The green movement" branches further into offices, shops, and factories as the working world learns that recycling makes both dollars and sense

A mericans are being buried under an avalanche of trash that shouldn't even exist.

According to waste-collection industry estimates, people in the United States each year throw away more than 1 million tons of aluminum cans and foil; 4.5 million tons of office paper; 10 million tons of newsprint; and earth-rupturing quantities of glass bottles and jars, metals, and plastics.

Landfills in many US communities are near capacity, and only 23.4 percent of the garbage consists of food and yard waste. The remainder is divided as follows: paper and paperboard, 42.1 percent; glass, 9.4 percent; metals, 9.2 percent; plastics, 6.5 percent; and other waste, 9.4 percent.

Moreover, most landfill waste is unnecessary, because nearly all such material could be recycled. Marcy R. Wydman, president of WITT Company, a manufacturer of recycling containers in Cincinnati, Ohio, observes: "The recovery and reuse of one ton of paper saves seventeen trees, diverts ninety-six gallons of water from the pulping process, and reduces the energy required to make the paper from virgin materials by the equivalent of two-and-one-half barrels of oil. With the average office worker throwing away at least a half-pound of paper each day, or more than 125 pounds a year, recycling makes good environmental sense.

"Including high-grade paper and beverage cans, businesses generate valuable office recyclables. Their recovery means less waste, less use of landfill space, and reduced trash-disposal costs."

There aren't enough recycling facilities in the US to handle what's already being hauled away by curbside collection programs (*see related story, next page*). Still, processing capability is bound to increase as organizations realize the economies that can be attained through recycling.

Public concern at last is mounting. Michael Peters Design, a New York marketing firm, learned that 78 percent of the consumers it surveyed in 1990 would be willing to pay more for "environmentally benign" products. And in the three years since that study was conducted, curbside programs in the US have burgeoned by more than 600 percent.

Another significant study was carried out by Gerstman + Meyers Inc., a New York City-based design-consulting organization. In 1989, Gerstman + Meyers found little consumer interest in environmentally clean packaging.

Only a year later, a second survey turned up a complete reversal in attitudes. Ninety-four percent of those questioned in 1990 said they believed that buying products in such packaging would contribute to the struggle to save Earth.

Companies that have established recycling policies are attracting and retaining top-quality employees.

"If you have a reputation for being a responsible business, people will be proud to work for you," says Jeffrey Hollender, chairman of Seventh Generation, a supplier of recycled paper in Colchester, Vermont.

Recycling doesn't represent an additional cost of doing business. By making your staff aware of why it's important, you'll *save* money, because you'll buy fewer supplies. If your company churns out substantial waste, you might even profit by selling it to a commercial recycler.

"Making a company 'green' can sound intimidating, indeed, to a small-business owner with too many things to do and too few people to do them," Mary Rowland writes in Your Company magazine. "But there's a lot of help and information available. You'll find handbooks, recycling services, and suppliers of 'benign' products.

"A good way to start, if you have the resources, is to have a consultant do an environmental audit, which may cost several thousand dollars. If you can't afford an audit, there are simpler things to do. You

must try to reduce waste, replace inefficient items, reuse whatever you can, recycle what you must dispose of, and buy recycled products. You can save the most money just by generating less trash."

WITT Company's Marcy Wydman lists these as the most essential steps:

• Make a firm personal commitment. Appoint a program coordinator, invest in recycling containers, and educate your employees as soon as the program begins.

• Instruct your coordinator to choose a waste-paper dealer, develop a collection system, select collection containers, meet with maintenance personnel, track the program to ensure that it runs smoothly, and analyze cost savings.

• Install recycling containers at locations where trash is thrown away most frequently. The most obvious areas are around copy machines, computers, common work centers, and individual desks and workstations. The best place for beverage-can-collection receptacles is near your cafeteria or lunchroom and in waiting rooms. To simplify separation and collection, color-code all containers.

• Organize your central storage area so that there's no chance for accidental mixing of trash with recyclable paper. Be certain that the location meets fire-code requirements. Many companies keep their main storage bins in the basement or near loading docks.

• Get everyone in the organization to participate. Begin with a signed kickoff memo that highlights the program's benefits and explains the separation and collection procedures. Explain where the revenue from the program will go. A share for an office party, for example, will build enthusiasm. After the memo is circulated, conduct a brief information session.

• Reinforce the recycling habit. In followup memos or on bulletin boards in heavy traffic areas, provide information on the amounts recycled, cost savings, and any problems that may exist.

• Besides a disposal program, put into effect other methods to reduce waste and reuse products. These include re-inking printer cartridges instead of throwing them away, eliminating unnecessary packaging, and circulating memos rather than making a copy for each employee.

• Because colored paper isn't collected in many programs, buy only white paper. Most important, purchase recycled white paper. When organizations express a preference for recycled products, more disposal companies will build recycling facilities to meet the market demand.

"Another approach to recycling that has been adopted by some companies is shredding paper for use as packing material," Patrick J. O'Connor reports in The Office magazine. "Some firms that didn't have shredders are buying them for that purpose.

"Aluminum and glass, as compared to paper, have very few categories. In offices,

the (recyclables) are mainly beverage containers. If they aren't returnable for a deposit or covered by a mandatory recycling program, these containers usually can be recycled locally through a commercial vendor or voluntary organization."

Some offices have too little waste to interest a recycling company. John Ortbal, author of *Buy Recycled! Your Practical Guide to the Environmentally Responsible Office*, recommends that firms with offices in multitenant buildings enter into cooperative recycling ventures.

> **'Companies that have recycling policies are attracting top-quality employees**

Ortbal, president of Services Marketing Group in Chicago, also suggests that you use as few photocopy sheets as possible by copying on both sides and using your copy machine's reduction features. In addition, written memos can be all but eliminated through telephone and voice-mail messages. If your company has a direct-mail list, Ortbal further advises that you weed out the names of prospects who haven't responded.

S ome big American companies are racking up huge savings through recycling.

Employees of Coca-Cola in Atlanta, Georgia, for instance, recycle nearly everything in sight. In one three-year period, they raised $50,000 for charity by selling otherwise useless junk. At AT&T's headquarters in New Jersey, the company saves $1.3 million a year from the recycling of office paper alone.

Bellcore, the New Jersey-based research arm of the Bell Telephone companies, makes $300,000 a year through the sale of recyclables and lower haul-away expenses. The company, which launched its recycling program in 1988, sells a videotape and other how-to-do-it materials to businesses that want to begin their own programs.

United Telephone of Florida (UTF), a Sprint company headquartered in Altamonte Springs, places its recycling focus on telephone directories. Through programs in thirteen counties, UTF in 1991 recycled more than 1,200 tons of directories. As a company publication points out, that kept 20,400 trees upright and saved 3,960 cubic yards of landfill space.

A UTF-sponsored program in Hardee County recruited the aid of schoolchildren and resulted in the return of 50 percent of all used directories. According to UTF, that's one of the highest return rates ever achieved in a voluntary collection program.

Steelcase Inc., based in Grand Rapids, Michigan, is one of the world's largest manufacturers of office furniture. In 1991, the company stopped sending fabric scrap to landfills. Instead, it was processed and used by the automobile industry as sound-dampening insulation. During the program's first six months, nearly forty tons of fabric were recycled.

The plan was set into motion when a fork-lift operator complained about the volume of discarded waste. Tom Hyde, a Steelcase project coordinator, organized a team of workers who knew that phase of production. Meeting weekly, they devised a collection system while management searched for and found a marketplace for the fabric scrap.

The Great Lakes Recycling Journal observes: "Fabric recycling at Steelcase is part of a large commitment to waste reduction. Other items now being recycled include office paper, corrugated (paper), sawdust, pallets, office ribbons, lubricants, tin, Styrofoam, telephone books, small batteries, plastics, foam, coatings, chemicals, and paint."

Long before US President Bill Clinton mandated drastic reductions in military expenditures, some armed-forces facilities were slashing costs through recycling projects.

Time magazine tells of one such effort that began in 1989: "J.J. Hoyt, recycling manager at the US Naval Base in Norfolk, Virginia, took over a solid-waste disposal program that had been costing taxpayers $1 million a year.

"A shrewd businessman, Hoyt was sensitive to hauling managers' needs and negotiated lucrative deals. Now, says one US Navy officer, 'not a tin can or newspaper falls to the ground on base.' (In 1992), Hoyt's program (earned) close to $800,000. 'The key is knowing the market,' he says."

On a more limited scale, entrepreneurs and small-office professionals can achieve the same kind of results.

Recycling programs often begin with a single idea. As one example, Levine/Schneider Public Relations in Los Angeles recycles all the paper, press releases, envelopes, cards, and labels that pass through its office each day.

"My challenge to all businesses is to get involved in doing something to recycle and conserve," says Michael Levine, the firm's president. "If not, we aren't meeting our obligations as good corporate citizens."

The Equity Group Inc., a financial public-relations firm in New York, has found an easy way to get second usage of most of its paper. Says spokeswoman Linda Latman: "We issue and print news releases on behalf of our clients and include them in the background kits we mail. Sooner or later, those releases become dated and obsolete.

"Instead of dumping them, we use the printless side of the press releases in our plain-paper fax machine and for drafts in

Process produces paper recycling

The Great Lakes Recycling Journal suggests a six-step process to make paper recycling successful in your office:

1. Appoint one of your most reliable employees to act as recycling coordinator. Working with him or her, motivate your employees to make recycling a commitment.

2. Talk to a waste-paper dealer or a local recycling center to determine what type of paper can be collected. Then, enter into a contract with a recycling hauler.

3. Set up a system that will enable your employees to separate paper at their desks quickly. For example, ask them to place computer paper in one bin, white office paper in another, and colored office paper in a third.

4. Prepare and distribute a list that describes which papers are "recyclable" and which are "trash." Most important, stress that recycling bins aren't garbage cans. Coffee grounds and the like must be disposed of elsewhere.

5. Publicize the results. Generate enthusiasm by calculating the total weight of the paper recycled by your staff in the past month. Even more compelling, estimate how many trees have been spared and how much landfill space has been conserved.

6. Buy recycled paper. Show your employees the end product of their efforts. And remind them that such paper can be recycled again and again.

Curbside collection ahead of its time?

Between 1989 and 1992, Time magazine reports, the number of curbside trash-collection programs in the United States alone soared from 600 to 4,000. Yet, much of what's being hauled away never is recycled.

According to testimony given before a US Congressional committee, *100 million tons* of newspapers are in storage nationwide because there are no places to recycle it.

Time remarks: "The problem is that the economics of recycling are out of whack. Enthusiasm for collecting recyclables has raced ahead of the capacity in many areas to process and market them. In recent years, many states and municipalities have passed laws mandating the collection of newspapers, plastics, glass, and paper. But arranging for processing—and finding a profit in it—has proved tricky."

The situation, however, may be only a short-term one. Some savvy processors have reaped substantial profits through the recycling of steel, aluminum cans, paper cartons, and cardboard.

Facilities to remove the ink from newsprint before it can be pulped to make new paper are tremendously costly. Still, smart deals can be made.

Many customers of Champion International Corporation, a major paper manufacturer, demand recycled paper. Champion Recycling Corporation, a subsidiary in Houston, Texas, built an $85 million de-inking plant. In turn, the city agreed to give Champion all its collections of old newspapers and magazines.

Says Champion International president Andrew Sigler: "This is a market-driven operation that's great for

Houston and gives us the assured supply we need for a profitable operation."

By the end of this century, recycling may be an economic necessity.

"Our members recognize that if you're not into recycling, you'll be out of business in ten years," says Allen Blakey, public relations director for the (US) National Solid Wastes Management Association. Based in Washington, DC, the trade group represents America's trash collectors.

Critics of recycling maintain that it will weaken the US economy, but Germany is thriving with a well-advanced national effort.

In December 1991, German retailers became obliged by law to reclaim such transport-packing materials as pressed foam and cardboard boxes. And, by mid-1995, German manufacturers will be required to collect 80 percent of their packaging waste.

The Duales System Deutschland, a recycling program initiated by private industry, had distributed collection bins to more than half of Germany's 80 million people by late 1992. Its goal is to reach everyone in the nation.

In Japan, recycling results are somewhat mixed. Time notes: "Japan's recycling rate is almost double that of the US—40 percent of municipal waste versus 17 percent. But the Japanese program shares some of the problems familiar to American recyclers. Milk cartons, one of the favorite recycling items, are piling up high in warehouses."

Hiroshi Takatsuki of Kyoto University compares his land's plight with that of the US: "Japan emphasized collection before coming up with an appropriate infrastructure for reuse."

our laser printer. In addition to releases, we use the other side of bad photocopies in the fax machine and the printers."

Manko, Gold, & Katcher, an environmental and land-use law firm in Bala-Cynwyd, Pennsylvania, initiated a basic recycling program that has become a model for many practices. It began when Jonathan Rinde, one of the firm's attorneys, commented to his associates: "Since we're an environmental law firm, maybe we should really try to use both sides of paper to reduce the paper flow.

"Perhaps we shouldn't use colored paper because it's more difficult to recycle. And what about those eight-and-one-half-by-fourteen-inch *yellow* pads that lawyers have been using for hundreds of years?"

The firm discovered that few of its vendors sold recycled legal pads. That prompted Rinde to recommend a radical departure from legal-profession tradition. He wanted to use *eight-and-one-half-by-eleven-inch white* pads. Rinde claimed that the smaller size would be both a paper reduction and recycling aid.

"But lawyers have *always* used eight-and-one-half-by-fourteen-inch yellow pads," one colleague argued. Another protested: "Let's not get carried away with all these new ideas!" Even though recycled paper at that time was more expensive, Rinde eventually won his point. Manko, Gold, & Katcher made the apparently unprecedented switch to small, white legal pads.

"All of us are feeling pretty terrific about what we're doing," says Mary McCullough, one of the firm's employees. "We now recycle newspapers, cans, and bottles. Also, we found legal pads with good-quality recycled paper. We use ceramic mugs or glasses instead of paper cups whenever possible. And our building recently started a recycling program. We like to think we had something to do with that."

NIBCO Inc., based in Elkhart, Indiana, manufactures faucets, industrial valves, and other flow-control devices at nine plants. Its recycling program involves each of its 4,500 employees.

Every work area is supplied with two wastebaskets: one for recyclable office paper and computer paper, the other for office-generated trash. Discarded office and computer papers are picked up each night by a commercial hauler and taken to a recycling firm hired by the company.

Aluminum cans are placed in lined containers throughout each NIBCO factory and emptied into a central aluminum-recycling bin once a week. Employees who live in areas not served by Elkhart's extensive

city recycling program are encouraged to bring all their home recyclables to work.

NIBCO buys only recycled paper products for office use. The office-supply requisition sheet itself is printed in soy-based inks on recycled carbonless paper. Further, the advertising department selects recycled paper for catalogs, price sheets, stationery, and all in-house printing.

Global Turnkey Systems Inc., a sixty-five-employee maker of customized computer software and hardware systems, went all out when it launched a recycling program at its facility in Waldwick, New Jersey. Laura Madaras, Global's corporate communications manager, conceived the plan and brought it to chief financial officer Michael Winer. What began as a recycling effort later turned into a wide-sweeping conservation campaign.

Madaras was named to head the drive. The early steps included the use of personal ceramic mugs bearing the corporate logo to replace paper and foam coffee cups, installation of bins and individual receptacles for various types of paper, pass-along memos in place of individual ones, centralized collection of aluminum cans, and a company policy of buying only recycled paper whenever possible.

Early in 1991, Winer decided to go beyond recycling and into total energy conservation. Heading a ten-employee volunteer cost-cutting team, he saw potential savings everywhere.

"By recycling paper," Winer notes, "you're saving energy, because paper producers don't need to create new paper. But you also can save your own electricity, water, and utilities in-house by initiating conservation procedures."

The team met every two weeks at lunch to discuss such energy-saving topics as high-efficiency light bulbs, energy audits, and water usage. Soon, conservation efforts swept through the company.

Initially, the energy-savings blueprint included the elimination of inefficient personal heaters, air-vent balancing, a strict policy of shutting off all unused lights and computers, and the installation of sun film on windows. That added up to a five-month saving of nearly $3,000.

Next, Global Turnkey cut its water usage by 40 percent when it installed low-flow faucet aerators on sinks and in the lunchroom. The sale of eighteen tons of used paper a year brought in monthly revenue of about $150. And with less trash going out, disposal services were slashed by $442 a month.

It all added up to about $10,000 in annual savings. Global used the money to buy

rolls, doughnuts, and bagels for employees; purchase recycling containers and energy-saving mechanisms; and make donations to local charities.

ompanies whose products require packaging and glass are coming forth to do their share. Dry Creek Vineyard in Healdsburg, California, for example, has asked glass suppliers to buy only recyclable cardboard boxes for its bottles.

Peterson and Sons Winery in Pavilion Township, Michigan, is the state's smallest winery. Even so, it has its own home-devised bottle-washing equipment and a recycling program. The company pays a refund of twenty-five cents for each of the 3,000 or so wine bottles that it sells annually.

Printers also are becoming aware of the need to recycle what they sell. In Kalamazoo, Michigan, TS Print Center operates two shops. Several years ago, Suzanne Cook, the company's president, volunteered to print brochures promoting Earth Day events in Kalamazoo. She inserted recycling tips in each envelope.

About 30 percent of her customers, Cook says, request that their printing be done on recycled paper. She suggests that they have all of it done that way, explaining that printers like recycled paper because it folds and dyes more easily.

"It looks beautiful," she adds. "There's even gloss-finished recycled paper. Many people are unaware that recycled paper exists. Once the demand increases, costs will go down and the stock will be easier to obtain."

Recycling has emerged as a popular community-service activity. One of the most spectacular events unfolds on the second Saturday of every month at the American Mall in Allen County, Ohio. Some 500 pickup trucks, vans, and other vehicles head for the mall to donate their garbage to the Tri-Moraine Audubon Society.

"We fill two forty-five-foot tractor trailers with about 35,000 pounds of newspapers, glass, and aluminum cans each month," says an enthusiastic Audubon officer. "It gets pretty lively. Our volunteers unload six cars at a time, but it still gets backed up."

Does that give you an idea for a Kiwanis club project? And, what about your own business or practice? Have you looked at ways to buy and sell recycled products? It's good citizenship, and, in the "green-conscious" 1990s, it's also an extremely smart business strategy.

ENVIRONMENTALISTS ARE ON THE RUN

Business leaders, local officials, and angry citizens
are demanding an end to rules based on
silly science and bad economics.
This time, they just might win.

Ann Reilly Dowd

HERE'S A PREDICTION that doesn't exactly sound like big news: In 1994, with the possible exception of a much needed reform of the Superfund law governing toxic waste dumps, no major environmental legislation will get through Congress. Ho-hum, you say? Wrong. The reason for this likely non-event is momentous—though largely unreported: For the first time since the green lobby swept through Washington more than two decades ago, environmental activists are on the run.

What's driving them back is a loose but powerful coalition of business leaders fed up with excessive regulation; state and local government officials tired of footing the bill when Washington issues new cleanup calls; and a growing pack of farmers, ranchers,

REPORTER ASSOCIATE *LaWanda Stone*

and other landowners angry at the way environmental laws increasingly erode private property rights. This crowd has no interest in rolling back or weakening most existing environmental protections—a good thing, since these by and large retain broad public support. Rather, their aim is to ensure that any *new* rule-making is based on sound science and sensible economics. Says Billy Tauzin (D-Louisiana), one of the movement's leaders in the House of Representatives: "We can no longer ignore the costs government imposes when it regulates. The heartbeat of this movement is a call for restraint and responsibility as the cornerstone of our nation's regulatory system."

Three reforms, dubbed the "unholy trinity" by opponents, dominate the anti-environmentalists' agenda. First and foremost, they hope to enact legislation requiring an assessment of risks and a cost-

benefit analysis whenever a federal agency issues a major new rule. Second, state and local officials want to pass a "no money, no mandate" law that would prohibit the federal government from imposing expensive new requirements without providing the wherewithal to pay for them. Third, property-rights advocates are demanding compensation when federal environmental actions severely limit the use and lower the value of private property.

Congressional support for these broad-based reforms is astonishingly strong. Last spring, despite stiff opposition from the green lobby, the Clinton Administration, and Democratic congressional leaders, the Senate passed an amendment sponsored by J. Bennett Johnston (D-Louisiana) that requires risk assessment and cost-benefit analysis on all major new environmental rules. The final vote: 95 to 3. A majority of

From *Fortune,* September 19, 1994, pp. 91-92, 96. © 1994 by Time Inc. Magazine Company. All rights reserved. Reprinted by permission.

members in both the House and Senate are also co-sponsoring "no money, no mandate" legislation. On the private property front, opponents have derailed the Clinton Administration's proposed Biological Survey, which would have empowered Uncle Sam to inventory all flora and fauna on every inch of America, including your backyard.

But while the reformers may have the votes, they don't control the legislative agenda; the only way they can get their bills enacted is to attach them as amendments to whatever environmental or safety legislation the congressional leadership decides to move. To counter this tactic, green activists and their allies on Capitol Hill are prepared to pursue a "kill strategy"—and deep-six any legislation that provides a vehicle for such reforms. Likely result: continued gridlock.

Even so, the political momentum is clearly shifting away from the environmentalists. To better understand why—and what drives the reform rebellion—consider the case of Montana rancher John Shuler. One snowy September night he thought he saw a grizzly bear lumbering past his living room window. Wearing only his skivvies, he grabbed his rifle and raced outside to find three bears rampaging through his sheep herd. When he fired in the air to scare them away, a fourth grizzly emerged from the darkness and turned to attack. Fearing for his life, Shuler shot the bear, which eventually died. For his crimes against an endangered species, the Environmental Protection Agency fined him $4,000.

NOW TRAVEL WITH US to Pretty Prairie, Kansas (pop. 600). The town faces a potential financial crisis over an EPA requirement that it spend as much as $450,000 to build a new water-treatment plant or dig a new well. The EPA's goal: to reduce nitrates in the water from 20 to ten parts per million, thereby lowering the risk of so-called blue-baby syndrome, a treatable blood condition affecting babies under 6 months. But only four babies that age now reside in Pretty Prairie, and all are red-cheeked and cooing. The town's sensible solution: Buy the kids bottled water. No way, said the EPA. So the town offered to buy all 600 residents bottled water. The EPA still wants either that plant or a well.

Or consider the paper industry, picked by the EPA as a model for a new, more cost-effective regulatory scheme designed to approach pollution control holistically rather than source by source. Problem is, the rules adopted under this new tack will still cost the industry $12 billion over three years, more than its total profits over the past decade. Most incredible: a new rule to reduce methanol that requires the installation of steam strippers and scrubbers—at $3.6 billion over three years—even though less expensive venting could do the job. Says Red Cavaney, president of the American Forest and Paper Association: "We'll have almost no new money for needed productivity and quality improvements or capacity expansion. This is out of control."

It wasn't always that way. From Earth Day 1970 through the late 1980s, federal regulators focused on the big, obvious sources of pollution, like oil- and coal-powered plants belching black smoke into the atmosphere and chemical companies dumping pollutants into the waterways. "In those days we could use relatively blunt instruments, like technology standards," says Harvard economist Dale Jorgenson. "The costs were relatively cheap vs. the benefits. And America was in a stronger position fiscally and vis-à-vis its international competitors."

But beginning with the Bush Administration, Congress and the White House set ever more sweeping and costly goals. Among them: cleaning up toxic waste dumps, protecting an expanded list of endangered species, reducing greenhouse gases, and phasing out a whole new range of chemicals found to be toxic in laboratory animals. Result: The annual cost of environmental compliance, says the EPA, rose from $42 billion in 1977 to roughly $130 billion today, a pace well ahead of inflation.

What's more, America's cleanup bill is considerably larger than those of its principal competitors. U.S. environmental spending amounts to 2.2% of GDP, vs. 1.6% to 1.8% in Germany and 1% to 1.5% in Japan, says Paul Portney, an expert at Resources for the Future, a Washington think tank. The EPA predicts that by the year 2000 the U.S. total will hit $178 billion, or 2.8% of GDP—assuming no new environmental initiatives.

A big part of the problem is that America's environmental policymaking has increasingly been driven more by media hype and partisan politics than by sensible science. Take Alar, a growth regulator that farmers used successfully for 20 years to improve the quality and appearance of apples. In early 1989 the EPA's Science Advisory Board deemed Alar a probable human carcinogen, based on tests involving high doses administered for long periods to mice. With actress Meryl Streep in the lead, environmentalists issued high-pitched warnings. And CBS's *60 Minutes* magnified the message.

Not surprisingly, panic set in. Parents poured apple juice down the drain. Stores pulled apple products off the shelves. U.S. apple growers lost some $100 million. But after five years of serious study, experts at the American Medical Association, Congress's Office of Technology Assessment, and the World Health Organization concur that in the trace amounts present on apples, Alar poses no real threat to human health. Richard Adamson of the National Cancer Institute says the risk is less than that incurred by eating a well-done hamburger or a peanut butter sandwich.

SADLY, THE CASE OF ALAR is more the rule than the exception. No one doubts, for instance, that prolonged exposure to asbestos increases the risk of cancer. But responding to public pressure, the EPA forced state and local governments to spend billions of dollars on removing asbestos from schools—even though the risk of premature death it caused was no more than 0.025 in a million. (By comparison, it's ten in one million for playing high school football and 1,200 for long-term smoking.) Now scientists at EPA and the National Academy of Sciences agree that removal actually poses greater risks because it releases particles into the air.

Despite the waves of panic that roll over America each year, some 500 scientists surveyed by the American Council on Science and Health have concluded that the threat to life from environmental hazards is "negligible." Smoking, drugs, and alcohol, they calculate, directly account for nearly 70% of the roughly one million premature deaths in America each year. Most of the rest stem from poor medical care, reckless driving, and unhealthy diet. Says ACSH President Elizabeth Whelan: "We're swishing at ants while the elephants run wild."

The woes arising from headline hysteria are often compounded by foolish lawmaking. Classic example: the infamous Delaney clause, which governs safety in food additives and literally requires federal officials to achieve "zero risk." In 1958, when the law was passed, zero technically meant a risk of no more than one in a million. But now sophisticated measuring techniques routinely allow scientists to measure potential threats down to one in a *trillion*—a million times less than one in a million.

More damage was inflicted in the 1980s

when a Democratic Congress—wary of Republican regulators appointed by Ronald Reagan and George Bush—passed a passel of sweeping environmental statutes and then deliberately barred the feds from considering costs when setting standards. Among the laws bearing this restriction are the Clean Air Act, the Clean Water Act, the Superfund Act, the Resources Recovery and Conservation Act, and the Safe Drinking Water Act. Says Harvard economist Robert Stavins: "Even when they want to do the right thing, regulators' hands are often tied."

But even when they aren't so bound up, the regulators' record is spotty. One reason, says John Graham, director of Harvard's Center for Risk Analysis, is the federal government's "obsession with the concept of a carcinogen." Typically, substances are classified as carcinogens if they produce malignancies in rodents at very high doses. But Graham points out the obvious: "The dose makes the poison." And the government rarely takes that into account. Whelan calls the phenomenon "mouse terrorism."

Nor is there any effort to systematically set overall environmental priorities, either within the EPA or across the federal government. Indeed, a 1987 EPA study concluded that there was an inverse relationship between what staffers considered the biggest risks and where EPA resources were being directed. Instead, the money moved with public opinion. Since then, little has changed. Laments Dale Jorgenson: "If we just regulated smarter, we could get the same environmental quality for half the cost."

SINCE THE LATE 1980s, Congress has taken a few important steps to grant companies greater flexibility in achieving environmental goals. Under the Clean Air Act, for example, it created a market in sulfur dioxide emissions that allowed utilities to trade pollution rights.

But such market-based innovations remain rare. The more common practice is still to rely on stiff technology or performance-based rules that push up compliance costs and undermine creative pollution-control efforts. Take natural gas, the clean, efficient darling of fossil fuels. Every President since Jimmy Carter has touted its virtues. Even so, the regulatory regime actively discourages fuel-switching, since it's cheaper and easier to meet EPA's percentage reduction goals with a dirty plant than with a clean one. And if you build a new plant that burns natural gas, you risk being classified as a "new source" of pollution and entering an even more terrifying regulatory hell.

Amoco tried to break out of this vicious circle by performing a joint study with the EPA of its Yorktown, Virginia, refinery. The idea was to figure out whether the company could achieve greater pollution control for less money if it was allowed to look at reducing emissions from the plant as a whole, rather than from specific sources. The answer was a resounding yes. Example: Amoco found it could achieve a far greater reduction in benzene emissions by spending

> ## "Forcing us to spend on unreal risks prevents us from tackling real ones, like lead paint or violence."

$6 million to improve the way it loads gasoline into barges than by spending $30 million upgrading its waste-water treatment system. But because EPA regulations focus on sewage systems and ignore barges, that route wasn't an option under existing laws. Overall, Amoco concluded it could achieve the same level of pollution control for 75% less if allowed to take a holistic approach.

RATHER THAN embrace these promising new experiments, however, many green activists continue to push ambitious and costly command-and-control-style initiatives. The most troubling may be a proposed ban on chlorine, advocated by Greenpeace, the National Resources Defense Council, and other environmental groups. Their charge: Chlorine is contributing to higher dioxin levels in soil and water, which may in turn lead to sterility in animals and humans. EPA administrator Carole Browner has launched a study of how to phase out at least some uses of chlorine.

In response, chemical industry executives point out that there is no evidence that chlorine has led to either cancer or birth defects in humans. Indeed, a chlorine plant explosion that sent a cloud of dioxin over Seveso, Italy, in 1976 produced no medical problems except a higher incidence of acne and nonfatal liver disorders.

What is certain is that the cost of banning chlorine would be astronomical—and crippling for many U.S. industries. Today, 85% of all pharmaceuticals, 96% of all pesti-

cides, 98% of all municipal water treatment, and much of the paper, plastics, and baking industries depend on chlorine as a component or disinfectant. Replacing it would cost U.S. consumers $90 billion, according to an industry-funded study by Charles River Associates, a Boston consulting firm.

Moreover, such a ban could perversely increase health risks. The government of Peru is suing the U.S. for classifying chlorine as a possible carcinogen. Based on that listing, Peru removed chlorine from its water supply and thus helped pave the way for a cholera epidemic that killed thousands. Insists Edgar Woolard Jr., chief executive of Du Pont, which manufactures many chlorine-based chemicals: "There may be some chlorine compounds that should be taken off the market, but very few. Independent scientific analysis will show that the benefits far outweigh the risks. The thought of banning it is just foolish."

Like business executives, many mayors and governors—including numerous liberal Democrats—are also fed up with Washington's costly one-size-fits-all approach to regulation. Up in Anchorage, sewage can be so heavily diluted with rainwater and snow that it contains virtually no organic matter. But the EPA insists on strict compliance with a regulation that forces municipal water-treatment plants to remove 30% of organic materials before discharging treated water into the ocean. To meet this target, Anchorage has had to recruit local fish processors to dump 5,000 pounds of fish guts into its sewage system each day—just so it can then clean up to the EPA's standards.

In Aspen, Colorado, Mayor John Bennett threatened to stand in front of government bulldozers rather than pay as much as $12 million to clean up lead deposits that were the remains of silver mining on Smuggler Mountain a hundred years ago. But even after blood testing showed that Aspen residents had below-average lead levels, the EPA refused to take the town off its Superfund cleanup list. Eleven years and $8 million later, Aspen is still fighting the EPA.

Columbus, Ohio, figures it will have to spend more than $1 billion between 1991 and 2000 to meet EPA mandates. By the turn of the century the average household there will pay $856 for environmental protection, more than for police or fire departments. And that will include spending some $24,000 a year to test for 43 pesticides not even used in the region. "Forcing us to expend scarce resources on unreal risks prevents us from tackling real ones like lead paint or violence on our streets," says Mayor John Lashutka. "That's the tragedy."

THE TRAGEDY that farmers, ranchers, and landowners complain about is the rigidity—and frequent absurdity—of strict enforcement of laws designed to protect wetlands or endangered species. When such laws come into play, the value of any affected property can plummet overnight. But the government is not required to compensate owners for such losses.

It gets worse. In some towns in Riverside County, California, the only people who saved their homes from forest fires last summer were those who broke the law by digging fire breaks around them, thereby upsetting the habitat of the endangered Stephen's kangaroo rat. In North Carolina, a 79-year-old man can't harvest 40 acres of mature timber because authorities found an abandoned red-cockaded woodpecker's nest there.

"Regular Joes are terrified of the environmental laws," says David Howard, vice president of the Alliance for America, a coalition of 552 private property groups nationwide. "Under the current regulatory system, you are guilty until proven innocent, and most people don't have the money to fight the federal government in the courts. So rather than trying to work with the government to protect the species, the answer is often SSS, short for 'shoot, shovel, and shut up.'"

Folks who run afoul of the wetlands laws have suffered even greater humiliations. Ocie Mills and his son Carey spent 19 months each in a Florida jail for dumping clean builders' sand on an otherwise dry lot that a federal district court later ruled was probably not a wetland. Bill Ellen, a noted environmental engineer who runs a nonprofit wildlife rescue center in

Virginia, spent six months in jail because during the construction of a wildlife refuge, he put two truckloads of fill in an area previously deemed not a wetland. Says University of Chicago law professor Richard Epstein: "These laws are berserk."

Altering those laws and others like them anytime soon hinges on breaking the current congressional stalemate on environmental issues. Voters may ultimately do that by their actions at the ballot box in

> On eco reform, "the Clinton Administration talks the talk, but it doesn't always walk the walk."

1994 and 1996. But a concerted push from the White House could make something happen sooner.

FOR NOW, however, Bill Clinton's stance in this debate is—no surprise—a straddle. While he has signed an executive order encouraging (but not requiring) agencies to perform risk assessments and cost-benefit analysis, the President has sided with environmentalists in opposing the so-called unholy trinity of legislative reforms. Vice President Al Gore and First Lady Hillary Rodham Clinton have actively lobbied against them. Charges lobbyist Wayne Valis, who heads a coalition of business groups for reform: "This Administration talks the talk, but it doesn't always walk the walk."

Might it do better in the future? In an interview with FORTUNE, EPA administrator Browner agreed that a new partnership between the regulated and the regulators is key. Indeed, she recently proposed a new "Common Sense" initiative designed to sweep away the legal impediments that bar companies like Amoco from taking a holistic approach to pollution control. Says Browner: "We need to create incentives for plant managers in companies all across the country to look for ways to get the most pollution control for the least amount of money. I need those guys working with me."

Three former EPA administrators—Russell Train, William Ruckelshaus, and William Reilly—believe what's ultimately needed is a new federal agency of scientists and economists that would assess risks, weigh costs and benefits, and help policymakers set governmentwide regulatory priorities. Another option might be for the President to create a high-level commission and charge it with hammering out a consensus on how to inject greater rationality and cost effectiveness into environmental rule-making. Such a body's members would include Administration officials, Congressmen, business and labor leaders, and environmental activists.

True, the risk that this exercise might simply produce a toxic waste dumpload of blather would be high. But if it were modeled on the bipartisan group led by Alan Greenspan that successfully tackled the controversial issue of Social Security reform in Ronald Reagan's first term—and coupled with, say, a two-year moratorium on any new environmental mandates—a commission could spark meaningful change. Increasingly, it appears, an angry American public isn't going to settle for less.

Combating Drugs In the Workplace

MINDA ZETLIN

Minda Zetlin is a New York-based writer.

George was one of the owners of a small, family-run business in the Midwest. One day, while walking around his manufacturing plant, he found a package of suspicious-looking white powder.

Bewildered, he summoned the local police; their investigation turned up an entire cocaine-dealing ring operating on his premises. In fact, the drug was being transported inside the stuffed animals his company manufactured.

Although names and identifying details have been changed, the above story is true. The point is a simple one: No matter who you are or what your company does, your workplace can be affected by drug abuse. And if your image of the typical drug abuser is a minority, inner-city teenager, think again. "Sixty-eight percent of drug users are currently employed," says Lee Dogoloff, executive director, American Council for Drug Education. "Seventy-six percent are white, which you would never know by watching the evening news." This, he says, explains the current concern with drugs in the workplace: "That's where they are."

Corporate America is beginning to think so too. Five years ago, an American Management Association survey of human resources managers showed that less than half their companies had addressed the issue of drugs at all; this year, the same survey showed 85 percent had established specific drug-abuse policies. Sixty-three percent were conducting some form of drug testing. (The possibilities include random testing of all employees, testing for "cause," as when an employee presents suspicious behavior or is recovering from a drug problem, testing as a routine part of post-accident investigation, or as a condition of hire.)

"Most major corporations now do pre-employment testing," Dogoloff says. Some managers only began such testing because most other companies in their communities were doing it. "They started thinking, 'Gee, what kind of candidates are coming to us?' "

Though most human resources managers believe testing is an effective weapon against workplace drug abuse, it does have passionate opponents. "Drug testing is an invasion of privacy," says Shelly Ginenthal, director of human resources at Macworld Communications Inc. "Besides, the accuracy is often in question, and a false positive can do a lot of damage to a person's reputation."

Whether or not you are in favor of it, drug testing alone is not enough, experts say. That belief is echoed by respondents of the AMA survey: Less than 9 percent of its survey respondents depend on testing alone to combat drug abuse. Most also provide drug education, supervisory training, employee assistance programs, or some combination of these.

Drug education is particularly effective, many companies have found. According to the survey, those companies that conducted drug education had a 55 percent lower test-positive rate than those that didn't. "A person who understands how a drug like marijuana interferes with coordination will have a different view of the crane operator's pot break—especially if he or she is on the receiving end of a bucket of concrete," Dogoloff explains.

PROCESS OUTWEIGHS POLICY

The foundation of an effective anti-drug program, experts agree, is a clear and coherent drug policy. "The first thing a company's management needs to do is figure out why drug use is unacceptable in its workplace and what it's going to do about it," Dogoloff explains. "To me, the process by which you figure your policy out is more important than what the policy is at the end. The thing not to do is hire some expert to come sit alone in a room and write up a policy for your company."

Instead, he suggests bringing together those areas of the company that must deal directly with drug problems: human resources, legal, safety, an EAP or a health department, and a representative who can speak for employees—whether or not they're represented by a union.

For one thing, he adds, you're more likely to create a policy that fits your company's philosophy, corporate culture and the industry it's in. Besides, "these are the same people who will have to live with the policy and implement it when it's done."

Whatever drug program or policy you wind up with, experts caution against ignoring the most common workplace drug: alcohol. Most do not make a distinction between alcohol abuse and illegal drug abuse—since drug abusers often use both at once.

"Alcohol is the overwhelming drug of choice," notes Jim Kelley, a partner in the Washington, D.C., law office of Morgan, Lewis & Bockius. Unfortunately, he says, many companies see alcoholism as a "run-of-the-mill" addiction. And because the media focus has been on illegal drugs, many companies have had a tendency to overlook alcohol abuse.

THE CORPORATE QUANDARY

Whatever you do, when faced with a drug abuse problem, "the first rule is: don't do nothing," Dogoloff says. "If you leave it alone, it's going to get worse."

MANAGED CARE— DOES IT WORK?

Talk to employee assistance program (EAP) professionals about drug rehabilitation, and you'll often hear the same complaint: a substance abuser comes to them for help and they recommend treatment—only to find the company's insurance won't pay for it.

At issue is the concept of managed care: reducing medical expenses, and thus insurance premiums, by ensuring that employees receive only such treatment that is deemed medically necessary. The idea has spawned an industry: Most major companies now have managed care companies overseeing employees' medical expenses and ruling out those seen as inappropriate; many of these managed care companies are subsidiaries of insurance firms. HMOs, though fundamentally different, operate on managed care principles, as well.

Managed care's detractors claim that this kind of care serves to treat employees only when they're really ill, and refuses treatment earlier, when illness might be prevented. Further, they point to the fact that both managed care companies and HMOs profit most by denying treatment. (HMOs can cut expenses, and thus raise profits, by denying treatment. And, although managed care companies may not gain directly by denying treatment, every time they do, they save money for the company that hired them.)

Managed care providers argue that it is the complete lack of control on medical spending that has driven insurance premiums into the stratosphere. Further, they claim, each individual case is evaluated according to the patient's needs and *not* the bottom line. So how can they

produce these savings that companies hire them to create? "If you're making decisions based on the client's needs, you're going to save money, because there's been a lot of inappropriate hospitalizations, people staying in the hospital longer than they need to, and that type of thing," says Jeff St. Romain, national account manager consultant for Human Affairs International, a managed care company and subsidiary of Aetna.

Whether good or bad, managed care has a profound effect on the treatments available to drug abusers. Most often at issue is an EAP's recommendation of inpatient treatment, which is frequently turned down in favor of much less expensive outpatient sessions. Frustrated EAP professionals are left scrambling for free beds at government-sponsored facilities, or finagling free beds from programs they've sent paying clients to in the past. In extreme cases, some have even doubled as social workers, counseling substance abusers themselves after coverage was turned down.

"The whole idea is to deny treatment," says Tom Ruggieri, LCSW, coordinator of the faculty-staff assistance program at the University of Maryland in College Park. "We've had employees who stay at home detoxing, in withdrawal for three or four days because we can't get inpatient treatment approved."

"HMOs, in particular, want the financially easy way out," says Valetta Evans, EAP manager for the American Red Cross. "Some have programs that don't do much at all, with only one meeting a week. Others will say: 'Okay, even if the person needs inpatient treatment, they have to fail at outpatient treatment first.' This is a tragedy. It just doesn't make sense."

Another EAP manager described one employee receiving drugs at home from a live-in boyfriend who was also physically abusing her. An insurance company denied inpatient treatment. Here was one case, he claimed, where inpatient treatment was clearly needed to get her out of a home environment in which going straight would be all but impossible.

But managed care professionals question this assessment. "You don't put someone in an inpatient program for housing reasons," St. Romain says. "What is insurance for? It's for medical conditions, not for housing. Companies can't afford to take on these kinds of situations."

Further, they argue, inpatient programs, especially ones of fixed duration, too often have been used as a rather costly panacea. "The idea is to go in for 28 days to straighten out—as if there were something magic about that length of time," St. Romain says. "I guess the magic is that insurance companies usually cover about 30 days of treatment."

"HMOs invariably want to manage treatment case by case," notes Glenn Young, chief operating officer of Health New England, an HMO in Springfield, Mass. "A program that automatically runs 28 or 21 days is not managing case by case."

And, he adds. "There's another aspect to this that EAP managers don't always talk about. The same company that instituted the EAP also decided to offer healthcare through an HMO or another managed care program. When the company's executives contracted for it, they knew what it meant. Often the two programs clash."

—M.Z.

As an employer, you are in a good position to help a drug abuser face reality, adds Ginenthal. "A lot of companies are quick to fire a drug abuser, but once that person is at large, the chances that he or she will get treatment diminish greatly." Often, the threat of dismissal will get a drug user into treatment when nothing else can, she adds. "So much of your identity and self-worth is tied to your job."

What's more, says Tom Ruggieri, LCSW, coordinator of the faculty-staff assistance program at the University of Maryland in College Park, "There are plenty of studies that show it's cheaper to rehabilitate someone than recruit, hire and train a new person."

Some job-related drug problems have straightforward solutions. Let's say an employee comes to work drug-impaired and relapses several times despite repeated rehabilitation treatment. You'd probably fire him: You'd have little choice. Or let's say someone stopped by your office to tell you she'd seen one of your employees smoking a joint at a private party Saturday night. You'd probably ignore this rumor without further substantiation.

But some drug-abuse incidents are not so clear-cut, presenting problems not only of good management, but also of good ethics. Following are five such dilemmas, each drawn from real life, though names and identifying details have been changed. *Management Review* asked for comments from

four experts: a corporate manager (**Norm Bush,** president and chief operating officer at ENSCO Inc., a Virginia-based research and development company), a human resources executive (**Shelly Ginenthal,** director of human resources at Macworld Communications Inc., located in San Francisco), an employee assistance program professional (**Dale Masi,** D.S.W., professor at the University of Maryland School of Social Work and president of Masi Research Consultants Inc.) and an attorney who specializes in this area (**Jim Kelley** of Morgan, Lewis & Bockius). Their answers illustrate the conflicting concerns of safety, fairness, productivity and compassion that confront managers when dealing with this difficult issue.

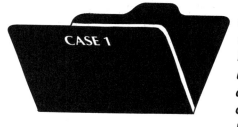

Charles operates heavy equipment for a power company. One evening, on his own time and away from company premises, he is arrested for driving while intoxicated. A search of his car turns up packets of cocaine, a loaded gun and drug paraphernalia. Under police questioning, he admits he's been dealing drugs. Without Charles' arrest and confession, the company would have no knowledge of his dealing, and there was no evidence that he has been using or selling drugs at work. But the power company has recently instituted a drug-abuse policy forbidding employees to sell drugs. The policy does not specify whether this stricture applies only to the workplace, or to outside locations as well. Charles promises to go straight and offers to subject himself to drug testing. Should he be allowed to keep his job?

NORM BUSH:

Although this is a serious charge, I would hate to condemn him on his first incidence without understanding what history was involved. A lot would depend on *how* we learned about the problem: If he was hiding it and we found out through other means, it would indicate that he wasn't trying to correct the situation.

If he came forward, though, and I felt he was being honest, I would want to give him a chance through drug testing—which would be reasonable in this situation—and counseling. Then, because the case is so severe, I would talk to his counselors and get their opinion as to whether we should retain him or not. I would at least want to look at the possibility that the employee may change.

DALE MASI:

Selling drugs is a separate issue from taking drugs. How you found out about it doesn't matter. If your company has a policy that says drug dealing will not be permitted, then you should follow the policy.

If the policy doesn't specify that drug dealing is only prohibited on company premises, then that policy needn't be limited to company premises. And, unless you're part of the federal government, you have the right to write a policy that applies to employees' off hours.

SHELLY GINENTHAL:

I would assume the policy refers only to the workplace. Employers don't really govern what you do outside, so I don't think the company's policy could be enforced. I would have stayed out of this entirely and really stuck to the performance issues: Has the employee's arrest affected his attendance? If it has, he might be suspended and referred to an EAP, which could suggest a drug program. Although the company can offer assistance, it cannot demand that he receive treatment. Then I would continue to monitor his performance carefully.

JIM KELLEY:

Is Charles protected by a union contract or not? That will become the major point. In the absence of a union contract, most employers would terminate him, especially if they were serious about eradicating drugs in the workplace. There is particular concern about drug dealers: The theory is that employees who sell drugs are likely to sell to their coworkers, since that's an obvious, accessible market. And even though Charles was caught off company premises, the policy is enforceable; most state laws don't protect illegal conduct.

But if Charles has a union contract, the picture changes. Under most common contracts, it's questionable whether the company can enforce his termination, unless it can prove some relation to job performance.

THE REAL-LIFE OUTCOME

This is the only case in this article in which names and details have not been changed, because they are a matter of public record. In 1985, the Florida Power Corp. dismissed Charles Waters under the circumstances described. However, Waters *was* protected by a union contract, and his union, the International Brotherhood of Electrical Workers, filed a grievance. A labor arbitrator reviewed the case, found that the anti-drug policy was unclear in its application to off-premises activity and ordered Waters reinstated with back pay.

Florida Power fought the arbitration by filing to have it vacated in district court. The company won its filing, but the union appealed to the U.S. Court of Appeals, Eleventh Circuit, and that court reinstated the arbitrator's decision.

Andrea is a brilliant, young computer designer who recently won an award for her work. However, she has been showing up to work with bloodshot eyes and slurred speech. Her company sends her to its EAP for testing, and her system is found to contain painkillers for which she has a prescription. She had started taking them to help with a back problem, which has long since improved, but she has now become dependent on the painkillers. She lies about her symptoms to get more drugs. EAP professionals send her to a rehabilitation clinic. After staying clean for four months, she again comes to work impaired. Should she be fired?

NORM BUSH:

I would consider the circumstances of Andrea's situation. She didn't get into this for kicks. She got involved because of a real problem, and *then* she got hooked. I would be more sympathetic to her than to someone who started taking drugs recreationally.

I would probably put her on probation and give her more time. I might invite her to work part time while getting treatment. In general, I would hang in there longer before I gave up on this situation. But she'd have to be working toward getting off the dependence. I hired her to do the work at a certain quality level, and she's not meeting that level.

DALE MASI:

It depends on what the policy is. If the policy says that a drug user who has a relapse should be fired, then you should follow the policy. If she were the porter that cleaned up the plant, would you give her another chance? I don't think so. And all employees obviously have to be treated equally.

I don't think firing on the first relapse is a good policy. It's better to give employees a second chance and fire on the third incidence of drug use. But even if you have a bad policy, you can't start making exceptions. You shouldn't give mixed signals. It's not fair to the other employees.

SHELLY GINENTHAL:

I would let her know in what areas her performance wasn't satisfactory and give her a referral back to the EAP. We would go through all the counseling again, and we would have many conversations about how important it is to stay off the drugs. Then I would warn her that this was her last chance.

It doesn't really matter whether the drug is legal or illegal. I'm not looking at the drug problem. I don't see a big difference between a person using drugs, or having a marital problem, or working a second job during the night and coming in too tired to function. What I care about is her performance, and she's not performing. She needs to get that fixed, and I'm willing to supply her with whatever she needs to do it.

JIM KELLEY:

The drugs Andrea is using are not legal: They were fraudulently obtained, even if she does have a valid prescription. Abuse of prescription drugs is a major problem in the workplace, and many drug policies address this circumstance exactly. If you don't have a specific policy, essentially, you have to evaluate the relationship between Andrea's lapse and her job performance. You might want to accommodate her if she's still doing a good job.

You might also have legal problems if you fire her: Under many state disability statutes and the federal Rehabilitation Act (which applies to government contractors), she might qualify as disabled. If she were an alcoholic, most courts would say you have to give her another chance. They are less understanding about drugs, but they might still take that view with a drug user who was in a rehabilitation program.

THE REAL-LIFE OUTCOME

The policy in Andrea's company is that an employee who tests positive for drugs within a year of rehabilitation is terminated, and so it was determined that she had to leave. However, because the drugs she was abusing were legally obtained, she was allowed to resign, rather than be fired.

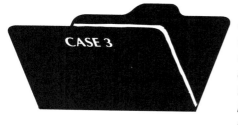

CASE 3

Nancy is a security guard in a manufacturing plant. For several months, she has been coming to work impaired by marijuana and depressants. Laura, Nancy's immediate supervisor, has discussed the problem with her several times, each time suggesting that Nancy seek counseling at the company's EAP. To let Nancy know that she cares, Laura has even gone to Nancy's home. Laura has the power to fire Nancy if she does not go to the EAP, but she lets the situation drag on. Laura is not doing her job effectively. Is it time for Laura's boss to step in?

DALE MASI:

It's very common for supervisors to avoid confronting drug users and holding them responsible for their behavior. Laura has got to remain uninvolved in Nancy's problem, while dealing with Nancy's performance. Going to Nancy's home is inappropriate; Laura is not a social worker.

As Laura's supervisor, I would tell Laura that she is responsible for Nancy's behavior. It's going to affect Laura's performance evaluation unless she handles the situation quickly. And that's the only way you'll get Laura to move.

SHELLY GINENTHAL:

I would try to get Laura some training. But because this is a safety issue, I would probably go over Laura's head and deal with the employee first. If it weren't a safety issue, I would coach and counsel Laura, give her an opportunity to handle the situation, or show her how it's done by meeting with her and Nancy together. I would send Laura to the EAP, and I would certainly want her to learn how to use the EAP in supervising people in crisis.

JIM KELLEY:

I would deal very severely with both supervisor and employee, es-

pecially given the nature of the job. At a minimum, I would give Laura a very serious counseling session. While she may believe she's being compassionate, she isn't helping Nancy—and she's harming the company.

As for the employee, this guard is worse than no security at all; I would get her off the job very quickly. Then I would give her a reasonable period of time to think about it—say, three days or a week—either without pay or as sick leave. During those few days, Nancy must decide whether she wants to go to the EAP. If not, she should be subject to disciplinary action, including discharge. Remember, an individual has to have an element of choice in going to an EAP—even if the option is losing her job.

NORM BUSH:

Because Nancy is in a position where security is paramount, she would be terminated immediately. When we hire someone in security, that person has to understand better than anyone how important it is. Because we deal with the Defense Department, we cannot tolerate any deviations at all that might jeopardize our classified material. If that happens, and the government decides we're not secure, they can cancel our con-

tract and put the entire company out of work.

As for Laura, I would counsel her and tell her I want Nancy removed. I'd explain that by trying to be understanding and sympathetic with Nancy, she'd failed to understand my concerns for the company. If she delayed further, I might have to put someone else in charge of security in the future.

THE REAL-LIFE OUTCOME

After several months of inaction—during which she'd been patiently briefed by her company's EAP head—Laura still had not dealt effectively with Nancy's drug problem. One day, Laura's boss, fed up with the situation, simply appeared at the security department and ordered Nancy to accompany him to the EAP. According to the EAP head, this forced Nancy to deal honestly, both with her counselor and herself, about what she was doing. As a result, he has high hopes for Nancy's recovery.

David is a former drug user who has spent time in jail. For the past three years he has been straight, and he now operates a forklift at a small construction company. Lately, however, he's begun having seizures, or "flashbacks," as a result of his earlier use of the drug PCP. He has been carefully evaluated by EAP professionals, and found to be clean of current drug use; indeed, they say flashbacks of this nature are quite common in ex-addicts. Mishandling of David's machine could be potentially dangerous to him and his coworkers. However, he has already had flashbacks while at the controls, and in each case the seizure caused him to release a handle, which simply stopped the machine. It is the only work he is qualified to do within this company. Should he continue on the job?

SHELLY GINENTHAL:

That's a tough one. I'd go right to David himself and really enlist his help in solving this problem. Then I'd put the situation to his co-workers—I'd maintain confidentiality about his prison record—and try to have them come up with a solution, rather than try to impose one. For instance, a coworker could be assigned to keep an eye on him at all times, ready to react if something happened. I would probably ask them to try this on a trial basis, so the situation could really be monitored.

NORM BUSH:

What I'd be tempted to do is retrain him for a different job and get him out of a potentially dangerous situation—where he could cause harm to himself and his coworkers. Even if it involved a cut in pay, it might mean a more permanent future.

JIM KELLEY:

Terminate him. You have no choice: He is physically unable to do the only work you have for him. Just because he's been lucky a couple of times doesn't mean this is a risk you or your company should take. It's unfortunate because he's clearly made an effort to stay away from drugs.

This is the kind of thing you tell high school kids about when you're warning them about the dangers of drugs.

DALE MASI:

I would not let the EAP make the decision. It's a medical decision, and I would want a brain scan and a full medical examination. I'd want to see what a psychiatrist who specializes in flashbacks had to say. I'd do that before assuming the seizures are flashbacks. It's a mistake people make often, and many patients are misdiagnosed. If the seizures aren't flashbacks, it may be possible to treat them.

If the people who do the examination are willing to sign off on him, and give him a clean bill of health, I'd let him go back to the forklift. Otherwise he might have to be retrained for another job in the company. If not, my hunch is you're eventually going to have to let him go.

THE REAL-LIFE OUTCOME

Company executives took a good look at David's history with seizures, including the fact that all of his seizures had been non-violent, and carefully considered the workings of the forklift he was operating. They took into consideration that he was drug-free. Eventually, executives decided that he posed no threat and allowed David to continue working the forklift. There have been no accidents so far.

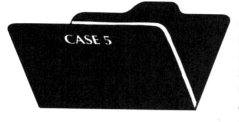

CASE 5

Joe has been working at a large manufacturing company for about 20 years. Seven years ago, he had a serious alcohol problem. The company does not have a formal EAP, but Craig, his manager, gave Joe a referral to a rehabilitation program. With Craig's support, Joe stopped drinking. Recently, in the wake of a divorce, Joe has begun appearing at work under the influence again. This time, Craig has decided to fire him. The company's HR department wants to veto Craig's decision: Joe is only nine months away from retirement. Early retirement might be a solution, but Joe refuses that option, claiming the benefits are too low. How would you handle this?

NORM BUSH:

If the guy has been productive all these years, there is no way I would fire him with retirement only nine months away. I would try to get a bit more creative and figure out what to do, even if I had to keep him on the payroll at $1 a week until he retired. I would also make an evaluation as to whether he intended to continue working past retirement. And I would try to get the EAP to help him. If Craig insists that he still wants Joe out of the workplace, I would respect his decision, but tell him that we can't fire Joe.

SHELLY GINENTHAL:

I wouldn't allow Joe to be fired. Instead, I would somehow negotiate a deal that would get him out of the office. I would counsel Joe on what help was available and explore other options. It seems Craig should be satisfied just having Joe out of the picture. After all, the problem isn't that he needs to fire Joe, it's that he needs someone who can do the job.

JIM KELLEY:

I'd bring him in and say, "Look, Joe, you're late, you're often absent, and we can't deal with your unreliability. We would like to put you in a treatment program, or at least have you diagnosed." Whatever you do, Joe won't be left with nothing. Under federal law, you become vested in your retirement benefits after five years, although the benefits are much higher if he makes it to retirement.

But just because he's eight or nine months shy of retirement is no basis to say that we'll carry him so he can vest completely. If he looks you in the eye and says, "I don't have a problem," then you have to apply your disciplinary rules as if he were anyone else. As a manager, there's no common-sense reason to do otherwise.

DALE MASI:

The chances are probably still very good for rehabilitation. Joe's been clean for years, and it was a crisis that caused him to drink again. What you need to do is get him back to the EAP—and he will go back there if he knows that his only other choice is going on early retirement. Even if rehabilitation takes up almost all of Joe's remaining work time, it will pay for itself in lower medical expenses, since medical benefits are usually part of a retirement package.

As for Craig, he's getting involved emotionally when he shouldn't be, and he needs help. He's taking it personally that his employee is drinking again, even though Joe's just been through a personal crisis.

THE REAL-LIFE OUTCOME

Angry both at Joe and the HR department, Craig made it his personal mission to fire Joe before the nine months were up. Eventually, he succeeded.

Embracing Diversity

Charles Garfield

Charles Garfield, contributing editor to Executive Excellence, *is CEO of the Charles Garfield Group in Oakland, CA (510) 272-9500. He is also the author of* Second to None *and* Peak Performers.

To understand certain issues and to change the way we approach people and problems, we need diversity in our organizations.

IN 1987, THE HUDSON INSTITUTE published *Workforce 2000: Work and Workers for the 21st Century,* a landmark study funded by the U.S. Department of Labor. The study projected that 25 million people would join the American workforce between 1987 and 2000. Of the new entrants, only 15 percent would be white males, almost 61 percent would be women, and 29 percent would be minorities (minority women were counted twice).

Diversity studies such as this tend to focus on differences in gender, culture, and ethnic background, but the definition of "diversity" also includes other differences—for example, the differences between young and old workers, between abled and disabled workers, and between straight and gay workers. All of these groups can—and do—contribute to the workforce. Unless we understand and draw on the diverse talents of our rapidly changing labor pool, unless we actively cultivate the leadership of women and minorities, we will be hard pressed as a nation to remain competitive in the coming years.

The seeds of a crisis are already present. A 1990 study conducted by the Hudson Institute and Towers Perrin shows that corporations are facing short-

ages of technical, professional, and secretarial workers and are experiencing high turnover because of "skills gaps." Some 70 percent of companies in the study reported difficulties in recruiting scientists and technical workers. Of the consumer products companies, 89 percent reported difficulties in finding workers with technical training, while the same percent of health-care companies couldn't find enough scientists.

As reasons for these difficulties, the study cites a lack of "leading edge" recruitment and training strategies and scarcity of progressive "support structures" for women and minority workers, such as daycare centers and mentor programs. These problems will be compounded as we enter an era of labor shortages.

Demographic changes in the workplace and in the marketplace compel us to learn more about one another. Minority markets in the United States now buy more than any of the countries with which we trade. Blacks, Asians, and Hispanics had a combined spending power of $424 billion in 1990, and their spending power is projected to reach $650 billion by the year 2000. Older Americans now control more than 50 percent of all discretionary income and spend more than $800 billion annually. It stands to reason that the workforce and its leadership must reflect the diversity of the markets they serve if they are to serve those markets well.

Business in a Multicultural World

Global competition, like domestic demographics, is exerting a significant pressure on us to learn about unfamiliar

cultures. Lewis Griggs, a San Francisco-based film maker and diversity consultant, told me that he was rudely awakened to the need for understanding different cultures when his own lack of such understanding stymied a potential business deal:

"I was involved in the start-up of a genetic engineering company, in the course of which I had a meeting with some Japanese pharmaceutical executives and became amazed at my own ineptitude because of the cultural differences. I discovered that it didn't matter what degree I had (an MBA from Stanford) or how skilled I was in business negotiations in this country or in a certain cultural style of business protocol and etiquette effectiveness. All this became totally irrelevant when my naivete about cultural differences became the reason that this meeting could go nowhere, that no trust could be established.

"What happened to me was really a shock of recognition that if this were true for me, it was true for a lot of Americans, and indeed was one of the main reasons for our trade deficit and our lack of competitiveness and our lack of ability to perform at a peak level internationally."

While ignorance of our foreign neighbors is troublesome, far more dangerous, says Griggs, is ignorance of our domestic neighbors. "Only 10 percent of us do business with foreigners, but 100 percent of us do business with Americans who are different from ourselves—Americans who are of Asian descent or African-Americans or Hispanics or Arabs or whatever. We all have cultural differences right here at home, the ignorance of which gets us into as much trouble as it does overseas."

The Faces of Diversity

Perhaps the most frequently discussed aspect of diversity is gender differences—not surprisingly, considering that women constitute more than 50 percent of the workforce, while the male viewpoint has overwhelmingly dominated the corporate scene. Theoretical arguments about nature versus nurture aside, the observers of both genders I interviewed agreed that men and women bring different styles and perspectives to work.

For example, Nancy Kaltreider, a professor of clinical psychiatry at the University of California at San Francisco, believes there's a big difference in male and females styles in the workplace: "I think women have a way of listening, of gathering information, of encouraging consensus as a part of their style, and less of a need to be seen as powerful leaders. I have found that women will encourage discussion of emotion-laden aspects of the work more.

"Women tend to humanize and to be aware of personal issues that are occurring in people's lives outside of the work situation, and women may be self-revealing in ways that tend to make the environment a little more relaxed. When women meet together on a work-focused activity, there is often an integration of meaningful personal events outside the office. For example, the first few minutes are more likely to involve discussion of the recent graduation of a child, death of a parent, etc. than the recent 49ers game. This acknowledgement seems to bring more unity to both lives. It is not uncommon for someone to bring light refreshments as symbolic celebration of a work or personal event. Women nurture each other better."

Price Cobbs, a University of California psychiatrist and a corporate consultant on diversity issues, agrees: "Women are not as afraid to get into the personal aspects of themselves as they relate to work. I find many men just beginning to be even remotely comfortable tapping the personal parts of their lives. They just want to stay with name, rank, serial number, and let me tell you what I do and how well I've done it."

Diversity—whether in the form of gender, culture, ethnicity, or some other attribute—has broad implications for how work is viewed, organized, and approached. Harold Epps of Digital Equipment Corporation in Boston has observed that diversity forces traditional managers to address a wider range of issues than they would in a homogeneous environment: "Women and people of color force white men to expand the way they approach particular issues."

Without an understanding and appreciation of the needs, backgrounds, and unique contributions of diverse groups, communication is difficult and misunderstandings are inevitable—even with the best of intentions.

A word of caution: It is tempting to reduce diversity to convenient categories in order to understand and manage it. But it is dangerous to pigeonhole individuals. People are defined not merely by what makes them "diverse" but by a broad range of personal characteristics. The point is, we are as diverse as we are numerous; each of us can be considered a segment of one.

By ignoring, suppressing, or eliminating diversity, we unwittingly stem the flow of innovation, the lifeblood of the corporation. Variety is not only the spice of life but, increasingly, the source of business success. To thrive, our organizations require diversity.

The Aging of America Is Making 'Elder Care' a Big Workplace Issue

Employees Who Juggle Jobs and Parental Needs Hand Bosses a New Challenge

Taking Days Off for Mom

Sue Shellenbarger

Staff Reporter of The Wall Street Journal

Faith Meurrens sees the work force of the future when she looks around her Omaha, Neb., office.

The 12 software designers she manages at U S West Communications Inc. are experienced, highly skilled and, at an average age of 42, about five years older than the typical U.S. worker. Only two have small children, but most have missed work lately to care for an aged relative.

Jerrie Cippera took time off to move her father from his Nebraska farm to a nearby town. Linda Smith rushed to Wyoming after her father had a stroke. Candace Sorenson's mother had a hip replacement. Duane Skaff wound up helping with three aged relatives. Two others, plus Ms. Meurrens and her boss, took time off when parents were hospitalized.

"Elder care is the biggest personal issue we face in maintaining productivity from day to day," Ms. Meurrens says.

BIGGER THAN CHILD CARE

The tip of a very disruptive iceberg has surfaced in the workplace, and is changing people's lives and job performance to a degree few had anticipated. "In the coming years, elder care will have a greater impact on the workplace than child care" or any other work-family issue so far, says Sally Coberly, an aging specialist at the Washington Business Group

on Health. "As the baby boom moves deeper into middle age, the need for elder-care services will simply explode."

About 22% of the work force expects to assume elder-care responsibility over the next three to four years, compared with 15% to 16% who have the responsibility now, says Boston consulting firm Work/ Family Directions Inc. By 2005, 37% of U.S. workers will be aged 40 to 54, the prime time for caring for elderly parents. By 2020, more than one in three employees will be providing elder care, says Andrew Scharlach, a University of California at Berkeley professor on aging.

Some companies' internal research suggests those numbers are understated. At New York Life Insurance Co.'s headquarters in Manhattan, 52% of 2,858 employees surveyed said they expected to have elder-care responsibilities within five years, compared with 50% for child care. Last November and December, employee calls for elder care from the work-family referral service at U S West Inc., parent of U S West Communications, exceeded child-care calls for the first time.

AN ISSUE FOR MOST EVERYONE

"This is really a demographic revolution, one for which we as a society are totally unprepared," says Dr. Scharlach. The number of people 85 or older who rely on their children will nearly double by 2030 and more than triple by 2050, the Census Bureau says, with families providing 80% of needed long-term care.

The revolution is touching even the highest ranking executives. Just before

Lawrence Perlman was promoted to chairman and chief executive officer of Ceridian Corp. in Minneapolis, he had to take time off from his job to make several trips to Palm Springs, Calif., to help his dying father. The experience "certainly sensitized me" to the elder-care issue, he says. Hugh McColl, chairman and chief executive of NationsBank Corp., lost time from work recently due to his father's long hospital stay.

Yet elder care remains largely undiscussed at most companies, a painful reminder of mortality that no one wants to face. "It's a hidden issue, a big shadow out there," says Max Johnson, a human-resources executive at Principal Financial Group, a Des Moines, Iowa, insurer.

THE STRESS

Few employees or their bosses are prepared for the disruptive force of elder-care concerns. Aged relatives' needs tend to erupt in periodic crises and stretch on for several years. That process of decline is more stressful for many employees than child-rearing, raising a thicket of sadness, anger, guilt and fear of loss.

Elder-care crises often strike in twos and threes, straining employee and employer to the limit. The odyssey of Mr. Skaff, a financial-system manager in Ms. Meurrens's group, was only beginning when he got the call everyone dreads from his mother's parish pastor in Sioux City, Iowa.

"Duane, I hate to be the bearer of bad news. But when I stopped by your mother's house today, I found a heavy smell of gas," the pastor said. Mr. Skaff's mother, fiercely independent at 88, had absentmindedly turned on her stove without lighting it, and the pastor "just happened to arrive at the right time," Mr. Skaff says. "She could have killed herself."

Traumatized by worry over his mother, Mr. Skaff moved her to his home in Omaha, then to a nursing home. But soon, another crisis arose when he found his wife's mother sprawled, gravely ill, on the floor of her Omaha home, where she had been caring for her wheelchair-bound husband, a stroke victim. The ensuing months were a nightmare, with Mr. Skaff helping care for his mother and in-laws. Briefly, his mother-in-law moved into his home, where his teenage daughter was already recuperating from a car accident.

Mr. Skaff was pulled away from work so much that he started going to the office late at night when his wife was home from her job. Other times, he worked nights or weekends, stretching the limits of e-mail from his home computer. "If my job hadn't given me flexibility, I don't know what I would have done," he says.

Such crises thrust care-givers, usually the children or close relatives of the sick, into a bureaucratic maze of trying to make successive care arrangements in a badly fragmented long-term-care system. The nation's patchwork of nursing homes, foster homes, adult day centers and home health-care agencies offer a dizzying array of often-unsatisfactory options. And about half the time, working care-givers live 100 miles or more from the relative, further snarling their efforts.

THE COST TO EMPLOYERS

Dr. Scharlach estimates productivity losses from elder care at $2,500 per employed care-giver per year, based on time missed from work and the cost of replacing care-givers who quit their jobs altogether. He estimates the lost output to elder care in the U.S. at $17 billion.

NationsBank was stunned to learn in focus-group and case studies that it was losing an estimated $1 million a year to absences for elder care. The company is starting an employee-help line and other elder-care programs this month.

While child-care problems tend to hit younger employees who often hold marginal jobs, employees with elder-care problems tend to be "older, more experienced, more advanced in their careers and therefore more valuable to us," Mr. McColl says. Women's increasingly crucial role in the work force intensifies the impact, says Michael Losey, president, of the Society for Human Resource Management, Alexandria, Va. "This isn't the old days, when the care-giver was a clerk-typist and she could walk away [from the work force], take care of an elder for a few years, then walk back in again."

As families fragment and scatter, more employees are tending to grandparents, stepparents and aunts and uncles, as well as parents. When a 25-year-old American Express Co. employee approached his boss in Florida recently about an elder-care problem, the manager was incredulous. "How old can your parents be?" the manager wondered. It turned out the employee was caring for his 85-year-old grandparent, says Barbara Katersky, American Express's vice president, employee relations. "We have a significant percentage of employees in that situation," she says.

Elder-care crises are taxing not only for employees, but for managers and coworkers. When Judi Renard's Alzheimer's-afflicted mother began wandering onto the freeway and hailing cars, Ms. Renard was frequently torn from her job processing customer orders for U S West Communications in Phoenix by calls from the police, saying, "Come and get her." Her mother would also accidentally set her house on fire or call Ms. Renard to remove imagined intruders. Though Ms. Renard tried not to miss work, she felt she had no choice.

Her absences posed "a challenge for all of us involved to be able to keep the business rolling," says her then-boss Susan E. Olson. Seeing Ms. Renard was under "amazing pressure," Ms. Olson called a meeting of her staff to explain Ms. Renard's situation. She invited a company health specialist to talk about Alzheimer's. In response, some employees worked overtime to cover for Ms. Renard and others just worked harder.

But "as Judi's manager . . . I felt at a loss over what to do, what to say, how to help her," Ms. Olson says. When her employees had child-care problems, she found it easier to discuss a range of options. But elder care "is sort of a scary thing," she says. Sometimes, she would sit in her office and talk with Ms. Renard about her rage and sadness at her mother's plight. Elder care "is an issue that we all are faced with," says Ms. Olson.

For U S West, Ms. Olson's strategy retained a skilled employee. Several years later, after moving her mother to three different long-term-care facilities, Ms. Renard still visits her in a nursing home, but works mostly uninterrupted. She has even been promoted.

PROBLEMS WITH HELP

When elder-care responsibilities hit an employee, they often must give up work, or work as they had come to know it. A seven-year study by the New England Research Institute in Watertown, Mass., found that when managers deny flexibility or elder-care demands grow too heavy, 3.3% of employees with such responsibilities quit their jobs while 8.3% change employment. Another 14% cut their work hours and 15% change their schedules.

Carolyn Johnson, a former field manager for a media-research concern, had a big problem finding someone to care for her mother, who has multiple sclerosis, in Ms. Johnson's Baltimore home. No one she hired would come until 8 a.m., and they were often late, making it hard for her to get to her job on time.

And few of the aides were reliable. Ms. Johnson fired one after she learned she was moonlighting as a prostitute. Another had a drug habit and abruptly quit. A third was dismissed after her mother complained she had yanked her earrings from her ears. Another asked her mother, "Do you think I get a kick out of pulling you back and forth in your wheelchair?"

At the office, a new boss wouldn't accommodate Ms. Johnson with a less rigid schedule. Instead, he increased her travel demands, requiring more overnight trips. The change "was a slap in the face," Ms. Johnson says. She resigned and started her own home-based business. Ms. Johnson, 45, also talks about aging issues to groups of care-givers.

Some managers find it hard to understand elder-care decisions like Ms. Johnson's. In the past, nursing homes were the accepted solution. But today, amid rising concern about the quality of life in old age, many employees see them as something to avoid as long as possible. That can leave a manager who put his own parent in a nursing home feeling "confused and even angry that the employee can't make the same decision he did," says Hank Linden, director of the employee-assistance program at American Express.

Elder care also unearths family issues that can be hard to decipher in the workplace. Some managers resent their employee suddenly becoming responsible for an aged parent and wonder why siblings aren't helping.

If an employee fears a manager's disapproval, says Ms. Katersky, the American Express employee-relations executive, "the talk goes underground. The employee suffers in silence while the manager wonders, 'What the hell happened to this employee who was a star and now isn't performing well?' "

The problem intensifies when employees are tapped for promotions or transfers. A telecommunications executive on the East Coast recently rejected a $1 million offer to become CEO at a West Coast firm because he didn't want to move far from his widowed mother, says E. Pendleton James, a New York recruiter.

An informal survey of U S West employees involved in a re-engineering of the company's service-delivery operations found that about 18% were weighing the impact of any transfer on their elderly parents—even more than the number who mentioned children as a factor.

Indeed, elders seem certain to become an increasingly visible presence in the workplace—much like new babies were in the 1980s. When Bernie Santore's workday as an assistant customer-service manager for First National Bank of Maryland stretches beyond the hours of her mother's adult day-care center, she sometimes brings her mother to the office. The 85-year-old woman sits in a back room, sipping tea and reading, while Ms. Santore or a co-worker checks on her periodically.

So far, the bank has been accommodating. "We'd be a little foolhardy not to recognize that care-givers need support," says Diane Murphy, a benefits manager for the bank.

Is U.S. Business Obsessed With Ethics?

That's the view of many foreign managers who resent distinctive American ethical practices being forced upon them.

David Vogel

DAVID VOGEL is professor of business and public policy at the University of California at Berkeley. This is adapted from an article that appeared originally in the fall 1992 issue of *California Management Review*.

In a number of important respects, the increased globalization of the economies of the United States, Western Europe, and Japan is making business practices more uniform. The structure and organization of companies, manufacturing technologies, the social organization of production, customer relations, product development, and marketing—all are becoming increasingly similar throughout the advanced industrial economies. One might logically think that a similar trend would be taking place with respect to the principles and practices of business ethics.

But business ethics have not yet globalized; the norms of ethical behavior continue to vary widely in different capitalist nations. During the past decade, highly publicized incidents of misconduct on the part of business managers have occurred in virtually every major industrial economy. Yet, while interest in business ethics has increased substantially in a number of countries in Europe, and to a lesser extent in Japan, no other capitalist nation approaches the United States in the persistence and intensity of public concern with the morality of business conduct.

During the past 15 years, more corporate officers and prominent businessmen have been jailed or fined in the United States than in all other capitalist nations combined. Likewise, the fines imposed on corporations in the United States have been substantially greater than in other capitalist nations. This both reflects the high standards that exist for corporate conduct in the United States and also serves to reinforce the perception that business misconduct is more pervasive in the United States. The American penchant for evaluating and comparing corporate social and ethical performance also informs consumer judgments of business. Various private, nonprofit organizations in the United States regularly "rank" corporations in terms of their behavior on such dimensions as women and minority employment, military contracting, concern about the environment, and animal testing; one annual guide, the Council on Economic Priorities' *Shopping for a Better World*, has sold close to 1 million copies since 1989. Such rankings are virtually unknown outside the United States, as are awards for "excellence in ethics." The Japanese may be obsessed with ranking corporations, but they appear to have overlooked this particular dimension of corporate performance.

Similarly, the number of companies that have been subject to consumer boycotts on the basis of their social policies has increased substantially in the United States in recent years. By contrast, consumer boycotts are much less com-

From *Across the Board,* November/December 1993, pp. 31-33. Adapted from *California Management Review,* Vol. 35, No. 1, Fall 1992. © 1992 by the Regents of the University of California. Reprinted by permission.

mon in Europe and virtually unknown in Japan (the most recent took place in the early 1970s and it involved the prices of televisions). A number of consumer boycotts have taken place in Britain, but far fewer than in the United States—even after taking into account the relative sizes of the two economies.

More generally, the debate over the role of business in Europe has focused on how to organize the economy, while in the United States it has emphasized standards of conduct for companies whose private ownership is assumed. This in turn may be due to another distinctive characteristic of American society: namely, the considerable emphasis that historically has been placed on the social obligations of business. Because corporations played a critical role in the development of cities and the shaping of communities in the United States, they long have been perceived as social institutions with substantial responsibility for the moral and physical character of the communities in which they have invested. Both the doctrine of corporate social responsibility and the practice of corporate philanthropy date back more than a century in the United States. By contrast, in both Europe and Japan, the responsibility of business historically has been defined more narrowly.

Ironically, it may be precisely because the values of "business civilization" are ingrained so deeply in American society that Americans tend to become so upset when the institutions and individuals they have looked up to—and whose values and success they have identified with—betray their trust.

Protestant Work Ethics

An important key to understanding the unique interest of Americans in the subject of business ethics lies in the United States' Protestant heritage: "The United States is the only country in the world in which a majority of the population has belonged to dissenting Protestant sects," according to Samuel P. Huntington's *American Politics: The Promise of Disharmony* (Harvard University Press). This has important implications for the way in which Americans approach the subject of business ethics. By arguing that one can and should do "God's work" by creating wealth, Protestantism raised the public's expectations of the moral behavior of business managers.

Thus, thanks in part to the role played by Reformed Protestantism in defining American values, the United States remains a highly moralistic society. Compared to the citizens of other capitalist nations, Americans are more likely to believe that business and morality are, and should be, related to each other, that good ethics is good business, and that business activity both can and should be consistent with high personal moral values.

While the high expectations of business conduct shared by Americans have a strong populist dimension, this particular understanding of the proper relationship between business and morality is not in any sense anti-business. It also is shared by much of the American business community. Indeed, the latter appear as concerned about the ethical lapses of their colleagues as is the American public. A survey of key business leaders that was conducted by Touche Ross (now Deloitte & Touche) in 1987 reported that more than two-thirds believe "that the issue of ethics in business has not been overblown in the current public debate."

Admittedly, some of these expressions of concern about business ethics amount to little more than public relations. But it is impossible to read through the various reports on business ethics in the United States without being struck by the sincerity of the concerns of the executives whose views they report.

Where else but in the United States would a group of nationally prominent executives establish and fund an organization such as the Business Enterprise Trust in order to offer annual awards for outstanding ethical behavior by corporations and individual managers? While the belief that good ethics and high profits go hand-in-hand certainly is not confined to American businessmen, they seem to articulate it more frequently than do their counterparts in other capitalist nations. One senses that many of the latter are a bit more cynical about the relationship between ethics and profitability. For example, in Germany: "Insider trading doesn't have much of a stigma. Tax evasion is a gentleman's sport," according to a March 23, 1987 *BusinessWeek* article.

Because the moral status of capitalism in Europe traditionally has been problematic, there appears to be much more cynicism about the ethics of business in Europe and in Japan. Europeans, in part due to the legacy of aristocratic and precapitalist values, have tended to view the pursuit of profit and wealth as somewhat morally dubious, making them less likely to be surprised—let alone outraged—when companies and managers are discovered to have been "greedy." For their part, "some Japanese seem almost inured to the kind of under-the-table favors whose disclosure sparked the [1991 Nomura Securities Co. Ltd. and The Nikko Securities Co. International Inc.] scandals," according to an Aug. 26, 1991 *BusinessWeek* article. As one Japanese investor told the magazine, "It's so much a part of Japanese culture and tradition that the people don't think they're doing anything wrong."

A Japanese political consultant mused to the *Washington Post National Weekly Edition* in September 1991: "I wonder sometimes when the Japanese people will rise up and say, 'We've had enough.' But the only answer I can give for sure is, 'Not in this century, at least.'"

Not surprisingly, many Europeans regard the current level of interest of Americans in the ethics and morality of business conduct—to say nothing of other aspects of American society—as somewhat excessive. Corporate codes of conduct, ethics-training programs, lists of "ethical" and "unethical" companies—all are seen as signs of an "unusually moralizing society," one that "people in old and cynical Europe often find difficult to take . . . seriously," according to the *Washington Post* article. The extent of moral scrutiny and self-criticism that pervade contemporary American society prompted *The Economist* to publish an editorial titled, "Hey, America, Lighten Up A Little."

Is the Whistle-Blower Always a Traitor?

The United States is distinctive not only in the intensity of public concern with the ethical behavior of business, but also in the way in which business ethics are defined. For one, Americans tend to emphasize the role of the individual as the most critical source of ethical values, while in other capitalist nations relatively more emphasis is placed on the corporation as the locus of ethical guidance.

Business ethics in the United States have been affected strongly by the "tradition of liberal individualism that . . . is typical of American culture," according to the *Journal of Business Ethics*. Not surprisingly, a frequent characteristic of business-ethics cases developed in the United States is that they require the individual to decide what is right on the basis of his own values. While the company's goals and objectives or the views of the individual's fellow employees are not irrelevant, in the final analysis they are not intended to be decisive. Indeed, they often may be in conflict.

By contrast, "in European circumstances it is not at all evident that managers, when facing a moral dilemma, will navigate first and foremost on their personal moral compass," the *Journal of Business Ethics* said. Rather, managers are more likely to make decisions based on their shared understanding of the nature and scope of the company's responsibilities. The legitimate moral expectations of a company are shaped by the norms of the community, not the personal values or reflections of the individual.

One possible outcome of the tension between the interests and values of the company and those of the individual employee is whistle-blowing. Critics of business in the United States have urged increased legal protection for whistle-blowers—and, in fact, some regulatory statutes in the United States explicitly protect those who publicly expose violations of various company policies.

By contrast, the idea that there could even be such tension between the individual and the organization is thoroughly alien to Japanese business culture, where whistle-blowers would be regarded more as traitors than heroes. Only a handful of European countries have laws protecting whistle-blowers. And few non-American companies have established formal mechanisms, such as the appointment of ombudsmen, to enable employees to voice their moral concerns about particular corporate policies. Workers in many other capitalist nations may well feel a greater sense of loyalty toward the businesses for which they work and greater respect for those in authority.

Check Checklists at the Door

A second critical difference between business ethics in the United States and other capitalist countries has to do with the role of law and formal rules. Notwithstanding—or perhaps because of—its traditions of individualism, Americans tend to define business ethics in terms of rules; the writing on business ethics by Americans is replete with checklists, principles, and guidelines for individual managers to follow in distinguishing right from wrong.

Americans' tendency to think of ethics in terms of rules is reflected in the widespread use of corporate codes among U.S.-based companies. Such codes are much less common in Europe, although their use recently has increased in Britain. One French observer notes: "The popularity of codes of ethics in the United States meets with little response in Europe. America's individualism does not correspond to the social traditions of Europe. These large differences make fruitless all desire to imitate the other's steps."

One French manager, whose company recently had been acquired by an American company, stated at an executive-training session I taught in 1991: "I resent having notions of right and wrong boiled down to a checklist. I come from a nation whose ethical traditions date back hundreds of years. Its values have been transmitted to me by my church and through my family. I don't need to be told by some American lawyers how I should conduct myself in my business activities."

Henri-Claude de Bettignies, who teaches business ethics at the French business school INSEAD, added at the 1991 Tokyo Conference on the Ethics of Business in a Global Economy: "Some European leaders perceive corporate codes of conduct as a device which deresponsibilizes the individual, i.e., he does not have to think for himself, he just needs to apply the codes of conduct which he has learnt and which—through training—have programmed him to respond in a certain 'corporate' way."

By contrast, European businesses appear to place greater emphasis on informal mechanisms of social control within the company. Indeed, European managers frequently profess astonishment at the apparent belief of many American executives and government officials that a company's adoption of a code actually can alter the behavior of its employees.

Is Bribery Always Unethical?

There is a third critical difference between business ethics in the United States and other capitalist nations around the world. Americans not only tend to define business ethics in terms of rules and procedures, but also believe that American rules and procedures should be applied universally.

For example, no other nation requires the foreign subsidiaries of its multinational corporations to follow the laws of their home country as frequently as does the United States. Thus, the United States is the only nation that restricts its companies from making payments to secure contracts or other benefits outside its borders.

A survey of European executives that was reported in *The New York Times* in March 1978 stated that, "Nearly 40 percent would never complain about bribery by a business rival—or answer charges of bribery against themselves." Similarly, in no other nation have corporations been criticized so frequently for exporting products that do not conform to the health and safety standards of their "home" country.

Universalism also has a second dimension having to do with the importance of the distinction between "us" and "them." American business culture—and American society—attaches considerable importance to treating everyone in the same arm's-length manner. By contrast, the Japanese—and, to a lesser extent, the citizens of Southern Europe—define their responsibilities in more particularistic terms: Managers and government officials place less value on treating everyone equally and attach much more importance to fulfilling their obligations to those individuals and institutions with whom they have developed longstanding and long-term relationships. (Significantly, it is very difficult to translate the phrases "equal opportunity" and "level playing field" into Japanese.) On this dimension, the United Kingdom and much of northern Europe are much closer to the United States.

All these dimensions are, in fact, interrelated. To summarize the American approach: Business ethics is about individuals making moral judgments based on general rules that treat everyone the same. By contrast, business ethics in Europe and Japan have more to do with managers arriving at decisions that are based on shared values, often rooted in a particular corporate culture, applied according to specific circumstances, and strongly affected by the nature of one's social ties and obligations.

Regulatory rules and standards, especially within the European Community and between the United States and Western Europe, certainly are becoming more similar. For example, a strengthening of environmental regulation has occurred in virtually all capitalist nations, while legal restrictions on insider trading—a decade ago, largely confined to the United States—are now the norm in Europe. Similar-

ly, a number of European nations recently have enacted legislation banning sexual harassment. The prosecution of white-collar criminals also has increased recently in Europe. In 1989, the first Swede to be found guilty of insider trading was sentenced to five years in prison.

Not only are many American legal norms and standards of corporate conduct being adopted in other capitalist nations, but as globalization proceeds and world commerce increasingly is driven by multinational corporations, these companies may well come to adopt common ethical standards. These developments are important. But they continue to be overshadowed by the persistence of fundamental national differences in the ways in which business ethics are defined, debated, and judged.

ETHICS
ARE STANDARDS LOWER OVERSEAS?

The conventional wisdom
says so, but others say we are too full
of "high-toned notions."

Andrew W. Singer

ANDREW W. SINGER is editor and publisher of *Ethikos*,
a New York-based publication that examines ethical issues in business.
This is an expanded version of an article that first appeared in *Ethikos*
in March 1991.

When American business people venture abroad, a common view is that they're wandering into an ethical no-man's-land, where each encounter holds forth a fresh demand for a "gratuity," or baksheesh.

William C. Norris, who founded and for many years headed Control Data Corporation, says, "No question about it. We were constantly in the position of saying how much we were willing to pay" to have a routine service performed overseas. Norris recalls frequently facing situations such as: "The computer is on the dock, it's raining, and you have to pay $100 to get it picked up. . . ."

In South America, firms often face a "closed bidding system" when dealing with that region's large, nationalized companies, says John Swanson, a senior consultant of communications and business conduct at Dow Corning Corporation. He says that his company has been locked out of the South American market at times because it refused to pay the bribes necessary to get that business.

In Japan, bids for Government construction jobs are routinely rigged, according to one former U.S. Government official who asked to remain anonymous—a result of Japanese firms purchasing "influence" from politicians.

Donald E. Petersen, former chairman and chief executive officer of the Ford Motor Company, cites ethical challenges in much of the developing world. "Give me a military dictator with absolute power, and it doesn't matter if he's South American or African or Asian—you've got problems."

Is the United States More Ethical?

Is this common perception borne out by reality? Are business standards overseas in fact lower than those at home? In 1987, Touche Ross, the accounting firm (now Deloitte & Touche), surveyed a range of U.S. business executives, members of Congress, and business school deans. Asked to rank the top five countries in terms of ethical standards, respondents placed the United States first, followed by the United Kingdom, Canada, Switzerland, and West Germany.

Some differences were found among respondent groups. Business school deans, for instance, put Japan at the top of their list—while business executives did not rank Japan among their top five at all.

When asked about the survey, William Norris says, "I agree with the second group. Control Data tried unsuccessfully for 15 years to get into the Japanese market. They kept us out with laws and subterfuges until they could catch up [to the U.S. computer industry]. Then they opened up to U.S. firms. I think that is very unethical."

Referring to the *keiretsu*, the famed Japanese business groups, Norris says, "In our country, we call that collusion."

Many U.S. executives agree that from a business ethics standpoint, the Japanese are a special case. Take gift giving. "It is an important part of how they conduct themselves," says Donald Petersen. Often, there is little thought given to the idea: "Give me the business and I'll give you a gift."

When dealing with the Japanese, Petersen found that it was futile to try to convince them of the superiority of the

American approach to business, in which, for instance, the receipt of gifts of any value in the course of a business transaction is frowned upon as a potential conflict of interest. His solution when dealing with the Japanese was simply to present the policy of accepting no gifts of any value as an American idiosyncrasy.

Bruce Smart, former U.S. Undersecretary of Commerce for International Trade, says that the Japanese are very consistent in sticking to their standards. However, those standards—which accept practices such as companies buying influence from politicians—may sometimes be looked at askance by U.S. eyes. Still, if by business ethics one means consistency with standards, "then the Japanese are probably very ethical," says Smart. Probably fewer Japanese executives cheat on their business expense sheets than Americans, Smart opines.

Underdeveloped Nations: "You'll be Tested Constantly"

In general, U.S. executives see only minor differences in business ethics as practiced in the United States, Canada, and Northern Europe. But most agree that there are some departures in the practice of business ethics when it comes to Southern Europe—Italy and Spain, for instance—and a tremendous difference in the underdeveloped nations.

"Based on my 40 years at Ford, there were no more difficult problems with ethical standards in Europe than here," says Petersen. But among the underdeveloped nations—particularly those countries with autocratic governments in which power is absolute and concentrated—it is often ordinary practice to hold out a hand for a bribe, or to take a company official for a slow walk through customs, until he gets the message that a "grease" payment is required.

Petersen maintains that a company can adhere to high standards—prohibiting bribery or even grease payments—and still function. "It's difficult. You'll be tested constantly, and at times you'll think you've lost business. But if you have a service that they want, they'll come around."

A "Holier-Than-Thou" Attitude

Not all agree that the United States is justified in taking such a superior position. "We have a tendency to take a 'holier-than-thou' attitude," says John A. Seeger, management professor at Bentley College in Waltham, Massachusetts. He maintains that U.S. standards are artificial and naïve rather than too high.

"We are often prepared to pay bribes because we hear that's expected—but that's because we hear from people who want bribes," says Seeger, explaining that managers don't often speak with the people who don't pay or receive bribes. "We expect to be held up, and so we get held up. It is the classic self-fulfilling prophecy."

When discussing overseas ethical standards, there is a danger of stereotyping people. Seeger, in fact, recently wrote a prize-winning management case based on a real incident in which the owner of a Persian Gulf company, Sameer Mustafa, an Arab, refused to bribe the engineer in charge of a Gulf construction project—and suffered economically as a result. Not *only* Americans have an abhorrence of bribery, Seeger suggests.

Kent Druyvesteyn, staff vice president of ethics at General Dynamics Corporation, agrees that we should put away ideas of American superiority when discussing ethics. Too often, says Druyvesteyn, ethical discussions take the form of: "We really do things well here. But when we go abroad, they do things so badly."

William S. Lipsman, associate general counsel of the Sara Lee Corporation, recently returned from a two-year assignment in the Netherlands. He says that he found litigation ethics standards in Europe to be higher than those in the United States. Business there is conducted on a more personal basis, Lipsman explains. "The concept that you, as a business leader, would sue another business without first sitting down at a meeting, face-to-face, is unheard of."

Bruce Smart doesn't even place the United States in the top echelon when it comes to national business standards. The Canadians, British, Australians, and perhaps even the Germans rate higher, in his view. His thinking: A kind of noblesse oblige still exists among the business classes in those countries. Conversely, in the United States, where there is a less entrenched business group, the prevailing attitude is that you make it whatever way you can. This attitude reached its apotheosis in the 1980s with the insider trading scandals on Wall Street, which Smart describes as "the biggest ethical blot on U.S. business" in recent memory.

Whether U.S. standards are in fact higher than those abroad is likely to remain a moot point. But in one respect the United States stands alone: It is the only nation that has sought to legislate moral business conduct overseas.

Can We Legislate Morality?

Passed in the late '70s in the wake of Watergate and the overseas bribery scandals, the Foreign Corrupt Practices Act (FCPA) made it a felony for U.S. companies to obtain business by paying off foreign government officials. From its inception, the FCPA has been controversial. "Managers in other countries often chuckle at the United States hoping to export its morality in the form of the Foreign Corrupt Practices Act," says Gene Laczniak, management professor at Marquette University in Milwaukee.

"It's anachronistic in today's world," says William Norris, the former Control Data chief. "It's like the antitrust laws in many ways. The world has passed it by." (The antitrust laws, enacted at the turn of the century, originally embodied a strong ethical element: The Government didn't want the nation's enormous "trusts" to run roughshod over the "little guy." That worked fine as long as the U.S. economy was an isolated system, say critics. But now antitrust laws may be inhibiting large U.S. firms from competing in the international arena.) In any case, says Norris, most U.S. companies don't want to become involved in activities such as bribing foreign officials.

R. John Cooper, executive vice president and general counsel of Young & Rubicam Inc., the New York-based advertising agency, makes a similar argument. The FCPA was enacted at a time when the competitive position of U.S. companies in the world was stronger—or at least perceived to be stronger—than it is today, Cooper points out. In 1970, the United States was the source of 60 percent of the world's direct foreign investment. By 1984, according to the United Nations, that figure had dropped to 12 percent. Japanese,

The Murky Land of the FCPA

The Foreign Corrupt Practices Act (FCPA) became law in 1977, in the wake of foreign bribery scandals involving U.S. companies that shook the governments of Belgium, the Netherlands, Honduras, Italy, and Japan. One of the most notorious incidents involved an estimated $25 million in concealed payments made overseas by Lockheed Corporation in connection with sales of its Tristar L-1011 aircraft in Japan. This culminated in the resignation and subsequent criminal conviction of Japanese Prime Minister Kankuie Tanaka.

The FCPA, which makes it a crime for a U.S. corporation to bribe officials of foreign governments to obtain or increase business, is controversial, in part, because it seeks to forge a distinction between "bribes" (which it deems illegal) and "gratuities" (which the FCPA permits). The difference is murky, according to the FCPA's critics.

"The law marked the difference between gratuities paid to low-level officials and payments made to authorities," writes Duane Windsor in his book, *The Foreign Corrupt Practices Act: Anatomy of a Statute.* "In many countries a payment to a customs official is a matter of course and a matter of economic necessity. A customs official may backlog an order or hinder a shipment by elaborately checking each imported item. The detrimental effect to the shipment is obvious. In response, lawmakers sought to delineate gratuities and bribes very clearly. But in reality the definition of gratuities was so vague that some people felt it had a chilling effect [on business]." **—A.W.S.**

European, and East Asian firms have picked up much of the slack, launching economic forays even into America's own backyard.

The United States risks becoming economically hamstrung by statutes such as the Foreign Corrupt Practices Act, suggests Cooper. "We have to reexamine some of these high-toned notions."

In the late 1980s, Young & Rubicam and three of its executives were indicted on a conspiracy charge under the FCPA. The Government asserted that the company had "reason to know" that one of its Jamaican agents was paying off that country's Minister of Tourism to obtain advertising business. In order to avoid a lengthy trial, the company paid a $500,000 penalty, says Cooper.

One outcome of that experience is that Young & Rubicam now has a policy that forbids even facilitating payments. Facilitating (or grease) payments are considerations to secure some ordinary service in a country, such as getting a ship unloaded in a harbor, or having a telephone installed. These are permitted under the FCPA.

Shouldering an Ethical Burden

According to Cooper, Young & Rubicam's recent experience "puts us in a position in which we're very reluctant to engage in a very common practice in some foreign countries: hiring people with relationships, who have the ability to generate business from official sources." The company can't go near such people, Cooper says. With increasingly heated international competition, the act is out of date, he says. It puts too much of a burden on U.S. corporations to know everything about their foreign agents—a burden not shouldered by foreign competitors.

The FCPA might have been an "overreaction" on the part of Congress to events such as Watergate and the overseas bribery scandals, suggests John Swanson of Dow Corning. (See box on this page.) "We're competing out there with strong and vibrant economies—Japan, the Common Market. We're a player but not a dominant player. We can't have

this legislation that is clearly not understood [but which] has such an effect on the viability of trade."

The FCPA brings back bitter memories for William Norris. Some years ago, Control Data Corporation was prosecuted by the U.S. Government under the Foreign Corrupt Practices Act for making payments in Iran.

"I never felt we did anything wrong," says Norris, explaining that the company was conforming to the laws of Iran. (In 1978, Control Data Corporation pleaded guilty to three criminal charges that it made improper payments to unnamed foreign officials. It was fined $1,381,000 by the U.S. Customs Service.) Looking back on his long tenure as Control Data's chief executive, Norris says that settling—and not fighting—that case was one of the few things that he ever regretted.

But the FCPA also has its defenders. "It's a tough trade-off," admits Marquette's Laczniak, but the bottom line is that the "U.S. public doesn't want its companies to secure business by paying huge sums of money to foreign officials." The FCPA, in other words, is really just a reflection of the prevailing values of American society.

"I have sort of a hard time arguing that it should be repealed," says Bruce Smart. Bribing foreign officials tends "to run counter to the idea of democratic representative government. If we countenance bribery, we make it more difficult for those people to find a better way to do business."

As for the idea that U.S. standards have to be adjusted to reflect the new economic realities: "That's an ancient argument, morally," says General Dynamics's Druyvesteyn. "It's one that goes back to Deuteronomy, in the Bible. 'Sure, things are rough. We've had a drought, and the sheep aren't fat. We may have to add a little to the weight.'"

The Slippery Slope of Grease Payments

What about facilitating, or grease, payments, which are permitted under the FCPA as long as they are documented? Such payments are the norm for doing business in some parts of the world. Indeed, government employees are often intentionally underpaid in the expectation that they will receive such gratuities.

The issue of facilitating payments is addressed in Dow Corning's ethics code. "The company felt in the early 1980s that if it didn't put it in the code, it would be like the ostrich with its head in the ground," explains John Swanson. Because grease payments are going on in many parts of the world, they should be recognized.

If the company sends a person to Mexico, and his household possessions are locked up on the dock, and he can't get them delivered to his house without a facilitating payment, then Dow Corning will pay it, says Swanson. "We don't like it. But to get that person to work a few weeks early, we will do it."

What did William Norris do when a big computer was stuck on the dock for want of a $100 payment? "I told them to pay the $100." To fail to make the grease payment in that instance would be "carrying it too far," says Norris. In many other cases, though, Control Data refused to yield to such extortion, and the company lost sales as a result.

"It depends upon what amount of money is involved," says Gene Laczniak. "If you are paying small amounts of money to individuals just to do their jobs [and that is part of the country's culture], then that is just the cost of doing business in that part of the world. But if the money is paid to sway people to make decisions that they would not otherwise make, then that is subverting the nature of the free market system," says Laczniak. "I don't think anyone wants the system to work that way."

Joanne Ciulla, a professor at the University of Pennsylvania's Wharton School, acknowledges that facilitating payments can be somewhat problematic. In many developing countries, bureaucracies are hopelessly inefficient, she says. One is, in effect, paying for an efficient service within an inefficient system.

This presents some moral problems. If everyone uncomplainingly pays facilitating payments, a government has no incentive to be efficient. On the other hand, there is not a whole lot one company can do to change the system. Ciulla is reluctant to recommend that companies "fight windmills" by banning such payments in toto. What companies can do, she suggests, is put pressure on governments to clean up their act. Airing such concerns might have an impact in the long run.

The argument that U.S. global standards are too high, however, is "totally absurd," in Ciulla's view. People sometimes overlook the deleterious effects that bribery has on developing countries, where the widespread practice impedes the development of a free market, she says. "How do you develop if you can't open a fruit stand without paying a bribe?"

She notes that even where bribery and corruption is widely practiced, it's not condoned—at least officially. Even in the Dominican Republic—considered by many to be one of the most corrupt places on earth—no one says bribery is okay, Ciulla points out. No one bribes publicly, it's done privately.

Barbara Burns, a public relations consultant and a member of the board of directors of the International Public Relations Association, says that in some South American countries, notably Brazil, it is not unusual for public relations professionals to pay to have favorable stories for corporate clients placed in publications, often by remunerating a journalist. "But everyone knows which publications these are—so placement is not so valuable to the client," says Burns. "And if you start paying off, it undermines your credibility, and finally your business." She adds that there are also many high-quality publications in Brazil that can't be "bought."

From a company's point of view, the practice of giving grease payments can be economically hazardous—apart from possible legal sanctions. "It's very hard to figure out the expenses. How do you anticipate costs?" asks Ciulla. Governments change, and a "contact" may fall from favor. How much additional extortion might one face down the road?

Integrity has Its Rewards

Adhering to higher standards doesn't have to have negative economic consequences, suggests Dow Corning's Swanson. Some years ago, Dow Corning surveyed its top customers. These customers found the company wanting in certain areas, namely response time and certain quality issues. On the positive side, the customers said: "We know you're a company of integrity, and that you stand behind your products, people, and service." Because of the company's integrity, says Swanson, "they gave us a three-year period of grace to improve our response times and quality. Otherwise, they might have taken their business to a foreign competitor."

U.S. standards are too high, then? "I don't carry that feeling with me," says Donald Petersen. "In general, I wouldn't want to see us say it's okay to reduce our standards to those of others."

And while William Norris is opposed to legislation like the FCPA—which was badly drawn and arbitrarily enforced, in his view—he doesn't recommend that U.S. companies compromise their high standards when operating abroad, either. "I don't think it's necessary to reassess those standards," says Norris. "It's better to lose a deal now and then than to lower standards, which will demoralize the workforce." In the long run, he sees high ethical standards simply as part of a quality management approach toward business.

Ethics in the Trenches

Robert D. Haas

ROBERT D. HAAS is chairman and CEO of Levi Strauss & Co.

Human-rights violations, child labor—how does a company deal with such problems?

A quick scan of today's headlines shows that ethical dilemmas are everywhere. Prudential-Bache Properties Inc. is sued by its investors, who allege it sold limited partnerships misleadingly; corruption and mismanagement cause the fortunes of Gitano Group Inc. to collapse; and executives of the American subsidiary of Honda Motor Co. Ltd. are charged by federal prosecutors with accepting bribes from dealers in exchange for franchises and hot-selling models.

What's going on? Have our ethical standards deteriorated, or are these headlines just a result of intensive media scrutiny? Can companies afford to be ethical in today's fiercely competitive environment, or are ethics a costly and convenient luxury?

I believe—and our company's experience demonstrates—that a company cannot *sustain* success unless it develops ways to anticipate and address ethical issues as they arise.

Drawing Multinational Lines

At Levi Strauss & Co., we're integrating ethics and other corporate values (such as empowerment and diversity) into every aspect of our business—from our human-resources programs to our vendor relationships. Let me illustrate our approach to linking ethics and business conduct with an area of increasing importance to many multinational corporations—the sourc-ing of products in the developing world.

Levi Strauss operates in many countries and diverse cultures. We must take special care in selecting our contractors and those countries where our goods are produced in order to ensure that our products are being made in a manner that is consistent with our values and reputation. In early 1992, we developed and adopted a set of global-sourcing guidelines that established standards our contractors must meet to ensure that their practices are compatible with our values. For instance, our guidelines ban the use of child and prison labor. They stipulate certain environmental requirements. Working hours can't exceed 60 hours a week, with at least one day off in seven. Workers must be present voluntarily, have the right of free association, and not be exploited. At a minimum, wages must comply with the law and match prevailing local practice.

We also recognize that there are issues beyond the control of our contractors in some countries, so we developed a list of country-selection criteria. We will not source in countries where conditions, such as the human-rights climate, would run counter to our values and have an adverse effect on our global brand image. Our decision to undertake a phased withdrawal from China, for example, was due largely to human-rights concerns. We remain hopeful that the human-rights climate will improve so we can reverse our decision.

Similarly, we will not source in countries where circumstances expose our traveling employees to unreasonable risk; where the legal environment makes it difficult or jeopardizes our trademarks; and where political or social turmoil threatens our commercial interests. In mid-1992 we suspended sourcing in Peru due to concerns regarding employee safety. Recently, we were able to lift the suspension because conditions in Peru have im-proved, although we still have not placed any business in that country.

To develop our guidelines, we formed a working group made up of 15 employees from a broad cross-section of the company. The working group spent nine months at the task, during which time its members researched the views of key stakeholder groups—sewing-machine operators, vendors, contractors, plant managers, merchandisers, contract productions staff, shareholders, and others. The working group then used an ethical-decision-making model to guide its deliberations. The model is a process for making decisions by taking into consideration all stakeholders' issues.

Once our guidelines were in place, training sessions were held for 100 in-country managers who would have to enforce them with our 700 contractors worldwide. Training included case studies and exercises in decision-making. The managers then made presentations on the guidelines to our contractors, conducted on-site audits, and worked with them to make those improvements identified as necessary.

Vexing Dilemmas

Drafting these guidelines was difficult. Applying them has forced us to find creative or unconventional solutions to vexing ethical dilemmas.

For example, we discovered that two of our manufacturing contractors in Bangladesh and one in Turkey employed underage workers. This was a clear violation of our guidelines, which prohibit the use of child labor. At the outset, it appeared that we had two options:

● instruct our contractors to fire these children, knowing that many are the sole wage earners for their families and if they lost their jobs, their families would face extreme hardships; or

● continue to employ the underage children, ignoring our company's stance against the use of child labor.

Courtesy Levi Strauss & Co.

Fourteen underage former workers at two Levi Strauss & Co. contractors' manufacturing plants in Bangladesh, including these children, now attend school.

Other companies facing this issue might have simply instructed contractors to fire underage workers on the spot. For Levi Strauss, this was undesirable. But we couldn't ignore our corporate values either. Looking beyond the obvious options, we came up with a different approach that led to positive benefits all around.

The contractors agreed to pay the underage workers their salaries and benefits while they go to school. (They do not work during this time.) Levi Strauss pays for books, tuition, and uniforms. When the children are of working age, they will be offered full-time jobs in the plant, which they are not required to take. Today, 14 children are attending school in Bangladesh, while another six are in school in Turkey.

And how did Levi Strauss benefit? We were able to retain three quality contractors who play an important role in our worldwide sourcing strategy. At the same time, our values and brand image were protected.

At times, adhering to these standards has added costs. To continue working for us, some contractors had to add emergency exits and staircases, improve ventilation or bathroom facilities, reduce crowding, and invest in water-treatment systems. The costs of these requirements were passed on to us in the form of higher unit prices. In other cases, we have forgone cheaper sources of production due to unsatisfactory working conditions or concerns about the country of origin.

> **In today's world, an exposé on working conditions on *60 Minutes* can undo years of effort to build brand loyalty.**

Conventional wisdom holds that these added costs place us at a competitive disadvantage. Certainly, they limit our options and squeeze profit margins. But over the years, we have found that decisions that emphasize cost to the exclusion of all other factors do not best serve a company's—or its shareholders'—long-term interests. Our five straight years of record sales and earnings, and a doubling of the size of our business in as many years, support our conclusion.

Moreover, as a company that invests hundreds of millions of advertising dollars each year to create consumer preference for our products, we have a huge stake in protecting that investment. In today's world, an exposé on working conditions on *60 Minutes* can undo years of effort to build brand loyalty. Why squander an investment when, with foresight and commitment, reputational problems can be prevented?

But don't take our word for it. There is a growing body of research evidence from respected groups that shows a positive correlation between good corporate citizenship and financial performance. These studies underscore that companies driven by values and a sense of purpose that extends beyond just making money outperform those that focus only on short-term profits. The former have higher sales, sustain higher profits, and have stocks that outperform the market.

These findings mirror our experience. Our values-driven approach has helped us:

● identify contractors who really want to work for Levi Strauss;

● gain customer and consumer loyalty because they feel good about having us as a business partner or about purchasing our products;

● attract and retain the best employees;

● improve the morale and trust of employees because the company's values more closely mirror their own personal values;

● initiate business in established and emerging markets because government and community leaders have a better sense of what we stand for and what to expect from us; and

● maintain credibility during times of unplanned events or crisis.

The conclusion is clear: There are important commercial benefits to be gained from managing your business in a responsible way that best serves the enterprise's long-term interests. The opposite is equally clear: There are dangers of not doing so.

Exporting Rights

Levi Tries to Make Sure Contract Plants in Asia Treat Workers Well

Inspector in Malaysia Checks Safety, Labor Practices Despite Local Wariness

Heeding Customer concerns

G. Pascal Zachary

Staff Reporter of The Wall Street Journal

PARIT BUNTAR, Malaysia—Amid the drone of sewing machines and the whir of fans overhead, Im Choong Hoe rushes past rows of busy seamstresses toward a fire extinguisher hanging on a wall.

This is Mr. Hoe's big moment. As an inspector for Levi Strauss & Co., the world's biggest supplier of brand-name apparel, he routinely travels around Southeast Asia to visit Levi's hired factories from Bangladesh to Indonesia. But rather than examining Levi jeans and shirts for flaws, he is searching for health and safety hazards and abuses of worker rights.

In many ways, his whole day depends on the condition of this fire extinguisher. In this plant of 1,000 workers, a fire would be disastrous, he says, and "lots of people" would die. "We can't afford that."

A few years ago, the idea of a U.S. multinational worrying about foreign contract workers' rights would have seemed hard to believe. But as reliance on foreign factories has soared and harsh conditions have been documented by the news media, a growing number of U.S. companies, such as Levi, Nordstrom Inc., Wal-Mart Stores Inc. and Reebok International Ltd., are espousing standards for hired factories that cover everything from wages and safety to the workers' right to organize.

"This is an issue that virtually all [multinationals] are going to have to address," says David Baron, an ethics professor at Stanford's Graduate School of Business at Palo Alto, Calif. "Most will choose to be more vigilant than before."

Pressure Increasing

For their own self-interest, if nothing else. In Europe and the U.S., unions and some politicians are pushing for retaliatory measures against exporting countries where workers lack clout and labor laws are either weak or routinely flouted. And companies such as Levi discern a greater tendency by some customers to shun products from sweatshops. Some outside observers agree. A growing number of people "don't want to buy a shirt made by children in Bangladesh or forced labor in China," says Simon Billeness, an analyst at Franklin Research & Development Corp., a Boston investment firm.

In the 1980s, Levi shifted about half of its manufacturing to hired factories such as this one in Malaysia, where today the best-paid seamstresses make about one-tenth the wages of those in the U.S. But Levi ignored working conditions at its contract factories; at one point, it didn't even know how many it had.

Then in late 1991, the closely held San Francisco company got a jolt. A contractor in the U.S. territory of Saipan was accused of keeping some imported Chinese women as virtual slaves. After finding that the workers were being paid below the island's legal minimum, Levi fired the contractor. It then formed a committee of top managers to review the way it monitored contractors. In early 1992, it became the first multinational to adopt a wide-ranging set of guidelines for its hired factories, covering the treatment of workers and the environmental impact of production. Levi even promised to inspect the factories regularly and cancel contracts with those that violated the rules.

Image Worries

Ethics aside, Levi was frankly concerned with its image among hip customers. "Anyone seeking to protect their brand and company reputation will realize these policies make business sense," says Robert Dunn, who helped design Levi's rights plan. "The alternative is to put ourselves at risk."

Levi's move paid quick dividends. When Wal-Mart was blistered in an NBC report for selling shirts made by Bangladeshi children, Levi cited its guidelines, which specifically rule out child labor, to persuade retailers to keep selling Levi garments from Bangladesh. (The retail chain subsequently instituted its own guidelines.) When an inspection disclosed that one of Levi's own contractors employed children, Levi—rather than order the contractor to fire underage workers whose wages were important to their families—decided to pay them while they attended school on the factory site until reaching age 14.

Levi has halted production entirely in Burma and China in response to what it considers systemic labor inequities. But because China is a major source of cheap labor, the decision sparked fiery debate within the company. A Levi committee recommended that it continue to do business with Chinese factories, seeking to reform rather than punish, but chief Executive Robert D. Haas chose to drop China instead. A few board members have objected to the decision, which Levi is currently reviewing.

Levi wins some praise for showing concern for the welfare of foreign workers who make its products but aren't on its payroll. "It is a healthy development that helps employers see that humane treatment won't bankrupt a company," says Lee Swepston, human-rights chief at the International Labor Organization, a United Nations agency in Geneva.

But because most companies don't make a priority of social welfare, skeptics say the intense competition in world markets will ultimately un-dermine scattered moves to establish standards. "High-minded efforts usually evaporate because people with far less scruples decide to low-ball labor, and dictates of the market eliminate these ethical assays," says Larry Byrnes, director of the Council on Hemispheric Affairs in Washington.

Geopolitics also can play a role. Although foreign governments usually don't take issue with the practices of individual companies, they often bristle at Western suggestions that they adopt U.S. or European labor standards. They see such efforts as thinly disguised attempts to hobble their manufacturers.

A typical exchange occurred in May when Malaysia's Prime Minister Mahathir Mohamad visited the White House. Mr. Mahathir said he can tolerate criticism of his country's lax labor regulations but warned that any Western move "to force us to bow to your demands" for a minimum wage and greater recognition for unions would amount to "twisting our arms, and that we will not accept."

Even if companies voluntarily adopt guidelines en masse, it may be hard to improve working conditions overseas without government oversight. "Corporations will find it problematic to police them on their own," says Sen. Tom Harkin, an Iowa Democrat who has sponsored a bill to ban goods made by foreign child labor.

Difficulties of the Job

The difficulties of looking out for contract workers are illustrated by Mr. Hoe's four-hour inspection of a Malaysian plant. He is no Upton Sinclair looking for muck to rake. A mild-mannered native of Singapore, he looks as if he stepped out of a Levi ad, wearing a blue denim chambray shirt, brown Dockers and loafers. Given the time constraints and the need for diplomacy, he is resigned to missing abuses—and to periodic embarrassments.

A few months ago, he was stunned when a Levi contractor in Indonesia—to whom he had given a clean bill of health—was found strip-searching female workers to determine whether they, as they claimed, were menstruating—and thus entitled to a day off with pay, according to the law of that Muslim country. Levi learned of the practice—and canceled the contractor—only after workers complained to an Indonesian rights commission.

Fluent in several Chinese dialects as well as English, Mr. Hoe is sharp and curious but eschews surprise inspections as impolite. He relies heavily on interview with bosses and reviews of company records. "I think of the contractor as family," he says. After 60 formal inspections and countless informal ones over two years, he has learned that patience and "a sense of humor" are the best ways to calm wary factory managers.

The very existence of the guidelines rankles some contractors, and not only because they usually end up bearing the cost of meeting Levi's demands. For example, Choy Ming Bil, who heads the Malaysian Textile Manufacturers Association, calls Levi's scrutiny "irritating" and accuses its inspectors of "splitting hairs" by examining employer wage records. He says that if Levi really were concerned about worker welfare it wouldn't alter its clothing designs so often, thus lowering productivity and piece-rate bonuses.

A Mixed Reception

At this Malaysian factory, a trio of managers are polite but clearly impatient with Mr. Hoe. Yet, they are accommodating. After all, Levi means business; this factory makes on average 150,000 garments, worth millions of dollars at wholesale, for Levi each year.

After entering a white-walled, air-conditioned office, everyone exchanges business cards, and Mr. Hoe accepts a cup of tea. Then he takes a 10-page questionnaire from his briefcase and carefully begins asking nearly 100 detailed questions, such as "Are first-aid supplies available in the facility?" and "Do workers have a right to refuse overtime?"

Before answering, the managers sometimes confer in Chinese. Gradually, a picture of a typical worker emerges: female, logging 55 hours over a six-day workweek, earning $6 to $12 a day depending on overtime. No medical benefits but free visits to a company doctor. Two-month maternity leaves and 16 paid holidays a year. An 80-cent "meal allowance" when overtime cuts into the dinner hour. No breaks during the day other than a 45-minute lunch—the workers' preference, the managers say, because it allows them to quit earlier.

"This is a good company to work for," Mr. Hoe declares.

Then he asks about health and safety. He hardly pauses when a manager asserts that no worker has had a reportable accident in years and that there are no accident records.

Mr. Hoe is eager to take up the subject of fire. Ever-present in his mind is a May 1993 toy-factory fire in Thailand that killed more than 200 people, and he has vowed to do whatever he can to prevent such a disaster at a Levi contractor. The last time he inspected this plant, he was pleased to find ample exits and no mezzanines, the makeshift second floors that can be difficult to evacuate. In Latin America, Levi has tried either to bring such mezzanines to the level of U.S. building codes, complete with fire exits, or to remove them. Some contractors have stopped doing business with Levi over the issue, though most have agreed to the changes.

Mr. Hoe knows that his plant holds yearly fire drills, but he wants it to do more. The managers tell him they have formed a fire-fighting team that gets training from a municipal fire brigade. Mr. Hoe smiles.

When the questionnaire is completed, the group breaks for a two-hour lunch. Afterward, Mr. Hoe

insists on trolling the factory floor. The managers scurry alongside him, trying to keep up with his brisk stride. The group walks only a dozen yards before Mr. Hoe spots that fire extinguisher and races toward it. He quickly finds a certificate that shows the extinguisher was recharged just two months earlier. "This is wonderful," he says.

Now there is a bounce in his step. In the next half-hour, he goes over the entire plant. He never speaks to any workers; he puts all questions to the managers. He criticizes a few blocked aisles. He checks on the progress of a waste-water treatment facility being built at Levi's insistence. The facility, for water dirtied in washing clothes, will meet not only Malaysian but U.S. standards.

He then checks a shabby but clean men's bathroom. Though a women's bathroom is empty, he is too shy to look inside. "I'm sure it's OK," he says.

Passing the office of the workers' union, Mr. Hoe notes that the door is padlocked but doesn't ask why. He accepts the managers' assurance that the union fairly represents the workers, so he doesn't find out that some years ago management formed a house union to kill an organizing drive likely to result in an independent union. The step was legal in Malaysia but appears to violate a Levi guideline endorsing workers' "right of free association." Mr. Hoe admits that he avoids union issues in Malaysia because wages seem adequate, and gross abuses, which abound in Bangladesh and India, are rare here.

Yet he offers just restrained praise for this factory, terming it "only average. The best plants have piped-in music and air conditioning." However, Levi's guidelines call only for factories to meet prevailing local standards. "I don't want to challenge them on luxuries," he says.

Returning to the managers' office, he reviews a sampling of time cards and pay records and finds no irregularities. Then he thanks the man-

agers for their "support," adding that he knows "your own corporate values and the upkeep of your image really makes you do a good job"— rather than any implied threat from Levi.

The stress on cooperation makes sense, Mr. Hoe says, but it upsets some outsiders, who charge that Levi's inspections are too easily manipulated by management. "On paper, Levi's guidelines sound good, but the company isn't doing enough to get independent answers," says Kenneth Perkins, an official with the union that helped the organizing drive that failed.

If a factory has a union, Levi inspectors ought to meet with union leaders and other workers off the premises, Mr. Perkins says. He terms the union at the plant inspected by Mr. Hoe a sham because the employment contract is "dictated by the management" and the union leadership "nonexistent." However, he says the workers' pay is slightly above average.

Levi concedes that it can do more to monitor its roughly 700 contract factories and that its handful of full-time inspectors and about 50 part-time ones are constantly refining their methods to close loopholes. When Mr. Hoe began inspecting plants two years ago, for example, he never checked workers' birth certificates in Bangladesh, as he now does routinely, or wage records anywhere. Just this year, he began inspecting factories in Indonesia every three months, as opposed to yearly elsewhere, because of concern that contractors may flout the nation's new minimum wage.

"It's going to take us a while to get this right," says Mr. Dunn, one of the program's architects.

Levi's defenders say that on balance its program, and efforts like it, are beneficial. Says Alice T. Marlin of the Council on Economic Priorities: "It's easy to poke holes [in the guidelines] if you compare them with what's ideal. But this is a good beginning."

Ethics and Social Responsibility in the Marketplace

- Marketing Strategy and Ethics (Articles 40–42)
- Ethical Practices in the Marketplace (Articles 43–46)

From a consumer viewpoint, the marketplace is the "proof of the pudding" or the place where the "rubber meets the road" for business ethics. In other words, what the company has promulgated about the virtues of its product or service has little meaning if the company's actual marketing practices and its treatment of the consumer contradict its claims.

At its core, marketing has a very noble and moral dual purpose: to satisfy human needs and wants and to help people through the exchange process. Marketing involves the coordination of the variables of product, price, place, and promotion to address effectively and efficiently the needs of consumers. Unfortunately, at times the unethical marketing practices of some firms have cast a shadow of suspicion over marketing in general. Since marketing is the aspect of business that is most visible to the public, it has perhaps taken a disproportionate share of the criticism directed toward the free enterprise system.

This unit takes a careful look at the strategic process and practice of incorporating ethics into the marketplace. The first subsection *Marketing Strategy and Ethics*, contains three articles describing how marketing strategy and ethics can be integrated in the marketplace. The first article provides a comprehensive and pragmatic conceptual base for combining social responsibility, ethics, and marketing strategy. The next article covers three areas of ethical challenge for sales managers. The last article in this subsection reveals how environmentally friendly furniture is gaining a following in the marketplace.

The second subsection is on *Ethical Practices in the Marketplace*. The first two articles delineate the impor-

tance of having an organizational culture that encourages and supports sound ethical behavior. "The Ethics of Bootstrapping" explores some critical ethical issues faced by a struggling start-up venture, while the last unit article reveals three consumer product companies that have exemplified ethical leadership in their domestic and global operations.

Looking Ahead: Challenge Questions

Does an organization have a responsibility to reveal product defects to consumers? Why or why not?

Given the competitiveness of the business arena, is it possible for marketing personnel to behave ethically and both survive and prosper? What are some suggestions you would make that could be incorporated into the marketing strategy for firms that want to be both ethical and successful?

In "The Ethics of Bootstrapping" article, Scott Cook makes the following comments: "What I've learned, and what all too many bootstrappers can miss, is that being truthful is good business. . . . Being ethical isn't a fairyland, Boy Scout idea, nor is it naive. I wanted to build a business for the long term. And trust is one of the most important sources of your power." Do you agree with this sentiment? Why or why not?

Which area of marketing strategy do you believe is most subject to public scrutiny in regard to ethics—product, pricing, place, or promotion? Why? What are some examples of unethical techniques or strategies involving each of these four variables?

Unit 4

Marketing By Professionals: Some Ethical Issues and Prescriptions

Patrick E. Murphy, Ph.D. and
Gene R. Laczniak, Ph.D.

Patrick E. Murphy, Ph.D., is a Professor of Marketing at The University of Notre Dame in Notre Dame, Indiana. Gene R. Laczniak, Ph.D., is a Professor of Business at Marquette University in Milwaukee, Wisconsin.

Introduction

Ethical issues facing the professions is a relatively longstanding concern. It is common practice to mention the "professional obligation" of certain practitioners to behave ethically. Examples of such professional duties are the obligations of medicine to provide health, of law to provide justice and of clergy to provide spiritual guidance. Another almost universal characteristic of the professions is the presence of a formal code of ethics and the existence of enforcement mechanisms for the code. We focus here, though, mostly on ethical questions revolving around the marketing and advertising techniques used by professionals such as accountants, dentists, lawyers and physicians.

The use of marketing and advertising techniques by professionals is an emotional and controversial topic. As Exhibit 1 recounts, the debate has raged for some time. From the Supreme Court decisions in 1976 *(Virginia State Board of Pharmacy v. Virginia Citizens Consumer Council)* and in 1977 *(Bates v. State Bar of Arizona)* that struck down prohibitions on such advertising, this issue has generated much debate in various professional communities. Feelings run deep on both sides, as exemplified by the following comment by former Chief Justice Warren Burger: "The public should never, never, never employ a lawyer or doctor who finds it necessary to advertise." His statement can be contrasted with one by a FTC official who said: "At bottom, the prejudice against advertising is that it creates pressure to compete." Related to the competition issue, is the feeling that advertising will place undue emphasis on price at the expense of the provider's quality of service. A final point of contention is that consumers seem generally much more favorably disposed to the use of advertising than many professionals.

In this article, we review the forces that have and will cause professionals to increase their marketing and advertising expenditures. We summarize the arguments for and against the use of these techniques. Then, we examine a few specific ethical issues relating to accountants, lawyers and the medical community. We conclude with **Ideas for Executive Action,** which should help advertising and marketing by professionals remain on a high ethical plane.

Exhibit 1

Legal Advertising: An Old Controversy

Over half a century ago, James F. Brennan, a California attorney, wrote a spirited argument against the prohibition, legal advertising and solicitation of clients by lawyers. Young, inexperienced, poor lawyers, he said, are forbidden to advertise or to solicit clients. But there is a sense in which this is *not* true of those attorneys who are wealthy and well established. The wealthy lawyer goes to his club and solicits the business of other wealthy persons on the golf course, at poolside, during dinner, at cocktail parties, and at other social functions. Because he has plenty of leisure, he may join philanthropic organizations and, through his activities there, may meet other persons who may be inclined, after talking to him, to retain his services.

Moreover, many lawyers work for large firms, engaged not exclusively in the practice of law but in other forms of activity closely related to law. Such firms and associations as banks, insurance companies, brokerage houses, utilities, unions, and large corporations of every kind may have one or more lawyers on their payrolls. Banks and insurance companies may advertise services related to setting up trusts and drawing up wills, all of which is the kind of work that is best done by lawyers and is likely to be done by the company's attorneys or in consultation with them. Thus, *these* attorneys benefit from the advertising done by the companies or associations with which they are affiliated; but the novice who is attempting to set up a solo practice is forbidden to advertise or to solicit.

Still others are fortunate enough to marry into the law business or to inherit one. They can afford to entertain the people who have lucrative law business to give.

All of this, Brennan said, was unfair to the impoverished young lawyer when he is denied the right to solicit business in the only way open to him. Even worse, he pointed out, was the fact that the bar associations were loaded with lawyers who worked for the big casualty insurers. It was curious, he said, that they were so eager to prevent others from soliciting business.

> Is it for the public interest or for their own interest? If the injured party has no independent legal advice as to his legal rights, these casualty insurance companies can settle with him on what they advise him his legal rights are.....If (plaintiffs') attorneys file more than three personal injury cases in one year, an investigation is made in the county clerk's office and elsewhere to ascertain how they got their cases. Why not investigate attorneys for bank and trust companies, title insurance companies and casualty insurance companies to ascertain how they get their cases?

Brennan noted that an attorney may know of legal rights that a party has but of which the party himself is ignorant. Yet, if the attorney informs the party of his legal rights and offers to assist him, he violates the rule and may be disbarred.

From *Business Insights*, Spring/Summer 1990, pp. 5-9. © 1990 by the Center for Business Development and Research, College of Business Administration at the University of Southern Mississippi. Reprinted by permission.

A poor man should be able to have a lawyer as well as the rich man, and he is more in need of one. The attorney who handles personal injury cases is the poor man's lawyer.

Forces Stimulating Marketing by Professionals

There are a number of developments in the last two decades that have moved professionals out of their traditional mode of operation. The ones we believe to be the most important are: emerging legal developments, growing competition and marketing's applicability to professional practice in areas such as new service development and franchising.

Legal Developments. Historically, most state and national professional organizations historically had prohibitions against advertising in their codes of conduct. The *Virginia Board of Pharmacy* case ruled "unconstitutional" a Virginia statute declaring that advertising of prescription drug prices by any pharmacist constituted unprofessional conduct. The *Bates v. State Bar of Arizona* case challenged the state bar association's ban on publicizing legal fees. The case was appealed to the Supreme Court, and it ruled in June 1977 that attorneys have First Amendment freedom of speech rights to advertise fees for routine services and that consumers have the right to receive such information. But the Court did not foresee major changes in the way that lawyers and other professionals practiced. They wrote: "We suspect that with advertising, most lawyers will behave as they always have. They will abide by their solemn oath to uphold the honor and integrity of the profession and the legal systems." The major professional associations followed the edict of the Court and relaxed advertising restrictions for dentists in 1977, and for the accounting, legal and medical professions in 1978. These decisions, then, set in motion the marketing and advertising of the professions.

Two subsequent Supreme Court cases reaffirmed the right of professionals to advertise. The first decision (the *Zauder* case in 1984) ruled that the use of illustrations or pictures in newspaper advertisements serves an important communicative function. The second case (*Shapero v. Kentucky Bar Association* in 1988) stipulated that states may not prohibit direct mail advertising aimed at specific target markets. The obvious conclusion that can be drawn is that marketing and advertising can now be legally used by professionals to promote their practice.

Growing Competition. The world of the 1990s is much more competitive for everyone, including professionals. There appears to be two reasons for this growing level of competition. First, law, architecture, dentistry and several other professions have become overcrowded with the number of new professionals entering the field. Professional schools continue to graduate large numbers of students every year. This means that the newer professionals, especially, must use marketing and advertising techniques to attract clients.

The mentality of most professionals toward promotion has also changed. They have moved from the traditional "country club" contact method of publicizing their service to a more sophisticated marketing perspective. This is not only due to the changing legal climate, but also because they see marketing as a viable mechanism to compete effectively in this changing environment. Competition probably will not diminish in the future, and most professionals (some reluctant, however) have recognized that marketing and advertising will continue to play a major role in this competitive world.

A third competitive development is the growth in different types of professional providers. Medicine and dentistry were dominated by individual practitioners who did not view themselves as competing directly with their colleagues. Now, in medicine for example, these individual purveyors are competing with clinics, group practices, HMOs as well as hospitals. In the accounting field, the so-called Big Six (reduced from eight) is not only competing with one another, but also with smaller firms, consulting organizations and specialty companies which provide highly specialized services (e.g., auditing for health care organizations). The pressure then is on all types of professional service providers to market themselves more aggressively against the new competitive forms.

Marketing's Applicability to Professional Practice. Some professionals have found that marketing concepts such as branding, new service development, alternate delivery mechanisms and franchising can be applied to their situation. If the professional wants to meet the needs of the time conscious and mobile consumer of the 1990s, such new approaches must be explored. Just as Burger King has found consumers to be loyal to their "brand", Humana has found that its brand of medicine is preferred by some consumers. The use of brand or corporate names has made it much easier to franchise legal, dental, optical and medical clinics. Such retailing of the professions began even before the Bates decision, but has gained popularity in the 1980s. Dental World, Omnidentix Systems, Nu Vision Centers and Sterling Optical are some of the best known professional services franchises.

As mentioned, even the more traditional professional practices have expanded their product line and altered their distribution network. For instance, ambulatory surgery, alcoholic rehabilitation, psychological counseling, personal injury law and management consulting by public accounting firms are recent additions to the product portfolio of service providers. Furthermore, professionals have begun using immediate care medical centers, satellite offices and expanded hours to appeal to time conscious consumers. These developments often necessitated some type of advertising to inform consumers of the change in service distribution by the professional.

The Status of Advertising by Professionals

Though 15 years have passed since the Virginia Board and Bates decisions, the use of marketing and advertising by professionals is still a controversial topic. We now review some of the strongest arguments on both sides of the issue.

The Case for Advertising by Professionals. Several arguments can be advanced. Probably the strongest is that consumers demand such information. Individuals are in need of information about legal, medical, optical and dental services. They are used to getting information about other products and services via the newspaper and television. At minimum, consumers want to know the location of the provider and the range of services offered. Word of mouth is still the most effective information source for all products; but dissatisfied consumers, newcomers to an area and the poor may not have access to this source. Consequently, advertising offers them an easily accessible vehicle for gaining information about professionals. From an ethical standpoint, it is argued that according to the principle of distributive justice, the poor, elderly and market illiterates are more likely to be served if advertising of these services is permitted.

A second argument, and the one that legal decisions are mostly based upon, is the First Amendment right of free speech. Professionals should be able to communicate with consumers in any nondeceptive manner that they choose. Critics view advertising as "undignified", but Justice Blackmun noted in the majority opinion of Bates: "The assertion that advertising will diminish the attorney's reputation in the community is open to question. Bankers and engineers advertise, and yet these professions are not regarded as undignified."

Third, proponents contend that the costs to consumers are lower when advertising is present. This is an extension of the competition argument which states that more information in the market place will have the effect of driving down prices. In the absence of advertising, the professionals could collude and keep prices artificially high. The Federal Trade Commission has used this argument extensively and has found in one study that in cities where lawyers intensely advertised, legal fees have declined by 5%—13%. When the FTC analysis is combined with the consumer information argument, supporters suggest that advertising contributes to the efficient functioning of the market place/economy.

A final reason to support increased marketing by professionals is that it allows a new entrant to gain access to the market more easily. In the absence of advertising, it may take years for a new lawyer or accountant, or a new type of practice to make enough contacts to attain a thriving business. A specific example is Hyatt Legal Services, a legal services chain with over 200 offices nationwide employing over 600 attorneys. Hyatt spent several million dollars on T.V. ads using CEO Joel Hyatt as spokesperson to build its client base. Although this firm is one of the most successful, there are undoubtedly many more professionals who received at least modest aid from advertising.

The Case Against Advertising by Professionals. The critics of marketing and advertising by professionals articulate a number of variations on a common theme. Namely, it is "unprofessional" for individuals who consider themselves to belong to a professional community to lower themselves to use common business practices. The logical extension of this argument is that advertising undermines the relationship of trust which exists between a professional person and a client. One CPA spokesperson perceives that the best way to build a practice is to get involved in one's community. The emphasis should be on "quality control, not marketing concepts". This critic foresees a long term detrimental impact of the marketing orientation of current CPAs: "By cheapening our profession with distasteful advertising and gimmicks, will we slip undistinguished into the maze of financial service providers who also are certified, i.e., planners, life underwriters, etc.?"

A similar sentiment was expressed by a lawyer who felt that advertising contributes to the negative image of that profession. A survey conducted by a Florida bar association found that professionals are very conscious of their image with the public, and some believe that the "dignity" of the profession is compromised with the use of mass market advertising. The view that marketing by professionals has an impact on all practitioners, not just those who advertise, is well articulated by a Florida lawyer: "Advertising is a broad brush, which stains all lawyers. We tend to be perceived as greedy, self-interested people who do not care about our clients and are only interested in making a buck."

Another view expressed by critics of marketing and advertising is that the focus has shifted away from the professional's major job of healing, advising and counseling toward an emphasis on issues of lesser importance—generating a profit. They ask, do consumers want to shop for the lowest price for a heart transplant as one would for a used car? Probably not. Certainly there are some unethical professionals who do use advertising unscrupulously. Furthermore, consumers are interested in more than price. Most want a competent, knowledgeable practitioner who can solve problems; price is secondary in importance. In the final analysis, however, the Supreme Court has affirmed the right of professionals to market and to advertise their services.

Ethical Issues in Marketing by Accountants

Accountants were also reluctant to embrace marketing and advertising concepts. Times changed dramatically during the 1980s. Many accounting firms both developed advertising campaigns and employed staff people in a marketing capacity. Some of the largest ones, like Arthur Andersen, initiated consulting divisions which were engaged in extensive marketing efforts. Consequently, questions regarding the ethics of these practices became more prevalent.

The definitive position on advertising in the accounting field is contained in Section 502 (Advertising and Other Forms of Solicitation) of the AICPA Code of Professional Conduct. The emphasis in the code is on *informational,* as opposed to persuasive, advertising. Section 502 delineates what is prohibited by the code as well as what is considered ethical in advertising by accountants. For example, past experience is acceptable to mention in advertising as well as the CPA designation. However, the advertiser cannot use self-laudatory statements unless they are based on verifiable facts. Certain advertising of the largest CPA firms (Deloitte, Haskins & Sells, and Price Waterhouse) has been contested on ethical grounds. Accounting firms that are concerned about the ethical posture of their advertising need to develop guidelines that delineate what is expected. For example, Arthur Andersen has a detailed book outlining the firm's position on ''Ethical Standards/Independence'', which includes the complete AICPA code as an appendix.

Ethical Questions Regarding Lawyer Advertising

Some law firms have openly embraced marketing. As one CEO of a prepaid legal service commented, ''We don't have attorneys that sit in the office and practice. We market law. That's all we do.'' The law firms that have most extensively used advertising are those specializing in personal injury, medical malpractice, immigration law or divorce. Lawyers now spend over $50 million on advertising, a ten-fold increase since 1980. The percentage of lawyers who advertise has increased from three percent to 32 percent over those years.

The American Bar Association has developed both a Model Code of Professional Responsibility and Model Rules of Professional Conduct. The state bar associations follow one of these two documents to serve as the official standard of conduct for lawyers. Several of the clauses are quite similar to those governing accountants. Alleged violations are reviewed by a state bar committee which can recommend one of several sanctions (e.g., reprimand, suspension or disbarment).

There are many potential ethical issues stemming from attorney advertising and marketing. Exhibit 2 lists some pertinent questions that could be asked about potentially unethical legal advertising. The sundry ethical issues include fear generating T.V. ads dramatized with sirens, ambulances, wrecked vehicles, or individuals being placed on stretchers, and ads that vow to help you ''collect cash''. An in-depth examination of law practice marketing listed over 20 categories of ethical issues including use of customer testimonials, non-informational adver-

tising and cold call solicitations. The study concluded with the following admonition:

> Inevitably, the standards which will govern all of lawyer business-getting activity will be those of honesty and fairness. Misleading and false statements and overreaching conduct will characterize prohibited marketing behavior.....The responsibility for ensuring that law practice marketing plans comply with ethical prescriptions rests squarely with the lawyers.....Lawyers who accept any marketing advice without scrutinizing its ethical propriety risk are wasting money on strategies which must be abandoned for ethical reasons. More importantly, they risk censure from the bar.

Exhibit 2

Some Ethical Questions About Lawyer Advertising

The principal difficulty, though, lies in determining just what is, for instance, misleading, or unfair, or dignified. Consider the following:

- A personal injury ad says, ''No recovery—no fee''. Is this misleading or deceptive for failure to mention the client may be responsible for litigation costs?
- Is a ''24-Hour Legal Hotline'' dignified?
- ''Real People, Not a Professional Corporation or Legal Clinic''. Is this misleading to the public and unfair to other lawyers?
- An ad seeking drunk driving cases shows a liquor bottle, a wrecked car, and a drunk. Is this dignified?
- ''Twenty Years of Successful Criminal Practice''. Is this self-laudatory; does it contain information about past performance; and does it create an unjustified expectation?
- ''Low Rates''. Is this sufficient fee information, or deceptive?
- In an advertising circular, ''Bring this coupon in for a Free Consultation. Is this dignified or deceptive?
- ''The Worst Injury of All May Be Not Being Properly Represented.'' Is this misleading or unfair?
- ''Full Compensation for Your Injuries''. Does this create unjustified expectations?
- ''Everyday our lawyers are in court representing innocent people charged with crimes they didn't commit.'' Is this potentially fraudulent or deceptive?
- A T.V. ad for personal injury cases shows an accident, flashing lights, and injured persons being loaded into ambulances. Is this dignified or deceptive? Does it appeal to anger, fear or greed?
- ''We took the fear out of legal fees.'' Is this deceptive? Is it telling the public to be fearful of lawyers and legal fees?
- A lawyers' referral service sells all referrals from certain counties to lawyers for a monthly fee. The service advertises an ''800'' phone number in the yellow pages, with a nationwide answering service based in Tennessee. The service has been approved only by a local bar association in California. Does this meet the letter and spirit of Rule 7.3?

Source: ''Lawyer Advertising—Marketing, Professionalism, the Future,'' *Res Gestae,* August 1988, 63.

Ethical Issues Facing Medical and Dental Marketing

Of all the professions, medicine has resisted marketing and advertising most vehemently. Survey results indicate that physicians are more skeptical than other professionals toward the benefits of marketing. It may be that they perceive marketing to be primarily a selling activity and far removed from their view of the responsibilities contained in the Hypocratic Oath. Although the medical community was covered by the *Bates* decision, the American Medical Association was charged by the FTC with conspiring with state and local medical societies to suppress all forms of medical advertising. The Supreme Court handed down another decision in 1982. It affirmed the right of physicians to advertise in a truthful, nondeceptive manner.

The majority of medical advertising is undertaken by clinics, HMOs and hospitals. One of the earliest, and most controversial, hospital ads was undertaken by Sunrise Hospital of Las Vegas. There are a number of codes developed by various associations to help insure ethical advertising. The Advertising Guidelines of the Council of Medical Specialty Societies contains 13 points which stipulate that the use of incomplete information, heavy fear appeals and misleading messages are unacceptable. Many of these ethical guidelines should hold for the advertising of any product. One especially ethically charged medical area is cosmetic surgery. It is heavily advertised in some parts of the country, such as California. A number of ethical hazards of advertising cosmetic surgery has been noted by critics, including the possibility of creating oversimplified expectations. The worst case scenario is where ads manipulate individuals to demand services that are downright unhealthy (suction-assisted lipectomy, i.e., fat suction is an especially controversial procedure). Another issue pertains to promoting the professional qualifications of individuals performing cosmetic surgery. Some physicians advertise themselves as specialists without the proper training or certification—a morally, medically, and legally dubious practice. Defenders of cosmetic surgery have noted three reasons why advertising such surgery may be ethically justifiable: (1) Medicine should serve human wants, and one's appearance may improve an individual's quality of life; (2) Patients demanding this surgery are not sick and are more free to "shop around" and find the best deal; and (3) The surgical costs are voluntarily borne by the consumer.

Ideas for Executive Action

The three interested parties—professional associations, practitioners and ad agencies—must all work together to insure that advertising by the professions is on the highest ethical plane. We propose a specific suggestion for each of them.

(1) **Professional associations must continue to place emphasis on advertising issues through updated codes and guidelines, enforcement and conference sessions devoted to the topic.**

Professional societies in law, accounting, medicine and dentistry have had to change their posture toward advertising. As one practitioner aptly noted: "The question is thus not whether but how physicians shall be permitted to advertise their services." It is in this spirit that associations should look at their role to assist and guide, but **not discourage,** advertising by their professionals. For example, the Indiana State Bar Association Lawyer Advertising Committee has recommended that the association publish articles outlining changes in rules governing legal advertising and prepare a brochure to be disseminated to the public so that they can better be protected from false and misleading advertising. Professional organizations need to scrutinize the marketing programs of their members keeping ethical questions in the limelight and holding sessions that discuss such questions at association meetings. Furthermore, sanctions must be enforced so that violators know they will be prosecuted.

(2) **Professionals who employ ad agencies must hold them to high levels of integrity and continuously monitor the messages they develop.**

Professionals need to be careful in the type of agency they select to do their advertising. One recommendation would be to monitor other noncompeting professional ads and to find out what agency prepares the ads that have high integrity and credibility. Just because an agency contends that they are an "expert" in legal or medical advertising does not make them an acceptable choice. Professionals can further monitor the effect of the ad on their clientele by asking their impression of it and doing some informal research on their own.

(3) **Ad agencies and marketing consultants who wish to serve professionals should position themselves as being sensitive to the unique needs of the professional community.**

Many agencies and consultants see the growing professional advertising market as an extension of their regular business. This is possibly a mistake. Professionals are different in their orientation. Taking the high road in marketing and advertising is not just expected; it is a necessity. Therefore, marketers should develop campaigns and programs that are unquestioned in terms of integrity. Understanding the philosophical perspective of a professional is more than a semantic challenge.

References

Abbott, Andrew, "Professional Ethics," *American Journal of Sociology,* Vol. 88, 1983, 855-885.

Balzer, John E., "Attorney Advertising: Who's Really Afraid of the Big Bad Lawyer," *New England Law Review,* March 1988, 727-760.

Braun, Irwin and Marilyn Braun, "Following a Decade of Advertising: Professionals Still Face Restraints," *Marketing News,* August 14, 1987, 21.

"CMSS Develops Guidelines for Physician Advertising," *Annals of Emergency Medicine,* December 1981, 100.

Dugas, Christine, "Marketing: The Prescription for Professional Practices?" *Ad Forum,* February 1983, 42-44.

Folland, Sherman, R. Parameswaran and John Darling, "On the Nature of Physicians' Opposition to Advertising," *Journal of Advertising,* Vol. 18, 1989, 4-12.

Hite, Robert E. and Cynthia Fraser, "Meta-Analyses of Attitudes Toward Advertising by Professionals," *Journal of Marketing,* July 1988, 95-105.

"Is Dignity Important in Legal Advertising?" *ABA Journal,* August 1, 1987, A-1 and A-2.

"Lawyer Advertising—Marketing, Professionalism, the Future," *Res Gestae,* August 1988, 59-64.

Leiser, Burton M., "Professional Advertising: Price Fixing and Professional Dignity versus the Public's Right to a Free Market," *Journal of Business and Professional Ethics,* Spring/Summer 1984, 93-110.

Macklin, Ruth, "Commentary on Leiser," *Journal of Business and Professional Ethics,* Spring/Summer 1984, 114.

"Major CPA Firms Accused of Violations of Professional Conduct," *The Practical Accountant,* April 1986, 43-44.

Morreim, E. Haavi, "A Moral Examination of Medical Advertising," *Business & Society Review,* Winter 1988, 4-6.

Moss, Frederick C., "The Ethics of Law Practice Marketing," *Notre Dame Law Review,* Vol. 61, 1986, 601-696.

North, Sterling, "Lawyers in the Age of Advertising," *New England Business,* August 3, 1987, 22-25.

Stafford, David C., "Advertising in the Professions," *International Journal of Advertising,* 1988, 7, 189-220.

Stewart, Larry, "Advertising: The Need For a Strong ATLA Policy," *ATLA Advocate,* July 1989, 2 and 4.

"Suggestions for Lawyer Advertising—Avoiding Deceptive & Unprofessional Ads," *Res Gestae,* February 1989, 394-398.

Trapani, Christopher, "Advertising v. Solicitation: Shapero Ends the Controversy Over Targeted Direct-Mailings by Attorneys," *Florida Bar Journal,* February 1989, 31-33.

Walsh, William J., "CPAs and Advertising: Another Voice," *Journal of Accountancy,* November 1986, 178-180.

"What Forms of Advertising Are Permissible Under the Ethics Code?" *Journal of Accountancy,* November 1986, 98-99.

*This paper is abstracted from a chapter entitled, "The Ethics of Social, Professional and Political Marketing", which will appear in The Higher Road: A Path to Ethical Marketing Decisions, to be published by Allyn & Bacon.

Three ethical challenges for sales managers

Gene R. Laczniak and Patrick E. Murphy

Gene R. Laczniak is Professor of Business in the marketing Department at Marquette University. Patrick E. Murphy is Chairman of the Marketing Department at the University of Notre Dame.

Personal selling accounts for more than eight million jobs in the United States. For every position in advertising, there are more than thirty jobs in personal selling. The express purpose of most selling is to convince the customer that the salesperson's product or service represents the *best* solution to the customer's needs. Thus, it is little wonder that because of its financial magnitude and persuasive aspects, personal selling is an area of marketing that generates many ethical questions.

Three areas call upon the sales manager to exercise a high degree of ethical propriety: Administration of sales territories, setting of sales quotas, and competitive considerations.

Within the selling process, special ethical responsibilities fall upon the sales manager. Many of the ethical issues with which the sales manager must grapple differ little from those found within the domain of most administrators. For example, the issue of employing, promoting, and firing personnel, and the inherent obligation in justice that managers conduct such affairs even-handedly are concerns of all supervisors. Further, many of the issues related to mainstream sales management fall under the jurisdiction of the law. The Equal Employment Opportunity Act, for instance, forbids discrimination against employees on any basis except performance-related criteria. Similarly, in the area of salary administration, just and prompt reimbursement of sales force expenses, as well as the accurate payment of salary, commissions, and bonuses are ethical (and legal) responsibilities implicit in honest compensation management.

However, there are at least three areas that are almost unique to sales management and which call upon the sales manager to exercise a high degree of ethical propriety. These are the administration of sales territories, the setting of sales quotas, and various competitive considerations.

The administration of sales territories

Obviously, the selling territory assigned to the sales representative goes far toward determining the potential sales levels and (possibly) compensation levels that the sales rep can attain. Thus, the assignment and administration of territories must be undertaken by the sales manager with special care. Sometimes it is necessary to reassign territories because of selling efficiencies. Loss of income to the individual sales rep or increased degrees of selling responsibility must be taken into consideration in such shifting of assignments. Also, certain accounts become important enough over time to become designated national accounts. That is, there are customers who become so important that they are handled exclusively by top management or headquarters personnel. In such situations, the sales manager seems to have an ethical responsibility to provide early notification to the sales rep who will lose future national (sometimes called "house") accounts. It also seems incumbent upon management to consider providing that sales rep with some sort of financial reward, additional new accounts, or expanded territory to make up for the loss of the key customer.

Sales managers should encourage sales representatives to ask for help when they face an ethically troublesome sale.

The setting of sales quotas

Often a large proportion of compensation in the area of personal selling is determined by commissions and bonuses. Attainment of sales quotas by the sales force will determine the level of financial remuneration that they receive. If sales quotas are not perceived as fair by sales reps, pressures for unethical behavior can increase. If the sales force regularly falls short of established quotas, there will be a decline in the morale of the reps. While a review of the various methods used to establish sales quotas is beyond the scope of this book, clearly, such decisions should be made with the degree of equity that allows for the realistic assessment of the quotas. All members of the sales force should have a fair chance to attain their quotas and receive a just wage, given the constraints of the territories they serve.

Competitive considerations

The written, promotional material that is developed by headquarters to accompany the product becomes an important sales aid for members of the selling team. Sales managers have a special responsibility to avoid alienating buyers via product misrepresentation or providing the sales force with materials that can be used carelessly to disparage competitors. Since the sales manager is typically responsible for overseeing sales materials as well as the sales force, the responsibility to see that this information passes ethical muster falls on the sales manager.

Ideas for ethical action

The following suggestions are offered to help sales managers establish a better ethical climate in which their sales reps might operate.

First, develop, circulate and promote a detailed and explicit sales ethics policy statement. Topics covered in this statement should address the major questions that arise in the course of the seller/buyer interaction. Issues such as gift-giving, bribery, entertainment, and conflicts of interest, should be treated in as much detail as the organization's selling experience allows. It is also imperative that such policy statements address any special issues that may come up in the sales force's handling of the product. For example, sellers of farm herbicides may have special obligations concerning safety disclosures. Pharmaceutical sales reps may have extraordinary responsibilities with regard to highlighting a new drug's potential side-effects to busy physicians.

The selling organization must also make clear that policy statements on ethics will be enforced. When this occurs, it should be done visibly and vigorously. Sales managers must take special care to reprimand ethical violations even-handedly—something that is not always the case. One national poll of sales managers, for instance, indicated that sanctions are more likely to be meted out when the unethical action caused negative outcomes for the selling organization, or when the sales rep involved was a poor performer to begin with.

Second, sales quotas should always be realistically set by management. Pressure to attain management-established sales quotas, even though possibly unrealistic, will create an environment whereby the sales rep is likely to become the rationalizer. In such situations, the exaggeration of product characteristics, overselling a client, bribery, or kickbacks may occur as the seller seeks a mechanism to achieve the needed sale and move toward meeting quota.

The implication here is that sales managers have a particular responsibility to monitor sales force behavior closely. This takes many traditional forms, including occasionally accompanying sales reps on calls and carefully auditing the sales call reports that most organizations routinely require. Individuals who have historically submitted questionable expense vouchers or accumulated extraordinary sales only during contest periods are candidates for special monitoring on the part of management. Prudent scrutiny may help purge members of the sales force who might later cause embarrassment or even legal action against the organization because of unethical actions.

Asking for help

Third, sales managers should encourage sales representatives to ask for help when they face an ethically troublesome sale. As noted previously, sales representatives operate with a great deal more independence than other line employees. However, this independence may foster a climate that creates a moral vacuum. The organization should designate someone who can be approached when sales reps are troubled by ethical concerns. The idea of a "sales chaplain" has been suggested as a mechanism for providing the guidance that salespeople might need in the ethical realm. This "chaplain" could be a retired sales executive or perhaps someone trained in ethics and familiar with the workings of the organization. His or her role would be to provide ethical guidance and counsel on issues that less experienced sales reps may not have previously encountered.

Fourth, if ethical problems persist in the selling environment, management should take pro-active measures. If there appears to be a persistent problem of unethical sales

Collusion to improve the ethical climate of the industry does not violate federal antitrust law.

behavior in an industry—for instance, a climate of kickbacks or payoffs—top management should consider meeting with competitors to hammer out an industry-wide code of sales ethics that will level the competitive playing field. Collusion to improve the ethical climate of the industry does not violate federal antitrust law. The defense industry, one certainly deserving of censure for past unethical selling practices, has developed such an industry-wide code.

Ethical abuse may stem from many factors, such as continuing unethical sales practices by competitors or improper requests by buyers. If sales reps become aware of continuing abuses and their immediate supervisor provides no help, there should be a mechanism by which they can "blow the whistle." The whistleblowing mechanism allows employees to have someone in the organization whom they can approach concerning moral conduct when their immediate line manager seems unwilling or unable to resolve a situation that has been repeatedly reported. The sales chaplain (or some other ethical ombudsman) may be the individual who is designated by the organization as the one to approach in such difficult instances. Importantly, protection from retribution against the employee who has bypassed the chain of command should be built into the whistleblower mechanism.

The Green Movement Sows Demand for Ecofurniture

Cheryl Powell

Staff Reporter of The Wall Street Journal

Environmentally friendly furniture is gaining a following.

A few small specialized furniture makers are going green, with midrange to high-priced lines of bedroom, living room and even children's furnishings. The furniture often is made of recycled wood, plastics or paper. Generally the finishes are water-based instead of chemical or polyester resin-based, which even after drying may emit potentially harmful gases.

These qualities are important for people like Susan Springer of Berkeley, Calif. Ms. Springer, 45, a former fashion designer, says that she has an asthma attack if she is near furniture with a chemical finish. If she sits on chemically treated foam cushions, she says her arms and legs tingle and her pulse rate jumps. She had to have her bed custom-made, with nontoxic-finished hardwood and a prewashed cotton cover and no foam or fire retardant. It cost about $1,000 in 1980.

"If money were no object, it wouldn't be a problem. I'd get all my furniture custom-made," she says. "But I just really have to search. It's hard."

Most furniture makers use polyester-resin sprays, which leave a clear finish. Many are reluctant to switch to water-based finishes, which leave a yellowish tint. Some don't have a policy on what kind of wood they use.

"We don't feel like we're out raping the planet when we cut a tree down. It can be replanted," says Larry Runyan, director of manufacturing services for the American Furniture Manufacturer's Association. "Right now, I don't see how you can manufacture environmentally friendly furniture."

But a few small specialized firms do. One cataloger, Seventh Generation Inc. in Colchester, Vt., offers a line of home furnishings made of wood from 19th-century New England buildings scheduled for demolition. Items such as a book shelf for $89 and coffee table for $199 have nontoxic finishes. Michael McDonough, a New York architect and designer, is launching Eco-Furnitures Inc. to sell his line of children's furniture made of compressed recycled newspapers. The papier-mache-like line will be available in toy and specialty stores this fall; a set of two chairs and a table will retail for about $180.

And ecologically sensitive furniture is making some inroads into the mainstream. The latest edition of Spiegel's catalog features a hardwood chest for $399 the catalog says is environmentally approved by the British chapter of Friends of the Earth.

David Molder, an environmental activist in Pittsburgh, appreciates the growing number of available products. He recently purchased a Wellspring futon mattress, made by Rising Star Futon of Bend, Ore., filled with recycled, chemical-free plastics from 480 two-liter bottles. "You're saving all the waste that goes into making cotton," says Mr. Molder.

Still, home-furniture makers trail the office-furniture industry, which is being driven by employers concerned about workplace safety and air quality. Such major companies such as Herman Miller Inc. began ecological programs years ago.

"More and more often we are being asked to fill out surveys about what we're doing environmentally before they'll buy our furniture," says Paul Murray, environmental affairs manager at the Zeeland, Mich., firm.

But when it comes to the home, most people think more about how a table or chair looks than what it's made of. "Food, you eat. Cosmetics and clothes, you put on your body. Furniture doesn't seem to affect you personally as much," says Pamela Diaconis, spokeswoman for Ikea U.S. Inc., a unit of Ingka Holding B.V., Netherlands.

But that may be changing. Agnes Bourne, who owns an interior design and furniture business in San Francisco, says customers are agreeable to green furniture, as long as the price isn't too high. Many of her customers are proud to tell friends they have ecologically sensitive furniture, Ms. Bourne says. Moreover, they enjoy seeing the results of their recycling efforts. "People are wondering: 'I'm doing all this work, so where is it going?' " she says. "Now they know."

Managing for Organizational Integrity

By supporting ethically sound behavior, managers can strengthen the relationships and reputations their companies depend on.

Lynn Sharp Paine

Lynn Sharp Paine is associate professor at the Harvard Business School, specializing in management ethics. Her current research focuses on leadership and organizational integrity in a global environment.

Many managers think of ethics as a question of personal scruples, a confidential matter between individuals and their consciences. These executives are quick to describe any wrongdoing as an isolated incident, the work of a rogue employee. The thought that the company could bear any responsibility for an individual's misdeeds never enters their minds. Ethics, after all, has nothing to do with management.

In fact, ethics has *everything* to do with management. Rarely do the character flaws of a lone actor fully explain corporate misconduct. More typically, unethical business practice involves the tacit, if not explicit, cooperation of others and reflects the values, attitudes, beliefs, language, and behavioral patterns that define an organization's operating culture. Ethics, then, is as much an organizational as a personal issue. Managers who fail to provide proper leadership and to institute systems that facilitate ethical conduct share responsibility with those who conceive, execute, and knowingly benefit from corporate misdeeds.

Managers must acknowledge their role in shaping organizational ethics and seize this opportunity to create a climate that can strengthen the relationships and reputations on which their companies' success depends. Executives who ignore ethics run the risk of personal and corporate liability in today's increasingly tough legal environment. In addition, they deprive their organizations of the benefits available under new federal guidelines for sentencing organizations convicted of wrongdoing.

These sentencing guidelines recognize for the first time the organizational and managerial roots of unlawful conduct and base fines partly on the extent to which companies have taken steps to prevent that misconduct.

Prompted by the prospect of leniency, many companies are rushing to implement compliance-based ethics programs. Designed by corporate counsel, the goal of these programs is to prevent, detect, and punish legal violations. But organizational ethics means more than avoiding illegal practice; and providing employees with a rule book will do little to address the problems underlying unlawful conduct. To foster a climate that encourages exemplary behavior, corporations need a comprehensive approach that goes beyond the often punitive legal compliance stance.

An integrity-based approach to ethics management combines a concern for the law with an emphasis on managerial responsibility for ethical behavior. Though integrity strategies may vary in design and scope, all strive to define companies' guiding values, aspirations, and patterns of thought and conduct. When integrated into the day-to-day operations of an organization, such strategies can help prevent damaging ethical lapses while tapping into powerful human impulses for moral thought and action. Then an ethical framework becomes no longer a burdensome constraint within which companies must operate, but the governing ethos of an organization.

How Organizations Shape Individuals' Behavior

The once familiar picture of ethics as individualistic, unchanging, and impervious to organizational influences has not stood up to scrutiny in recent years. Sears Auto Centers' and Beech-Nut Nutrition Corporation's experiences illustrate the role organizations play in shaping individuals' behavior – and how even sound moral fiber can fray when stretched too thin.

In 1992, Sears, Roebuck & Company was inundated with complaints about its automotive service business. Consumers and attorneys general in more than 40 states had accused the company of misleading customers and selling them unnecessary parts and services, from brake jobs to front-end alignments. It would be a mistake, however, to see this situation exclusively in terms of any one individual's moral failings. Nor did management set out to defraud Sears customers. Instead, a number of organizational factors contributed to the problematic sales practices.

In the face of declining revenues, shrinking market share, and an increasingly competitive market for undercar services, Sears management attempted to spur the performance of its auto centers by introducing new goals and incentives for employees. The company increased minimum work quotas and introduced productivity incentives for mechanics. The automotive service advisers were given product-specific sales quotas – sell so many springs, shock absorbers, alignments, or brake jobs per shift – and paid a commission based on sales. According to advisers, failure to meet quotas could lead to a transfer or a reduction in work hours. Some employees spoke of the "pressure, pressure, pressure" to bring in sales.

Under this new set of organizational pressures and incentives, with few options for meeting their sales goals legitimately, some employees' judgment understandably suffered. Management's failure to clarify the line between unnecessary service and legitimate preventive maintenance, coupled with consumer ignorance, left employees to chart their own courses through a vast gray area, subject to a wide range of interpretations. Without active management support for ethical practice and mechanisms to detect and check questionable sales methods and poor work, it is not surprising that some employees may have reacted to contextual forces by resorting to exaggeration, carelessness, or even misrepresentation.

Shortly after the allegations against Sears became public, CEO Edward Brennan acknowledged management's responsibility for putting in place compensation and goal-setting systems that "created an environment in which mistakes did occur." Although the company denied any intent to deceive consumers, senior executives eliminated commissions for service advisers and discontinued sales quotas for specific parts. They also instituted a system of unannounced shopping audits and made plans to expand the internal monitoring of service. In settling the pending lawsuits, Sears offered coupons to customers who had bought certain auto services between 1990 and 1992. The total cost of the settlement, including potential customer refunds, was an estimated $60 million.

Contextual forces can also influence the behavior of top management, as a former CEO of Beech-Nut Nutrition Corporation discovered. In the early 1980s, only two years after joining the company, the CEO found evidence suggesting that the apple juice concentrate, supplied by the company's vendors for use in Beech-Nut's "100% pure" apple juice, contained nothing more than sugar water and chemicals. The CEO could have destroyed the bogus inventory and withdrawn the juice from grocers' shelves, but he was under extraordinary pressure to turn the ailing company around. Eliminating the inventory would have killed any hope of turning even the meager $700,000 profit promised to Beech-Nut's then parent, Nestlé.

A number of people in the corporation, it turned out, had doubted the purity of the juice for several years before the CEO arrived. But the 25% price advantage offered by the supplier of the bogus concentrate allowed the operations head to meet cost-control goals. Furthermore, the company lacked an effective quality control system, and a conclusive lab test for juice purity did not yet exist. When a member of the research department voiced concerns about the juice to operating management, he was accused of not being a team player and of acting like "Chicken Little." His judgment, his supervisor wrote in an annual performance review, was "colored by naïveté and impractical ideals." No one else seemed to have considered the company's obligations to its customers or to have thought about the potential harm of disclosure. No one considered the fact that the sale of adulterated or misbranded juice is a legal offense, putting the company and its top management at risk of criminal liability.

An FDA investigation taught Beech-Nut the hard way. In 1987, the company pleaded guilty to selling adulterated and misbranded juice. Two years and two criminal trials later, the CEO pleaded guilty to ten counts of mislabeling. The total cost to the company— including fines, legal expenses, and lost sales—was an estimated $25 million.

Such errors of judgment rarely reflect an organizational culture and management philosophy that sets out to harm or deceive. More often, they reveal a culture that is insensitive or indifferent to ethical considerations or one that lacks effective organizational systems. By the same token, exemplary conduct usually reflects an organizational culture and philosophy that is infused with a sense of responsibility.

For example, Johnson & Johnson's handling of the Tylenol crisis is sometimes attributed to the singular personality of then-CEO James Burke. However the decision to do a nationwide recall of Tylenol capsules in order to avoid further loss of life from product tampering was in reality not one decision but thousands of decisions made by individuals at all levels of the organization. The "Tylenol decision," then, is best understood not as an isolated incident, the achievement of a lone individual, but as the reflection of an organization's culture. Without a shared set of values and guiding principles deeply ingrained throughout the organization, it is doubtful that Johnson & Johnson's response would have been as rapid, cohesive and ethically sound.

Many people resist acknowledging the influence of organizational factors on individual behavior – especially on misconduct – for fear of diluting people's sense of personal moral responsibility. But this fear is based on a false dichotomy between holding individual transgressors accountable and holding "the system" accountable. Acknowledging the importance of organizational context need not imply exculpating individual wrongdoers. To understand all is not to forgive all.

The Limits of a Legal Compliance Program

The consequences of an ethical lapse can be serious and far-reaching. Organizations can quickly become entangled in an all-consuming web of legal proceedings. The risk of litigation and liability has increased in the past decade as lawmakers have legislated new civil and criminal offenses, stepped up penalties, and improved support for law enforcement. Equally – if not more – important is the damage an ethical lapse can do to an organization's reputation and relationships. Both Sears and Beech-Nut, for instance, struggled to regain consumer trust and market share long after legal proceedings had ended.

As more managers have become alerted to the importance of organizational ethics, many have asked their lawyers to develop corporate ethics programs to detect and prevent violations of the law. The 1991 Federal Sentencing Guidelines offer a compelling rationale. Sanctions such as fines and probation for organizations convicted of wrongdoing can vary dramatically depending both on the degree of management cooperation in reporting and investigating corporate misdeeds and on whether or not the company has implemented a legal compliance program. (See the insert "Corporate Fines Under the Federal Sentencing Guidelines.")

Such programs tend to emphasize the prevention of unlawful conduct, primarily by increasing surveillance and control and by imposing penalties for wrongdoers. While plans vary, the basic framework

is outlined in the sentencing guidelines. Managers must establish compliance standards and procedures; designate high-level personnel to oversee compliance; avoid delegating discretionary authority to those likely to act unlawfully; effectively communicate the company's standards and procedures through training or publications; take reasonable steps to achieve compliance through audits, monitoring processes, and a system for employees to report criminal misconduct without fear of retribution; consistently enforce standards through appropriate disciplinary measures; respond appropriately when offenses are detected; and, finally, take reasonable steps to prevent the occurrence of similar offenses in the future.

There is no question of the necessity of a sound, well-articulated strategy for legal compliance in an organization. After all, employees can be frustrated and frightened by the complexity of today's legal environment. And even managers who claim to use the law as a guide to ethical behavior often lack more than a rudimentary understanding of complex legal issues.

Managers would be mistaken, however, to regard legal compliance as an adequate means for addressing the full range of ethical issues that arise every day. "If it's legal, it's ethical," is a frequently heard slogan. But conduct that is lawful may be highly problematic from an ethical point of view. Consider the sale in some countries of hazardous products

Acknowledging the importance of organizational context in ethics does not imply forgiving individual wrongdoers.

without appropriate warnings or the purchase of goods from suppliers who operate inhumane sweatshops in developing countries. Companies engaged in international business often discover that conduct that infringes on recognized standards of human rights and decency is legally permissible in some jurisdictions.

Legal clearance does not certify the absence of ethical problems in the United States either, as a 1991 case at Salomon Brothers illustrates. Four top-level executives failed to take appropriate action when learning of unlawful activities on the government trading desk. Company lawyers found no law

Corporate Fines Under the Federal Sentencing Guidelines

What size fine is a corporation likely to pay if convicted of a crime? It depends on a number of factors, some of which are beyond a CEO's control, such as the existence of a prior record of similar misconduct. But it also depends on more controllable factors. The most important of these are reporting and accepting responsibility for the crime, cooperating with authorities, and having an effective program in place to prevent and detect unlawful behavior.

The following example, based on a case studied by the United States Sentencing Commission, shows how the 1991 Federal Sentencing Guidelines have affected overall fine levels and how managers' actions influence organizational fines.

Acme Corporation was charged and convicted of mail fraud. The company systematically charged customers who damaged rented automobiles more than the actual cost of repairs. Acme also billed some customers for the cost of repairs to vehicles for which they were not responsible. Prior to the criminal adjudication, Acme paid $13.7 million in restitution to the customers who had been overcharged.

Deciding before the enactment of the sentencing guidelines, the judge in the criminal case imposed a fine of $6.85 million, roughly half the pecuniary loss suffered by Acme's customers. Under the sentencing guidelines, however, the results could have been dramatically different. Acme could have been fined anywhere from 5% to 200% the loss suffered by customers, depending on whether or not it had an effective program to prevent and detect violations of law and on whether or not it reported the crime, cooperated with authorities, and accepted responsibility for the unlawful conduct. If a high ranking official at Acme were found to have been involved, the maximum fine could have been as large as $54,800,000 or four times the loss to Acme customers. The following chart shows a possible range of fines for each situation:

What Fine Can Acme Expect?

	Maximum	Minimum
Program, reporting, cooperation, responsibility	$2,740,000	$685,000
Program only	10,960,000	5,480,000
No program, no reporting no cooperation, no responsibility	27,400,000	13,700,000
No program, no reporting no cooperation, no responsibility, involvement of high-level personnel	54,800,000	27,400,000

Based on Case No.: 88-266, United States Sentencing Commission, Supplementary Report on Sentencing Guidelines for Organizations.

obligating the executives to disclose the improprieties. Nevertheless, the executives' delay in disclosing and failure to reveal their prior knowledge prompted a serious crisis of confidence among employees, creditors, shareholders, and customers. The executives were forced to resign, having lost the moral authority to lead. Their ethical lapse compounded the trading desk's legal offenses, and the company ended up suffering losses – including legal costs, increased funding costs, and lost business – estimated at nearly $1 billion.

A compliance approach to ethics also overemphasizes the threat of detection and punishment in order to channel behavior in lawful directions. The underlying model for this approach is deterrence theory, which envisions people as rational maximizers of self-interest, responsive to the personal costs and benefits of their choices, yet indifferent to the moral legitimacy of those choices. But a recent study reported in *Why People Obey the Law* by Tom R. Tyler shows that obedience to the law is strongly influenced by a belief in its legitimacy and its moral correctness. People generally feel that they have a strong obligation to obey the law. Education about the legal standards and a supportive environment may be all that's required to insure compliance.

Discipline is, of course, a necessary part of any ethical system. Justified penalties for the infringement of legitimate norms are fair and appropriate. Some people do need the threat of sanctions. However, an overemphasis on potential sanctions can be superfluous and even counterproductive. Employees may rebel against programs that stress penalties, particularly if they are designed and imposed without employee involvement or if the standards are vague or unrealistic. Management may talk of mutual trust when unveiling a compliance plan, but employees often receive the message as a warning from on high. Indeed, the more skeptical among them may view compliance programs as nothing more than liability insurance for senior management. This is not an unreasonable conclusion, considering that compliance programs rarely address the root causes of misconduct.

Even in the best cases, legal compliance is unlikely to unleash much moral imagination or commitment. The law does not generally seek to inspire human excellence or distinction. It is no guide for exemplary behavior – or even good practice. Those managers who define ethics as legal compliance are implicitly endorsing a code of moral mediocrity for their organizations. As Richard Breeden, former chairman of the Securities and Exchange Commission, noted, "It is not an adequate ethical standard to aspire to get through the day without being indicted."

Integrity as a Governing Ethic

A strategy based on integrity holds organizations to a more robust standard. While compliance is rooted in avoiding legal sanctions, organizational integrity is based on the concept of self-governance in accordance with a set of guiding principles. From the perspective of integrity, the task of ethics management is to define and give life to an organization's guiding values, to create an environment that supports ethically sound behavior, and to instill a sense of shared accountability among employees. The need to obey the law is viewed as a positive aspect of organizational life, rather than an unwelcome constraint imposed by external authorities.

An integrity strategy is characterized by a conception of ethics as a driving force of an enterprise. Ethical values shape the search for opportunities, the design of organizational systems, and the decision-making process used by individuals and groups. They provide a common frame of reference and serve as a unifying force across different functions, lines of business, and employee groups. Organizational ethics helps define what a company is and what it stands for.

Many integrity initiatives have structural features common to compliance-based initiatives: a code of conduct, training in relevant areas of law, mechanisms for reporting and investigating potential misconduct, and audits and controls to insure that laws and company standards are being met. In

addition, if suitably designed, an integrity-based initiative can establish a foundation for seeking the legal benefits that are available under the sentencing guidelines should criminal wrongdoing occur. (See the insert "The Hallmarks of an Effective Integrity Strategy.")

But an integrity strategy is broader, deeper, and more demanding than a legal compliance initiative. Broader in that it seeks to enable responsible conduct. Deeper in that it cuts to the ethos and operating systems of the organization and its members, their guiding values and patterns of thought and action. And more demanding in that it requires an active effort to define the responsibilities and aspirations that constitute an organization's ethical compass. Above all, organizational ethics is seen as the work of management. Corporate counsel may play a role in the design and implementation of integrity strategies, but managers at all levels and across all functions are involved in the process. (See the chart, "Strategies for Ethics Management.")

During the past decade, a number of companies have undertaken integrity initiatives. They vary according to the ethical values focused on and the implementation approaches used. Some companies focus on the core values of integrity that reflect ba-

Management may talk of mutual trust when unveiling a compliance plan, but employees often see a warning from on high.

sic social obligations, such as respect for the rights of others, honesty, fair dealing, and obedience to the law. Other companies emphasize aspirations – values that are ethically desirable but not necessarily morally obligatory – such as good service to customers, a commitment to diversity, and involvement in the community.

When it comes to implementation, some companies begin with behavior. Following Aristotle's view that one becomes courageous by acting as a courageous person, such companies develop codes of conduct specifying appropriate behavior, along with a system of incentives, audits, and controls. Other companies focus less on specific actions and more on developing attitudes, decision-making processes, and ways of thinking that reflect their values. The assumption is that personal commit-

The Hallmarks of an Effective Integrity Strategy

There is no one right integrity strategy. Factors such as management personality, company history, culture, lines of business, and industry regulations must be taken into account when shaping an appropriate set of values and designing an implementation program. Still, several features are common to efforts that have achieved some success:

☐ *The guiding values and commitments make sense and are clearly communicated.* They reflect important organizational obligations and widely shared aspirations that appeal to the organization's members. Employees at all levels take them seriously, feel comfortable discussing them, and have a concrete understanding of their practical importance. This does not signal the absence of ambiguity and conflict but a willingness to seek solutions compatible with the framework of values.

☐ *Company leaders are personally committed, credible, and willing to take action on the values they espouse.* They are not mere mouthpieces. They are willing to scrutinize their own decisions. Consistency on the part of leadership is key. Waffling on values will lead to employee cynicism and a rejection of the program. At the same time, managers must assume responsibility for making tough calls when ethical obligations conflict.

☐ *The espoused values are integrated into the normal channels of management decision making and are reflected in the organization's critical activities:* the development of plans, the setting of goals, the search for opportunities, the allocation of resources, the gathering and communication of information, the measurement of performance, and the promotion and advancement of personnel.

☐ *The company's systems and structures support and reinforce its values.* Information systems, for example, are designed to provide timely and accurate information. Reporting relationships are structured to build in checks and balances to promote objective judgment. Performance appraisal is sensitive to means as well as ends.

☐ *Managers throughout the company have the decision-making skills, knowledge, and competencies needed to make ethically sound decisions on a day-to-day basis.* Ethical thinking and awareness must be part of every managers' mental equipment. Ethics education is usually part of the process.

Success in creating a climate for responsible and ethically sound behavior requires continuing effort and a considerable investment of time and resources. A glossy code of conduct, a high-ranking ethics officer, a training program, an annual ethics audit – these trappings of an ethics program do not necessarily add up to a responsible, law-abiding organization whose espoused values match its actions. A formal ethics program can serve as a catalyst and a support system, but organizational integrity depends on the integration of the company's values into its driving systems.

---

ment and appropriate decision processes will lead to right action.

Martin Marietta, NovaCare, and Wetherill Associates have implemented and lived with quite different integrity strategies. In each case, management has found that the initiative has made important and often unexpected contributions to competitiveness, work environment, and key relationships on which the company depends.

Martin Marietta: Emphasizing Core Values

Martin Marietta Corporation, the U.S. aerospace and defense contractor, opted for an integrity-based ethics program in 1985. At the time, the defense industry was under attack for fraud and mismanagement, and Martin Marietta was under investigation for improper travel billings. Managers knew they needed a better form of self-governance but were skeptical that an ethics program could influence behavior. "Back then people asked, 'Do you really need an ethics program to be ethical?'" recalls current President Thomas Young. "Ethics was something personal. Either you had it, or you didn't."

The corporate general counsel played a pivotal role in promoting the program, and legal compliance was a critical objective. But it was conceived of and implemented from the start as a company-wide management initiative aimed at creating and maintaining a "do-it-right" climate. In its original conception, the program emphasized core values, such as honesty and fair play. Over time, it expanded to encompass quality and environmental responsibility as well.

Today the initiative consists of a code of conduct, an ethics training program, and procedures for reporting and investigating ethical concerns within the company. It also includes a system for disclosing violations of federal procurement law to the government. A corporate ethics office manages the program, and ethics representatives are stationed at major facilities. An ethics steering committee, made up of Martin Marietta's president, senior executives, and two rotating members selected from field operations, oversees the ethics office. The audit and ethics committee of the board of directors oversees the steering committee.

The ethics office is responsible for responding to questions and concerns from the company's employees. Its network of representatives serves as a sounding board, a source of guidance, and a channel for raising a range of issues, from allegations of wrongdoing to complaints about poor manage-

ment, unfair supervision, and company policies and practices. Martin Marietta's ethics network, which accepts anonymous complaints, logged over 9,000 calls in 1991, when the company had about 60,000 employees. In 1992, it investigated 684 cases. The ethics office also works closely with the human resources, legal, audit, communications, and security functions to respond to employee concerns.

Shortly after establishing the program, the company began its first round of ethics training for the entire workforce, starting with the CEO and senior executives. Now in its third round, training for senior executives focuses on decision making, the challenges of balancing multiple responsibilities,

Strategies for Ethics Management

Characteristics of Compliance Strategy

Ethos	conformity with externally imposed standards
Objective	prevent criminal misconduct
Leadership	lawyer driven
Methods	education, reduced discretion, auditing and controls, penalties
Behavioral Assumptions	autonomous beings guided by material self-interest

Characteristics of Integrity Strategy

Ethos	self-governance according to chosen standards
Objective	enable responsible conduct
Leadership	management driven with aid of lawyers, HR, others
Methods	education, leadership, accountability, organizational systems and decision processes, auditing and controls, penalties
Behavioral Assumptions	social beings guided by material self-interest, values, ideals, peers

Implementation of Compliance Strategy

Standards	criminal and regulatory law
Staffing	lawyers
Activities	develop compliance standards train and communicate handle reports of misconduct conduct investigations oversee compliance audits enforce standards
Education	compliance standards and system

Implementation of Integrity Strategy

Standards	company values and aspirations social obligations, including law
Staffing	executives and managers with lawyers, others
Activities	lead development of company values and standards train and communicate integrate into company systems provide guidance and consultation assess values performance identify and resolve problems oversee compliance activities
Education	decision making and values compliance standards and system

and compliance with laws and regulations critical to the company. The incentive compensation plan for executives makes responsibility for promoting ethical conduct an explicit requirement for reward eligibility and requires that business and personal goals be achieved in accordance with the company's policy on ethics. Ethical conduct and support for the ethics program are also criteria in regular performance reviews.

Today top-level managers say the ethics program has helped the company avoid serious problems and become more responsive to its more than 90,000 employees. The ethics network, which tracks the number and types of cases and complaints, has served as an early warning system for poor management, quality and safety defects, racial and gender discrimination, environmental concerns, inaccurate and false records, and personnel grievances regarding salaries, promotions, and layoffs. By providing an alternative channel for raising such concerns, Martin Marietta is able to take corrective action more quickly and with a lot less pain. In many cases, potentially embarrassing problems have been identified and dealt with before becoming a management crisis, a lawsuit, or a criminal investigation. Among employees who brought complaints in 1993, 75% were satisfied with the results.

Company executives are also convinced that the program has helped reduce the incidence of misconduct. When allegations of misconduct do surface, the company says it deals with them more openly. On several occasions, for instance, Martin Marietta has voluntarily disclosed and made restitution to the government for misconduct involving potential violations of federal procurement laws. In addition, when an employee alleged that the company had retaliated against him for voicing safety concerns about his plant on CBS news, top management commissioned an investigation by an outside law firm. Although failing to support the allegations, the investigation found that employees at the plant feared retaliation when raising health, safety, or environmental complaints. The company redoubled its efforts to identify and discipline those employees taking retaliatory action and stressed the desirability of an open work environment in its ethics training and company communications.

Although the ethics program helps Martin Marietta avoid certain types of litigation, it has occasionally led to other kinds of legal action. In a few cases, employees dismissed for violating the code of ethics sued Martin Marietta, arguing that the company had violated its own code by imposing unfair and excessive discipline.

Still, the company believes that its attention to ethics has been worth it. The ethics program has led to better relationships with the government, as well as to new business opportunities. Along with prices and technology, Martin Marietta's record of integrity, quality, and reliability of estimates plays a role in the awarding of defense contracts, which account for some 75% of the company's revenues. Executives believe that the reputation they've earned through their ethics program has helped them build trust with government auditors, as well. By opening up communications, the company has reduced the time spent on redundant audits.

The program has also helped change employees' perceptions and priorities. Some managers compare their new ways of thinking about ethics to the way they understand quality. They consider more carefully how situations will be perceived by others, the possible long-term consequences of short-term thinking, and the need for continuous improvement. CEO Norman Augustine notes, "Ten years ago, people would have said that there were no ethical issues in business. Today employees think their number-one objective is to be thought of as decent people doing quality work."

NovaCare: Building Shared Aspirations

NovaCare Inc., one of the largest providers of rehabilitation services to nursing homes and hospitals in the United States, has oriented its ethics effort toward building a common core of shared aspirations. But in 1988, when the company was called InSpeech, the only sentiment shared was mutual mistrust.

Senior executives built the company from a series of aggressive acquisitions over a brief period of

> At NovaCare, executives defined organizational values and introduced structural changes to support those values.

time to take advantage of the expanding market for therapeutic services. However, in 1988, the viability of the company was in question. Turnover among its frontline employees – the clinicians and therapists who care for patients in nursing homes and hospitals – escalated to 57% per year. The company's inability to retain therapists caused customers to defect and the stock price to languish in an extended slump.

After months of soul-searching, InSpeech executives realized that the turnover rate was a symptom of a more basic problem: the lack of a common set of values and aspirations. There was, as one executive put it, a "huge disconnect" between the values of the therapists and clinicians and those of the managers who ran the company. The therapists and clinicians evaluated the company's success in terms of its delivery of high-quality health care. InSpeech management, led by executives with financial services and venture capital backgrounds, measured the company's worth exclusively in terms of financial success. Management's single-minded emphasis on increasing hours of reimbursable care turned clinicians off. They took management's performance orientation for indifference to patient care and left the company in droves.

CEO John Foster recognized the need for a common frame of reference and a common language to unify the diverse groups. So he brought in consultants to conduct interviews and focus groups with the company's health care professionals, managers, and customers. Based on the results, an employee task force drafted a proposed vision statement for the company, and another 250 employees suggested revisions. Then Foster and several senior managers developed a succinct statement of the company's guiding purpose and fundamental beliefs that could be used as a framework for making decisions and setting goals, policies, and practices.

Unlike a code of conduct, which articulates specific behavioral standards, the statement of vision, purposes, and beliefs lays out in very simple terms the company's central purpose and core values. The purpose – meeting the rehabilitation needs of patients through clinical leadership – is supported by four key beliefs: respect for the individual, service to the customer, pursuit of excellence, and commitment to personal integrity. Each value is discussed with examples of how it is manifested in the day-to-day activities and policies of the company, such as how to measure the quality of care.

To support the newly defined values, the company changed its name to NovaCare and introduced a number of structural and operational changes. Field managers and clinicians were given greater decision-making authority; clinicians were provided with additional resources to assist in the delivery of effective therapy; and a new management structure integrated the various therapies offered by the company. The hiring of new corporate personnel with health care backgrounds reinforced the company's new clinical focus.

The introduction of the vision, purpose, and beliefs met with varied reactions from employees, ranging from cool skepticism to open enthusiasm. One employee remembered thinking the talk about values "much ado about nothing." Another recalled, "It was really wonderful. It gave us a goal that everyone aspired to, no matter what their place in the company." At first, some were baffled about how the vision, purpose, and beliefs were to be used. But, over time, managers became more adept at explaining and using them as a guide. When a customer tried to hire away a valued employee, for example, managers considered raiding the customer's company for employees. After reviewing the beliefs, the managers abandoned the idea.

NovaCare managers acknowledge and company surveys indicate that there is plenty of room for improvement. While the values are used as a firm reference point for decision making and evaluation in some areas of the company, they are still viewed with reservation in others. Some managers do not "walk the talk," employees complain. And recently acquired companies have yet to be fully integrated into the program. Nevertheless, many NovaCare employees say the values initiative played a critical role in the company's 1990 turnaround.

The values reorientation also helped the company deal with its most serious problem: turnover among health care providers. In 1990, the turnover rate stood at 32%, still above target but a significant improvement over the 1988 rate of 57%. By 1993, turnover had dropped to 27%. Moreover, recruiting new clinicians became easier. Barely able to hire 25 new clinicians each month in 1988, the company added 776 in 1990 and 2,546 in 1993. Indeed, one employee who left during the 1988 turmoil said that her decision to return in 1990 hinged on the company's adoption of the vision, purpose, and beliefs.

Wetherill Associates: Defining Right Action

Wetherill Associates, Inc. – a small, privately held supplier of electrical parts to the automotive market – has neither a conventional code of conduct nor a statement of values. Instead, WAI has a *Quality Assurance Manual* – a combination of philosophy text, conduct guide, technical manual, and company profile – that describes the company's commitment to honesty and its guiding principle of right action.

WAI doesn't have a corporate ethics officer who reports to top management, because at WAI, the company's corporate ethics officer *is* top management. Marie Bothe, WAI's chief executive officer, sees her main function as keeping the 350-employee company on the path of right action and looking for opportunities to help the community. She delegates the "technical" aspects of the business—marketing, finance, personnel, operations—to other members of the organization.

Creating an organization that encourages exemplary conduct may be the best way to prevent damaging misconduct.

Right action, the basis for all of WAI's decisions, is a well-developed approach that challenges most conventional management thinking. The company explicitly rejects the usual conceptual boundaries that separate morality and self-interest. Instead, they define right behavior as logically, expediently, and morally right. Managers teach employees to look at the needs of the customers, suppliers, and the community – in addition to those of the company and its employees – when making decisions.

WAI also has a unique approach to competition. One employee explains, "We are not 'in competition' with anybody. We just do what we have to do to serve the customer." Indeed, when occasionally unable to fill orders, WAI salespeople refer customers to competitors. Artificial incentives, such as sales contests, are never used to spur individual performance. Nor are sales results used in determining compensation. Instead, the focus is on teamwork and customer service. Managers tell all new recruits that absolute honesty, mutual courtesy, and respect are standard operating procedure.

Newcomers generally react positively to company philosophy, but not all are prepared for such a radical departure from the practices they have known elsewhere. Recalling her initial interview,

one recruit described her response to being told that lying was not allowed, "What do you mean? No lying? I'm a buyer. I lie for a living!" Today she is persuaded that the policy makes sound business sense. WAI is known for informing suppliers of overshipments as well as undershipments and for scrupulous honesty in the sale of parts, even when deception cannot be readily detected.

Since its entry into the distribution business 13 years ago, WAI has seen its revenues climb steadily from just under $1 million to nearly $98 million in 1993, and this in an industry with little growth. Once seen as an upstart beset by naysayers and industry skeptics, WAI is now credited with entering and professionalizing an industry in which kickbacks, bribes, and "gratuities" were commonplace. Employees – equal numbers of men and women ranging in age from 17 to 92 – praise the work environment as both productive and supportive.

WAI's approach could be difficult to introduce in a larger, more traditional organization. WAI is a small company founded by 34 people who shared a belief in right action; its ethical values were naturally built into the organization from the start. Those values are so deeply ingrained in the company's culture and operating systems that they have been largely self-sustaining. Still, the company has developed its own training program and takes special care to hire people willing to support right action. Ethics and job skills are considered equally important in determining an individual's competence and suitability for employment. For WAI, the challenge will be to sustain its vision as the company grows and taps into markets overseas.

At WAI, as at Martin Marietta and NovaCare, a management-led commitment to ethical values has contributed to competitiveness, positive workforce morale, as well as solid sustainable relationships with the company's key constituencies. In the end, creating a climate that encourages exemplary conduct may be the best way to discourage damaging misconduct. Only in such an environment do rogues really act alone.

MANAGING BY VALUES

Is Levi Strauss' Approach Visionary—Or Flaky?

Talk, talk, talk. As a black mid-level executive at Levi Strauss & Co. in the early 1980s, that's all Louis Kirtman got from the white men above him in top management. Levi's had long enjoyed a reputation as a socially responsible employer. But that didn't mean much to Kirtman as he watched black executives he thought were highly qualified passed over for plum jobs, while his own career seemed stalled on a lonely plateau. Top management always mouthed diversity, Kirtman says, "but in the end, they chose people they were comfortable with" for key positions.

Fast forward to 1994, and Kirtman is a much happier man. As president of Levi's Britannia Sportswear division, the 48-year-old executive is a step away from joining the company's senior management ranks. Life changed for him in 1985, when senior executives began feeling heavy pressure from above to make "workplace diversity" a reality rather than a topic of conversation. The chief of Levi's then-ailing European division tapped Kirtman to help rescue the unit. The young executive made the most of his opportunity and landed on the fast track. "We started to improve at Levi's," he says, "when we stopped talking about values like diversity and started behaving that way."

Levi Strauss is embarked on a grand social experiment. It is struggling mightily, though not always successfully, to live up to a singular, lofty vision of how to run a modern corporation—a vision set forth by none other than Chairman and Chief Executive Robert D. Haas, the great-great-grandnephew of founder Levi Strauss. The vision combines traditional liberal idealism with a set of management precepts straight out of the '90s zeitgeist of inclusion and "empowerment." Haas calls it "responsible commercial success." More conservative executives might call it flaky.

Haas believes the corporation should be an ethical creature—an organism capable of both reaping profits and making the world a better place to live. Creating tangible opportunities for minority employees such as Kirtman is only one part of the equation. Haas is out to make each of his workers, from the factory floor on up, feel as if they are an integral part of the making and selling of blue jeans. He wants to ensure that all views on all issues—no matter how controversial—are heard and respected. The chairman won't tolerate harassment of any kind. He won't do business with suppliers who violate Levi's strict standards regarding work environment and ethics. A set of corporate "aspirations," written by top management, is to guide all major decisions.

If many of these goals sound familiar, it's because countless other companies have tried to embrace them to one degree or another. Xerox, Johnson & Johnson, and MCI are all noted for their efforts to promote diversity of background and thought among their workers. Nike, Microsoft, and Federal Express are well known for pushing authority down through the ranks and allowing employees plenty of input when it comes to running the business.

Some companies approach diversity and empowerment as competitive tools. "We don't encourage homogeneity here," says Timothy F. Price, president of business markets at MCI Communications Corp. "The price you pay for conformity is lack of creativity." Others are learning to give ethnic minorities, homosexuals, and women protection and respect out of a late 20th century defensiveness: In an ever more litigious society, they fear being sued.

No company, however, has embraced a values-based strategy the way Levi's has. Sitting in his San Francisco office wearing a pair of pointy-toe boots, a plaid shirt, and stone-washed 501s, Haas explains why: "We are not doing this because it makes us feel good—although it does. We are not doing this because it is politically correct. We are doing this because we believe in the interconnection between liberating the talents of our people and business success."

Haas points to a study issued on May 30 by Gordon Group Inc. for the California Public Employees' Retirement System (CalPERS). Its conclusion: Companies that involve employees more often in decision-making boast stronger market valuations than those that don't. The report suggested that CalPERS might see stock gains by pressuring companies to improve workplace conditions. Says Richard H. Koppes, the pension fund's general counsel: "This is one of the screens we'll use in looking for what companies we target."

Levi's, of course, won't be on Koppes' list. Ever since the $1.6 billion leveraged buyout Haas led in 1985, the world's largest apparel maker has been a private company. CalPERS would probably like a piece, though. Record sales and earnings for five of the past six years culminated in a 36% rise in profits last year, to $492 million on sales of $5.9 billion. And Morgan

From *Business Week*, August 1, 1994, pp. 46-52. © 1994 by McGraw-Hill, Inc. Reprinted by special permission.

WHAT LEVI'S ASPIRES TO

NEW BEHAVIORS

Management must exemplify "directness, openness to influence, commitment to the success of others, and willingness to acknowledge our own contributions to problems."

DIVERSITY

Levi's "values a diverse workforce (age, sex, ethnic group, etc.) at all levels of the organization.... Differing points of view will be sought; diversity will be valued and honestly rewarded, not suppressed."

RECOGNITION

Levi's will "provide greater recognition—both financial and psychic—for individuals and teams that contribute to our success...those who create and innovate and those who continually support day-to-day business requirements."

ETHICAL MANAGEMENT PRACTICES

Management should epitomize "the stated standards of ethical behavior. We must provide clarity about our expectations and must enforce these standards throughout the corporation."

COMMUNICATIONS

Management must be "clear about company, unit, and individual goals and performance. People must know what is expected of them and receive timely, honest feedback...."

EMPOWERMENT

Management must "increase the authority and responsibility of those closest to our products and customers. By actively pushing the responsibility, trust, and recognition into the organization, we can harness and release the capabilities of all our people."

DATA: LEVI STRAUSS & CO.

running its business? Haas says no, but plans to spend $500 million starting this summer to restructure Levi's manufacturing, marketing, and distribution systems. He feels the company is in a temporary lull; in the long run, he insists, the cultivation of a culture devoted to such values as diversity and empowerment will make Levi's all the more responsive in the marketplace.

The jury is still out on that. BUSINESS WEEK had the opportunity to travel within the world of Levi's this spring and glimpse firsthand how Haas's experiment is proceeding. The following set of snapshots provides ample evidence that Haas is a long way from realizing his vision. "We are only a few steps along in our journey," he agrees. "We are far from perfect. We are far from where we want to be. But the goal is out there, and it's worth striving for."

'WHAT'S NEXT, CRYSTALS?'

Margaret P. Lourenco wasn't so sure about this values stuff when she first came to Levi's. A 32-year-old, can't-sit-still financial planner, she left J.P. Morgan & Co. in New York for San Francisco in 1990. She remembers well her reaction when she was first given the "Aspiration Statement," the corporate credo at the center of Haas's values-based strategy. "When I first read it," she recalls, "I said 'Phew, what are we going to have next, crystals?' "

A lot of people have that reaction. Printed on paper made from recycled blue denim, the Aspiration Statement hangs on office and factory walls throughout Levi's. To emphasize its gravity, Haas made sure it was crafted by top management, not the human resources department. At Levi's, one-third of an employee's evaluation is based on "aspirational" behavior: Ignore issues such as diversity and empowerment, and you might not get your raise.

After the button-down atmosphere at Morgan, Lourenco was bemused by the "I'm O. K., you're O. K." nature of Levi's culture. But then she took a chance and politely criticized her boss for what she considered heavy-handed behavior. To her surprise, he agreed and changed his act. "I found that Aspirations isn't about New Age feel-good," she says. "It's about being open and direct. It's about getting rid of hidden agendas."

For his part, F. Warren Hellman worries that all this management-speak risks clogging up the works at Levi's. Doing the right thing is fine, he says, but "there's a danger that this will degrade into a touchy-feely, I-don't-want-to-offend-you, creativity-stifling style of management." Hellman is hardly a disinterested observer. A San Francisco investment banker, he's Bob Haas's distant cousin and a Levi's director.

Don't get the idea that Hellman is not foursquare behind the chairman. Even though he thought it was a terrible idea to leave such a potentially lucrative market, he joined the unanimous board vote to pull $40 million of Levi's business out of China in protest of human-rights violations there. "Basically, we love Bob," Hellman says. "Bob has made a fortune for everyone, and you owe Bob one." Still, he says, "the challenge for Levi's

Stanley & Co. estimates that the stock—94% of which is in Haas family hands—has appreciated 1,300% since the LBO [leveraged buyout].

But this year, sales have slowed to a crawl, and operating profits will likely decline. A big problem is that Levi's is proving clay-footed when it comes to developing new products and getting goods into its retail outlets. Has the company's emphasis on "values" distracted it from the nuts and bolts of

is to be sure that decisions are not just 'nice' decisions, but decisions that are meant to enhance shareholder value."

"I haven't seen the word 'nice' anywhere in the Aspiration Statement," growls Robert D. Rockey Jr., president of Levi Strauss North America. Openness and respect don't equate with niceness, he says. "Honesty is the key." Levi's 360-degree review process, which requires that an employee be evaluated not just by his or her superior but also by subordinates and peers, isn't always pleasant. Rockey says his own evaluation "upset my self-image. I thought I was more visionary. I thought I was more caring. I was afraid to be personal." The reviews caused Rockey to loosen up somewhat, to command less, to listen more. But as his fellow workers can attest, the former Navy reserve captain still feels no need to be nice.

'WE'RE NOT A PERFECT COMPANY'

As far as some of the company's customers are concerned, Levi's has been a little too nice to its competition for the past few years. W. Barger Tygart, J. C. Penney Co.'s top merchandiser, finally has his wrinkle-free Dockers. But he had been clamoring for them for a year while Haggar Apparel Co. and Farah Manufacturing Co. soaked up sales in the hottest segment of the men's pants business. "They don't have the flexibility" to move fast on fashion trends, Tygart gripes. Levi's admits that it already has lost at least $200 million in sales by being slow into the wrinkle-free market. This year, the missed opportunity will contribute to Levi's first profit decline since 1988.

It has been a long time since retailers have been happy with Levi's customer support. Good thing the company offers high-quality clothes and a great brand name. "If you weren't Levi's," an executive at California's Mervyn's department stores once told the company, you'd be gone." Tygart notes that Levi's might take 25 to 30 days just to replenish a standard lot of pants; Haggar or Farah do it in 10. "That's 15 or 20 days when all we're selling is the competing product," Tygart says.

Such problems raise the question of whether Levi's emphasis on values is distracting. Haas insists that is not the case. Levi's, he argues, allowed its product development and customer service in the U.S. to slip because the company had been struggling to keep up with heady growth at home and explosive growth overseas. We're not a perfect company," he says. "We could be doing a better job in customer service."

Haas believes the problems would be worse if it weren't for the company's free exchange of ideas. "If anything," he says, "I think our values help address the problems because we get more two-way communication." Levi's is counting on communication more than ever as it moves toward a solution: This summer it is heading full bore into a $500 million effort to remake its product-development and distribution systems. Warehouses will be relocated, computer systems will be overhauled, employees will be uprooted—and some of them may lose their jobs. Levi's executives acknowledge this will test the values strategy. "An environment of uncertainty produces a lot of fear," says one. "It's easy to regress to old behaviors in a situation like that."

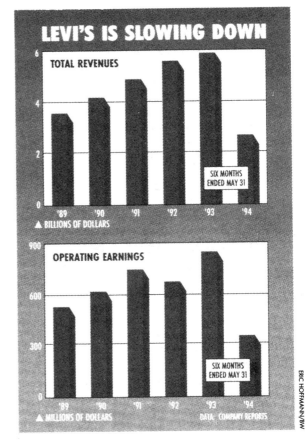

Not surprisingly, Levi's whole approach to the reengineering is uniquely, well, aspirational. More than 6,000 of the company's 36,000 employees were asked to provide advice on what Levi's should be doing differently. With that input in hand, nearly 200 of the company's key managers took over an entire floor of cubicles at headquarters and spent more than a year planning at a cost of $12 million. The company's Diversity Council, which is a direct link to senior management for groups representing blacks, Asians, Hispanics, gays, and women, also played a role in the decisions made.

The process took much longer and involved far more people than advisers at Andersen Consulting thought wise. But Haas says orienting the organization toward a common goal will prove more efficient in the long run. He sees the Aspiration Statement serving as a mountain climber's rope. "It allows individuals to take risks that they couldn't take if they weren't bound together by a common understanding," he says.

'I'M NOT A 35-YEAR-OLD WOMAN'

A diverse workforce, unafraid to volunteer idiosyncratic ideas and opinions, leads to better marketing decisions, insists Daniel M. Chew, Levi's director of corporate marketing. That doesn't mean market research and focus groups can be dispensed with. But an employee base that's more reflective of the customer base can make a company hipper and more responsive, Chew believes.

Long gone are the days when everyone wore the same kind of Levi's. Today, the company sells 200 styles of blue jeans alone. There is no way, Haas says, that top management can stay on top of fashion trends without help from deep within the organization. "I'm not a 35-year-old woman," says Haas. "I'm no hip-hopper. I'm not the target customer."

An example of diversity in action: While the gritty, independent hipsters in Levi's "501 Blues" TV ads have drawn young customers like a strong magnet, they didn't click for Levi's Hispanic employees and customers. "Why is that guy walking down the street alone?" they asked. "Doesn't he have any friends?" Scenes of friends and family would resonate better in their culture, they said, and given that Hispanics buy 50% more Levi's than the average customer, this was important information. So, Levi's launched a fresh series of 501 ads for the Hispanic market that downplayed individuality to emphasize camaraderie instead. Sales in the Hispanic community have been booming.

But even at Levi's, diversity at the top is a troublesome goal. Haas's executive management committee is composed of seven middle-aged white men and one middle-aged white woman. While Haas openly recognizes the disparity between word and deed at the upper echelon, he explains that building talent takes a long time. Levi's has doubled the percentage of minority managers, to 36%, since Haas became CEO in 1984. Women have climbed from 32% of the management ranks to 54% in the same period. In both cases, Levi's vastly outperforms the average U.S. corporation, according to federal labor statistics.

Louis Kirtman, who is Levi's top black executive, says the company still has work to do, but he's happy with the fact Levi's has moved more than a dozen minorities and women into mezzanine-level management slots. A Hispanic man now runs Levi's South American sourcing operation. Women head up Levi's operations in Britain and Mexico. When some of the senior managers in their fifties move on, Kirtman says, "you'll see the real change occur."

Of course, all this talk about the importance of diversity is a thorn in the side for some white males at Levi's. Several executives say, though not for attribution, that they've heard plenty of white males grumble about feeling "disempowered" as they try to advance within the corporation. Haas doesn't offer such employees much in the way of solace. For those white males "who focus on self-improvement and their contributions, the chances are good," Haas reflects. "We've eliminated the automatic promotions based on the old-boy network."

'PEER PRESSURE CAN BE BRUTAL'

Salvador Salas is a long way from the old-boy network. Fingertips wrapped in green adhesive tape to prevent cuts and scratches, Salas sews blue-jean waist-bands all day at the nonunion Kastrin Street factory in El Paso. If Haas's idealism is running into reality when it comes to white male egos in the executive suite, consider the factory floor. Empowerment and teamwork can be alien, uncomfortable concepts for those who have spent their working lives taking orders.

Salas likes his job, but he's not so sure about the new team system Levi's is introducing in its 27 U. S. sewing plants. Instead of grouping workers by function—all the zipper-sewers in one area, all the belt-loop attachers in another—Levi's has created multitask teams of 20 or 30 workers each. They are responsible for completing individual orders by assembling full pairs of pants, from waist to hem. After 18 months of teamwork in El Paso, turnaround time from order to shipment has dropped from seven days to three. But the workers aren't all getting along.

Under the team system, a worker's incentive pay is tied to team performance. A poor performer or absent worker affects everybody's paycheck. When someone is perceived to be faking sick days or lollygagging on a sewing machine, tempers flare. Says Salas: "Somebody's fooling around, and somebody else calls attention to that, and the first guy will just flip him off." Supervisor Gracie Cortez says that "it gets tough out there." She finds herself intervening to prevent "big fights." Says plant manager Edward Alvarez: "Peer pressure can be vicious and brutal."

Kastrin Street plant workers got two weeks of training before the team system kicked in, part of it devoted to group dynamics. Alvarez allows it "wasn't enough." Since then, 4 of 39 teams have undergone one-day let's-get-along sessions with a private consultant. But even that hasn't done the trick. "We're trying to find a more effective way to do it," Alvarez says.

While most Levi's plants are nonunion, Levi's gets credit—even from the union leaders it does have—for running some of the safest most worker-friendly factories in an industry notorious for abuses. "Here, I can get up and go to the restroom or get a drink when I need to," says rivet setter Emerio Ponce, who has worked for another apparel maker in El Paso. "I wasn't used to that."

Still, critics charge that Levi's pays a lot more attention to workers and training at headquarters than in the factories. Milton Moskowitz, coauthor of *The 100 Best Companies to Work For In America,* dropped Levi's from the list in the most recent edition, partly because of what he sees as a double standard. Although Haas has assured, for instance, that the partners of gay employees get health benefits—something that resonates loudest in San Francisco—he has shut down a pants factory in San Antonio in favor of moving the business to low-wage Costa Rica. The decision idled 1,100 workers.

Levi's President Thomas W. Tusher says the company simply had no choice: The San Antonio plant made Dockers, which require twice the labor content of blue jeans. Levi's had to move to a low-wage country to compete on price in what has become a brutal market for casual all-cotton slacks. Other companies make similar decisions every day. But because of Levi's self-conscious reputation as an employer who cares, it opens itself up to plenty of criticism.

Haas's standard reply is that guaranteed employment is not a part of Levi's values system. Such a pledge would be "unwise and dishonest," he says. Still, as the restructuring program goes forward, more dislocations and layoffs are likely. When they come, Bob Haas will have a lot more explaining to do.

'WE DON'T SUPPORT CHILD LABOR'

The simple truth is, living up to a value system as comprehensive as Levi's is hard. It takes hours and hours of work. Today, near the Levi's contractor in Dhaka, Bangladesh, you can see young girls in pigtails, clutching textbooks to their red-and-white school uniforms as they file into class. But not long ago, these same girls—11, 12, 13 years old—toiled full-time as seamstresses, earning $384 a month sewing Dockers casual pants.*

In 1992, to square its international sourcing practices with its own ethical code, Levi's began cracking down on child-labor violations by enforcing International Labor Organization standards that bar employment of children under the age of 14. Two Bangladeshi contractors admitted to Levi's that they hired children and agreed to fire them.

They also argued to Levi's officials, however, that the girls and boys provided their families' sole economic support—most of them were the oldest children in large, single-parent families. "We don't support child labor," says Robert H. Dunn, Levi's corporate-communications and community-affairs chief. "But our intention is not to have a devastating effect on families."

Levi's could have ignored its code or it could have canned the kids and forgotten about them. Instead, it worked out a compromise with the contractors: If they continued to pay wages and agreed to hire the children back when they turned 14, Levi's would send them to school and foot the bill for uniforms, books, and tuition.

The deal sounds expensive all the way around. But between the two, Levi's and its contractor have spent just a few thousand dollars. Besides, says Haas, such actions pay dividends in terms of brand image and corporate reputation. Just ask such companies as Wal-Mart Stores and Nike, which have come under

*Levi Strauss & Co. said its contract garment workers in Bangladesh are paid $384 a month. Levi's now says these workers actually earn an average of only $50 a month, including overtime pay. The $384 figure is based on a formula known as Purchasing Power Parity that reflects the purchasing power of the U.S. dollar in Bangladesh and is meant, Levi says, to give some context to the wages paid in different countries. *Editor*

fire for their Third World subcontracting practices. "In today's world, a TV expose' on working conditions can undo years of effort to build brand loyalty," says Haas. "Why squander your investment when, with commitment, reputational problems can be prevented?"

'IT'S A MATTER OF LEADERSHIP'

Bob Haas doesn't have to meet with stock analysts. He feels no pressure from Wall Street for neat, predictable quarterly results. Even the banks that funded his leveraged buyout are off his back: The company's mammoth cash flow has shaved debt to 4.6% of total capital. Would the company behave any differently if it were publicly traded? "It would take a lot more fortitude on the part of Levi's executives," Haas says. But he insists that "this is not a matter of structure, it's a matter of leadership."

Public company or not, Levi's experiment in corporate culture will attract attention and invite criticism. Noted apparel consultant Alan G. Millstein speaks for the many cynics when he says: "The company has the P. C. mindset. The Haases think they talk to God."

Now that enough operational problems have cropped up to slow financial results, Haas has given his critics some ammunition they didn't have before. But he goes out of his way to say that you can't abandon management-science efforts simply because things get tough. Too many managers, he feels, use that as an excuse to hide their "resistance to the idea that the soft sides and hard sides of management can be combined."

It's not so much that they can't be combined but that they may have unintended consequences when they are. Dealing with the surprising, often contradictory results of managing by values may be a manager's toughest task. Many managers are likely to ask themselves: Is it worth the trouble? Many, perhaps, would say "no."

"People are comfortable with the traditional ways of doing business," Haas says. "They might say, 'We aspire to do the things you've done, but we don't have time for it, the stock market wouldn't value it, or we're not as prosperous as Levi Strauss is.' " When it comes to managing by values, Haas has a ways to go to meet his own exacting standard. But he can't be faulted for bowing to what's comfortable.

By Russell Mitchell in San Francisco, with Michael Oneal in New York and bureau reports

Scott Cook founded Intuit, maker of the check-writing-software product Quicken, in 1984 with $151,000, after being turned down by venture capitalists for the $2 million he thought he would need. The start-up cash was quickly exhausted on product development, and the Menlo Park, Calif., company scraped through three desperate years before hitting its stride. Today Intuit has 400 employees. Sales last year were $44 million, and this year's revenues are expected to reach $80 million. Despite dozens of competitors in the category, Intuit has a 70% market share.

This article is derived from conversations between Cook and associate editor Leslie Brokaw.

The Ethics of
BOOTSTRAPPING

At no time is there more pressure to cut ethical corners than when your company's survival—and your own economic well-being—is at stake

SCOTT COOK

When you're a little, struggling start-up, you're confronted by ethical questions almost every day. Your company has no visible track record, or a very limited one. Or, like us in our early years, a very shoddy one. We had a poorly selling product for several years, we had no money, and our two closest competitors were corporate subsidiaries that together spent $7 million on marketing during our launch year alone.

That's the test of your ethics, when you're staring straight at the shame of failure. Each week your ethics are challenged by the promises you make. How much do you embellish your financial condition, the resources behind you, the success of your customers? What do you tell employees? Prospects? To get the sale, do you promise things you know you can't deliver? Do you make promises to your employees that you know in your heart you can't keep? I found I couldn't do those things. I just couldn't get my enthusiasm up for it; I had to do what felt

> **W**hat I've learned, and what all too many bootstrappers can miss, is that being truthful is good business. You may solve some temporary bind by fibbing, but it will come back to haunt you. It's not just wrong; it also doesn't work.

right. Of course, no one would argue that businesspeople should do otherwise. But they *do* do otherwise, all the time. Because it's business we're talking about, and because it's cutthroat and you can rationalize almost anything, and because—especially when you're bootstrapping as we were—*it's a matter of survival.*

But what I've learned, and what all too many bootstrappers can miss, is that being truthful is good business. Apart from moral judgments, consider expediency—and expediency is what bootstrapping amounts to. Business is about doing right by the customer and by your business partners, which include vendors and employees. If you do right by them, your business will flourish. If you don't, your business won't. You may solve some temporary bind by fibbing, but it will come back to haunt you. It's not just wrong; it also doesn't work. Being ethical isn't a fairyland, Boy Scout idea, nor is it naïve. I wanted to build a business for the long term.

And trust is one of the most important sources of your power.

Let me give you an example. We sell our software to retailers and dealers, who resell it to their customers, the end-users. It is common in our industry, as in a lot of industries, for salespeople to "load" the dealer with too much product. There is an old slogan, "a loaded dealer is a loyal dealer," because he won't want to push the competitor's product until he gets rid of yours first. With that in mind, some companies invent elaborate schemes to get dealers to buy more than they need; their salespeople overstate demand, exaggerating how well their product is going to sell or how big a promotion is.

Well, we don't do that. We don't think it's right to tell dealers they're going to sell 100 units a month when they're really going to sell 40—or, in our case with the major chains, 10,000 units when 4,000 is more like it.

Is this an issue of ethics or smart business? Frankly, I think the two merge. Although it means we sometimes miss higher revenues at the end of a quarter—that's why other companies load dealers, to maximize numbers so salespeople can get their commission checks or show off to the president—in the long run, being honest has served us better. For one thing, if you produce a large chunk of product and then don't get orders for three months, your manufacturing facility sits idle. That kind of boom-and-bust cycle is inefficient—it's hell on manufacturing people, who find it much easier to produce a level, constant volume of product.

We'll actually tell accounts they've ordered *too much*, that we'd like to ship them less because we think they're overbuying. And because of that, they've started to trust us in surprising ways. When we launch a new product—we've brought out three in the last year—we get into all the chain stores instantly. They don't even question it, because they know we're not going to screw them. What's more, many of the accounts now say, "We trust you, how much should we order?" Normally that would never happen. They would try to figure it out themselves, or they'd ask the salesperson and cut that recommendation in half. Instead, they're relying on our advice in ways that are very untypical for chain-store buyers and very helpful in building long-term partnerships.

> What happens if you lie, and are successful? Your customers may know you lied, and employees will definitely know you've lied, and you've set up a culture in which lying's OK—or worse, in which lying is linked with success.

It's amazing how uncommon it is to think about sales that way; so many companies seem to be out to snooker dealers as much as possible. That attitude is everywhere, probably because managing a company for short-term revenue is so much easier. It's all in the numbers. If the revenues aren't there, some presidents yell a lot, and people learn to run around and get short-term sales. Those presidents tell their people, "I don't care if the demand isn't there, go and sell them." That's easy; any idiot can do that. And many idiots do.

Ethical temptations continue to come up for us. For instance, we offer a consistent price to all our major accounts; it's the best price we can afford. But some of those accounts will call and say, "Hey, if you knock 5% off your price, I'll place a big order right now." Well, more volume is better, especially for a bootstrapped company, right?

Wrong. It probably wouldn't mean any extra sales to end-users. What it *would* mean is less revenue per unit—5% less—and, more important, it would mean you lied. *All* your customers are concerned that they have the best deal, and when we say, "Nobody gets a better price than this," that's got to be true. If we trim prices for certain accounts, we're lying. It's common, but ultimately it will hurt you.

Some customers are always looking for you to bend your rules, but if you hold out, the benefits can be enormous—and not just financially. Recently we pitched a hot, exclusive promotion idea to a large wholesale distributor. We were going to offer a special version of a product if the consumer bought other software at the same time—a dealer-created bundle.

The wholesaler turned us down, so we offered it to a second wholesaler, who took it. Soon dealers started changing wholesalers to get this special product, and the first wholesaler was livid. Its reps screamed at our director of sales that we had to offer the same deal to them.

We arranged a Saturday conference call with this wholesaler's chairman, and he was *angry*. He threatened to stop promoting our products, start pushing our competitors' products—nothing illegal, but things that would hurt our business. I need to get this same promotion, he said; what are you going to do for me?

And we said, "No, we offered the promotion to you first. You turned it down. The other wholesaler bought it on the agreement that it was an exclusive for them. For us to give it to you would mean going back on our word." He said, "So don't give me the promotion. Give me a million dollars in cash and I'll simulate it." And I said we couldn't do that; it was ethically wrong. The call ended when we agreed to disagree, and we said we'd talk a few days later. We went away really nervous.

Monday morning the wholesaler's reps called and said they understood our point of view, they respected it, they knew we had come to them with other good ideas, and in fact they thought our ideas were so good they wanted to elevate us into their top rank of vendors. They'd compensate for this promotion problem in another way.

It came totally out of the blue. We thought we'd have a year of really hard sliding with that account, because once an account is pissed at you, it tends to stay pissed. But not at all; our stand enhanced our relationship.

What's clear is that if that wholesaler's management had pushed us around and succeeded, we would have lost their respect. And there was great temptation. I mean, it was *really* tempting to do something that would have been against our word.

And this is the point: while a lot of bootstrapping companies think about the *consequences of failure*—"Gee, if I don't fib about this, I'm going to fail, and if I fail, I'll lose all my money, and my wife and kids, and my self-respect"—I don't think they consider the *consequences of success*. What happens if you lie, and are successful? Your customers may know you lied, and employees will definitely know you've lied, and you've set up a culture in which lying's OK—or worse, in which lying is linked with success.

The things that help make a company successful become the elements of its foundation, the stories through which new employees learn what's right and what's expected of them, and how they can succeed. Do you want those cultural legends to be about tricking others? You've got your choice.

If you create the right culture, people will do the right thing. I remember when we were working on one ad, our graphic designer came to see me, and she seemed hesitant about it. I said, "What do your guts tell you?" She said, "I just don't think we're being straight with people." If her guts told her that, she was probably onto something. She talked to the marketing vice-president about it, and we never ran the ad.

You have to realize that as a CEO, you're a role model and an example. People learn from your actions more than you ever believe. Now, we're not perfect; there are tough judgment calls every day, by people at every level in the company, and we don't always get it right. But I know that our chances of getting it right are highest only if our culture demonstrates the right values for people. The underpinnings of how you run the company give people rules they live by, and people will really believe in them and hold them dear.

It's a rare thing, this opportunity to create a culture; there's almost no place in our world where you can do that. Normally, you take culture as a given. American culture is American culture; we lament that politicians can't lead us better, that kids don't study harder, that too many people are crooks.

But when you create a company, you *can* create a culture—not in wide variance with what surrounds you, but you can move values, subtly and not so subtly, in the direction you want. It's the most powerful thing you can do, to seed that culture the right way, because ultimately, that will become more important to the success or failure of your company than you are. The culture you establish will guide and teach all your people in all their decisions. And if you've got a choice about the culture you create, why build it on a foundation of fraud?

THE 5TH ANNUAL BUSINESS ETHICS AWARDS FOR EXCELLENCE IN ETHICS

Focus: Consumer Products Companies

MARGARET KAETER

CORPORATE LEADERSHIP. Those two words, six simple syllables, hold increasingly complex meaning for the business world as we approach the twenty-first century. No longer defined simply as being the best business within a niche, corporate leadership today means leading the world, providing a role model for every entity the business touches. It means measuring success not always in terms of shareholder return, but in terms of employee loyalty, supplier relationships, consumer education, and the company's impact on the planet. ⚜ This year's Business Ethics Award winners—Merck, Aveda, and Levi Strauss—have always taken seriously their role as corporate leaders. But what sets them apart is their attention to detail, says Alice Tepper Marlin, executive director of the Council on Economic Priorities. "A lot of companies intend to be wonderful on social responsibility but they don't get down to specifying what they mean so the employees know what to do." ⚜ We know, of course, what they've done. Merck has built a reputation for putting human lives above profits, Aveda has built environmentalism into every aspect of its business operation, and Levi Strauss has taken its commitment to community activism onto the global stage to become a champion for human rights. But the question we put before each of them is, "Why? What is the advantage of extending our view of corporate leadership when it means forging new roads and redefining company success?" ⚜ Their responses underscore the importance of developing a values-based corporate culture—and a vision of business as a powerful force for good. Such a model doesn't guarantee painless solutions to societal woes nor a smooth avenue toward higher earnings, but it can provide a pathway for companies seeking to integrate their purpose with their profits.

Past Winners

▶ **Avis,** for its ground-breaking efforts in creating 100 percent employee ownership at a major corporation. Honored in 1992.

▶ **Beth Israel Hospital,** for its exceptional support of women in the workforce. Honored in 1991.

▶ **H.B. Fuller,** for adopting the highest global environmental standards. Honored in 1989.

▶ **Herman Miller,** for enlarging the concept of employee ownership. Honored in 1989.

▶ **Johnson & Johnson,** for sustaining ethics-based decision making over four decades. Honored in 1989.

▶ **Monsanto,** for making great strides in reducing environmental pollution. Honored in 1991.

▶ **Patagonia,** for dedication to the natural world and a spirit of adventure in outdoor clothing. Honored in 1990.

▶ **Polaroid,** for innovation in employee ownership and involvement. Honored in 1991.

▶ **Quickie Designs,** for making possible an active lifestyle for the disabled. Honored in 1990.

▶ **Springfield Remanufacturing,** for its innovations combining employee ownership with financial education for employees. Honored in 1992.

▶ **Stonyfield Farm,** for a commitment to nutrition, sustainable agriculture, and support of family farmers. Honored in 1991.

▶ **Weirton Steel,** for using employee ownership as a turnaround strategy in the struggling steel industry. Honored in 1992.

This Year's Honorable Mentions

▶ **Clorox** For its wide-ranging community youth work.

▶ **Tom's of Maine** For its environmental stewardship.

▶ **Esprit de Corp.** For incorporating environmentalism into all aspects of the workplace and marketing.

DETAILS, DETAILS, DETAILS
AVEDA

Minneapolis, Minnesota
Ownership status:
Privately owned.
Annual sales:
$50 million, (estimated as of August, 1993). Sales have increased by 35 percent annually since 1988.
Annual net earnings:
Not available.
Number of employees:
345.

PHOTOGRAPH COURTESY AVEDA.

FOUNDED IN 1978 by the son of an Austrian herbalist, Aveda has always paid attention to the environment. The mission to produce natural products and educate consumers on environmental issues came before the company and continues to drive every action, from writing a corporate memo to entering new markets.

Aveda views its mission not as competing for a slice of the cosmetics pie, but as creating a new pie. All of the company's seven hundred cosmetics and body care items are made solely from natural, sustainable ingredients, and the company searches the world for organically grown materials. "The reason this company has been so successful is not because it's about competing, but because it's about integrity," says Melisse Shaban, Aveda's general manager. "Imagine if all companies took the approach we do to ingredients and recycling. It would have an enormous impact on the world."

Aveda, for example, has never entered the lucrative hair color market because most hair dyes can't be created with natural ingredients. "We walk away from business that could make us a more significant player in our industry," says Shaban. "The intention never was to have a multi-million-dollar company, but to make a product and set an example."

At this they have definitely succeeded. At times, it's difficult to sort the Aveda products from the Aveda messages. The company frequently conducts educational campaigns on such environmental issues as deforestation and pesticide use, for example. "If you tell consumers the consequences of their choices, they will pick the right thing," says Shaban. "When you make the product and the information available, people will respond."

That message also is ingrained in the corporate culture. On-site daycare and a cafeteria featuring organically grown foods complement the home office's wooded set-

Aveda Highlights

▶ First signer of CERES Principles.
▶ Sponsors annual Earth Day programs within salon network to raise money for environmental causes.
▶ Launched recycling program for product containers.
▶ Uses only recycled, unbleached paper, and non-toxic soy inks in advertising, packaging, and stationery.
▶ Sponsors lectures, seminars, and retreats at the Aveda Spa on issues relating to environmentalism in business.

ting. While, inside the offices, the mission is strong. "They have a very impressive attention to detail," says CEP's Alice Tepper Marlin. "They actually test all ingredients to determine they aren't contaminated by pesticides." Indeed, the company has a list of specifications for every item it uses.

The goal, says Shaban, is to achieve a balance. "You must have a focus other than profit. People—employees and customers—want the opportunity to do the right thing, so it's the job of a company to make it easier for individuals to make a choice. We spend

more on creating our product than any other cosmetic manufacturer. We could do things differently and make it cost less, but that's not what's important to us."

Aveda's employees don't work there because it's a growing, thriving company, she explains. They work for Aveda because it offers a way for them to realize their personal visions of a better planet. "We're a company that has a belief. Our people and products match those beliefs. The pride our employees have for this company goes to the core of our selves."

CRITERIA FOR THE BUSINESS ETHICS AWARDS

1. The company's commitment to ethics and social responsibility must have a history and an ongoing vibrancy. It must be as vital to the company as a good product.
2. The company's social programs must have depth and sincerity. They cannot be mandated by law or done to avoid taxes.
3. Ethical and social concerns must genuinely be part of the company's culture, not an add-on program like a foundation.
4. The company must show potential for having a substantial presence in the world, and for making a positive impact on the business community.

LEVI STRAUSS

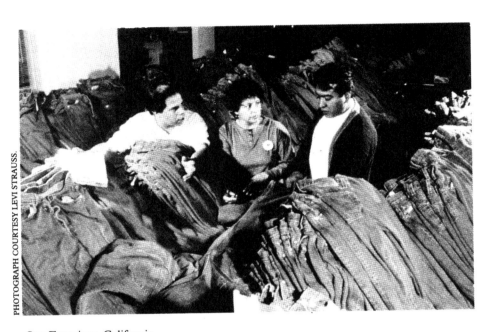

PHOTOGRAPH COURTESY LEVI STRAUSS.

San Francisco, California
Ownership status:
Privately owned.
Annual sales:
$5.6 billion in 1992, the sixth straight year of record sales.
Annual net earnings:
$360 million in 1992.
Number of employees:
34,000.

W HEN PEOPLE THINK OF Levi Strauss & Co., they invariably think of the company's flagship product — the blue jeans that have adorned cowboys, students, and weekend carousers since the company's founding in 1853.

But just as its blue jeans have been durable, surviving more than a century, so too have the company's values. "The family that founded this company has very strong personal, family, social and religious values," says Tepper Marlin. "They brought those values to the company."

The Haas family still owns the world's best-known clothing company. And its values still guide the operations. "We have a tradition of ethical behavior," explains Robert Dunn, vice president of corporate affairs and executive vice president of the Levi Strauss Foundation. "We have articulated a vision that goes beyond selling our product, and we have committed to it.

Levi Strauss Highlights

▶ Instituted comprehensive environmental and ethical principles to guide decision making.
▶ Recently introduced Business Partner Terms of Engagement to help choose contractors and suppliers.
▶ Recruits and manages a diverse workforce—more than half of all U.S. employees belong to minority groups. Fourteen percent of top management was non-caucasian in 1991 and 30 percent was female.
▶ First U.S. company to offer health care coverage for unmarried domestic partners.

Ethics at Levi Strauss is not an option, it's a ground rule, a part of every decision. If there is a conflict, ethical values must prevail."

For example, says Dunn, a Levi Strauss performance evaluation holds managers accountable for ethical behavior; the salary increase or bonus they receive is, in part, determined by their ethical decisions. "We have a self-selecting process," Dunn says. "If people think ethics are important, they want an af-

filiation with a company like this. People want to feel that they can engage in a business activity that reflects their personal values."

As a sign to these employees, Levi Strauss' executive management committee decided in 1993 that it no longer was only responsible for managing the company. It renamed itself the Global Leadership Team. "They agreed that they wanted to be clear about the vision of the organization, that they wanted to reinforce ethics as an overriding value for all decisions."

The committee has made good on that promise. After developing its Business Partner Terms of Engagement and sending representatives to visit many of its international operations, the company decided to discontinue working with contractors in China and Burma because these countries violated the human rights guidelines in the new document. The move was criticized by some business analysts as being short-sighted because the company would lose sales, especially in the rapidly expanding Chinese consumer market.

But Dunn argues such a move ultimately will prove to be a profitable one. "We may not have an accounting system that works to account for the full cost or benefit of a decision, but setting an ethical course is consistent with being profitable," he explains. "For us, acting ethically means taking into account the legitimate claims of everyone who might be affected by a decision and trying to resolve everyone's concerns. It will catch up with a company if they only think of one group, such as the shareholders or customers."

Some observers have criticized the company's decision to close some of its U.S. manufacturing facilities and transfer those jobs to the developing world, where they say Levi Strauss underpays workers. Still, the company argues that it has demonstrated a solid commitment to its employees. It routinely pays higher wages than other manufacturers in all parts of the world. Also, it attempts to locate plants in the countries where the product is sold as a way to bolster local economies.

"The experience of this company is that when we do what we believe is right, the company has benefited from standing by its convictions," Dunn says. "It may be disadvantageous in the near term in ways that are easily quantifiable, but it's difficult to assess the ways it might benefit us because we've honored our ethical values. We have attracted good people and have developed strong relationships with suppliers and consumers while winning the trust and confidence of investors."

A POWERFUL PRESCRIPTION
MERCK & CO.

Whitehouse Station, New Jersey
Ownership status:
161,200 shareholders.
Annual sales:
$9.66 billion in 1992.
Annual net earnings:
$2.44 billion in 1992.
Number of Employees:
38,000.

PHOTOGRAPH COURTESY MERCK.

THERE ARE FEW BUSINESSES in a position to so thoroughly exploit customers as a pharmaceutical manufacturer. If you desperately need a drug, you're likely to mortgage your home to get it.

And while some companies have built their business on the basis of that exploitation, Merck & Co. has become the world's largest prescription drug company by leading the way in lowering prices, donating medication, and helping fund research efforts in developing countries. Just this spring the company proposed a system to ensure price restraints on medication. It included requiring independent outside auditors to certify that price increases meet specific criteria as well as cutting prices found to be in excess *and* paying that excess money into a government fund for improving health care access.

"If adopted industry-wide, our pricing proposal could produce an estimated $7-9 billion in savings on prescription drug costs in the three-year period between 1994 and 1996," says Merck chairman and CEO P. Roy Vagelos. "It is clear that the American people deserve cost containment as we move to a reformed health care system."

Such a move is typical of the way this 102-year-old organization operates. It is, in fact, the cornerstone of the company's foundation. Witness this 1950 quote by former president and chairman George Merck: "We try to remember that medicine is for the patient. We try never to forget that medicine is for the people. It is not for profits. The profits follow, and if we have remembered that, they have never failed to appear. The better we have remembered that, the larger they have been."

Indeed, Merck takes great pride in measuring its success not by the number of dollars it passes along to shareholders, but in the number of lives it gives to the world. "Merck is most fortunate in that our business is saving lives and fighting disease. That is corporate citizenship of the highest order, because

Merck Highlights

▶ Has been a leader is assuring price increase restraint on human drugs.
▶ Launched education initiative to revitalize elementary science and math education.
▶ Donates medical supplies to organizations and countries in need ($30 million worth in 1991).
▶ Donates medication—and the money to administer it—to prevent river blindness, which afflicts three million people in Africa and Latin America.
▶ Gave $1 million grant to a Costa Rican organization, INBio, to help search for new medicines from the Costa Rican rainforest; also contracted to give the project a percentage of royalties from the sale of those drugs.
▶ Is an industry leader in compensation—average employee made $57,000 in 1991.

we measure our success by how much we help people around the world," says Robin Hogen, executive vice president of the Merck Company Foundation. "Business does not operate in a social vacuum. Companies rise and fall based on how well they serve society. If your competition does it better than you do, they win and you lose—which is why serving society is the true foundation of our free enterprise, capitalist system."

While Merck's philanthropic efforts have become a model for other pharmaceutical companies, it also has extended this socially responsible view to other arenas. Although the company has had some problems with toxic chemical releases, it has pledged to the EPA that it will reduce them by 90 percent by 1995. "Merck's fundamental mission is providing society with products that promote the health and well-being of all, and health and well-being are possible only in a healthy environment," explains Vagelos.

Likewise, its employee benefits programs are considered among the best in the country. Health insurance, on-site daycare, company-sponsored health programs, and employee stock ownership plans are generous; It has long been recognized as one of the best companies to work for in America. "It seems to be an especially well-run company," says Tepper Marlin. "When you spend your time thinking of saving lives it becomes natural to treat employees well and reach out into the community."

Developing the Future Ethos and Social Responsibility of Business

Business ethics should not be viewed as a short-term, "knee-jerk reaction" to recently revealed scandals and corruptions. Instead, it should be viewed as a thread woven through the fabric of the entire business culture—one that ought to be integral to its design. Businesses are built on the foundation of trust in our free enterprise system. When there are violations of this trust between competitors, between employer and employees, or between businesses and consumers, the system ceases to run smoothly.

From a pragmatic viewpoint, the alternative to self-regulated and voluntary ethical behavior and social responsibility on the part of business may be governmental and legislative intervention. From a moral viewpoint, ethical behavior should not exist because of economic pragmatism, governmental edict, or contemporary fashionability—it should exist because it is morally appropriate and right.

This last unit is composed of five articles that provide some ideas, guidelines, and principles for developing the future ethos and social responsibility of business. "The Challenge of Ethical Behavior in Organizations" begins this section by examining some critical areas of challenge that ethical organizations are likely to face in the future. The next article points out the importance of establishing an ethical work environment and suggests steps and ingredients that a company can utilize in building a busi-

ness ethics program. "Can a Company Be Too Ethical?" takes a look at some companies that have been criticized for ignoring core business concerns at the expense of so-called humanitarian projects. "High Explosives" covers some salient ethical land mines that need to be avoided. The last article, "How to Make Diversity Pay," reflects that, while many companies dawdle, smart ones are betting that a diversified workforce will prove vital in the twenty-first century.

Looking Ahead: Challenge Questions

In what areas should organizations become more ethically sensitive and socially responsible in the next five years? Be specific and explain your choices.

Do you agree with the author of "High Explosives" in regard to the prognostication of the 10 explosive ethical issues that management will face in the 1990s? Why or why not? What other ethical issues or land mines do you envision? Discuss the basis of your prediction.

Obtain codes of ethics or conduct from several different professional associations (for example, doctors, lawyers, CPAs). What are the similarities and differences between them?

How useful do you feel that codes of ethics are to organizations? Why?

Unit 5

The Challenge
of Ethical Behavior
in Organizations

Ronald R. Sims

Ronald R. Sims is Associate Professor in the School of Business Administration at the College of William and Mary. His research interests include ethical behavior, experiential learning, employee and management training and development, and organizational transitions. His articles have appeared in a variety of scholarly and practitioner-oriented journals.

ABSTRACT. This paper is designed to do three things while discussing the challenge of ethical behavior in organization. First, it discusses some reasons why unethical behavior occurs in organization. Secondly, the paper highlights the importance of organizational culture in establishing an ethical climate within an organization. Finally, the paper presents some suggestions for creating and maintaining an ethically-oriented culture.

It has often been said that the only constant in life is change, and nowhere is this more true than in the workplace. As one recent survey concluded, "Over the past decade, the U.S. corporation has been battered by foreign competition, its own out-of-date technology and out-of-touch management and, more recently a flood of mergers and acquisitions. The result has been widespread streamlining of the white-collar ranks and recognition that the old way of doing business is no longer possible or desirable" (*U.S. News & World Report*, 1989, p. 42).

As the twenty-first century approaches, companies face a variety of changes and challenges that will have a profound impact on organizational dynamics and performance. In many ways, these changes will decide who will survive and prosper into the next century and who will not. Among these challenges are the following:

(1) *The challenge of international competition.*
(2) *The challenge of new technologies.*
(3) *The challenge of increased quality.*
(4) *The challenge of employee motivation and commitment.*
(5) *The challenge of managing a diverse work force.*
(6) *The challenge of ethical behavior.*

While these challenges must all be met by organizations and managers concerned about survival and competitiveness in the future, this paper will focus on the challenge of ethical behavior. More specifically, this paper will (1) discuss some reasons' unethical behavior occurs in organizations, (2) highlight the importance of organizational culture in establishing an ethical climate within the organization, and finally, (3) present some suggestions for creating and maintaining an ethically-oriented culture.

Ethics and the challenge of ethical behavior

The imperatives of day-to-day organizational performance are so compelling that there is little time or inclination to divert attention to the moral content of organizational decision-making. Morality appears to be so esoteric and qualitative in nature that it lacks substantive relation to objective and quantitative performance. Besides, understanding the meaning of ethics and morality requires the distasteful reworking of long-forgotten classroom studies. What could Socrates, Plato, and Aristotle teach us about the world that confronts organizations approaching the twenty-first century? Possibly a gap in philosophical knowledge exists between organizational executives and administrators of different generations. Yet, like it or not, there has and will continue to be a surge of interest in ethics.

The word "ethics" is often in the news these days. Ethics is a philosophical term derived from the Greek word "ethos" meaning character or custom. This definition is germane to effective leadership in organizations in that it connotes an organization code conveying moral integrity and consistent values in service to the public. Certain organizations will commit themselves to a philosophy in a formal pronouncement of a Code of Ethics or Standards of Conduct. Having done so, the recorded idealism is distributed or shelved, and all too often that is that. Other organizations, however, will be concerned with aspects of ethics of greater specificity, usefulness, and consistency.

Formally defined, *ethical behavior* is that which is morally accepted as "good" and "right" as opposed to "bad" or "wrong" in a particular setting. *Is it ethical*, for example, to pay a bribe to obtain a business contract in a foreign country? *Is it ethical* to allow your company to withhold information that might discourage a job candidate from joining your organization? *Is it ethical* to ask someone to take a job you know will not be good for their career progress? *Is it ethical* to do personal business on company time?

The list of examples could go on and on. Despite one's initial inclinations in response to these questions, the major point of it all is to remind organizations that the public-at-large is demanding that government officials, managers, workers in general, and the organizations they represent all act according to high ethical and moral standards. The future will bring a renewed concern with maintaining high standards of ethical behavior in organizational transactions and in the workplace.

Many executives, administrators, and social scientists see unethical behavior as a cancer working on the fabric of society in too many of today's organizations and beyond. Many are concerned that we face a crisis of ethics in the West that is undermining our competitive strength. This crisis involves businesspeople, government officials, customers, and employees. Especially worrisome is unethical behavior among employees at all levels of the organization. For example, a recent study found that employees accounted for a higher percentage of retail thefts than did customers (Silverstein, 1989). The study estimated that one in every fifteen employees steals from his or her employer.

In addition, we hear about illegal and unethical behavior on Wall Street, pension scandals in which disreputable executives gamble on risky business ventures with employees' retirement funds, companies that expose their workers to hazardous working conditions, and blatant favoritism in hiring and promotion practices. Although such practices occur throughout the world, their presence nonetheless serves to remind us of the challenge facing organizations.

This challenge is especially difficult because standards for what constitutes ethical behavior lie in a "grey zone" where clear-cut right-versus wrong answers may not always exist. As a result, sometimes unethical behavior is forced on organizations by the environment in which it exists and laws such as the Foreign Corruption Practices Act. For example, if you were a sales representative for an American company abroad and your foreign competitors used bribes to get business, what would you do? In the United States such behavior is illegal, yet it is perfectly acceptable in other countries. What is ethical here? Similarly, in many countries women are systematically discriminated against in the workplace; it is felt that their place is in the home. In the United States, again, this practice is illegal. If you ran an American company in one of these countries, would you hire women in important positions? If you did, your company might be isolated in the larger business community, and you might lose business. If you did not, you might be violating what most Americans believe to be fair business practices.

The effective management of ethical issues requires that organizations ensure that their managers and employees know how to deal with ethical issues in their everyday work lives. Therefore, organizational members must first understand some of the underlying reasons for the occurrence of unethical practices.

Unethical behavior: why does it occur in organizations?

The potential for individuals and organizations to behave unethically is limitless. Unfortunately, this potential is too frequently realized. Consider, for example, how greed overtook concerns about human welfare when the Manville Corporation suppressed evidence that asbestos inhalation was killing its employees, or when Ford failed to correct a known defect that made its Pinto vulnerable to gas tank explosions following low speed rear-end collisions (Bucholz, 1989). Companies that dump dangerous medical waste materials into our rivers and oceans also appear to favor their own interests over public safety and welfare. Although these examples are better known than many others, they do not appear to be unusual. In fact, the story they tell may be far more typical than we would like, as one expert estimates that about two-thirds of the 500 largest American corporations have been involved in one form of illegal behavior or another (Gellerman, 1986).

Unfortunately, unethical organizational practices are embarrassingly commonplace. It is easy to define such practices as dumping polluted chemical wastes into rivers, insider trading on Wall Street, over-charging the government for Medicaid services, and institutions like Stanford University inappropriately using taxpayer money to buy a yacht or to enlarge their President's bed in his home as morally wrong. Yet these and many other unethical practices go on almost routinely in many organizations. Why is this so? In other words, what accounts for the unethical actions of people in organizations, more specifically, why do people commit those unethical actions in which individuals knew or should have known that the organization was committing an unethical act? An example recently provided by Baucus and Near (1991) helps to illustrate this distinction.

Recently, a federal court judge found Allegheny Bottling, a Pepsi-Cola bottling franchise, guilty of price fixing. The firm had ended years of cola wars by setting prices with its major competitor, Mid-Atlantic Coca-Cola Bottling (New York Times, 1988). Since evidence showed most executives in the firm knew of the illegal price-fixing scheme, the court not only fined Allegheny $1 million but also sentenced it to three years in prison — a sentence that was suspended since a firm cannot be imprisoned. However, the unusual penalty allowed the judge to place the firm on probation and significantly restrict its operations.

In another case, Harris Corporation pleaded no contest to charges that it participated in a kickback scheme involving a defense department loan to the Philippines (Wall Street Journal, 1989). Although this plea cost the firm $500,000 in fines and civil claims, Harris's chief executive said the firm and its employees were not guilty of criminal conduct; he maintained that top managers

pleaded no contest because the costs associated with litigation would have been greater than the fines, and litigation would have diverted management attention from firm operations.

Although both cases appear to be instances of illegal corporate behavior, there is an important distinction between them. In the first case, Allegheny's executives knew or should have known the firm's activities were illegal; price fixing is a clear violation of anti-trust law. Further, the courts ruled that evidence indicated the firm had engaged in the illegal act. In contrast, it is not clear that Harris Corporations' managers committed an illegal act. Some areas of the law are very ambiguous, including the area relevant to this case, the Foreign Corrupt Practices Act, and managers may not at times know what it legal or illegal; thus, a firm may inadvertently engage in behavior that is later defined as illegal or unethical (Baucus and Near, 1991).

One answer to the question of why individuals knowingly commit unethical actions is based on the idea that *organizations often reward behaviors that violate ethical standards.* Consider, for example, how many business executives are expected to deal in bribes and payoffs, despite the negative publicity and ambiguity of some laws, and how good corporate citizens who blow the whistle on organizational wrongdoing may fear being punished for their actions. Jansen and Von Glinow (1985) explain that organizations tend to develop *counternorms,* accepted organizational practices that are contrary to prevailing ethical standards. Some of these are summarized in Figure 1.

The top of Figure 1 identifies being open and honest as a prevailing ethical norm. Indeed, governmental regulations requiring full disclosure and freedom of information reinforce society's values toward openness and honesty. Within organizations, however, it is often considered not only acceptable, but desirable, to be much more secretive and deceitful. The practice of stonewalling, willingly hiding relevant information, is quite common. One reason for this is that organizations may actually punish those who are too open and honest. Look at the negative treatment experienced by many employees who are willing to blow the whistle on unethical behavior in their organizations. Also, consider for example, the disclosure that B. F. Goodrich rewarded employees who falsified data on quality aircraft brakes in order to win certification (Vandevier, 1978). Similarly, it has been reported that executives at Metropolitan Edison encouraged employees to withhold information from the press about the Three Mile Island nuclear accident (Gray and Rosen, 1982). Both incidents represent cases in which the counternorms of secrecy and deceitfulness were accepted and supported by the organization.

Figure 1 shows that there are many other organizational counternorms that promote morally and ethically questionable practices. Because these practices are commonly rewarded and accepted suggests that organizations may be operating within a world that dictates its own set of accepted rules. This reasoning suggests a second answer to the question of why organizations knowingly act unethically — namely, because *managerial values exist that undermine integrity*. In a recent analysis of executive integrity, Wolfe explains that managers have developed some ways of thinking (of which they may be quite unaware) that foster unethical behavior (Wolfe, 1988).

One culprit is referred to as the bottom-line-mentality. This line of thinking supports financial success as the only value to be considered. It promotes short-term solutions that are immediately financially sound, despite the fact that they cause problems for others within the organization or the organization as a whole. It promotes an unrealistic belief that everything boils down to a monetary

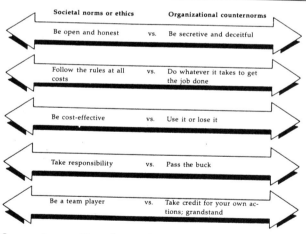

Societal norms or ethics		Organizational counternorms
Be open and honest	vs.	Be secretive and deceitful
Follow the rules at all costs	vs.	Do whatever it takes to get the job done
Be cost-effective	vs.	Use it or lose it
Take responsibility	vs.	Pass the buck
Be a team player	vs.	Take credit for your own actions; grandstand

Source: Jansen, E. and Von Glinow, M. A.: 1985, 'Ethical Ambivalence and Organizational Reward Systems', *Academy of Management Review* **10**(4), pp. 814–822.

Fig. 1. Societal norms vs. Organizational counternorms: an ethical conflict.

game. As such, rules of morality are merely obstacles, impediments along the way to bottom-line financial success.

A similar bottom-line mentality, the *"political bottom line,"* is also quite evident in the public sector.

For example, when it comes to spending money, the U.S. Congress has no equal. Although much of this expenditure is for purposes of national concern, a sizable portion is devoted to pork-barreling. Pork-barreling refers to the practice whereby a senator or representative forces Congress to allocate monies to special projects that take place in his or her home district. In many cases, the projects have little value and represent a drain on the taxpayers. They do, however, create jobs — and political support — in the home district. This practice is common, because many members of Congress believe it will help them get votes in the next election.

In some more extreme — and definitely ethically questionable — situations, such actions are designed to reward some large-scale campaign contributors in the home district. A case in point is the Maxi Cube cargo handling system. Funds for testing the Maxi Cube cargo handling system were written into the fiscal 1989 defense budget during the final Senate-House Appropriations conference at the request of Rep. John Murtha of Pennsylvania. The $10 million item was specifically targeted for a Philadelphia businessman (and contributor to Murtha's campaign) who was to manufacture the truck in Murtha's home district. The only problem was that the U.S. Army had clearly said that it had "no known requirement" for the handler. In response, Murtha was reported to be "mad as hell" at the "nitpicking" by the army. He pushed ahead anyway and used his position on the Appropriations committee to freeze a series of military budgeting requests until he got his pet project approved.

And Murtha is not alone. Rep. Les Aspin of Wisconsin got the Defense Appropriations committee to include $249 million to continue making a certain ten-ton truck (in Wisconsin, naturally) that the army was trying to phase out. It, too, was unneeded, but Aspin wanted the project for his home district. Is this legal? Yes? Is it ethical? That depends upon your point of view (Morgan, 1989). Clearly, Murtha and Aspin thought it was appropriate, given the realities of today's private and public organizations.

Wolfe also notes that managers tend to rely on an exploitative mentality — a view that encourages "using" people in a way that promotes stereotypes and undermines empathy and compassion. This is a highly selfish perspective, one that sacrifices concerns for others in favor of benefits to one's own immediate interests. In addition, there is a Madison Avenue mentality — a perspective suggesting that anything is right if the public can be convinced that it's right. The idea is that executives may be more concerned about their actions appearing ethical than by their legitimate morality — a public relations-guided morality. It is this kind of thinking that leads some companies to hide their unethical actions (by dumping their toxic wastes under cover of night, for instance) or otherwise justify them by attempting to explain them as completely acceptable.

It is not too difficult to recognize how individuals can knowingly engage in unethical practices with such mentalities. The overemphasis on short-term monetary gain and getting votes in the next election may lead to decisions and rationalizations that not only hurt individuals in the long run, but threaten the very existence of organizations themselves. Some common rationalizations used to justify unethical behavior are easily derived from Gellerman (1986):

** Pretending the behavior is not really unethical or illegal.
** Excusing the behavior by saying it's really in the organization's or your best interest.
** Assuming the behavior is okay because no one else would ever be expected to find out about it.
** Expecting your superiors to support and protect you if anything should go wrong.

Within the literature on corporate illegality, the predominant view is that pressure and need force organizational members to behave unethically and develop corresponding rationalizations; however, according to recent research this explanation only accounts for illegal acts in some cases (Baucus and Near, 1991). In their data, poor performance and low organizational slack (the excess that remains once a firm has paid its various internal and external constituencies to maintain cooperation) were not associated with illegal behavior, and wrongdoing frequently occurred in munificent environments.

According to the model developed from Baucus and Near's research (see Figure 2), illegal behavior occurs under certain conditions. For example, results from their research showed that (1) large firms are more likely to commit illegal acts than small firms; (2) although the probability of such wrongdoing increases when resources are scarce, it is greatest when resources are plentiful; (3) illegal behavior is prevalent in fairly stable environments but is more probable in dynamic environments; (4) membership in certain industries and a history of repeated wrongdoing are also associated with illegal acts; and, (5) the type of illegal activity chosen may vary

according to the particular combination of environmental and internal conditions under which a firm is operating (Baucus and Near, 1991).

Baucus and Near also suggest that conditions of opportunity and predisposition are antecedents of illegal behavior. That is, rather than tightening conditions creating pressure for illegal acts, it may be that loosening ambiguous conditions create opportunities to behave illegally. In terms of the model presented in Figure 2, large firm size provided more opportunity to engage in illegal activities than small size; the former condition may make it easy to hide illegal activities. Rules, procedures, and other control mechanisms often lag behind growth of a firm, providing organizational members with an opportunity to behave illegally because no internal rules prescribe such behavior.

Predisposition indicates a tendency or inclination to select certain activities — illegal ones — over activities because of socialization or other organizational processes. Baucus and Near (1991) avoid the assumption that a firm's managers or agents sub-

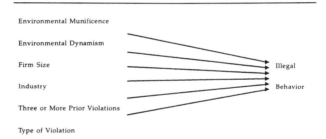

Source: 1991, Baucus, M. S. and Near, J. P.: 1991, 'Can Illegal Corporate Behavior Be Predicted? An Event History Analysis', *Academy of Management Journal* **34**(1), pp. 9—36.

Fig. 2. Modified model of the illegal corporation behavior process.

scribe to a different set of ethical standards than the rest of society. Instead, they recognize that organizations, and industries, can exert a powerful influence on their members, even those who initially have fairly strong ethical standards.

As noted above, organizations operating in certain industries tend to behave unethically. Certain industry cultures may predispose organizations to develop cultures that encourage their members to select unethical acts. If an organization's major competitors in an industry are performing well, in part as a result of unethical activities, it becomes difficult for organizational members to choose only unethical actions, and they may regard unethical actions as a standard

Lundberg: The first program was called "21 Jump Street," and its star was a teenager named Johnny Depp. We got him out in public—we sent him to malls. It's remarkable how fast information passes through teenage America. When a friend tells you something, it has tremendous credibility.

Stewart: You can influence word of mouth in a number of ways. For example, Lexus was running ads, but the company knew what owners said about the cars was really selling them. So they put the car in lobbies at ballets and local symphonies, where people who could afford a Lexus would see it.

Brown: Word of mouth is now becoming word of the keyboard. It used to be that when someone bought a product, they would pass their experience—satisfaction or dissatisfaction—on to a circle of acquaintances. Maybe 15 to 20 people would be affected by it. Now you have computer networks like Internet, which has more than 20 million users. People are increasingly using this medium for product and service information. Someone gets on and says, "I'm thinking of buying a printer." The network is flooded with thousands of comments. And those comments go to everybody else on the network.

I understand that the advertising on Prodigy's online network wasn't very successful. Now it has to charge customers more than anticipated.

Bender: It may not have anything to do with the advertising. When you've got a new medium, there's going to be some run-up time until people learn how to be creative in that medium.

Does everyone need to be involved in computer advertising right now?

Brown: When you lose your first customers because you haven't made the option available, it's time to think seriously about computer advertising.

Stewart: Some things won't sell by computer. You can provide information, but for something like a house, the customer will want to walk through it. Right now, it's probably not terribly important for real-estate agents to be online, because not many of their cus-

tomers will want to shop for a house that way. That may change as the penetration of computers grows.

Lundberg: It depends on the product and the company. A company with a 50-year history might risk damaging firmly established brand loyalty. But if you're the new guy on the block, maybe you do want to try something different—and irreverent.

Hughes: You're going to see the technology advance to such a level that consumers will be able to customize ads. You can see it right now when you go to entertainment complexes. When you visit the ET ride at Universal Studios, you punch in your name just before you get on. At the end of the ride, ET says "Goodbye" and calls you by name. In the future, messages will be totally customized for particular households.

If it's too personalized, aren't customers going to worry about who knows what?

Stewart: We're going to evolve to a point where we recognize that a name is intellectual property. If I have a name, I own it. If you make use of it without my permission, you owe me damages. If I choose to give my name to you for a particular purpose, then that's my decision. The business of selling mailing lists won't go away completely. People will identify themselves. But it will no longer be the broad spectrum. You won't do mailings to everyone who owns a particular car model.

Brown: You see it now. Almost half of southern California residents have unlisted telephone numbers. When you drive between LAX and Laguna Beach, you see all the walled communities. People are putting walls around themselves, and that includes their names and other information.

Stewart: We're in a transition period, and that's part of the confusion. We've moved away from big mass audiences, but we're not yet to the point where the consumer is fully in control. I think there will always be a place for mass advertising, although what we increasingly see ourselves doing is advertising advertising.

Bender: The package Time-Warner put together for Chrysler is a good example. Chrysler ads asked consumers to send

in for a multimedia kit, including a video. It contained all the information the customer could want on a particular class of automobile. Because it was multimedia, the customer could choose to throw the tape in the VCR or spend time browsing through the pages of the printed material.

Brown: In Ross Perot's presidential campaign ads and infomercials, he told the audience they could request more information. So the audience was self-selected. Those who were interested enough to request the information got it. There was no need to waste resources on those who didn't.

Bender: I have a fantasy. The next time I buy life insurance, I want to punch "Life Insurance" into my computer and get every company out there in the world. I want to say, "I'm 48 years old, I smoke, I have a wife and this many kids, and I have this

"Getting people to pay attention to advertising is not really a problem when the advertising is personally relevant."

David Stewart
University of
Southern California

much insurance now. Is there anything else you'd like to know? Now give me prices and tell me how you work this." I get a lot of phone calls now, but I don't get them all at once—and I don't get them when I want them.

Lundberg: This will happen, but it's not going to necessarily replace existing methods of communication. There will always be people who watch the football game on the couch with their head on a pillow. But right now, the media are moving from passive toward interactive.

Stewart: There is no magic formula. The misconception about advertising is that there is a magic bullet that does everything for everybody. The fact is that advertising is a whole array of tools, and it's inherently a creative enterprise. It works when you get it matched right with a particular audience. If you don't understand your audience, how can you possibly use the creative tools?

Those Mind-Boggling Promotions

Consumers' frustration has doomed some, but more are on the way.

Adam Bryant

Americans' love of a bargain notwithstanding, consumers are getting fed up with the increasingly complex promotions being served up by corporate marketing departments.

The often dizzying lists of conditions, choices and partners in today's promotions—a loose term for incentives that typically give shoppers something in addition to the basic product—leave many people feeling they need an accountant's eyeshade to scour ads for savings.

"There are so many schemes, and I don't think they pay," said Lou Nobiletti, a retired hotel executive in Hampton Bays, L.I., one of the many consumers who has given up on hunting for deals among the fine print and now looks only at prices when he shops. "They're too devious."

Such impatience often dooms big marketing efforts, notably a year-old "frequent buyer" program called Air Miles, which halted operations in the United States in May. The program enabled consumers to earn frequent-flier mileage on four airlines by buying products from a raft of big companies, including A.T.&T., Gillette, Citicorp and Procter & Gamble.

Some industry experts say Air Miles faltered because the rewards were too small, but many argue that it also required too much work, like mailing in proofs of purchase.

Consumers do embrace certain promotions, the ones that keep the fine print to a minimum and offer rewards they want. The General Motors Mastercard, for example, has been a runaway success. It gives consumers a 5 percent rebate on purchases that they can then use to reduce the price of a new G.M. car. In just over a year, the company has signed up six million accounts.

In contrast, General Electric offers a credit card with 27 marketing partners like Kmart and Macy's, which send a packet of coupons worth $250 to cardholders every three months. Each coupon has its own conditions, like $10 off a $50 purchase. For every $500 spent with the card, a shopper gets $10 that can be used only at the 27 retailers.

"You need an attaché case to really use this card," said Robert B. McKinley, president of Ram Research, a credit-card research firm in Frederick, Md. "Not only is it messy, but where are the coupons when you need them?"

Broad changes in consumer attitudes are difficult to prove. But interviews with consumers and marketing experts leave little doubt that many people are wearied by deals that tax their time-starved lives.

Judith Langer, president of Langer Associates, a New York-based research firm that conducts more than 200 focus groups a year, said that she often hears complaints from consumers about information overload. "The feeling is very much, 'It's too much, and I need to simplify my life,' " she said.

The publisher of The Tightwad Gazette newsletter, Amy Dacyczyn, can work up enthusiasm for almost any penny-pinching idea, including buying huge stuffed animals at yard sales and eviscerating them to make Halloween costumes. But she finds today's proliferating promotions a turnoff. "If I don't have time to sit down and figure them out, I ignore them," she said.

Nevertheless, surveys of the packaged goods industry—considered a bellwether of the broader marketplace—suggest that companies are spending a growing percentage of their marketing budgets on promotions, often joining forces in complex deals.

A joint Nabisco and Sony promotion that started this month can earn customers up to $23 worth of rebates. To reach that figure, they must buy four combinations of the companies' products chosen from a list of more than 45 items—including Nabisco cookies and crackers and Sony compact disks and video games—and then send away for the rebates. Ten million booklets are being distributed to help explain the offer.

GQ magazine has sponsored a program called Return on Invest-

courage ethical behavior, organizations can benefit from the following suggestions:

** Be realistic in setting values and goals regarding employment relationships. Do not promise what the organization cannot deliver.

** Encourage input throughout the organization regarding appropriate values and practices for implementing the cultures. Choose values that represent the views of employees at all levels of the organization.

** Do not automatically opt for a "strong" culture. Explore methods to provide for diversity and dissent, such as grievance or complaint mechanisms or other internal review procedures.

** Insure that a whistle-blowing and/or ethical concerns procedure is established for internal problem-solving (Harrington, 1991).

** Provide ethics training programs for *all* employees. These programs should explain the underlying ethical and legal (Drake and Drake, 1988) principles and present practical aspects of carrying out procedural guidelines.

** Understand that not all ethical situations are clear-cut. Like many basic business situations, the organization should recognize that there are ambiguous, grey areas where ethical trade-offs may be necessary. More importantly, some situations have no simple solution (Cooke, 1991).

** Integrate ethical decision-making into the performance appraisal process.

In conclusion, even though ethical problems in organizations continue to greatly concern society, organizations, and individuals, the potential impact that organizational culture can have on ethical behavior has not really been explored (Hellreigel *et al.*, 1989). The challenge of ethical behavior must be met by organizations if they are truly concerned about survival and competitiveness. What is needed in today's complicated times is for more organizations to step forward and operate with strong, positive, and ethical cultures. Organizations have to ensure that their employees know how to deal with ethical issues in their everyday work lives. As a result, when the ethical climate is clear and positive, everyone will know what is expected of them when inevitable ethical dilemmas occur. This can give employees the confidence to be on the lookout for unethical behavior and act with the understanding

that what they are doing is considered correct and will be supported by top management and the entire organization.

References

Alder, H. J. and Bird, F. B.: 1988, 'International Dimension of Executive Integrity: Who is Responsible for the World', in S. Srivastva, ed., *Executive Integrity: The Search for Human Values in Organizational Life* (Jossey-Bass, San Francisco), pp. 243–267.

Arlow, R. and Ulrich, T. A.: 1980, 'Auditing Your Organization's Ethics', *Internal Auditor* **39**(4), pp. 26–31.

Baumhart, R.: 1961, 'How Ethical are Businessmen?', *Harvard Business Review* **39**(4), pp. 26–31.

Baucus, M. S. and Near, J. P.: 1991, 'Can Illegal Corporate Behavior Be Predicated? An Event History Analysis', *Academy of Management Journal* **34**(1), pp. 9–36.

Brenner, S. and Molander, E.: 1977, 'Is the Ethics of Business Changing?', *Harvard Business Review* **55**(1), pp. 55–71.

Bucholz, R. A.: 1989, *Fundamental Concepts and Problems in Business Ethics* (Prentice-Hall, Englewood Cliffs, NJ).

Burns, S.: 1987, 'Good Corporate Citizenship Can Pay Dividends', *Dallas Morning News* (April 15), p. C1.

Carroll, A. B.: 1978, 'Linking Business Ethics to Behavior in Organizations', *Advanced Management Journal* **43**(3), pp. 4–11.

Cooke, R. A.: 1991, 'Danger Signs of Unethical Behavior: How to Determine If Your Firm Is at Ethical Risk', *Journal of Business Ethics* **10**, pp. 249–253.

Conklin, J.: 1977, *Illegal But Not Criminal* (Prentice-Hall, Englewood Cliffs, NJ).

Drake, B. H., and Drake, E.: 1988, 'Ethical and Legal Aspects of Managing Corporate Cultures', *California Management Review* (Winter), pp. 120–121.

Geis, G.: 1977, 'The Heavy Electrical Equipment Antitrust Case of 1961', in G. Geis and R. Meier, eds., *White-Collar Crime: Offenses in Business, Politics, and the Profession* (Free Press, New York), pp. 117–132.

Gellerman, S. W.: 1986, 'Why "good" Managers Make Bad Ethical Choices', *Harvard Business Review* (July–August), pp. 85–90.

Graham, J. W.: 1986, 'Principled Organizational Dissent: A Theoretical Essay', in B. M. Staw and L. L. Cummings, eds., *Research in Organizational Behavior*, Vol. 8 (JAI Press, Greenwich, Conn.).

Gray, M. and Rosen, I.: 1982, *The Warning* (Norton, New York).

Harrington, S. J.: 1991, 'What Corporate America is Teaching About Ethics', *Academy of Management Executive* **5**(1), pp. 21–30.

Hegarty, W. and Sims, H., Jr.: 1978, 'Some Determinants of Unethical Decision Behavior: An Experiment', *Journal of Applied Psychology* **63**(4), pp. 451–457.

Hellreigel, D., Slocum, J. W., Jr., and Woodman, R. W.: 1989, *Organizational Behavior* (West Publishing, St. Paul, MN).

5. FUTURE ETHOS AND SOCIAL RESPONSIBILITY OF BUSINESS

Hunt, J. G.: 1991, *Toward A Leadership Paradigm Change* (Sage, Newbury Park, CA).

Jansen, E. and Glinow, M. A.: 1985, 'Ethical Ambivalence and Organizational Reward Systems', *Academy of Management Review* **10**(4), pp. 814—822.

Morgan, D.: 1989, 'Truck Army Does Not Want to Be Tied Up in House Turf Battle', *Washington Post* (August 12), p. A2.

New York Times: 1988, 'Corporate Prison Term for Allegheny Bottling' (September 1), p. D2.

Nielsen, R. P.: 1988, 'Limitations of Ethical Reasoning as an Action (Praxis) Strategy', *Journal of Business Ethics* **7**, pp. 725—733.

Nielsen, R. P.: 1989, 'Changing Unethical Organizational Behavior', *Academy of Management Executive* **3**(2), pp. 123—130.

Otten, A. L.: 1986, 'Ethics on the Job: Companies Alert Employees to Potential Dilemmas', *The Wall Street Journal* (July 14), p. 17.

Posner, G. and Schmidt, W.: 1984, 'Values and the American Manger: An Update', *California Management Review* **24**(3), pp. 206—216.

Raelin, J. A.: 1987, 'The Professional as the Executive's Aide-de-Camp', *Academy of Management Executive* **1**, pp. 171—182.

Schermerhorn, J. R.: 1989, *Management for Productivity* (John Wiley, New York).

Schneider, J. B. and Rentsch, J.: 1991, 'Managing Climates and Cultures: A Futures Perspective', in J. Hage, ed., *Future of Organizations* (Lexington Books, Lexington, MA).

Silverstein, S.: 1989, 'One in 15 Employees in Study Caught Stealing', *Los Angeles Times* (December 2), p. D-1.

Stead, W. E., Worrell, D. L., and Stead, J. G.: 'An Integrative Model for Understanding and Managing Ethical Behavior in Business Organizations', *Journal of Business Ethics* **9**, pp. 233—242.

Touche Ross: 1988, *Ethics in American Business: An Opinion Survey* (Touche Ross and Co.).

Trevino, L. K.: 1986, 'Ethical Decision Making in Organizations: A Person-Situation Interactionist Model', *Academy of Management Review* **11**(3), pp. 601—617.

U.S. News & World Report: 1989 (January 16), p. 42.

Vandevier, K.: 1978, 'The Aircraft Brake Scandal: A Cautionary Tale in Which the Moral is Unpleasant', in A. G. Athos and J. J. Babarro, eds., *Interpersonal Behavior: Communication and Understanding Relationships* (Prentice-Hall, Englewood Cliffs, NJ), pp. 529—540.

Vitell, S. and Festervand, T.: 1987, 'Business Ethics: Conflicts, Practices and Beliefs of Industrial Executives', *Journal of Business Ethics* **6**, pp. 111—122.

Wall Street Journal: 1989, 'Harris Corp. Is Convicted in Kickback Plan', (June 5), p. A7.

Wolfe, D.: 1988, 'Is There Integrity in the Bottomline: Managing Obstacles to Executive Integrity', in S. Srivastva, ed., *Executive Integrity: The Search For High Human Values in Organization Life* (Jossey-Bass, San Francisco), pp. 140—171.

Worrell, D. L., Stead, W. E., J. G. and Spalding, J. B.: 1985, 'Unethical Decisions: The Impact of Reinforcement Contingencies and Managerial Philosophies', *Psychological Reports* **57**, p. 355.

Creating Ethical Corporate Structures

Patrick E. Murphy
University of Notre Dame

Patrick E. Murphy is Associate Professor of Marketing at the College of Business Administration, University of Notre Dame. Dr. Murphy holds the B.B.A. degree from the University of Notre Dame, the M.B.A. degree from Bradley University, and the Ph.D. degree from the University of Houston. He is currently editor of the Journal of Public Policy and Marketing.

ETHICAL BUSINESS PRACTICES stem from ethical corporate cultures, the author writes. How does an organization go about developing that kind of culture? The most systematic approach is to build and nurture structures that emphasize the importance of ethical considerations. This paper outlines several companies' experiences with three types of ethics-enhancing structures: corporate credos, programs such as training workshops and ethics "audits," and codes tailored to the specific needs of a functional area. *Ed.*

WHAT IS AN ETHICAL COMPANY? This question is not easy to answer. For the most part, ethical problems occur because corporate managers and their subordinates are *too* devoted to the organization. In their loyalty to the company or zest to gain recognition, people sometimes ignore or overstep ethical boundaries. For example, some sales managers believe that the only way to meet ambitious sales goals is to have the sales reps "buy" business with lavish entertaining and gift giving. This overzealousness is the key source of ethical problems in most business firms.

Employees are looking for guidance in dealing with ethical problems. This guidance may come from the CEO, upper management, or immediate supervisors.[1] We know that ethical business practices stem from an ethical corporate culture. Key questions are, How can this culture be created and sustained? What structural approaches encourage ethical decision making? If the goal is to make the company ethical, managers must introduce structural components that will enhance ethical sensitivity.

In this paper, I examine three promising and workable approaches to infusing ethical principles into businesses:
• corporate credos that define and give direction to corporate values;
• ethics programs where companywide efforts focus on ethical issues; and
• ethical codes that provide specific guidance to employees in functional business areas.

Below I review the virtues and limitations of each and provide examples of companies that successfully employ these approaches.

Corporate Credos

A corporate credo delineates a company's ethical responsibility to its stakeholders; it is probably the most general approach to managing corporate

Table 1	The Credo of Security Pacific Corporation	
Commitment to Customer The first commitment is to provide our customers with quality products and services which are innovative and technologically responsive to their current requirements, at appropriate prices. To perform these tasks with integrity requires that we maintain confidentiality and protect customer privacy, promote customer satisfaction, and serve customer needs. We strive to serve qualified customers and industries which are socially responsible according to broadly accepted community and company standards.	**Commitment to Employee** The second commitment is to establish an environment for our employees which promotes professional growth, encourages each person to achieve his or her highest potential, and promotes individual creativity and responsibility. Security Pacific acknowledges our responsibility to employees, including providing for open and honest communication, stated expectations, fair and timely assessment of performance and equitable compensation which rewards employee contributions to company objectives within a framework of equal opportunity and affirmative action.	**Commitment of Employee to Security Pacific** The third commitment is that of the employee to Security Pacific. As employees, we strive to understand and adhere to the Corporation's policies and objectives, act in a professional manner, and give our best effort to improve Security Pacific. We recognize the trust and confidence placed in us by our customers and community and act with integrity and honesty in all situations to preserve that trust and confidence. We act responsibly to avoid conflicts of interest and other situations which are potentially harmful to the Corporation.
Commitment of Employee to Employee The fourth commitment is that of employees to their fellow employees. We must be committed to promote a climate of mutual respect, integrity, and professional relationships, characterized by open and honest communication within and across all levels of the organization. Such a climate will promote attainment of the Corporation's goals and objectives, while leaving room for individual initiative within a competitive environment.	**Commitment to Communities** The fifth commitment is that of Security Pacific to the communities which we serve. We must constantly strive to improve the quality of life through our support of community organizations and projects, through encouraging service to the community by employees, and by promoting participation in community services. By the appropriate use of our resources, we work to support or further advance the interests of the community, particularly in times of crisis or social need. The Corporation and its employees are committed to complying fully with each community's laws and regulations.	**Commitment to Stockholder** The sixth commitment of Security Pacific is to its stockholders. We will strive to provide consistent growth and a superior rate of return on their investment, to maintain a position and reputation as a leading financial institution, to protect stockholder investments, and to provide full and timely information. Achievement of these goals for Security Pacific is dependent upon the successful development of the five previous sets of relationships.

ethics. The credo is a succinct statement of the values permeating the firm. The experiences of Security Pacific Corporation (a Los Angeles–based national bank that devised a credo in 1987) and of Johnson & Johnson illustrate the credo approach.

Security Pacific's central document is not an ethical code per se; rather, it is six missionlike commitments to customers, employees, communities, and stockholders. The credo's objective is "to seek a set of principles and beliefs which might provide guidance and direction to our work" (see Table 1).

More than 70 high-level managers participated in formulating a first draft of the commitments. During this process, senior managers shared and analyzed examples of ethical dilemmas they had faced in balancing corporate and constituent obligations. An outside consultant, hired to manage the process, helped to draft the language. Ultimately more than 250 employees, from all levels of the bank, participated in the credo formulation process via a series of discussion groups.

Once the commitments were in final form, management reached a consensus on how to communicate these guiding principles to the Security Pacific organization. Credo coordinators developed and disseminated a leader's guide to be used at staff meetings introducing the credo; it contained instructions on the meeting's format and on showing a videotape that explained the credo and the process by which it was developed. At the meetings, managers invited reactions by posing these questions: What are your initial feelings about what you have just read? Are there any specific commitments you would like to discuss? How will the credo affect your daily work? Employees were thus encouraged to react to the credo and to consider its long-run implications.

Security Pacific's credo was recently cited as a model effort, and it serves internally both as a standard for judging existing programs and as a justification for new activities.[2] For example, the "commitment to communities" formed the basis for a

and at $1,000 he can become a Sony television owner. A Nissan or Volkswagen could roll in at $10,000. With an annual income of $1,000, Eastern Europeans can afford only refrigerators, says a study by Whirlpool. At $2,000 they rate automatic washers. "Central Europe is passing through this threshold," says Ruggero Bodo, vice president for planning at Whirlpool Europe. "People in these markets are screaming for high-quality, good-performance convenience goods."

Consumers show astonishing resourcefulness in finding ways to buy what really matters to them. Recall that in the U.S. the first satellite dishes sprang up in the poorest parts of Appalachia. Notes Peter Kennedy Jr., a consultant with the Futures Group in Glastonbury, Connecticut: "The poorest slums of Calcutta are home to 70,000 VCRs. In Mexico, homes with color televisions outnumber those with running water."

Remember also that low average-income figures may conceal a lively luxury market. In Warsaw (average annual income: $2,500)

and North America: "You were a hero to present the best bookcase produced in Northern Europe to Scandinavians. Today it's not enough. You have to compete with a bookcase produced in Taiwan by a manufacturer who has access to all the technology, capital, and labor that you do."

After sizing up the global opportunities, RJR Nabisco International President Rick Thoman is investing heavily in Latin America. The company recently opened a bakery in Monterrey, Mexico. Clorox just completed deals in Argentina and Chile to consolidate its ownership of distributors there. Procter & Gamble, CPC, and PepsiCo are also stepping up their South American acquisitions.

These big labels like South America because it is youthful and increasingly affluent, and consumers have an abiding trust in international brand names. More important, trade and economic barriers that once complicated business are eroding, making ownership more practical. Says Thoman: "It's becoming a level playing field. The

Eastern Europe's consumers are starved for basic goods that bore Westerners.

well-dressed shoppers flock to elegant boutiques stocked with Christian Dior perfume and Valentino shoes. Even simple grocery stores have installed fancy gourmet counters featuring French cheese and wine. In China, where per capita income is less than $600, the Swiss company Rado is selling thousands of its $1,000 watches. Guinness is doubling its sales force to cope with the demand for Johnnie Walker Black whisky—most of which is now bootlegged.

Suppliers of everything from petrochemicals to chewing gum will have to meet world standards where none existed before. Make no mistake, the Second World and Third World seek only first-rate product. U.S. companies once viewed China as a place to unload lower-value merchandise. No more. "You can't sell a TV in Guangdong unless it's a 29-inch with flat-screen technology," says George Baeder of PacRim. "No self-respecting Cantonese would want anything less."

Why so demanding? Mass media have educated consumers worldwide about the best of everything, and advances in retailing have made it available. Explains Goran Carstedt, president of IKEA North America, the global furniture retailer with operations from Bahrain to Singapore, as well as in Europe

openness of markets augurs very well for Latin America."

Stitching the region together commercially are a series of trade agreements that will let goods flow across borders. Among them: Mercosur (Argentina, Paraguay, Brazil), Ancom (Peru, Bolivia, Ecuador, Colombia, Venezuela) and Caricom (Caribbean nations).

As such pacts take effect, companies are seeing the beginnings of a pan–Latin American market, much as in Western Europe. Despite the dominance of one language, Spanish, the region had tended to divide into a Europe-oriented market in Argentina and the southern cone, and an American orientation in the North. The dichotomy is blurring, at least from a marketing viewpoint. Says Thoman: "We can shoot commercials in Colombia and show them all over."

Even Brazil, ever on the verge, is once again showing signs of life. Although inflation may hit 2,000% this year, reform just could happen. If it does, the government may sell businesses it controls in steel, telecommunications, and petrochemicals, energizing a huge segment of the economy.

Latin America's promising picture grows far brighter if Congress approves NAFTA. Says Josephine Jimenez, director of Mont-

THE PAC RIM'S BOOMING BUYING POWER

Millions of households approaching $18,000 per year buying power
Indexed to Singapore prices

73.3	2000
32.5	1995
14.4	1991

What the added middle class will buy In millions	Between now and 1995	2000
Bedrooms	32	116
Living rooms	16	58
Kitchens	16	58
Bathrooms	32	116
Living space (sq. m.)	1,200	4,350
Large appliances	16	58
Televisions	24	87
Telephones	24	87
Cars	16	58

FORTUNE CHART / SOURCE: PACRIM

gomery Asset Management's six emerging markets funds: "NAFTA will change the course of Latin American economic history. The consumer is waiting to spend, and the U.S. is the least expensive place to shop in the world right now." Mexico, for instance, with a population of 83 million, needs six million housing units. The country produces only 700,000 cars a year. The U.S., with three times the population, manufactures 15 times more cars.

A S IN SOUTH America, opportunities in Eastern Europe are immense. A new market of more than 300 million hungry consumers is about as large as Western Europe's. Reform seems irreversible. Only a few years ago Warsaw was a drab city, full of decaying concrete, peeling paint, and empty stores. Today it's the heart of Europe's fastest-growing country. Poland's economy should grow 4% this year, leaving Western Europe in the recessionary dust. More than half of working Poles have found jobs in the private economy.

Per capita incomes in Eastern Europe remain surprisingly low. The average Romanian and Russian earn about $600 a year. The average Hungarian, the richest East European, takes in only $3,440 (vs. an average of $20,000 in the EC). Post-communism, state workers and the underclass of unemployed have struggled. Only a minority have so far prospered: traders, repairmen, and tiny manufacturers freed to flourish; managers of state companies set to go private; lawyers and accountants; stifled artists and writers finally playing to paying audiences.

Eastern Europe's consumers are starved for basic goods that bore Westerners: Hamburgers, refrigerators, pizzas, telephones, and many others fly out of the stores. Overwhelming demand forced supermarketer Ahold to double expansion plans in the Czech Republic.

Managers generally see Poland, Hungary, the Czech Republic, and Slovakia as Eastern Europe's best bets. In these four pioneers Whirlpool Europe is achieving sales growth averaging 6% a year, says Ruggero Bodo. That's three times the figure in Western Europe. In a recent marketing study, Whirlpool concluded that these Central Europeans have the advantage of being "geographically and culturally tied to Germanic countries" and that their "economies are less reliant on former Soviet markets."

Carmakers are rushing to invade the still small market. French automaker Renault says it sold 2,300 vehicles last year in Hungary, 2,000 in Poland, and 1,600 in the former Czechoslovakia. In Germany, by contrast, it sold more than 200,000. The potential is what's exciting. Western Europeans own 450 cars per 1,000 people, while Central Europeans own about 200 per 1,000.

T HE SCOPE of what non-Japanese Asia will need as we reach its century of dominance is hard to fathom. Consider just the broad categories: It will become a voracious consumer of petrochemicals, plastic, and energy. Already the world's biggest steel market—more than twice as large as the U.S.'s—it will increase consumption 4% to 5% annually (U.S. consumption is falling). The demand for housing will explode as wealth begins to distribute families—now stacked three generations per household—to roomier quarters.

Just how much of this huge market will the West grab? "What Western companies are doing is a toe in the water," says PacRim's Baeder. But Japanese, Taiwanese, and Korean rivals have been swimming in these markets for years, gaining an edge that may be impossible to beat. Consider plastics. In five years, Taiwan's Chi Mei has emerged as a world leader, overtaking GE Plastics, Monsanto, and BASF in production of ABS, the high-grade plastic used in computer keyboards and telephone cases. Other players are lurking in other areas. President Foods, a $1-billion-a-year Taiwanese company, envisions China alone as five regional markets, each capable of producing $5 billion of sales.

Whatever is going to happen is going to happen fast. Technology is radically changing development cycles in Asia. Consumer goods cycles in developing economies are beginning to parallel technology cycles, achieving greater advances in shorter times. Adds Baeder: "It's going to take China ten years to do what Taiwan did in 25." If that's the case, he says, then companies such as President will have an advantage over non-Asian multinationals. They can recognize where China is in its development because they've been through it already.

The People's Republic of China, 1.2 billion in number, is an infinity of hot sum-

mer days to a world of would-be lemonade salesmen. Smith New Court says average per capita income has reached $1,000 in the southern cities of Shenzhen and Guangzhou, and Shanghai is close. These figures may be low, considering the value of government subsidies for food and housing. By almost any measure, China will become Asia's largest consumer market after Japan by 2000.

That's good news for companies such as Nike, which recently recorded its first million-dollar sales month in China; in the U.S. it sells $1 million every three hours or so.

Opportunities are enormous in telecommunications, pharmaceuticals, and specialty chemicals. As the population shifts its protein source from vegetable to animal, a characteristic of economic growth, grain consumption increases dramatically—you've got to run seven times as much grain through a cow to produce the same protein you would get from eating grain itself. Should China increase its caloric intake an unremarkable 15%, the country would have to produce or import 150 million tons of grain. To trading companies such as Cargill this is no small chunk of feed, as it represents the entire worldwide traded grain market.

India is no less astounding in the scope and complexity of its growing market. Estimates of its middle class range from 100

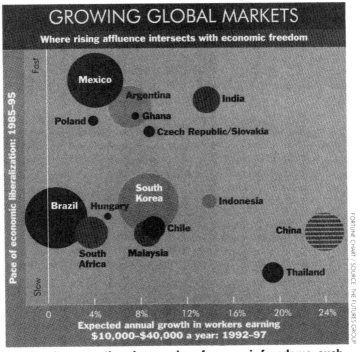

Middle-class growth and expansion of economic freedoms, such as market access, create opportunities (China data estimated).

million to 300 million, depending on what you're selling. While definitions vary, no one disputes that consumers with income to spend on branded goods are increasing faster than any other section of society. The growing reach of television, including the explosive 200% growth of urban STAR TV viewers since June 1992, is expanding markets as well. Says Titoo Ahluwalia, who heads MARG, a market research and consulting firm in Bombay: "It's not just that the middle class has more money. Communications is playing a big part. There is both a capacity and a propensity to buy branded products." This heady growth will likely continue if India can contain political instability, its caldron of religious disputes in particular.

The Southeast Asian countries of Malaysia and Indonesia are busily replicating the feats of tiny Singapore, which became a global player in a remarkably short time. One reason: Singapore's communications infrastructure, one of the best in the world, which the country used as a springboard to global trade.

Any attempt to talk about the global market invites overstatement. But what you can say calmly and conservatively is portentous enough. "People everywhere want to be part of the global consumer world," says Peter Kennedy of the Futures Group. As widely as their tastes may range, they will ever want the same things—quality, trust in the products they buy, and perhaps some prestige to top it off. Most certain of all: In this decade far more than before, consumers from Guangzhou to Gstaad will get what they want.

presents that are intended to "unduly influence" or "obligate" the recipient, as well as receiving gifts worth more than a nominal amount.

One might contend that it is easy for a large, profitable company like IBM to have an exemplary code. On the other hand, one could also argue that a real reason for the company's continued success is that its sales representatives do subscribe to these principles. Is this a perfect code? No. The gifts area could use more specificity and, even though the company spends millions of dollars a year on advertising, that subject is not addressed in any section of the code. Further, IBM's legal department administers the code, which may mean that problems are resolved more by legal than ethical interpretation.

When should a company use a tailored code of ethics? If a company has one dominant functional unit (like IBM), or if there is diversity among functional areas, divisions, or subsidiaries, then a tailored code might be advisable. It allows the firm to promulgate specific and appropriate standards. Tailored codes are especially useful to complex organizations because they represent permanent guidelines for managers and employees to consult.

When should they be avoided? If a firm's leaders believe specific guidelines may be too restrictive for their employees, then a tailored code is an unsatisfactory choice. Codes are not necessary in most small firms or in ones where a culture includes firmly entrenched ethical policies. If a credo is similar to the Ten Commandments, and programs are similar to religious services, then tailored credos can be considered similar to the Bible or to other formal religious teachings. They provide the most guidance, but many people do not take the time to read or reflect on them.

Conclusion

My research on ethics in management suggests several conclusions that the corporate manager may wish to keep in mind.

• **There Is No Single Ideal Approach to Corporate Ethics.** I would recommend that a small firm start with a credo, but that a larger firm consider a program or a tailored code. It is also possible to integrate these programs and produce a hybrid: in dealing with insider trading, for example, a firm could develop a training program, then follow it up with a strongly enforced tailored code.[7]

• **Top Management Must Be Committed.** Senior managers must champion the highest ethical postures for their companies, as James Burke of J&J does. This commitment was evident in all the companies described here; it came through loud and clear in the CEOs' letters, reports, and public statements.

• **Developing a Structure Is Not Sufficient by Itself.** The structure will not be useful unless it is supported by institutionalized managerial processes. The credo meetings at Security Pacific and the seminars at Chemical Bank are examples of processes that support structures.

• **Raising the Ethical Consciousness of an Organization Is Not Easy.** All the companies mentioned here have spent countless hours — and substantial amounts of money — developing, discussing, revising, and communicating the ethical principles of the firm. And in fact there are no guarantees that it will work. McDonnell Douglas has an extensive ethics program, but some of its executives were implicated in a recent defense contractor scandal.

In conclusion, let me add that managers in firms with active ethics structures — credos, programs, and tailored codes — are genuinely enthusiastic about them. They believe that ethics pay off. Their conviction should provide others with an encouraging example.

References

The author would like to thank Bernard Avishai, Gene Laczniak, Michael Mokwa, Lee Tavis, and Oliver Williams, C.S.C., for their helpful comments on an earlier version of this article.

1
P.E. Murphy and M.G. Dunn, "Corporate Culture and Marketing Management Ethics" (Notre Dame, IN: University of Notre Dame, working paper, 1988).

2
R.E. Berenbeim, *Corporate Ethics* (New York: The Conference Board, research report no. 900, 1987), p. 15, pp. 20–22.

3
A more detailed discussion of Chemical's comprehensive program, and of Johnson & Johnson's, appears in *Corporate Ethics: A Prime Business Asset* (New York: Business Roundtable, February 1988).

4
One of the case studies appears in "Would You Blow Whistle on Wayward Colleague?" *American Banker*, 17 June 1988, p. 16.

5
Touche Ross, *Ethics in American Business* (New York: Touche Ross & Co., January 1988).

6
Berenbeim (1987), p. 17.

7
G.L. Tidwell, "Here's a Tip — Know the Rules of Insider Trading," *Sloan Management Review*, Summer 1987, pp. 93–99.

Can a Company Be Too Ethical?

Impossible, say some executives. But others say too much of any good thing can have bad consequences.

Andrew W. Singer

ANDREW W. SINGER is editor and publisher of *ethikos,* a New York-based publication that examines ethical issues in business.

"A couple of years ago, we were competing on a government contract," recalls Norman Augustine, chairman and CEO of Martin Marietta Corp. "The low bid would win. Two days before we were to submit the bid, we got a brown paper bag with our competitor's bid in it."

Martin Marietta didn't "spend 10 minutes" debating what to do with this information, Augustine remembers. The company turned the price sheet over to the U.S. government. Martin Marietta also told its competitor what it had received.

"And we did not change our bid."

What happened? "We lost the contract," recalls Augustine. "As a result, some of our employees lost jobs. And our shareholders lost money."

Is this a case of a company being too ethical?

No, answers Augustine. The outcome was only unfavorable in the short term. "We helped establish a reputation that, in the long run, will draw us business." This he accepts as a matter of faith.

"To me, the subject of ethics deals with principles," explains Augustine, "what you believe to be right or wrong." And insofar as ethics deals with principles, it is not possible to be too ethical. "You can't have too much principle."

But not all agree.

"You can spend too much time, too much effort, on almost anything," says Edward Bowman, Reginald Jones Professor of Corporate Management at The Wharton School at the University of Pennsylvania. "It doesn't mean you shouldn't be ethical." But it does suggest that there are limits.

What happens to a company in a highly competitive industry where "sharp" practices are the norm? If it behaves too nobly, might not other corporations succeed in cutting it off at the knees? Or what about companies that pour heaps of money into safety or environmental compliance—above and beyond what is mandated by law? Won't that hurt the bottom line?

A company, too, can pay so much attention to "doing good" that its traditional business suffers. This was a criticism made against Control Data Corp. (now Ceridian Corp.) under William C. Norris in the 1980s. The company ignored its core business at the expense of so-called humanitarian projects, said critics (more on this shortly).

The question—Can a company be too ethical?—admits of no quick or simple answers. In fact, it is difficult even to arrive at a common definition of what one means by ethical. Strictly speaking, ethics is a discipline for dealing with questions of good or bad, right and wrong—but there is also

From *Across the Board,* April 1993, pp. 17-22. © 1993 by the Conference Board, Inc. Reprinted by permission.

a broader definition, at least in the minds of many executives and ethicists, that embraces issues of so-called social responsibility. (Superogatory duties, philosophers might call these.) Issues of bribe-taking, the stealing of competitive information, and sexual harassment clearly accord with most people's notion of ethics, but others, such as affirmative action, investing in South Africa, empowering workers, and hiring the hard-core unemployed can be addressed only if one accepts an expanded concept.

Nonetheless, asking the question sheds some light on how business leaders view ethics and the business enterprise. (For the purposes of this inquiry, we examine business ethics in both the strict and expanded senses of the word.)

Thomas Donaldson, John F. Connelly Professor of Business Ethics at Georgetown University, observes that what is understood as business ethics among executives has undergone a sea change in recent decades. In the '60s, for instance, "business executives tended to identify corporate ethics with philanthropy and social-oriented programs, like hiring the hard-core unemployed.

"Now it has to do more with *how one approaches business objectives*." Is one being attentive to all one's constituencies, or "stakeholders," including employees, customers, suppliers, and the community in which one operates?

Some people say a company can be too ethical if "it pays its employees like kings," notes Donaldson. They reason that it costs money to pay employees so handsomely, and a company's profit margin may deteriorate, which ultimately hurts shareholders and overall business health. In that case, a serious question arises if the company is behaving toward its shareholders, and others, in a less-than-ethical manner.

The Price of Ethics

Most will agree that ethics sometimes exacts a price in the short run. "You know that old definition of a pioneer: He's the one with the arrows in his butt," says Tom Stephens, chairman, president, and CEO of the Manville Corp. (formerly Johns-Manville, of asbestos notoriety).

Manville emerged from bankruptcy in 1988. Today, Stephens feels an obligation for his company to be more ethical than average—given its past and the fact that it was offered a second chance by the courts. (The company, once one of the world's largest manufacturers of asbestos, was subject to 150,000 lawsuits on behalf of individuals whose health was allegedly ruined from asbestos exposure.) Yet this stance has its perils from a short-term profit standpoint.

Take the issue of product labeling. In the late '80s and early '90s, Manville went beyond what the law required in terms of warning labels on its fiberglass products. After the

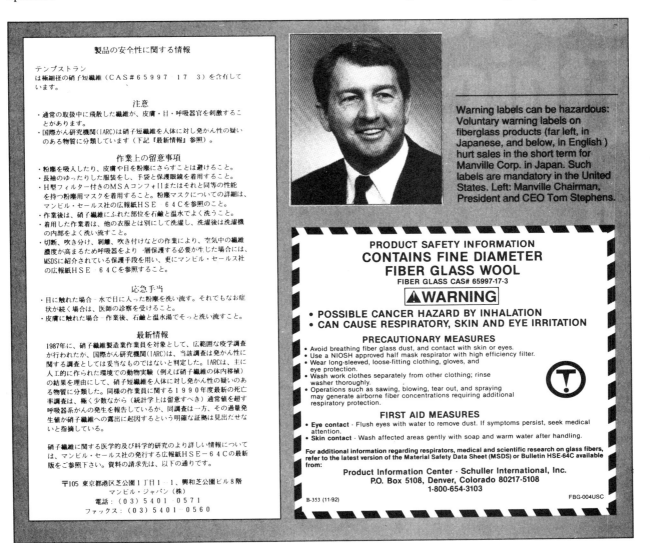

Warning labels can be hazardous: Voluntary warning labels on fiberglass products (far left, in Japanese, and below, in English) hurt sales in the short term for Manville Corp. in Japan. Such labels are mandatory in the United States. Left: Manville Chairman, President and CEO Tom Stephens.

International Agency for Research on Cancer suggested in 1987 that fiberglass was a "possible carcinogen," the company promptly affixed prominent cancer-warning labels to all its fiberglass products. (The company disputes the claim that fiberglass may be a carcinogen, however.)

This in itself is not so unusual: U.S. companies are expected to respond this way in accordance with the Occupational Safety and Health Administration's (OSHA) Hazard Communication Standard. But Manville went further: It put the warning labels on fiberglass products that it shipped to Japan, and translated those warnings into Japanese. Not only was this not required by law, but the Japanese government advised against it.

Government officials there warned "against using the 'C' word," recalls Stephens. (The Japanese have a particular dread of cancer—a legacy of Hiroshima.) They were afraid of frightening the public. Manville's business customers, in turn, were fearful of scaring their workers. Architects worried about alarming lawyers by specifying a possibly carcinogenic building material.

The Japanese said, "We'll tell them what the risks are," according to Stephens. No need to alarm people by affixing such a label.

"But a human being in Japan is no different from a human being in the U.S.," Stephens says. "We told them we had a policy. We had to have a label."

The Japanese response? "The Japanese trade minister said, 'You are very brave.' "

And it *did* have an impact on the company's Japanese sales. (Twenty-five percent of Manville's revenues are derived from outside the United States.) The company lost 40 percent of sales to Japan in one year.

Stephens, Augustine, and others who recount such stories usually add that their business losses are only in the short term. Manville, for instance, was later able to rebuild all of its Japanese business. But do some managers believe that a business can be too ethical—period—and not just in the short term?

Few are likely to say so publicly. "If you ask people directly, they're likely to give you the most socially responsible answer," observes John Delaney, professor of management at the University of Iowa. But Delaney, who has collected dozens of ethical dilemmas submitted by business executives (including those from a study he conducted of Columbia University business-school graduates), suspects that some executives privately believe a company can, in fact, be too ethical.

He offers this case, which was reported by a corporate auditor at a large, well-known pharmaceutical company:

"The FDA was reviewing our application to place a new drug on the market," the auditor told Delaney. The persistent questioning of the FDA reviewer regarding the application, however, made the auditor uneasy, so he asked to review his company's research-and-development records.

Photocopies of the data provided evidence of "double books." "One set of raw data, completely fabricated, had been provided to me to present to the FDA, while another set of raw data, showing failing results, were the true data," the auditor recalled to Delaney.

The auditor reported his findings, in accordance with corporate procedure, to the international legal department. Eventually, he was asked to testify before the company's board of directors.

"The corporation, as a consequence of the hearing, made me a 'deal.' They would give me all the resources possible to get the drug approval by the FDA. But they promised they would never market the drug. They did not want the embarrassment of the fraud uncovered. . . . I cooperated in the deal, and the company cooperated in its part. Ten years later, the drug is still not on the market."

Subsequent to this "deal," however, the company rewrote the auditor's job description. Its aim seemed to be to make it more unlikely that improprieties of this sort would be uncovered in the future. The new corporate policy prohibited "surprise" audits, for instance. And corporate audit policy was placed directly in the hands of the CEO.

According to Delaney, this suggests that the pharmaceutical concern saw real "costs" in being too ethical. It didn't want to be blatantly unethical—foisting a flawed drug on the public (nor did it fire or demote the whistle-blowing auditor)—but by the same token, it wasn't too keen about uncovering any more episodes of this sort. Hence, it curtailed the audit function. The company seemed to be saying, "Whoa, we don't want to be too ethical. That could lead to real trouble!"

Nor is this stance entirely without financial justification. Back in 1975, the Wharton School's Bowman co-authored "A Strategic Posture Toward Corporate Social Responsibility," a study of 100 companies in the food-processing industry that sought to establish if there was a connection between corporate social responsibility and profits. (Bowman acknowledges that social responsibility is not the same thing as ethics but suggests that the two are related.)

Did the link exist? "If you plot the relationship, the association is curvilinear," says Bowman. That is, as one moves from companies that exhibit little or no social responsibility to those that demonstrate a modest degree, profitability rises. It peaks somewhere in the middle.

(What constituted a socially responsible company? Such factors as concern for the environment and eagerness to hire minorities. An unusually responsible corporation might be one that granted employees paid leaves of absence to work in the local community, for instance.)

"But over on the far right [i.e., among the *most* socially responsible firms], profitability drops off." It is a matter of diminishing marginal returns.

"You can spend too much money on advertising, on computers, on research and development," says Bowman. "Can a company concerned with its overall health spend too much on social responsibility? The answer is yes."

Nonetheless, as a matter of record, "The number of firms that have gotten in trouble for being too ethical is very small," observes David Vogel, professor of business and public policy at the Haas School of Business at the University of California at Berkeley.

While acknowledging that ethics and profits are not always compatible, and a company facing constraints could in theory be too ethical for its own good—such as failing to lay off workers when its sales plummet—in point of fact, "few firms, when faced with that tension, don't give in to the economic constraints," says Vogel.

The Legacy of Control Data

One of the few examples in which a company might have been harmed by being too good, Vogel acknowledges, is Control Data, which may have sapped its resources with humanitarian programs in the early and mid-'80s.

of the brand's total sales of approximately 100 million deutsche marks.

Thus encouraged, Henkel's management took a similar step a few months after the relaunch of Pattex. This time the subject of umbrella treatment was Pritt, the company's number one brand around the world in glue sticks. Previously, Henkel had repositioned Pritt from "stick gluing" to "simple all-purpose gluing," but with little success. Nevertheless, the experience with Pattex gave top management reason to hope that a coordinated, standardized package design and communication strategy might do the trick this time.

Besides, the major subsidiaries had changed their tune: they endorsed an internationally harmonized Pritt line. In fact, the champion of the concept was the Benelux unit, one of Henkel's largest. Many executives in headquarters in Düsseldorf also viewed the Pritt decision as the next logical step after Pattex.

What more could central product management possibly ask for?

There was one potential problem, however, with the Pritt plan. A quickly arranged consumer survey in West Germany and Benelux had shown that the harmonized line might still be insufficient to turn the broader Pritt umbrella brand around. While comparative test results indicated some improvement over the current package design, they still put UHU, Pritt's global archrival, ahead along many consumer-perceived dimensions. But Pattex's encouraging performance and the unusually strong support from the leading subsidiaries persuaded the head office to proceed with the harmonized line anyway.

In the months that followed, while Pattex maintained its sales climb, the new strategy failed to im-

---

The "Learn to Speak Polaroid" campaign made all the right moves.

---

prove Pritt's ho-hum performance, to everybody's surprise. The brand did not lend support to the lesser products under its umbrella, and their sales continued to stall. Today worldwide sales still hover far below expectations, and Pritt remains a one-product brand standing for stick gluing and not much more.

What explains the success of one program in the face of heavy subsidiary opposition and the failure of the other in spite of warm local support? Henkel management has discovered two reasons. Headquarters let forceful subsidiary officers drown out early warnings based on research about Pritt, and they hastened the decision. It was a case of enthusiasm substituting for hard data. Moreover, when the early results disappointed hopes, the subsidiaries diverted

Pritt's promotion funds to other products in a search for immediate payoff. With no central follow-up, the local units did nothing to make up the lost promotion support.

Accordingly, the Pritt plan got neither the initial scrutiny nor the later subsidiary backup that Pattex had enjoyed. Combined, the two handicaps proved fatal to Pritt's global branding.

Winners and Losers

To ascertain why certain global marketing decisions succeed while others fail, I recently studied 17 cases of marketing standardization at 9 American and European multinationals. Nine of the ventures were successes, but in eight, the companies failed to meet their objectives. This article reports on the findings of the study.

A systematic comparison of the "winners" and "losers" reveals that the differences in outcome often depend on the processes underlying the decision making. In other words, my study shows that the ways global decisions are conceptualized, refined, internally communicated, and, finally, implemented in the company's international network have a great deal to do with their performance.

I have identified five pitfalls that handicap global marketing programs and contribute to their suboptimal performance or even demise. The pitfalls include insufficient use of formal research, tendency to overstandardize, poor follow-up, narrow vision in program coordination, and inflexibility in implementation. I'll take these up in turn.

Insufficient Research. Formal research is of course not alien to marketing decision making, yet many a global program has been kicked off without the benefit of a reality test. Nearly half of the programs examined included no formal research before startup. And most of the companies paid for this omission afterwards.

A case in point was Lego A/S, the Danish toy marketer, which undertook American-style consumer promotions in Japan a few years ago. Earlier, the company had measurably improved its penetration of U.S. households by employing "bonus" packs and gift promotions. Encouraged by that success, it decided to transfer these tactics unaltered to other markets, including Japan, where penetration had stalled. But these lures left Japanese consumers unmoved. Subsequent investigation showed that consumers considered the promotions to be wasteful, expensive, and not very appealing. Similar reactions were recorded in several other countries. Lego's marketers thus got their first lesson on the limitations of the global transferability of sales promotions.

Lego management examined consumer perceptions of promotions only *after* the program had failed. In the words of one headquarters executive close to the decision concerning Japan, "People at the head office in Billund and locally believed so much in the U.S. experience and its transferability that they didn't see any need to test the promotions."

This case typifies managerial complacency toward use of market information. At the extreme, it exhibits itself as "we know what we need to know," an attitude that discounts the necessity of research in the early phases of a program. This blinkered outlook often accompanies an assumption that one market's experience is transferable to others—as though the world has finally converged and market idiosyncracies have disappeared. Even managers' enthusiasm can get in the way of research. Henkel learned this point in its almost casual dismissal of Pritt's consumer survey results.

Shortcutting the early step of research in a decision process is likely to be costly. Of the cases in the sample, nearly two-thirds of the global programs that did not benefit from formal research before launch failed in their mission, while the same proportion of those that relied on research succeeded.

Overstandardization. Paradoxically, without some diversity of practice in the organization, marketing standardization will not work. When a program is burdened with too many standards, local inventiveness and experimentation close to the markets dry up. Local innovation is exactly what a global program needs to keep itself updated and responsive to evolving market conditions.

In the mid-1970s, when Polaroid introduced its pathbreaking SX-70 camera in Europe, the company employed the same advertising strategy—including TV commercials and print ads—it had used in the triumphant launch of the product in the United States. To headquarters in Cambridge, Massachusetts, the camera was a universal product with a universal consumer benefit: the pleasure of instant photography. Therefore, the communication approach should be standard around the world. Well, the product was surely universal, but the television commercials, featuring testimonials from personalities well-known in the United States, like Sir Laurence Olivier, were not necessarily transferable to Europe. At least, that's what Polaroid's executives there thought.

Unperturbed by subsidiaries' concerns, Cambridge set strict guidelines to discourage deviation from the global plan. Even local translations of the English spoken in the commercials had to get approval from the head office. As one senior European executive recalls, "We were treated like kids who have to be controlled every step along the way."

The Europeans were proved to be right. The testimonials by "unknown" personalities left consumers cold. The commercials never achieved much impact in either raising awareness of Polaroid for instant photography or pulling consumers into the stores for a closer look at the camera. Even though the SX-70 later became a winner in Europe, local management believes that the misguided introductory campaign in no way helped its performance.

Fortunately, the lesson was not forgotten a decade later, when Polaroid's European management launched a program of pan-European advertising to reposition Polaroid's instant photography from a "party camera" platform, which had eroded the brand's image and undermined camera prices, to a serious, utilitarian platform. But this time, headquarters didn't assume it had the answer. Instead, it looked for inspiration in the various advertising

Would local managers buy DEC's Europe-wide sales program?

practices of the European subsidiaries. And it found the answer in the strategy of one of the smallest subsidiaries, Switzerland's. With considerable profit, the Swiss unit had promoted the functional uses of instant photography as a way to communicate with family and friends. A pan-European task force charged with setting the advertising strategy tested the concept in major markets. These tests proved that the Swiss strategy was transferable and indeed produced the desired impact.

Thus was born the "Learn to Speak Polaroid" campaign. The two-year European project is considered one of the company's most successful advertising efforts. Subsidiaries outside Europe, including those in Australia and Japan, liked the strategy so much that they adopted it too. The experience is a source of pride for European management and a reaffirmation that "Europe can take care of itself."

What made the SX-70 and "Learn to Speak Polaroid" campaigns decidedly different was the decision-making processes involved. Promoting the SX-70 was a top-down process. But in "Learn to Speak Polaroid," the subsidiaries were offered the opportunity to influence the outcome, and they took it. Furthermore, "Learn..." was a product of the diversity found in the subsidiaries' communication strategies. The task force had the luxury of choosing among several solutions to the problem. It also had the wisdom to test the chosen strategy for confirmation of its impact around Europe.

Finally, and perhaps most important, even after adopting the pan-European program, local management retained the freedom to adapt the campaign to domestic tastes and needs. For example, where tests showed that the "Learn..." tag didn't convey the intended meaning in the local language, the subsidiary was free to change it. The message was more important than the words. Moreover, while the copy and layout for print ads remained fixed throughout Europe, local units could choose their preferred illustrations from a large set of alternatives prepared by the ad agency.

The contrasting outcomes of these two campaigns underscore a point clear to experienced marketers that, for a global program to achieve its aims, the scope of standardization need not be total. Any such program usually can attain its objectives through standardization of a few elements in the marketing mix of a product or service. Never too many elements, however, these are the leverage points around which the rationale for standardization is built.

With Pattex, for instance, the global branding strategy depended on the use of a successful brand for new products, uniform positioning of the entire range, and harmonized package designs. Local units, on the other hand, had authority over a set of decisions including communication strategy, pricing, and distribution channels. They could even decide on the package illustrations pertaining to the uses of adhesives. These matters, though important to the marketing success of Pattex in each country, did not impinge on the rationale or the crucial elements of standardization.

Nor did the flexibility allowed in the execution of "Learn to Speak Polaroid" advertising weaken the campaign. Deviations in execution didn't distract from the common mission; rather, they helped strengthen the effort by bringing local expertise to bear on the details. Overstandardization would have destroyed the incentive for local contribution, a price no global marketing program can afford to pay.

Poor Follow-up. Impressive kickoff meetings, splashy presentations to country heads, and the like are important attention-getters at the start of a campaign. But the momentum will be lost, as in the case of Pritt's promotional support, if these are not followed by lower key yet concrete steps to monitor progress and solve problems as they come along. These post-launch activities can determine whether a program survives the domestic organization's other priorities.

The differing experiences of Digital Equipment Corporation and another U.S.-based computer company, which I will call Business Electronic Systems (BES), are instructive. Not long ago, DEC's European operation installed a standardized sales management program in its 17 regional subsidiaries. Aimed to improve sales force productivity and customer service, the program touched on many aspects of overseeing

the region's 2,500-strong sales force. But as sales operations were traditionally considered a local matter, sales managers were at first predictably unenthusiastic about using the system. It was considered an infringement on their authority.

What gradually sold them on it was the continuity of attention the program got in the two years after its highly visible launch. Through watchful monitoring of progress toward full implementation, coordinating sessions among local sales managers, and periodic messages of reinforcement from top management, sponsors at regional headquarters made sure that the program received priority from subsidiary officials. The coordinating sessions for subsidiary sales managers were particularly helpful, highlighting the payoffs from use of the system and furnishing a forum for dealing with common problems. These sessions proved to be invaluable for taking a creative solution produced in one market and spreading it to the other 16.

At BES, which installed a standardized software-house cooperation program in Europe, the picture was much different. Regional headquarters conceived the program to help penetrate a market segment where BES was weak—small and medium-sized accounts. The program required a big change in sales force operation: no longer in control of the hardware and software package, the sales force had to determine its content jointly with a software house that had access to the smaller accounts. The success of the standardized program depended on how well the sales force carried out its new assignments in BES's eight country and subregional European operations.

Like DEC, BES gave the project a highly visible launch. Top management left no doubt that the software-house cooperation strategy enjoyed its

It took nonconforming managers to make Unilever's household cleaner a success.

wholehearted support. But the program never got the follow-up attention it needed. The responsibility for overseeing the project kept changing hands in the head office. Partly as a result of these switches in management, efforts to monitor progress in the subsidiaries dwindled.

The main problem, however, was the absence of a communication channel for sharing and building on subsidiary experiences. Each unit was obliged to find its own solutions to problems common to many. Hence the wheel was reinvented every time. Moreover, many country sales managers resented having to implement an unpopular program. Some gave up; others reluctantly carried on to the end, which came in three years. The reason: poor performance.

The quality of follow-up is of paramount importance when a global program introduces abrupt changes in local practice. As DEC's example shows, timely follow-up measures can go a long way to ensure subsidiary involvement and compliance. Without such measures, as BES learned, the program can easily succumb to local management's lukewarm interest.

Narrow Vision. A coordinating organization is needed to look after the health of a global marketing program because, as we have seen, a program's success depends so much on what happens after its launch—whether problems in implementation are resolved, and how the program's content is adapted to evolving internal and market conditions.

Two common mechanisms employed to manage a global program through its launch and beyond are those based, respectively, in the headquarters and a "lead market." Under a headquarters mechanism, the formal authority for a program rests with a central line or staff function like worldwide product management, regional management, or international marketing coordination. Under a lead market mechanism, a subsidiary is assigned the responsibility to define and manage a given program for all the participating "follower" countries. The choice of a lead market is usually a function of its expertise or experience with a particular product or service.

Though popular, both approaches have serious weaknesses. Headquarters, by definition removed from the firing line, nevertheless makes decisions that are supposed to keep the program fine-tuned to changing subsidiary market conditions. Similarly, the lead-market structure lacks the global perspective and information sources to coordinate international activities well. That is especially true when the lead market is also the home base for successful products that are globalization candidates. In these cases, management isn't always willing to adopt its "tried and proven" marketing ideas to different conditions prevailing elsewhere in the international organization.

But the main problem with both mechanisms is narrow vision; in each, only a single perspective is represented. As such they are not open to a continuous stream of inputs from local markets. Nor do they provide a forum for debating alternatives or sharing solutions to common problems. As a result, local management often justifiably regards headquarters or lead-market decisions as narrow, insular, top-down, and even dictatorial.

Unilever's experience with its household cleaner Domestos shows how a decision-making structure representing a single view can hamper global market-

ing. In the 1970s, the Anglo-Dutch company targeted Domestos for international expansion and assigned development of a global "reference mix" to the brand's lead market in the United Kingdom, where Domestos had been well established for a long time. But years and several market entries later, top management was still waiting for a repeat elsewhere of the UK's success story. Later analysis identified a key contributor to the problem: the lead market's insistence on a home-brewed recipe of positioning Domestos as a "lavatory germ killer" in markets already crowded with specialized and lower priced competition.

Where the product had won penetration, it had done so largely by deviating from the lead market's guidelines and staking out a whole new product category. In West Germany, Domestos was positioned as an all-purpose sanitary cleaner, and in Australia as a "bathroom plaque remover"—an innovative platform with potential for universal application, as consumers in many markets now show a growing concern with the appearance of their bathrooms.

To avoid the problems inherent in center-based or lead-market mechanisms, Unilever's detergent unit recently opted for a multisubsidiary structure to coordinate brands in Europe. The European Brand Group (EBG) is a decision-making body that includes executives from headquarters and a number of large subsidiaries.

So far, the company's experience with this mixed organization has been encouraging. As an example, EBG was instrumental in developing and launching a lemon-scented version of Vif, Unilever's successful abrasive liquid cleaner, across Europe in record time of a few months. Most important, the introduction outfoxed Procter & Gamble, which was known to be planning a similar move with its Mr. Clean; Vif Lemon won the race to market in every single country. Unilever management hopes that such gains in coordination will reinforce EBG's mandate to "view Europe as one business" and help speed up harmonization of marketing practices around the continent.

Rigid Implementation. Standardized marketing is a means of reaching an end, never an end in itself. When global marketers forget that obvious truth, standardization risks becoming rigid and ultimately self-defeating. Two common manifestations of rigidity are forced adoption and automatic piloting.

Forced adoption is the outcome of a tendency to ignore local units' reservations about implementing a standardized marketing program. Higher level management's typical reaction is to close the exit door on this ground: "After all, what's left of global marketing if the implementation isn't universal?" Theoretically, this is right. And ardent globalizers would argue that local resistance can be expected in any standardized effort and that without some central di-

Can you get lean without being mean? That depends a good deal on whether you're the downsizer or the downsizee. To an executive faced with intense competitive pressures to cut costs and bolster efficiency and productivity, paring the workforce may be the only way to save your company—and the majority of the jobs it provides the community. If you're the one whose position is suddenly made redundant, though, it's hard to see the up side to such restructuring.

The Path: Downsizing doesn't have to be a ruthless exercise. Large companies and small have demonstrated a willingness in recent years to restructure in a way that gives fair consideration to the viewpoints of all stakeholders. The key, according to experts in ethical downsizing, is to employ a holistic view of the process. It's more than just cutting payroll; it's reinventing your organization. And, when they can't avoid layoffs, responsible companies increasingly offer extensive outplacement services, consulting contracts, or even temporary jobs to the laid-off workers.

3. IT'S NOT EASY BEING GREEN

Having rushed headlong into a new age of corporate environmentalism, companies are scrambling to find ways to distinguish themselves as "greener than thou" businesses. Typically such efforts show up most crassly on the shelves of supermarkets, where everything from toilet paper to light bulbs promise to save the planet.

The greenish tint of marketing these days is creating increasing skepticism about corporate environmentalism.

All this environmentally correct hyperbole has certainly brought the issue to the attention of the consumer. What the consumer does with it is another matter entirely. More people are basing some of their purchasing decisions on environmental concerns, various surveys have indicated, but at the same time, the greenish tint of marketing in general is creating increasing skepticism about corporate environmentalism.

Last year's decision by the Federal Drug Administration to draft guidelines regulating environmental marketing claims will have some effect on the way companies connect their products to the future of the planet, says Kenneth Goodpaster. And we're likely to see a steady growth in "third-party" environmental certification groups. As a result, companies eager to trumpet their love for the earth in the future should do so with great care. "Some companies probably will be burned by consumer boycotts and other actions if they demonstrate they are taking advantage of environmental symbolism,"

he says. "There will be a winnowing process that will take place on into the future."

The Path: Quite simply: Walk the talk, but talk quietly. As Hoffman notes, the public wants to see companies "doing things that are ethically above the bottom line with regard to the environment." But beware: Even if you're doing the right thing, nobody can do everything right. And the more you advertise your greenness, the more a skeptical public—not to mention an aggressive competitor—may be attracted to your blemishes.

4. THE CHAINS THAT BIND US

In the past five years, a new professional has surfaced on the corporate landscape: the vice president of ethics. Responding to changes in federal sentencing guidelines and other factors (including PR fears), major corporations all across the country have instituted ethics programs, plugged in employee hotlines, and hired good people to act as the company's conscience.

The effect of all this activity has been mixed. In some cases, such programs have been integrated nicely into the way the company does business. In other instances, it's simply a gesture company officials hope will protect them in the event somebody somewhere in the company does the wrong thing and gets caught.

While the proliferation of such initiatives augurs well for business generally, there are signs of trouble, says Barbara Ley Toffler. "Ethics and standards change over time," she cautions, "and because there's been such a strong focus on ethics generally, there may be an equally strong inclination to lock into standards and ways of doing things that are not responsive to the rapidly changing way in which business is done."

The danger, Toffler says, is that all these ethics programs restrict the ability of companies to seek creative solutions to ethical dilemmas. "We run the risk that ethics will become something that constrains us rather than enabling us to exercise good judgment."

The Path: Ethics programs must be an integral part of a proactive management strategy. Companies that use them wisely integrate the principles those programs represent into the way they do business, realizing that they form a foundation from which creative solutions may arise.

5. CURSE OF THE BEAN COUNTERS

When the Center for Business Ethics opens its tenth annual conference this October, the major issue on the agenda will focus on control, trust, and accountability in financial reporting and accounting. "I am quite convinced that whole arena is ripe for ethical investigation and possible change," says Hoffman. "Accounting firms need to look very seriously at potential conflicts of interest they may have in their activities as consultants to corporations which they then audit."

But the disclosure question is a sticky one. Codes of ethics instruct accountants not to divulge any information about their clients, yet what if that client is bilking the public out of millions of dollars?

The Path: If Hoffman's concerns are legitimate, the accounting profession needs to come together in a hurry and modify its code of ethics. In the meantime, though, there's always been an excellent way to deal with unsavory clients or consultants: Stop doing business with them.

6. YOU'RE LIABLE TO SUFFER

We've all read the horror stories about product liability cases. The awards to nutty consumers continue to mount, while companies spend millions of dollars a year on insurance to protect them from unwarranted litigation. "The pendulum has swung very far in the direction of seller beware," says Goodpaster.

The trend may be peaking—or "bottoming out," as Goodpaster puts it—but until business and consumers come to some "shared consciousness about risk," the product liability question will continue to haunt companies. Consumers must take some responsibility for the ways in which they use products, and manufacturers must carefully weigh the hazards a product may create before bringing it to the marketplace.

The area of financial reporting and accounting is ripe for ethical investigation.

After all, the ludicrous product liability verdicts have something to do with the fact that many companies *have* built a well-deserved reputation for foisting hazardous products on an unsuspecting public in the past. What we're experiencing now is, to some degree, nothing more than payback time.

The Path: The classic example of a company properly handling a product liability emergency, of course, is Johnson & Johnson's Tylenol episode a decade ago. More recently, though, Pepsi's response to the bogus syringe-in-the-soda-can allegations demonstrates the power of good PR work: The company was prepared to pull the product off the shelves if the allegations proved true, and officials communicated that commitment to the public clearly and forthrightly. At the same time, they aggressively defended the integrity of their production processes, and effectively countered the claims. The lesson is clear: If you've done the wrong thing, correct it quickly and take full responsibility. If you're wrongly accused, defend yourself vigorously in the public eye. Don't wait for the issue to pass. It won't.

7. CLARENCE AND ANITA REVISITED

That crackling sound you've been hearing around the office is not the new carpeting. It's the sound of men and women walking around on egg shells. Sexual harassment suits have become such a prominent threat in most corporations, says Goodpaster, that co-workers are having to invent new ways of communicating. "They are watching what they say in meetings, putting things in the hypothetical, rather than categorical mode," he notes. "There's a tremendous amount of self-protective behavior."

That's not to say it's unwarranted. Until Supreme Court rings in several pending cases create some shared meaning of what constitutes an offensive work environment or unwelcomed attention, companies will continue to hope seminars and other sexual harassment awareness campaigns will keep them out of the courts.

The Path: Experts in the field advise three basic strategies: Educate your employees to help them become more sensitive to the issue. Establish a policy defining sexual harassment, post it prominently in the workplace, and clearly communicate the fact that it is not acceptable behavior in your company. Also, develop simple and convenient procedures for handling complaints.

8. NO SECRETS

It's no secret that technology has radically changed the way we do business in the past decade. But the proliferation of databases, faxes, and E-mail also has provided companies with the means to pry like never before.

"We are only beginning to see the full implication of data networks and potential intrusions on privacy," says Goodpaster. "That iceberg is just peeking up at the moment."

E-mail is only the most obvious temptation, and already stories of supervisors invading their employees' computer mail are becoming commonplace. The confidentiality of faxed material, and the use of increasingly sophisticated consumer databases also raise privacy concerns, Goodpaster says. "We're not talking about some constitutional sense of privacy, but privacy of information, and our right to control what information gets to be collected."

The Path: Company policies concerning privacy issues sound nice, but they're less than effective against a snooping supervisor who believes his E-mail raids are just another management tool. This is essentially a power issue, inasmuch as access to information equals power, so it should come as no surprise to discover that companies with empowered employees have the least trouble with privacy issues. Establish and nurture both formal and informal lines of communication as a means to empowering people, and when the issue arises you'll have created a forum within which the company can most effectively discuss it.

9. DIVERSE STROKES FOR DIVERSE FOLKS

It's a bit like a Mr. Rogers mantra—"Can you say multi-culturalism?"—but managing diversity is a challenge few companies can say they've mastered. Business better get used to it, says Michael Levett, because in the months and years ahead, the homogenized workforce will become as anachronistic as the manual typewriter.

The payoff for companies that meet the challenge? Lower recruitment and training costs, and higher productivity. Those who have trouble seeing past race, gender, or sexual preference increasingly will find themselves in court, battling discrimination suits.

The Path: It's obviously a lot less aggravating to fight discrimination before it happens than to defend your corporate practices in a courtroom. The first step is simple: Embark on a corporate mission to understand and appreciate the value of a diverse workforce.

From there, it gets harder. You'll need seminars, policies, mission statements, new employee programs, and a heart-felt determination to see the world beyond your own nose.

10. THE PRICE IS WRONG

Not long ago conventional wisdom told us that the free market was pretty good at setting prices. More and more, though, other forces seem to be at work. Last fall, allegations of predatory pricing were levelled at American Airlines and Wal-Mart, and drug companies endured several attacks from consumer groups and politicians aimed at forcing them to lower prices. Neither of the predatory pricing charges stuck, but public skepticism about corporate pricing decisions is intensifying. Several drug companies rolled back prices last year in response to the outcry, and Wal-Mart recently was forced to abandon plans to open a new store in a rural Massachusetts town when residents voted to deny the company zoning permits.

"The phenomenon of communities being protective of their own trade patterns is not a new one," says Goodpaster. "But I suspect Wal-Mart is bringing it to a head in certain communities."

Predatory pricing is extremely difficult to prove, certainly, and competitive forces still do a pretty good job of regulating prices. Companies that find themselves operating in areas that lack clearly perceived market forces, however, may find themselves fending off public criticism in the months ahead.

The Path: A few of the larger pharmaceutical companies have done a good job avoiding prolonged controversy over pricing by—you guessed it—lowering their prices. Others have scored PR points by donating their products to clinics serving the indigent. As in all situations involving the irascible public, it's usually best to respond quickly, clearly, and thoughtfully. If you're doing the right thing, state your case and keep doing it; if you're not, stop.

HOW TO MAKE DIVERSITY PAY

While many companies dawdle, smart ones are betting a diversified work force will prove vital in the 21st century.

Faye Rice

Ernest H. Drew, the amiable CEO of Hoechst Celanese, the chemical giant, remembers exactly when he became an advocate of a more diverse work force. He was attending a 1990 conference for Hoechst's top 125 officers, mostly white men, who were joined by 50 or so lower-level women and minorities. The group split into problem-solving teams, some mixed by race and sex, others all white and male. The main issue was how the corporate culture affected the business and what changes might be made to improve results. When the teams presented their findings, a light clicked on for Drew. "It was so obvious that the diverse teams had the broader solutions," he recalls. "They had ideas I hadn't even thought of. For the first time, we realized that diversity is a strength as it relates to problem solving. Before, we just thought of diversity as the total number of minorities and women in the company, like affirmative action. Now we knew we needed diversity at every level of the company where decisions are made."

Drew has since thrust Hoechst Celanese into a small group of pioneers: companies that have learned to attract, retain, and promote women and the profusion of ethnic groups streaming into the labor pool. Human resources experts estimate that only 3% to 5% of U.S. corporations are diversifying their work forces effectively. Employers agree with that assessment. A 1992 survey by the

REPORTER ASSOCIATE *Ricardo Sookdeo*

Hay Group showed that only 5% of 1,405 participating companies thought they were doing a "very good job" of managing the diversity of their work forces.

Such results might surprise those who remember how loudly the diversity drum was beaten seven years ago, when the Labor Department released its *Workforce 2000* report heralding dramatic demographic shifts in the U.S. work force by the millennium. Nearly 85% of the 25 million entering the labor pool would be women, minorities, or immigrants, it said; only 15% of new entrants would be white males, and their total share would shrink from 51% to 45%. The most recent studies by the U.S. Labor Department confirm those trends, although some percentages vary slightly.

Many companies vowed to master the management of diversity. They spent huge sums for consultants to whip it into the corporate culture mix. Yet in most cases the changes never took. At some companies, downsizing became the more urgent imperative. At others, it seems, the intention was never really sincere.

But companies such as Xerox, Avon, AT&T, IBM, Grand Metropolitan's Burger King, and Levi Strauss have stuck with their commitment to work force diversity, even in the face of restructuring, rising hostilities among some ethnic groups, and blistering competition. Why? After all, no study has so far proved conclusively that diverse work forces perform better. To many executives, it is just common sense. Says IBM chief Louis V. Gerstner Jr.: "Our marketplace is made up of all races, religions, and sexual orientations, and therefore it is

vital to our success that our work force also be diverse." Adds Ted Childs, director of work force diversity at IBM: "We think it is important for our customers to look inside and see people like them. If they can't, it seems to me that the prospect of them becoming or staying our customer declines."

Several academic studies, while not real-world evidence, suggest that diversity can enhance performance. At the University of North Texas last year, ethnically diverse teams of business students were pitted without their knowledge against all-white teams for 17 weeks. At first the homogeneous teams sprinted ahead, but by the study's end the heterogeneous groups were viewing situations from a broader range of perspectives and producing more innovative solutions to problems. Says Larry K. Michaelsen of the University of Oklahoma, one of three professors who conducted the experiment: "Cultural diversity in the U.S. work force has sometimes been viewed as a dark cloud. Our results suggest that it has a silver lining."

That seems especially likely as business moves toward management that values the intellectual contribution of every worker. No longer is the push to integrate or assimilate everyone into some homogeneous corporate type. At companies that are successfully managing diversity, different cultures and styles are embraced. The companies recognize that individuals' gender, ethnicity, and sexual orientation deeply inform the way they think about themselves. Says Robert L. Lattimer, managing director of Diversity Consultants in Atlanta, a division of Towers Perrin: "The whole point of

between a bond's (or other item's) selling price and its face value when it is selling below face value.

Discount House   A retail company which sells goods at prices below those generally prevailing, usually relying on selling large quantities in order to pay overhead expenses and generate sufficient profit.

Discretionary Income   That portion of disposable income, either of an individual or of a nation as a whole, which remains after paying for necessities.

Disposable Income   That portion of income, either of an individual or of a nation as a whole, which remains after payment of personal taxes to the government.

Distribution   The ways by which a company gets its product to the point of purchase by the final consumer. In statistics, the way in which a set of numbers tends to be more or less concentrated in different ranges or categories. Perhaps the most widely known distribution is the classical bell shaped curve, with the largest concentration of numbers at the mid point. *See* Channels of Distribution

Distributor   In general, any person or organization performing the function of product distribution. The term usually excludes retailers but includes wholesalers and dealers who sell to either retailers or industrial consumers.

Dual Distribution   The selling of products to two or more competing distribution networks, or the selling of two brands of nearly identical products through competing distribution networks. An example of the first case is found in the petroleum industry which sells to independent dealers as well as captive retailers. An example of the second case is found in the marketing of products under private label which are also being sold as nationally advertised brands. *See* Channels of Distribution, Distribution

Dumping   The act of selling large amounts of goods or securities without regard to the effect on the marketplace; or the selling of imported goods at a price lower than that charged in the country of origin. *See* Anti-Dumping Tariff

Durable Goods   Products that continue in service for an appreciable length of time such as automobiles or major household appliances. *See* Non-Durable Goods

Exports   Goods produced within a country and subsequently sold in another country. *See* Imports

Fair Trade Laws (Fair Trade Acts)   Statutes which exempt price maintenance agreements between manufacturers and distributors for certain trademarked items. While the use of fair trade agreements is diminishing, the absence of this special legal status would put such agreements in direct conflict with the restraint of trade provisions of the antitrust laws.

Franchise   The right to distribute a company's products or render services under its name, and to retain the resulting profit in exchange for a fee or percentage of sales.

Free on Board (FOB)   Delivered, without charge, to a specific location where ownership changes hands at the expense of the buyer.

Freight Absorption   Payment of transportation costs by the manufacturer or seller, often resulting in a uniform pricing structure.

Imports   A country's buying of goods or services which are manufactured or produced in some other country.

Industrial Goods   Those goods which are destined for use in, or consumption by, commercial businesses. The industrial goods market generally exhibits more uniform and rational buying patterns than the consumer goods market. *See* Capital Goods

Inventory   An asset composed of goods held for sale or raw materials and semi-finished goods held for use in their production.

Inventory Profit   Profit made by a company because it had inventory on hand during a period of rising costs and prices. If a company increases its selling prices as soon as its costs increase, it will realize more than its normal profit on the on-hand inventory which it purchased at historically lower costs.

Inventory Turnover Rate   The rate at which inventory is fully replaced each year. It is normally determined by dividing the cost of goods sold during the year by the average inventory level during the year. Also called stockturn rate.

Invoice   A detailed statement of goods or services provided, usually including a request for payment.

Jobber   One who buys from wholesalers and sells to retailers to eliminate the necessity of one-to-one contact between each wholesaler and retailer. Sometimes used synonymously with wholesaler.

Law of Supply and Demand   Those laws, generally relating to economic theory, which describe the behavior of prices through an understanding of such factors as the economic structure, the nature of products, and specific combinations of the supply and demand levels for products.

Life Cycle   The phases through which a product or business passes during its viable life. There are four generally accepted life cycle phases: (1) development, 2) growth, 3) maturity, and 4) decline. The duration and intensity of each phase depends upon the characteristics of each product or business.

Logo   The symbol or trademark which a company uses to identify itself such as on letterheads, signs or advertising.

Loss Leader   An item which a manufacturer or retailer sells at or below cost in order to either achieve greater market penetration or attract purchasers for other products in the product line.

Market   The potential buyers for a company's product or service; or to sell a product or service to actual buyers. The place where goods and services are exchanged. *See* Marketing, Marketplace

Market Analysis A sub-division of marketing research which involves the measurement of the extent of a market and the determination of its characteristics.

Marketing The total effort of a company in directing products from manufacturer to final consumer including advertising, selling, packaging, distribution, market research and other such functions.

* **Marketing Budget** A statement of the planned dollar sales and planned marketing costs for a specified future period.

† **Marketing Concept** A company belief that the best way to be successful is by identifying the needs and wants of a particular market segment and developing and implementing marketing strategies to satisfy those needs in ways that are more efficient than the competition's.

* **Marketing Management** The planning, direction and control of the entire marketing activity of a firm or division of a firm, including the formulation of marketing objectives, policies, programs and strategy, and commonly embracing product development, organizing and staffing to carry out plans, supervising marketing operations, and controlling marketing performance.

Marketing Mix The elements of marketing: product, brand, package, price, channels of distribution, advertising and promotion, personal selling, and the like.

* **Marketing Planning** The work of setting up objectives for marketing activity and of determining and scheduling the steps necessary to achieve such objectives.

Market Orientation A marketing philosophy which emphasizes the dynamics of the marketplace (particularly customer needs) as opposed to the product. *See* Product Orientation

Market Penetration Typically, market penetration refers to the advancement of one's products or services into a particular marketplace or market segment. *See* Market Share

Marketplace In general, the place where the business of a market is conducted. It is the place or circumstances where the buying and selling of goods and services occurs.

* **Market Potential (also Market or Total Market)** A calculation of maximum possible sales opportunities for all sellers of a good or service during a stated period.

Market Research The generation of empirical and statistical information concerning consumers or purchasers. Market research seeks, for example, to determine how purchasers behave and how they perceive the various characteristics of products.

Market Segment A group or segment of consumers who share some characteristics in common, such as age, sex, income, education, occupation, marital status or geographic location. A company usually directs its marketing effort at specific market segments.

Market Share A product's sales as a percent of all sales of similar products. Market share may also apply to a group of products or to a company in relation to its industry.

Market Skimming Exploiting only the prime market segment of a product's or company's marketplace which is either the most profitable, the least costly to reach, or requires the least amount of available resources.

Market Stimulation The act of increasing sales through the introduction or augmentation of an element of the marketing mix.

Mark Up As it relates to retail selling it is the retailer's expected margin expressed as a percentage of selling price (selling price minus cost divided by selling price). It differs from gross margin in that the latter is an achieved percentage of gain while the former is an intended percentage of gain.

† **Mass Marketing** Utilizing marketing strategies to attract as many customers from all market segments as possible. Usually involves the mass-production and mass-distribution of a single product; some toothpastes and laundry detergents are examples.

Mass Media Advertising The use of any advertising media whose audience consists of the general population such as with radio, newspaper or television advertising.

Middleman A person or business which buys and sells between manufacturers and consumers or similarly brings together two complementary interests.

Missionary Selling The initial sales efforts by a manufacturer into virgin markets. Typically, the missionary sales person will receive a salary rather than a commission for services.

* **Motivation Research** A group of techniques developed by the behavioral scientists which are used by marketing researchers to discover factors influencing marketing behavior.

Multinational A company which conducts operations in many countries.

Non-Durable Goods Products that do not last or continue in service for any appreciable length of time. Clothing is an example of non-durable goods.

Obsolescence The decrease in the value of an item which is caused by age, style change or new technology. An item may be obsolete even though it still functions in the way in which it was designed. *See* Planned Obsolescence

Patent A license granted by a government to an inventor giving, for a period of time, exclusive manufacturing rights to the invention. A patent has value and is often included as an asset on a company's balance sheet. In the United States, a patent can be protected for 17 years.

Personal Selling Any form of oral sales presentation or assistance to a customer. Traditionally the cornerstone of selling and promotional activities, it is one of the elements of the marketing mix.

* **Physical Distribution** The management of the move-

ment and handling of goods from the point of production to the point of consumption or use.

Planned Obsolescence Purposely designing obsolescence into a product. This can be achieved either by incorporating periodic changes which are stylistic rather than functional, or by designing a product with a physical life shorter than its useful life.

Point-of-Purchase Advertising The act of promoting a product at the location of purchase. A point-of-purchase display is designed to impel on-the-spot buying by customers. It is used more extensively in marketing consumer than industrial goods, because ultimate consumers are more susceptible to impulse buying.

Predatory Price Cutting The practice of selling goods or services at or below cost. Predatory price cutting may be employed to increase a company's market share or to sell unwanted merchandise. Note, however, that predatory price cutting does not refer to such selling of seasonal or perishable items.

Price Elasticity An economic concept which attempts to measure the sensitivity of demand for any product to changes in its price. If consumers are relatively sensitive to changes in price (i.e., higher price results in a lower demand for a product), then the demand for such a product is elastic. If, on the other hand, changing price does not affect the quantity purchased, then such a product is said to exhibit an inelastic demand characteristic. *See* Law of Supply and Demand

Price Fixing The illegal attempt by one or several companies to maintain the prices of its products above those that would result from open competition.

* **Price Leader** A firm whose pricing behavior is followed by other companies in the same industry. The price leadership of a firm may be limited to a certain geographical area, as in the oil business, or to certain products or groups of products, as in the steel business.

Price Out To calculate the price or cost of a set of actions; or to lower a price in an effort to drive high priced competition out of a market.

Pricing Policies The manner in which a company determines the prices of its goods or services. Three such methods used are: 1) to apply a standard markup to the cost of goods, 2) to maintain prices in line with competition, and 3) to charge what the market will bear.

Primary Market Demand The demand for goods and services in the market for which they were primarily intended.

Product Anything which a company sells. In the narrowest sense product refers to manufactured items. In popular terminology, however, product can also refer to services, securities and the like.

Product Differentiation The ability or tendency of manufacturers, marketers or consumers to distinguish between seemingly similar products. *See* Brand, Brand Differentiation

Productivity The rate at which production occurs (presumably to generate profit) in a given period of time.

Productivity may apply to a laborer, machine, company, industry or even an entire country.

* **Product Line** A group of products that are closely related either because they satisfy a class of need, are used together, are sold to the same customer groups, are marketed through the same type of outlets or fall within given price ranges. Example, carpenters' tools.

* **Product Management** The planning, direction, and control of all phases of the life cycle of products, including the creation or discovery of ideas for new products, the screening of such ideas, the coordination of the work of research and physical development of products, their packaging and branding, their introduction on the market, their market development, their modification, the discovery of new uses for them, their repair and servicing, and their deletion.

Product Market Erosion A decrease in demand for a product or service. Product market erosion might be caused, for example, by the introduction of a similar product which consumers purchase as a substitute.

* **Product Mix** The composite of products offered for sale by a firm or a business unit.

Product Orientation A marketing philosophy which emphasizes the product as opposed to the customer. Such an orientation usually involves efforts to perfect product design, improve production efficiencies, and reduce product cost without heeding the dynamics of the marketplace or changes in the competitive situation. *See* Market Orientation

Promotion The stimulation of sales by inducements or product exposure directed at either the channels of distribution or the final consumer. Promotion can refer to various forms of advertising, trade or consumer discounts, specially advertised discounts or the like. The promotion of a new product might include a combination of several of these. *See* Marketing Mix

Proprietary Product A product which is of such distinction as to be under patent, trademark or copyright protection. Also those products protected by proprietary market positions, such as through strength of distribution channels, production efficiencies, geographic location, etc.

† **Psychographics** Measurable characteristics of given market segments in respect to lifestyles, interests, opinions, needs, values, attitudes, personality traits, etc.

* **Publicity** Non-personal stimulation of demand for a product, service or business unit by planting commercially significant news about it in a published medium or obtaining favorable presentation of it upon radio, television, or stage that is not paid for by the sponsor.

Pull Strategy A marketing strategy whose main thrust is to so strongly influence the final consumer that the demand for a product "pulls" it through the various channels of distribution. Such a strategy is generally accompanied by large advertising expenditures to influence the consumer and relatively low markups to wholesalers and retailers. *See* Push Strategy

Push Strategy A marketing strategy whose main thrust is to provide sufficient economic incentives to members of the channels of distribution so as to "push" the product through to the consumer. Such a strategy is usually accompanied by high price markups, selective distribution and retail price support by the manufacturer. *See* Pull Strategy

* **Resale Price Maintenance** Control by a supplier of the selling prices of his branded goods at subsequent stages of distribution by means of contractual agreement under fair trade laws or other devices.

Restraint of Trade In general, activities which interfere with competitive marketing. Restraint of trade usually refers to illegal activities.

* **Retailing** The activities involved in selling directly to the ultimate consumer.

* **Sales Forecast** An estimate of sales, in dollars or physical units for a specified future period under a proposed marketing plan or program and under an assumed set of economic and other forces outside the unit for which the forecast is made. The forecast may be for a specified item of merchandise or for an entire line.

* **Sales Management** The planning, direction, and control of the personal selling activities of a business unit, including recruiting, selecting, training, equipping, assigning, routing, supervising, paying, and motivating as these tasks apply to the personal sales force.

* **Sales Promotion** (1.) In a specific sense, those marketing activities, other than personal selling, advertising, and publicity, that stimulate consumer purchasing and dealer effectiveness, such as display, shows and exhibitions, demonstrations, and various non-recurrent selling efforts not in the ordinary routine. (2.) In retailing, all methods of stimulating customer purchasing, including personal selling, advertising, and publicity.

Secondary Market Demand The demand for goods or services in a market other than that for which they were intended. *See* Primary Market Demand

Selective Distribution The use of only those means of distributing a product which are either most profitable, easiest to manage or control, or otherwise particularly beneficial or consistent with other marketing, production or financial considerations. *See* Distribution, Market Skimming

Sellers Market A condition within any market in which the demand for an item is greater than its supply. A market in which the seller maintains a more favorable bargaining position than the buyer. *See* Buyers Market

* **Selling** The personal or impersonal process of assisting and/or persuading a prospective customer to buy a commodity or a service or to act favorably upon an idea that has commercial significance to the seller.

Services In general, efforts expended to meet human needs which are primarily direct person to person activities or those activities not associated with the manufacturing or processing of a product, good, commodity or the like.

Shopping Goods Consumer goods which are purchased only after comparisons are made concerning price, quality, style, suitability and the like. Shopping goods are often purchased infrequently, consumed or used up slowly and are subject to advanced or deferred purchase decisions on the part of the consumer. Such items include, for example, furniture, rugs and shoes. *See* Convenience Goods, Speciality Goods

† **Social Marketing** The use of marketing strategies to increase the acceptability of an idea (smoking causes cancer); cause (environmental protection); or practice (birth control) within a target market.

Specialty Goods Consumer goods, usually appealing only to a limited market, for which consumers will make a special purchasing effort. Such items include, for example, stereo components, fancy foods and prestige brand clothes. *See* Convenience Goods, Shopping Goods

† **Target Marketing** Developing product and promotion strategies for a very well-defined group of potential customers to which a company decides to market goods or services.

Trade Advertising Advertising directed at the trade which distributes, sells or uses a product.

Trademark (Trade-Mark) An affixed sign or mark distinguishing articles produced or marketed by one company from those of another. Generally used to protect the goodwill or name of a certain class of goods, trademarks can be registered thus restricting use by others.

* **Ultimate Consumer** One who buys and/or uses goods or services to satisfy personal or household wants rather than for resale or for use in business, institutional, or industrial operations.

* **Value Added by Marketing** The part of the value of a product or a service to the consumer or user which results from marketing activities.

Wholesaler One who makes quantity purchases from manufacturers (or other wholesalers), and sells in smaller quantities to retailers (or other wholesalers). The wholesaler usually handles the products of many different manufacturers and in turn is only one of many suppliers to his customers. Similarly, the wholesaler will operate in a smaller geographic area than the manufacturer but a much larger area than the retailer. The wholesaler will usually rely on a small percentage profit from a large volume of sales, and may be expected to provide various services to the customer which would otherwise not be available.

Sources for the Glossary:
Terms designated by an asterisk (*) were taken from "Marketing Definitions: A Glossary of Marketing Terms," Committee on Definitions of the American Marketing Association.
Definitions for terms designated with a dagger (†) were developed by the Annual Editions staff.
The remaining terms were taken from "The Language of Business" (1975). The complete pocket glossary is available at either single list price or quantity discount price through Cambridge Business Research Inc., 4 Brattle St., Suite 306, Cambridge, MA 02138.

accountants, advertising by, 177, 178–179, 180
accounting, 233–234
"action bias," 28
Adler, Nancy, 24
advertising, 11, 115; by professionals, 176–181
Aetna Life & Casualty Co., 137, 140
affirmative action, 72–73, 75, 77, 224
age discrimination, 79–84
Age Discrimination in Employment Act (ADEA), 82
aging of America, elder-care programs and, 158–160
AIDS, privacy and, 49–51
Air Force, 106
Akers, Robert, 20
Alar, 146
alcoholism, employee assistance programs and, 149, 150, 151, 153, 154, 155
Allegheny Bottling, 212
Allied Tech, 94–95
American Airlines Inc., 135, 235
American Association of Retired Persons (AARP), 82
American Express, 42, 138, 159, 160
Americans with Disabilities Act (ADA), 44–45
Anchorage, Alaska, 147
Apple Computers, 41
apples, Alar and, 146
Arey, Mary Lou, 70
Aristotle, 21, 24
Aspen, Colorado, 147
Aspin, Les, 213
AT&T, 9, 39–40, 41, 87, 142, 239–240
Augustine, Norman, 226, 230–231
automation, 134–135
Aveda, 204, 205

"bad apple" argument, 123
"bad barrel" argument, 123
Bates v. State Bar of Arizona, 176–181
Beech-Nut Nutrition Corporation, 122–123, 187
Bell Telephone, 144
bid rigging, 98, 101
Bird, Frederick, 24
Blue Shield of Rhode Island, 135–136
Boisjoly, Roger, 99–100, 102
bootstrapping, 201–203
Boston Consulting Group (BCG), 90, 91
Bothe, Marie, 194–195
bottom-line-mentality, 213
bribery, 33, 97, 112, 113, 163, 166, 224–225
Bryan, John, 71
Bugai, Robert A., 107
BUMs (business update meetings), at Intel, 40
Burger King, 238, 239
Burke, James, 221, 225
Burma, 172, 206
burnout, 85–87
Bush, Norm, 150, 151, 152, 153, 154, 155
Business Partner Terms of Engagement, 206
business update meetings (BUMs), at Intel, 40

Cadbury Schweppes, 20
California Energy, 86

California Public Employees' Retirement Systems (Calpers), 196–197
capitalism, 28–29
case study method, of ethical education, 7–8, 153–154
Catchings, Phillip B., 90–91
categorical imperative, 7, 14–15, 17, 53
Ceridian Corp. See Control Data
Challenger disaster, 97, 99–100, 102
Champion International Corporation, 144
Chaplains, sales, 183
charity, ethical dilemma involved in nonvoluntary gifts to, 126–127
check-in-the-box mentality, 137–138
Chevron, 39, 42
child care, 137–140
child labor, 169–170
China, 172, 206
Chisholm, Tommy, 126–127
chlorine, ban on, 147
Chrysler Corp., 70, 123
Citicorp, 132
Civil Rights Act of 1964, 72
Cobbs, Price, 157
Coca-Cola Inc., 142
cognitive moral development theory, 124
Columbus, Ohio, 147–148
Commonwealth Electric Company, 98, 101
compliance approach, to ethics management, 188–190, 192
Connelly, Don, 127
consensus building, in Japanese businesses, 101
consequences, teleological theory and, 54
Continental Airlines, 122
Continental Bank Corp., 135
contingent workers, 135–136
contributions, ethical dilemma involved in nonvoluntary, 126–127
Control Data, 19, 167, 226, 228–230
corporate culture, 123
cost-benefit analysis, for environmental issues, 145–146, 147–148
credos, corporate, 219–222, 223, 225
cultural acceptability tests (CATs), 124
cultural diversity: differences in ethical values and, 165–168; multiculturalism and, 156–157
culture, corporate, 123
Cummins Engine Co., 12, 112, 136
Cyprus Amax Mineral Co., 134–135

decentralization, ethical consequences of, 32, 34
democracy, capitalism and, 28–29
Dennis, Helen, 79–80, 81, 84
dental advertising, 177, 179–180
deontological theory, 53–54
Department of Defense, 140
DePree, Max, 229, 230
Dial Corp., 239
dioxin, 147
Disclosure Rule, 14, 15, 16
distributive justice, 12
diversity, 28, 156–157, 165–168, 196, 198–199, 235, 236–240
Dodd, Dan, 119, 120
Dow Corning, 112–113, 130, 168
downsizing, 33, 88–93, 135, 232–233, 239
Drew, Ernest, 236, 237–239
drug testing, of employees, 47–48, 147–155
Dry Creek Vineyard, 143

Dunn, Robert, 206
DuPont Co., 70, 137
Dyess, Kirby, 41, 42

E. F. Hutton, 113
early retirement incentives (ERIs), 82
ecofurniture, 185
Eco-furnitures Inc., 185
elder care, aging of America and, 158–160
e-mail, 45, 234
embezzlement, 9
Emerson, Ralph Waldo, 32, 33
employee assistance programs (EAPs), 149, 150, 151, 153, 154, 155
empowerment, 134, 135
encouragement, 19
entertainment business, 224
environmental issues, 133, 145–148, 205, 233; corporate recycling and, 141–144
Equal Employment Opportunity Act, 182
Equity Group Inc., 143
espionage, corporate, 224
ethical audit, 110, 111, 112–113, 222
ethical behavior, 210–218
ethical education, case study method of, 7–8, 153–154
ethical relativism, 52–53
Europe, business ethics in, vs. Japan and United States, 161–164
European Collision Center, 134
Ewing, David, 96, 101

fairness, 19–20
families, employers and, 137–140
Family and Medical Leave Act, 140
Farrot Corporation, 126–127
federal sentencing guidelines, 56, 189
Federal Trade Commission (FTC), 176, 178, 180
Fel-Pro, 137, 139
"flexible work alternative," 83
flextime, 138, 139, 140
Ford Motor Company, 112; women managers at, 69–70
Foreign Corrupt Practices Act (FCPA), 166–168
Fulghum, Robert, 20
furniture, environmental-friendly, 185
Fyock, Cathy, 80, 82

G. D. Searle, 98
gender differences, diversity and, 157
General Dynamics, 113
General Electric, 97, 105, 110–111, 122, 132
General Motors, 70, 112
gifts: ethical issues involved in accepting, 11, 112, 222, 223, 224–225; exchange of, 165–166
Ginental, Shelley, 149, 150, 151, 152, 153, 154, 155
"glass ceiling" issues, 76
golden rule, 7, 9–10, 14, 15–16, 53–54
Golden Turnkey Systems Inc., 143
Goodpaster, Kenneth, 232, 233, 234, 235
government contracts, issues involved in, 97, 98, 100–101
grievance committees, 151
Griggs, Lewis, 156
Groen, Becky, 119, 120

Haas, Robert D., 196, 198, 199–200
Halfin, Mark, 24
Hall, Dan, 119, 120

Harris Corporation, 212
health care insurance, 113
health maintenance organizations (HMOs), 150
Hellman, F. Warren, 197–198
Herman Miller, 28, 229, 230
Hewlett Packard, 113
Hilby Wilson Inc., 20
HIV, privacy and, 49–51
Hoe, Choong, 171, 172–173
Hoechst Celanese, 236, 237–239
Hoffman, Michael, 232, 233–234
Honeywell, 83–84
human rights, 169
Hydraulic Parts and Components Inc., 100–101

Iacocca, Lee, 113, 123
IBM, 86, 115, 133, 223, 224, 225, 236, 238
incentive compensation plan, 193
industry-wide codes of ethics, 123, 184
insider trading, 110, 222, 223–224
InSpeech, 193–194
integrity, 23–27
integrity-based approach, to ethics management, 186–195
Intel, 40
intergenerational day-care centers, 138–139
Intuit, 201
Intuition Ethic, 14–15, 16
ISI, 137, 140

J. C. Penney, 9–10
James, William, 31, 102
Japan, 101–102, 161–164, 165–167, 227–228
job security. See security
John Hancock Insurance Co., 138
Johnson & Johnson, 113, 187–188, 220, 225
Johnson, Paul, 50
justice, 21; distributive, 12

Kaltreider, Nancy, 157
Kant, Immanuel, 7, 17, 24
Karen, Nancy P., 91, 93
Kelley, Jim, 150, 151, 152, 153, 154, 155
kickbacks, 100–101
Kirtman, Louis, 196, 199
Kissinger, Henry, 124
Kmart, 45
Kohlberg, Lawrence, 124
Kraines, Gerald, 86, 87

law, business ethics and, 7
layoffs, 113
legal advertising, 176–177, 179, 180
Levett, Michael, 232, 235
Levi Strauss & Co., 171–173, 196–200, 204, 206
liability, product, 234
lie detector tests, for employees, 224
literature, ethics and, 29
Lockheed Corporation, 167
Loftus, Denise, 79, 81, 82, 84
loneliness, 29
Lorenzo, Frank, 122
loyalty, and security, in corporate-employee relationship, 38–42, 133

MacIntyre, Alasdair, 21
Madaras, Laura, 143

Mahathir Mohamad, 172
Malaysia, 171, 172–173
Manville Corp., 227–228
Martin Marietta Energy Systems, 105–106, 191–193, 230–231
Masi, Dale, 150, 151, 152, 153, 154, 155
Maybelline Inc., 237
McDonald's, 80–81
McDonnell Douglas, 110, 115–116, 225
McDonough, Michael, 185
McMasters program, 81
medical advertising, 177, 179–180
mellowing factor, 10
Merck & Co., 204, 207
Mickens, Ed, 50
Mink, Patsy T., 108
moral content test, 124
moral reasoning, 115–116
moral relativism, virtue and, 21
Morton Thiokol, 99, 102, 105
Motorola, 19
multiculturalism, diversity and, 156–157

NASA (National Aeronautics and Space Administration), 100, 102, 109
National Retiree Volunteer Coalition (NRVC), 81
Nations Bank, 139, 159
nepotism, 113, 224
New York Life Insurance Co., 158
NIBCO Inc., 143
"no money, no mandate" law, 145, 146
Noer, David, 41, 85
Norris, William C., 226, 229–230
NovaCare Inc., 193–194
novels, ethics and, 29
Nynex Corp., 88, 89–91, 93

Oak Ridge National Laboratory, 105–106
Occupational Safety and Health Administration (OSHA), 228
Older Workers League (OWL), 83–84
ombudsman, 12
optimism, 19
oral warnings, in sexual harassment cases, 67–68
organizational ethics, 12
Orlov, Darlene, 57–58, 61–62
Ortbal, John, 142
outsourcing, of workers, 135–136

Paine, Lynn Sharp, 120, 121
paper industry, 146
Pastin, Mark, 18, 19
People Express Airlines, 230
Peru, 147
Pet Inc., 239
Peterson and Son Winery, 144
Picard, Sara, 94–95
place determination, 114
Polaroid, 83, 112, 117
political action committees (PACs), 223
polygraph tests, for employees, 224
pragmatism (James), 102
predatory pricing, 235
preferential treatment, 224
price fixing, 33, 212
price negotiation, 114
privacy rights, 149, 223, 234; electronic monitoring and, 43–48; HIV and, 49–51
product liability, 234
professional ethics, 7, 15, 17
promotion presentation, 114–115

property rights, environmental issues and, 145, 148
protestant work ethic, business ethics in United States and, 162
prudence, 21
Prudential, 40
psychological egoism, 54
Pulaski Furniture Corp., 134

quotas: racial, 72; sales, 183

racial discrimination, 72
rationalization, 52–53
Raychem Corp., 136
Raytheon Corporation, 132
recession, effect of, on ethical behavior, 130–132
reciprocal dealing, 224
records, in sexual harassment investigations, 67
recycling, 141–144
Remington Products Co., 140
Respect Inc., 70
Rest, James, 124
Reuters, 40
reverse discrimination, affirmative action as, 72
Riverside County, California, 148
rules, deontological theory and, 53–54
Russo, Thomas A., 58

"sales chaplains," 183
sales managers, ethical challenges for, 182–184
sales quotas, 183
sales territories, ethical challenges in administration of, 182
Sara Lee Corp., 70–71
Schacht, Henry B., 136
Schwartzkopf, William, 98, 101
Searfass, Denise, 137
Sears, Roebuck & Company, 187
Securities and Exchange Commission (SEC), 110
security, and loyalty, in corporate-employee relationship, 42, 133
Security Pacific Corporation, 220, 225
sexual harassment, 96, 234; myths of, 96–97; investigating, complaints, 66–68
Shapero v. Kentucky Bar Association, 177
Sheraton-Boston Hotel, 46
Skaff, Duane, 158–159
"skill gaps," 156
SLRPs (strategic long-range plans), at Intel, 40
Smilich, Jack, 126, 127
soapbox factor, in business ethics, 6
Social Security tax, child care and, 138
soft factor, in business ethics, 6
Sokol, David, 86
South Africa, divestment from, 8
Southland Corp., 135
speech, freedom of, and advertising, 178
Sprint, 142
Steelcase Inc., 142–143
strategic long-range plans (SLRPs), at Intel, 40
Stride Rite, 138–139
Swanson, John, 222–223

tampering, handling of Tylenol poisoning scare by Johnson & Johnson and, 113, 187–188

"tapering off," 83
technology, 134–135
telecommuting, 133
teleological theory, 54
temperance, 21
temporary workers, 135–136
theft, employee, 9, 52–55
Thrasher, Robert J., 89–90
Tillich, Paul, 96–103
Toffler, Barbara Ley, 232, 233
trust, 19
TS Print Center, 144
TV test, 7
Tylenol poisoning scare, handling of, by
    Johnson & Johnson, 113, 187–188

unions, 151
United States, business ethics in, vs.

Europe and Japan, 161–164
United Telephone of Florida (UTF), 142
US West Communications Inc., 158, 160
USF&G Corp., 135
utilitarianism, 7, 12, 15, 17, 54

values, 123; confusing virtue with, 21;
    culture and, 165–168
Virginia State Board of Pharmacy v.
    Virginia Citizens Consumer Council,
    176–181
virtue, 21–22
Vitti, Bernie, 95
Vocational Rehabilitation Act of 1973, 152

Wallace, Doug, 50–51, 95, 127
Wal-Mart, 172, 235
waste management, 112

Wetherill Associates, Inc. (WAI), 194–195
whistleblowing, 11, 96–97, 98, 100,
    104–109, 162–163, 184
white-collar crime, 56–62
Wilson, James Q., 21
Winer, Michael, 143
Wiretap Act, 44, 46
witnesses, in sexual harassment
    complaints, 66–67
WITT Company, 141–142
Wolfram, Edward P., 59
women, 76, 136, 157; lack of, in top
    management positions, 69–71; sexual
    harassment and, 63–65, 97
Wood, Graydon, 120, 121
Wydman, Marcy R., 141–142

Yankelovich, Daniel, 38, 85

Credits/ Acknowledgments

Cover design by Charles Vitelli

1. Ethics, Values, and Social Responsibility in Business

Facing overview—Photo by Pamela Carley.

2. Ethical Issues and Dilemmas Involving Employees and the Workplace

Facing overview—Digital Stock photo.

3. Business and Society

Facing overview—EPA-Documerica photo. 141—Illustration by Sam Ward.

4. Ethics and Social Responsibility in the Marketplace

Facing overview—Alcoa photo.

5. Developing the Future Ethos and Social Responsibility of Business

Facing overview—New York Stock Exchange photo by Howard Topple.

PHOTOCOPY THIS PAGE!!!*

ANNUAL EDITIONS ARTICLE REVIEW FORM

■ NAME: _____ DATE: _____

■ TITLE AND NUMBER OF ARTICLE: _____

■ BRIEFLY STATE THE MAIN IDEA OF THIS ARTICLE: _____

_____

_____

_____

_____

_____

■ LIST THREE IMPORTANT FACTS THAT THE AUTHOR USES TO SUPPORT THE MAIN IDEA:

_____

_____

_____

_____

_____

_____

■ WHAT INFORMATION OR IDEAS DISCUSSED IN THIS ARTICLE ARE ALSO DISCUSSED IN YOUR TEXTBOOK OR OTHER READING YOU HAVE DONE? LIST THE TEXTBOOK CHAPTERS AND PAGE NUMBERS:

_____

_____

_____

_____

_____

_____

_____

■ LIST ANY EXAMPLES OF BIAS OR FAULTY REASONING THAT YOU FOUND IN THE ARTICLE:

_____

_____

_____

_____

■ LIST ANY NEW TERMS/CONCEPTS THAT WERE DISCUSSED IN THE ARTICLE AND WRITE A SHORT DEFINITION:

_____

_____

_____

_____

_____

*Your instructor may require you to use this Annual Editions Article Review Form in any number of ways: for articles that are assigned, for extra credit, as a tool to assist in developing assigned papers, or simply for your own reference. Even if it is not required, we encourage you to photocopy and use this page; you'll find that reflecting on the articles will greatly enhance the information from your text.

ANNUAL EDITIONS: MARKETING 95/96
Article Rating Form

Here is an opportunity for you to have direct input into the next revision of this volume. We would like you to rate each of the 46 articles listed below, using the following scale:

1. Excellent: should definitely be retained
2. Above average: should probably be retained
3. Below average: should probably be deleted
4. Poor: should definitely be deleted

Your ratings will play a vital part in the next revision. So please mail this prepaid form to us just as soon as you complete it.
Thanks for your help!

Rating	Article	Rating	Article
	1. Portrait of a Changing Consumer		24. Consumer Behavior: Yesterday, Today, and Tomorrow
	2. Defining the New Marketing Concept		25. The Unhappy Consumer
	3. Beyond Quality and Value		26. From Choices to Checkout, the Genders Behave Very Differently in Supermarkets
	4. Operation Zero-Defect Marketing		
	5. Marketing Myopia (With Retrospective Commentary)		27. Marketing with Blinders On
	6. Executing the New Marketing Concept		28. Integrated Marketing Plans Help Small Businesses Stay Ahead
	7. The Marketing Concept: A Forgotten Aid for Marketing High-Technology Products		29. What's in a Brand?
			30. Whatever Happened to Run-Flat Tires . . .
	8. Relationship Marketing: Positioning for the Future		31. Flops
	9. Affinity Marketing: What Is It and How Does It Work?		32. Product Development: Minnesota Mining and Manufacturing
	10. Service Is Everybody's Business		33. Ten Timeless Truths about Pricing
	11. Improving America's Service		34. Stuck! How Companies Cope When They Can't Raise Prices
	12. The Little Extras Keep Customers Coming Back		35. How to Escape a Price War
	13. Waxing Customer Service and Cars		36. The Retail Revolution
	14. Strategic Green Marketing		37. Survival Tactics for Retailers
	15. From Witches to Anorexics, Critical Eyes Scrutinize Ads for Political Correctness		38. The Fall of the Mall
			39. TV or Not TV
	16. How to Find Out What They Want		40. The Death and Rebirth of the Salesman
	17. Operation: Oops!		41. Advertising That Works
	18. Churches Turn to Research for Help in Saving New Souls		42. Those Mind-boggling Promotions
			43. Where the Global Action Is
	19. The Ethnic Boom: Marketing to the Target		44. Going Global
	20. What Does "Hispanic" Mean?		45. Beware the Pitfalls of Global Marketing
	21. Baby Busters: The Neglected Generation		46. Electrolux: The Trick to Selling in Europe
	22. The Brave New World of Men		
	23. Marlboro Man Doing Diapers Now		

(Continued on next page)

ABOUT YOU

Name_____ Date_____

Are you a teacher? ☐ Or student? ☐

Your School Name _____

Department _____

Address _____

City _____ State _____ Zip _____

School Telephone # _____

YOUR COMMENTS ARE IMPORTANT TO US!

Please fill in the following information:

For which course did you use this book? _____

Did you use a text with this Annual Edition? ☐ yes ☐ no

The title of the text? _____

What are your general reactions to the Annual Editions concept?

Have you read any particular articles recently that you think should be included in the next edition?

Are there any articles you feel should be replaced in the next edition? Why?

Are there other areas that you feel would utilize an Annual Edition?

May we contact you for editorial input?

May we quote you from above?
